KU-483-242

Practical
Rails Plugins

Nick Plante and
David Berube

 Apress®

Practical Rails Plugins

Copyright © 2008 by Nick Plante and David Berube

All rights reserved. No part of this work may be reproduced or transmitted in any form or by any means, electronic or mechanical, including photocopying, recording, or by any information storage or retrieval system, without the prior written permission of the copyright owner and the publisher.

ISBN-13 (pbk): 978-1-59059-993-8

ISBN-10 (pbk): 1-59059-993-4

ISBN-13 (electronic): 978-1-4302-0654-5

Printed and bound in the United States of America 9 8 7 6 5 4 3 2 1

Trademarked names may appear in this book. Rather than use a trademark symbol with every occurrence of a trademarked name, we use the names only in an editorial fashion and to the benefit of the trademark owner, with no intention of infringement of the trademark.

Lead Editor: Clay Andres
Technical Reviewers: Justin Blake, Josh Martin
Editorial Board: Clay Andres, Steve Anglin, Ewan Buckingham, Tony Campbell, Gary Cornell,
    Jonathan Gennick, Matthew Moodie, Joseph Ottinger, Jeffrey Pepper, Frank Pohlmann,
    Ben Renow-Clarke, Dominic Shakeshaft, Matt Wade, Tom Welsh
Project Manager: Beth Christmas
Copy Editor: Marilyn Smith
Associate Production Director: Kari Brooks-Copony
Production Editor: Kelly Gunther
Compositor: Linda Weidemann, Wolf Creek Press
Proofreader: Nancy Bell
Indexer: Carol Burbo
Artist: April Milne
Cover Designer: Kurt Krames
Manufacturing Director: Tom Debolski

Distributed to the book trade worldwide by Springer-Verlag New York, Inc., 233 Spring Street, 6th Floor, New York, NY 10013. Phone 1-800-SPRINGER, fax 201-348-4505, e-mail orders-ny@springer-sbm.com, or visit http://www.springeronline.com.

For information on translations, please contact Apress directly at 2855 Telegraph Avenue, Suite 600, Berkeley, CA 94705. Phone 510-549-5930, fax 510-549-5939, e-mail info@apress.com, or visit http://www.apress.com.

Apress and friends of ED books may be purchased in bulk for academic, corporate, or promotional use. eBook versions and licenses are also available for most titles. For more information, reference our Special Bulk Sales–eBook Licensing web page at http://www.apress.com/info/bulksales.

The information in this book is distributed on an "as is" basis, without warranty. Although every precaution has been taken in the preparation of this work, neither the author(s) nor Apress shall have any liability to any person or entity with respect to any loss or damage caused or alleged to be caused directly or indirectly by the information contained in this work.

The source code for this book is available to readers at http://www.apress.com.

To my wife, Amanda, for . . . well, you know . . . everything.
—nap

To my parents.
—David Berube

Contents at a Glance

PART 1 ■■■ Introduction to Plugins for Ruby on Rails

PART 2 ■■■ Model Enhancement

PART 3 ■■■ Controller Enhancement

PART 4 ■■■ Login/Security Plugins

iv

PART 5 ▪▪▪ Search and Query Plugins

PART 6 ▪▪▪ Performance Optimization Plugins

PART 7 ▪▪▪ View/UI Enhancement

PART 8 ▪▪▪ Testing with Plugins

PART 9 ▪▪▪ Plugin Development Strategies

Contents

PART 1 ▪▪▪ Introduction to Plugins for Ruby on Rails

PART 2 ▪▪▪ Model Enhancement

PART 3 ■■■ Controller Enhancement

PART 4 ◼◼◼ Login/Security Plugins

PART 5 ■ ■ ■ Search and Query Plugins

PART 6 ■ ■ ■ Performance Optimization Plugins

PART 7 ■ ■ ■ View/UI Enhancement

PART 8 ■ ■ ■ Testing with Plugins

PART 9 ■■■ Plugin Development Strategies

About the Authors

NICK PLANTE is a programmer, author, entrepreneur, and (most of all) a nice guy. As a partner in Ubikorp Internet Services, Nick specializes in helping web-based software startups accelerate their development with Ruby and Rails. He is also a co-organizer of the New Hampshire Ruby User Group and the Rails Rumble coding competition and contributes to numerous open source projects.

Prior to his involvement in the Ruby community, Nick spent time in the trenches with Java, PHP, Flash/ActionScript, and C/C++. In his free time, he enjoys independent film, comic books, loud music, and talking about himself in the third person. If you feel like discussing any of these topics, he would be happy to hear from you. Nick's contact information can be found on his blog at `http://blog.zerosum.org`.

DAVID BERUBE is a Ruby developer, trainer, author, and speaker. He has used both Ruby and Ruby on Rails for several years, starting in 2003, when he became a Ruby advocate after he wrote about the language for *Dr. Dobb's Journal*. He wrote the Apress books *Practical Ruby Gems* and *Practical Reporting with Ruby and Rails*.

His professional accomplishments include writing Ruby software for The Casting Frontier, one of the world's most successful digital video sites for the commercial casting industry. Additionally, he has worked on several other Ruby projects, including the engine that powers CyberKnowHow's BirdFluBreakingNews searches and ThoughtBot's Rails engine that powers Sermo's "America's Top Doctor" contest.

David's journalism has been in print in more than 65 countries, in magazines such as *Linux Magazine* and *PHP International Magazine*. He has also taught college courses and has spoken publicly on topics such as "MySQL and You" and "Making Money with Open Source Software."

David lives in New Hampshire. His hobbies include basketball, music, and musicianship.

About the Technical Reviewers

JUSTIN BLAKE is a dedicated husband, proud father, and avid programmer. He has been using Ruby and Rails professionally since the pre-1.0 days, originally as an independent consultant and later as a full-time employee of Atlantic Dominion Solutions (http://www.techcfl.com).

Whenever possible, Justin frequents local tech conferences and the Orlando Ruby Users group. He enjoys writing plugins, open source software, and applications using Ruby, Rails, PHP, and Python.

When not hunched over a computer in his cave, writing code and reviewing books, Justin is a typical geek who appreciates a good comic book or video game. If all of this sounds intriguing and you simply must know more, you can find his musings at both http://mega.blaix.com and http://rorblog.techcfl.com.

JOSH MARTIN has been developing Ruby on Rails applications professionally since version 0.9.3 was released in 2004. With a background in agile web development, and with numerous startups under his belt, he continues to work as a professional consultant both nationally and worldwide.

Josh also has a strong passion for the open source community, maintaining his own public repository of Ruby on Rails plugins, and enjoys introducing new developers to the Ruby language. You can usually find him lurking on the Freenode IRC network under the alias of Skiz. And if you ever see him in public, be sure to ask what getting bit by a horse feels like.

Acknowledgments

Writing a book is hard work. Seriously! We wouldn't kid about that. However, the author's responsibility is just one part of it. Thanks to Jason Gilmore for getting the ball rolling and to Clay Andres for his editorial guidance throughout the remainder of this endeavor. Josh Martin and Justin Blake, our technical reviewers, routinely went above and beyond the call of duty in their work, making sure that all code samples were up to their own high standards and suggesting notes and tips to help you, the reader.

Special thanks go to Apress project manager *extraordinaire* Beth Christmas for keeping us (mostly) on track. Without her diligence, we surely would have been lost at sea long ago. Thanks also to Marilyn Smith for her copyedit polish and to Kelly Gunther and her production team for their magnificent work and for putting up with our last-minute changes.

In addition to the people directly involved with this project, we would like to thank Yukihiro "Matz" Matsumoto for creating such a fun, wonderful programming language. We would also like to thank the entire Rails core team, and all the contributors and plugin authors who have published even the smallest possible patch or extension to the framework. In particular, we would like to give a hearty thanks to the developers who are responsible for the plugins showcased in this book. Without their innovations, this effort would not have been possible.

Nick Plante and David Berube

First and foremost, I would like to thank my family—my wife Amanda, my mother and father, and my brother Matt—for supporting me in all things. I will never be able to thank you enough for all that you've given me.

Thanks to the folks that I work with on a daily basis, mostly Ian Koss and Ty Rauber, and all our partners and clients for giving me wonderfully strange challenges to work on and forcing me to continually reevaluate the way I work and the tools that I use. Thanks to all my friends and the other developers and software industry professionals I've worked with in the past as well, both the good ones and the bad ones—I've learned something from each of you. I would like to thank Steve Reber in particular for his mentoring (and enthusiasm for reality television).

Finally, in addition to the Ruby and Rails communities at large, I would like to thank all those people who have helped me personally, especially the NH Ruby regulars and the rest of the offRails crew. Many a chapter idea, tip, or refinement for this book wouldn't have been fully formed without your input. Without community, we're all isolated, and no idea or implementation is ever worth a damn in isolation.

Nick Plante

I would like to thank my parents, who I owe an inexpressible debt and whose counsel was invaluable. I would like to thank my two sisters, Rebecca Berube Leuser and Elizabeth Lee; both have shown great wisdom in their lives, and I'm fortunate to learn from their example.

I would also like to thank the many friends who have supported me—in particular, Wayne Hammar, Matthew Gifford, Andy Thomas, and John Dwyer.

I would also like to thank the vast array of professional associates I've worked with and learned from—in particular, Joey Rubenstein. Extra special thanks to Jason Gilmore for his patient explanations and excellent advice. He knows a tremendous amount about writing, and I'm extremely fortunate to have had a chance to work with him on three books. Thanks to Timothy Pope for Rails.vim and to Nick Plante, my coauthor, for his patience during this amazingly busy period of my life.

David Berube

Introduction

This is a book about Ruby on Rails and the Rails plugin system. But it's also a book about sharing, code reuse, and learning by example. Being the savvy, tuned-in Ruby developer you are, you already know that some incredibly awesome open source libraries and code snippets are available to help you accelerate your development projects. Much of this code is published through the Ruby Gems package system. However, code that is intended to modify or enhance the popular Ruby on Rails web framework is usually made available through its own convenient plugin system. These plugins serve a variety of purposes, and the framework makes it easy to package and distribute these extensions, all without making actual changes to Rails itself!

In this book, you'll find examinations of what we feel are some of the most powerful third-party extensions for Rails. If we've left out your favorite plugin, know that it wasn't an easy choice! We started with a list of more than 60 different plugins that we've used and enjoyed in various Rails projects and (with much consternation) whittled that down to what you see here. We picked those that felt the most practical for beginning to intermediate-level Rails developers.

In addition to showcasing some of the best Rails plugins, our other goal was to deliver a set of recipes for functional mini-applications. We've observed that most "recipe" books for Ruby and Rails are focused on the advanced user, delivering quick snippets and explanations about how to use a particular technique within an existing project. Although we feel that their approach is extremely useful (and own a number of these books ourselves), it isn't particularly well suited to developers who are new to the framework. Therefore, we wanted to spend a little extra time putting plugins within a real-world context, using them to build something tangible and immediately accessible to developers of all skill levels.

We hope that you'll find these projects to be an interesting way to explore the power of Rails plugins, and that they help you see how you can use plugins to accelerate the development of your own projects.

What's Included

The mini-applications we'll be building are intended to be showcases for the plugins that they utilize. Therefore, we won't concern ourselves too much with performance optimization, database tuning, or testing during the bulk of our chapter examples (unless the plugins we're discussing themselves focus on one of those areas!). This isn't to say that we feel those subjects aren't important; we very much do. When we're developing applications for our clients, for example, we always take a test-driven (or behavior-driven) approach, and we think that you probably should, too.

The plugins and examples we'll talk about are grouped together by their purpose or subject area:

- Plugins that modify and extend your application's *models* are discussed in Chapters 2 through 7.

- Plugins that operate at the *controller* level and affect the request/response cycle are discussed in Chapters 8 through 10.

- Plugins that deal with login and security concerns are the focus of Chapters 11 through 13.

- Plugins for searching and querying are covered in Chapters 14 through 16.

- Plugins to help you optimize your application's performance are covered in Chapters 17 and 18.

- Plugins that affect your application's views are discussed in Chapters 19 through 24.

- Plugins that change the way you test your code are the focus of Chapters 25 through 27.

We've tried to spend a good deal of time in each area in order to give you a taste of the different kind of functionality that plugins can provide.

The first and last chapters break from the mini-project per-chapter convention in order to provide an introduction to the plugin system itself and a brief tutorial on developing your own plugins, respectively.

What You Should Know

Although we've written the book with the beginning Rails developer in mind, we do make some basic assumptions about your familiarity with Rails concepts. We assume that you understand the basics of the Model-View-Controller (MVC) pattern and web frameworks in general, that you're familiar with HTML, and that you know the structure of a Rails project and basic Ruby syntax. In order to get right to the meat of the powerful features enabled by these plugins, we'll be skipping over these basics.

If you're unfamiliar with Rails, there are a number of great books already published that serve as excellent introductions. *Beginning Rails* by Jeffrey Allan Hardy, Cloves Carneiro Jr., and Hampton Catlin (Apress, 2007) and *Agile Web Development with Rails* by Dave Thomas and David Heinemeier Hansson (Pragmatic Bookshelf, 2006) are both highly recommended. David Black's *Ruby for Rails* (Manning, 2006) is also a fantastic title that will not only familiarize you with Ruby, but also teach you how Rails makes use of Ruby's metaprogramming capabilities. This will come in very handy if you plan on writing your own plugins or extensions to the framework. We touch on these topics briefly in the final chapter of this book, but our discussion is merely meant as a starting point and is specific to plugins. To really embrace the power of Ruby, you'll want to dive in further!

Code Requirements and Resources

All the examples in this book were tested using Ruby 1.8.6 with Rails 2.1 and, unless otherwise noted, should also work with Rails 2.0.2. Most examples were created using the SQLite 3 database engine as a back end, except when more advanced database features were needed (for instance, for the geocoding examples in Chapter 14); for those cases, we used MySQL 5.x. You'll need at least a passing familiarity with these technologies to get the most out of this book.

Having a basic understanding of the Subversion version control system will help, too. Note that we've also included several plugins whose most recent versions are available via the Git version control system rather than Subversion. Since Git plugin support was only recently introduced in Rails 2.1, there may be additional steps required for installing some of the plugins when using Rails 2.0.2. Don't worry—whenever this is the case, we'll let you know.

Be aware that the Rails world moves fast, and that plugins, like all good software, are often improved and refactored. Many of the contributions we've profiled here are very stable and pillars of the Rails plugin system, but a number of them represent newer upstarts and may change over time, just as the framework will. The README files and RDoc-based documentation provided with a plugin are always the definitive source of information about that plugin, so when in doubt, make sure to check the documentation.

Full source code for all the examples featured in this book, including the plugins themselves, can be found at http://railsplugins.com. If you have trouble installing any plugin found at a third-party web site or source code repository, we suggest downloading the code from the http://railsplugins.com site. Project archives will contain both the sample applications and the plugin code we've used. Additionally, all source code is available from the Source Code/Downloads area of the Apress web site (http://apress.com). Any errata can be found there as well.

PART 1

■ ■ ■

Introduction to Plugins for Ruby on Rails

In this first part of the book, we'll introduce you to the fundamentals of plugins: what they are, how they work, and how you can get started using them. Plugins come in a variety of forms, but almost all of them are installed and managed in just a few different ways, which we'll cover in Chapter 1. We'll also show you two concrete examples of plugins.

CHAPTER 1

■ ■ ■

The Power of Rails Plugins

Ruby on Rails is a powerful framework for building web applications. We won't waste precious space extolling its many virtues; if you weren't already aware of them, you probably wouldn't be reading this book. To put it succinctly, Rails makes good development practices easy and enjoyable, and allows you to build solid, well-structured, and (gasp!) maintainable applications quickly.

As most seasoned developers have learned through experience, a framework is only as good as it is extensible, and yet there's a certain trick to keeping such a thing simple and unencumbered. In fact, you might even say that these goals of simplicity and extensibility are directly at odds most of the time. Fortunately for us, Rails has found a nice balance in the form of its plugin architecture.

This book focuses on how you, as a developer, can leverage plugins to accelerate the development of your own projects. We'll demonstrate how major features can be added to existing applications with very little effort through a series of specific examples, allowing you to implement features that would traditionally take you far, far longer to develop on your own. We'll also show you how to create your own plugins to share with others. This chapter will get you started by giving you an idea of what plugins can do for you and then explaining how to find, install, and manage plugins.

What Can Plugins Do for You?

Plugins, in a nutshell, are bits of packaged code that provide either a modification to existing framework behavior or entirely new functionality. Some plugins are simple things that just make a new helper available in your views, such as the Gravatar plugin (`http://gravatarplugin.rubyforge.org`), which allows you to display a user's existing avatar icon from the popular Gravatar web service. On the other hand, some involve more complex functionality, such as adding geolocation capabilities to the default Active Record finder (GeoKit, Chapter 14) or providing a complete login/authentication system and user model (Restful Authentication, Chapter 11). The following are just some of things plugins can do:

- Extend an existing data model, allowing any resource to have items like ratings, tags, or comments associated with it, or allowing the model to act as something else entirely, such as a list or a tree data structure.

- Provide whole application subsystems, such as user authentication and authorization.

- Enhance your application views by wrapping easy-to-use helpers around popular third-party packages for graphing, media playback, web services access, and so on.

- Add Rake tasks to your Rails project, such as one to generate code coverage statistics or data model annotations.

- Change the way testing or other built-in facilities work.

As you can see, plugins serve a multitude of purposes. The plugin architecture in Rails is itself deceivingly simple, and the real magic comes from the metaprogramming capabilities inherent in an elegant dynamic language like Ruby, which allows any class to be opened and modified at runtime. This means that it's possible to change or extend any and all of the default behaviors in your models, controllers, and views.

Plugins are often used as a way to experiment with new ideas. In fact, features that eventually become part of the Rails core codebase can often begin life as plugins, as they provide a mechanism with which to share new ideas and functionality without directly modifying Rails itself.

Other features introduced as plugins simply have no place in the Rails core and are intentionally left out in the interest of keeping the core as general purpose and as slimmed-down as possible. These plugins serve purposes as diverse as payment processing (ActiveMerchant, Chapter 10), lightboxing images (Lightbox Helper, Chapter 19), testing HTML markup validity (Assert Valid Markup, Chapter 27), and interfacing with message queues (Workling, Chapter 18). They demonstrate exactly why the system works as well as it does; you can create a new project and elect to install only the specific pieces that make sense for your project, without worrying about the bloat of unused features. These less general-purpose plugins will remain plugins forever, existing as segmented architectural bits that can be maintained and updated on their own release schedule.

Like the basic foundation of open source software itself, the plugin architecture leverages the collective intelligence and experience of the entire Ruby on Rails community. Do you need to generate PDF documents on the fly? Bruce Williams and Wiebe Cazamier have written a tool, in the form of a plugin, that allows you to use LaTeX to do just this (RTex, Chapter 24). Do you need to handle image file uploads, create thumbnails, and store them at Amazon S3 (Simple Storage Service)? Rick Olson has already devised a way to do all that for you, too (Attachment Fu, Chapter 3).

The contributions made by the community in this area are staggering. Indeed, the popular plugin directory service at `http://agilewebdevelopment.com` counts more than 700 plugins in existence today, with new code being added by talented Rails developers every day. We can't cover them all here, but what we can do is get you started. However, before we can start exploring all the great uses for plugins and demonstrating examples with our sample applications, we first need to discuss the basic tools for discovering and installing plugins.

Managing a Wealth of Plugins

As you're no doubt aware, when you create a new Rails project, a number of helpful scripts are automatically available to you. One of these scripts is the plugin manager, available in `script/plugin` within the Rails project structure. This script is the gateway through which plugins can be discovered, installed, updated, and removed.

■**Note** We assume that you already have Rails installed and you are working with version 2.0.2 or later. If you don't already have Rails installed, refer to the instructions at `http://rubyonrails.org` or the book *Beginning Rails: From Notice to Professional* by Jeffrey Allan Hardy (Apress, 2007).

Let's create a new Rails project so we can start exploring the plugin system. Enter the following command:

```
rails plugin_explorer
```

Finding Available Plugins

Plugins are typically available through a series of plugin repositories. When you create a Rails application, the plugin manager comes with a predefined set of defaults. Change to the newly created project directory and issue the following command to tell the plugin manager to list the default set of plugins available to a virgin Rails project.

```
cd plugin_explorer
ruby script/plugin list
```

```
account_location             ➡
http://dev.rubyonrails.com/svn/rails/plugins/account_location/
acts_as_list                 ➡
http://dev.rubyonrails.com/svn/rails/plugins/acts_as_list/
acts_as_nested_set           ➡
http://dev.rubyonrails.com/svn/rails/plugins/acts_as_nested_set/
acts_as_tree                 ➡
http://dev.rubyonrails.com/svn/rails/plugins/acts_as_tree/
atom_feed_helper             ➡
http://dev.rubyonrails.com/svn/rails/plugins/atom_feed_helper/
auto_complete                ➡
http://dev.rubyonrails.com/svn/rails/plugins/auto_complete/
continuous_builder           ➡
http://dev.rubyonrails.com/svn/rails/plugins/continuous_builder/
deadlock_retry               ➡
http://dev.rubyonrails.com/svn/rails/plugins/deadlock_retry/
in_place_editing             ➡
http://dev.rubyonrails.com/svn/rails/plugins/in_place_editing/
javascript_test              ➡
http://dev.rubyonrails.com/svn/rails/plugins/javascript_test/
legacy                       ➡
http://dev.rubyonrails.com/svn/rails/plugins/legacy/
localization                 ➡
http://dev.rubyonrails.com/svn/rails/plugins/localization/
open_id_authentication       ➡
http://dev.rubyonrails.com/svn/rails/plugins/open_id_authentication/
```

```
scaffolding                    ➡
http://dev.rubyonrails.com/svn/rails/plugins/scaffolding/
scriptaculous_slider           ➡
http://dev.rubyonrails.com/svn/rails/plugins/scriptaculous_slider/
ssl_requirement                ➡
http://dev.rubyonrails.com/svn/rails/plugins/ssl_requirement/
token_generator                ➡
http://dev.rubyonrails.com/svn/rails/plugins/token_generator/
tzinfo_timezone                ➡
http://dev.rubyonrails.com/svn/rails/plugins/tzinfo_timezone/
tztime                         ➡
http://dev.rubyonrails.com/svn/rails/plugins/tztime/
upload_progress                ➡
http://dev.rubyonrails.com/svn/rails/plugins/upload_progress/
```

There are some interesting plugins in this list, but note that they're all in the same repository. Also note that the plugin repository itself is really just a Subversion (svn) source control repository, accessible via the HTTP protocol. You can open your web browser and plug in one of these URLs if you like. You'll see a directory listing that corresponds to the current Subversion revision for that plugin source. Feel free to read the plugin's README file or poke around in its source, but don't get sidetracked; we'll be talking about how plugins are internally structured in Chapter 28, where you'll learn how to create, test, and distribute your own plugin.

■**Tip** The list of sources is shared across projects and is stored in a file called .rails-plugin-sources in your home directory. If you see additional plugins or repositories in this list, it's most likely because you previously added them using the source command.

What if you want to add another repository in order to expand the list of available plugins? You can use the plugin manager's discover and source commands. If you use the discover command, the plugin manager will ask you whether you want to add repositories from a known list to your personal set.

```
ruby script/plugin discover
```

```
Add http://www.agilewebdevelopment.com/plugins/? [Y/n]
Add svn://rubyforge.org/var/svn/expressica/plugins/? [Y/n]
Add http://soen.ca/svn/projects/rails/plugins/? [Y/n]
...
```

If you rerun the list command, you'll notice that the list of plugins has been greatly expanded. It now includes all of the plugins located within the new repositories that you've discovered.

Note The list of repositories retrieved by the `discover` command is actually scraped from the following URL: `http://wiki.rubyonrails.org/rails/pages/Plugins`. Since this page is a wiki and it's publicly editable by just about anyone, you may want to use discretion when adding plugins. In general, it's not a good idea to install plugins named things like `acts_as_identity_theft`! If you add a repository and want to later remove it, you can use the `unsource` command.

You can manually add plugin repositories to the local set by using the `source` command. Try this:

```
ruby script/plugin source http://svn.railsplugins.com/plugins
```

```
Added 1 repositories.
```

If you want to just list plugins available at that repository, use the `list` command with the `--source` option.

It's important to note that sourcing a repository is not a prerequisite for installing plugins from that repository. When installing plugins, you can specify either the full path to the plugin or a short name for the plugin if the plugin's repository is in your sources list. We'll cover how to install plugins next.

RUBY GEMS

In addition to plugins, we'll be using a number of useful Ruby gems throughout this book. RubyGems is a general package management system for Ruby libraries, and is not specific to Rails. Gems and plugins cover a lot of the same ground, with the primary differences being internal structure and the fact that plugins are specific to Rails, following certain conventions that allow them to hook into the Rails initialization process. Often, you'll find that a Rails plugin will consist of a thin wrapper around a more powerful gem.

Gems have many features that are lacking in Rails plugins, including dependency management and proper versioning, and there are ongoing discussions about bridging this divide. In the meantime, if your application depends on any number of gems, you may wish to unpack them to the `vendor` directory to ease deployment and versioning concerns.

To make this easier, Rails 2.1 has added a mechanism for defining and associating gem dependencies with Rails projects using the `config.gem` directive in `environment.rb` and the `rake gem` family of Rake tasks. Running `rake gems:install` will install gems that are listed as dependencies on the local system, and `rake gems:unpack` will unpack those gems to the `vendor` directory automatically. For more information, see the excellent Railscast screencast resource at http://railscasts.com/episodes/110. If you're using Rails 2.0 or older, we recommend checking out the Gems On Rails plugin by Dr. Nic Williams, which provides equivalent functionality. Gems On Rails is available at `http://gemsonrails.rubyforge.org`.

For more information about Ruby gems in general, check out *Practical Ruby Gems* by David Berube (Apress, 2007).

Installing Plugins

A plugin can be installed by using the plugin manager's `install` command. Once installed, integration with your application can often be as simple as adding a line to your `environment.rb` configuration or adding declarative-looking statements to an existing model class.

To demonstrate how to install Rails plugins, as well as see how they work in practice, let's install a couple extremely useful plugins. First, we'll examine the simple Annotate Models plugin, by Dave Thomas, and then we'll take a brief look at a slightly more complex plugin, Exception Notification, by Rails core team member Jamis Buck.

Installing the Annotate Models Plugin

The Annotate Models plugin adds a comment summarizing the current database schema to the top of each Active Record model source file. These annotations are very useful, since otherwise the table attributes may not show up at all within the body of your model. It's certainly a best practice to have these attribute definitions handy when looking at your model source. Imagine adding new developers to your development team and making them examine SQL table schemas in order to understand your data models. Better to make those models as self-explanatory as possible, right?

If the plugin is listed in your local sources, you can simply issue a command like `script/plugin install annotate_models`. However, Annotate Models is not in your default local sources, and we don't want to bother to source the whole repository. Instead, we can just specify the full path to the plugin, including the repository:

```
ruby script/plugin  install http://svn.pragprog.com/Public/plugins/annotate_models
```

```
+ ./annotate_models/ChangeLog
+ ./annotate_models/README
+ ./annotate_models/lib/annotate_models.rb
+ ./annotate_models/tasks/annotate_models_tasks.rake
```

This output shows that the most recent version of the specified plugin has been checked out from its Subversion repository. It has been placed in the `vendor/plugins` directory of the project, which is where all per-project plugins are stored. Any plugins that are present within that directory structure are automatically loaded at startup. In this case, the Annotate Models plugin simply adds a Rake task to the default set of tasks for your Rails project. You can learn more about it by looking at the plugin's `README` file, which should now be located in your local source tree at `vendors/plugins/annotate_models/README`.

To test the newly installed plugin, you'll first need a model to annotate. Let's create one now. We'll generate a `Book` model that has some number of attributes.

```
ruby script/generate model book
```

```
      exists  app/models/
      exists  test/unit/
      exists  test/fixtures/
      create  app/models/book.rb
      create  test/unit/book_test.rb
      create  test/fixtures/books.yml
      create  db/migrate
      create  db/migrate/001_create_books.rb
```

Next, we'll edit the migration to specify a number of attributes. Edit the file db/migrate/
001_create_books.rb so it looks like this:

```
class CreateBooks < ActiveRecord::Migration
  def self.up
    create_table :books do |t|
      t.column :title, :string
      t.column :isbn, :string
      t.column :author, :string
      t.column :publisher, :string
      t.column :description, :text
    end
  end

  def self.down
    drop_table :books
  end
end
```

As of Rails 2.0.2, any new Rails project uses SQLite version 3 as its default database back
end unless otherwise specified. This means that when you run your database migration, a
database is automatically created for you in db/development.sqlite3. If you would prefer to
use MySQL or PostgreSQL, you can edit the config/database.yml file at this time.

Run the migration now by entering the following command:

```
rake db:migrate
```

```
== CreateBooks: migrating ====================================================
-- create_table(:books)
   -> 0.8761s
== CreateBooks: migrated (0.8762s) ===========================================
```

At this point, you have an application with a single data model, Book, which is, through
the magic of Active Record, associated with the books table in your database. A Book instance

has five attributes: a title, an ISBN, an author, a publisher, and a description. If you open your model code in `app/models/book.rb`, you can see the model definition:

```
class Book < ActiveRecord::Base
end
```

That isn't very descriptive, is it? Let's try out the Annotate Models plugin, to see how that can help us here. If you viewed the `README` file earlier (good initiative!), you already saw the instructions for use. It's very simple. The plugin provides a Rake task to annotate any model objects in the current project. Let's run it:

```
rake annotate_models
```

Annotating Book

That's all the output you'll see—nothing fancy. But if you open the model definition, you can see the results of this action:

```
# == Schema Information
# Schema version: 1
#
# Table name: books
#
# id          :integer(11)   not null, primary key
# title       :string(255)
# isbn        :string(255)
# author      :string(255)
# publisher   :string(255)
# description :text
#

class Book < ActiveRecord::Base
end
```

Now that's much clearer. Simply by looking at the model source, you can see which attributes are available. In addition, this information will be nice to have around if you plan on generating API documentation for this project with RDoc (the standard embedded documentation generator for Ruby).

As you can see, the Annotate Models plugin isn't at all complicated in terms of what it does. It is, however, universally useful and a great tool to have in your box of development tricks. As we examine numerous plugins throughout this book, you'll find that almost all of them do far more complicated things than Annotate Models, but few of them are as universally applicable across all projects.

Installing the Exception Notification Plugin

Moving on to a slightly more complicated example (which also has universal appeal), we'll next examine the Exception Notification plugin. If you have an application deployed in a production environment, exception notifications can be crucial to have in place.

Imagine that you're an experienced programmer learning Rails and you've just deployed your first big application. Unfortunately, your boss chewed you out this morning because for the past week, a big client was trying to use an obscure feature of the site that hadn't been properly tested by one of your subordinates. It turns out that a helper function was referencing a misnamed controller, which was causing an exception to be raised. Worse, the client waited an entire week to notify support about it. If you had had some warning, you could have fixed it before the complaint had escalated!

With exception notification in place, if your application experiences an unhandled exception, the details of that exception will be immediately packaged and sent to some e-mail address that you specify. The e-mail message will contain a wealth of information about the exception, including the current request, session, and environment data, in order to help you re-create and resolve the problem. It's an essential tool, particularly in the early production life stages of a new application.

First, let's install the plugin:

```
ruby script/plugin install ➥
http://dev.rubyonrails.org/svn/rails/plugins/exception_notification
```

```
+ ./exception_notification/README
+ ./exception_notification/init.rb
+ ./exception_notification/lib/exception_notifiable.rb
+ ./exception_notification/lib/exception_notifier.rb
+ ./exception_notification/lib/exception_notifier_helper.rb
+ ./exception_notification/test/exception_notifier_helper_test.rb
+ ./exception_notification/test/test_helper.rb
+ ./exception_notification/views/exception_notifier/_backtrace.rhtml
+ ./exception_notification/views/exception_notifier/_environment.rhtml
+ ./exception_notification/views/exception_notifier/_inspect_model.rhtml
+ ./exception_notification/views/exception_notifier/_request.rhtml
+ ./exception_notification/views/exception_notifier/_session.rhtml
+ ./exception_notification/views/exception_notifier/_title.rhtml
+ ./exception_notification/views/exception_notifier/exception_notification.rhtml
```

As before, the plugin has been checked out to your vendor/plugins directory, where it will be loaded on startup. It's important to note that if you install new plugins while you're running a development server, you'll need to restart the server. Plugins are loaded only on startup, even in development mode. For the Annotate Models plugin, this didn't matter so much, because the plugin was providing only a Rake task. In this case, the Exception Notification plugin will be mixed into your ApplicationController, extending Rails itself, so the server will need to be restarted before things will work properly.

Exception Notification, like many plugins, requires some minimal amount of integration into your project to function. This is typical of plugin installations. Although the plugin is already installed, you need to tell it how to talk to the rest of the application. In most cases, this means adding a line or two of declarative-looking code to a model class, or setting a configuration directive in environment.rb. The specifics depend on the plugin and its purpose. The README file that comes with the plugin will always document this process, so be sure to read it. In the case of Exception Notification, you'll need to include the `ExceptionNotifiable` mixin in your `ApplicationController` (app/controllers/application.rb):

```
class ApplicationController < ActionController::Base
  include ExceptionNotifiable
  ...
end
```

The act of mixing in this new module will make sure that the application fires off a notification e-mail whenever an exception is encountered. You also need to specify the e-mail recipients in your `config/environment.rb` file:

```
ExceptionNotifier.exception_recipients = %w(support@your-company.com)
```

You can further customize the plugin if you wish, to set the sender address of the e-mail, the text used to prefix the subject line of the e-mail, and so on. See that `README` file for details.

In any case, you can now restart the application. If it's running in production mode and an exception is generated from a request source other than localhost (that is, from any remote user), an e-mail will be sent to the intended recipient.

To test exception notifications while running locally in development mode, you need to tweak a few extra items. This is because Rails treats exceptions differently in production versus development mode (it also treats local requests specially). In production mode, we want to protect users from seeing the details of the exception that occurred. In development mode, we'll display any and all exception data to the user in an error template. These differences are reflected in the `rescue_action_in_public` and `rescue_action_locally` methods of the `ActionController::Rescue` module, and Exception Notification, being interested only in remote requests received while in production mode, hooks into only the former method.

To remedy this, so we can test the plugin locally, add the following two lines to the end of your `ApplicationController` class definition in app/controllers/application.rb (immediately before the end).

```
local_addresses.clear
alias :rescue_action_locally :rescue_action_in_public
```

■Note What this does is essentially force the requests that result in exceptions in the development environment to be handled the way that they would be handled for remote client requests in production, which, since we've mixed in `ExceptionNotifiable`, involves sending the exception notification e-mails. We've also told Rails to treat all requests as nonlocal—even requests from localhost. Again, this is for the purpose of testing our plugin only, and you'll probably want to remove this code after verifying that exception notifications are working. In most cases, you would prefer to see the standard `rescue_action_locally` behavior while in development, since it will display the error in your browser window and allow for quicker debugging.

Now you need to add something to your application to generate an exception. That should be easy enough, right? We've all done it. Edit your `config/routes.rb` file and add the following line before the default route specification:

```
map.connect '/foo', :controller => 'foo'
```

Since there is no `FooController`, this should cause an exception (in this case, a `NameError`) to be raised. If everything is configured correctly, your application will write the notification to your development log. To see this for yourself, start your server using `ruby script/server` and open a web browser. Surf to `http://localhost:3000/foo`, and you should be greeted with the default 500 Server Error page. If you look in your `log/development.log`, you'll see that the exception notification has been generated. It should look something like this:

```
Sent mail:
 From: Exception Notifier <exception.notifier@default.com>
Subject: [ERROR] application#index (NameError) ➥
"uninitialized constant FooController"
Mime-Version: 1.0
Content-Type: text/plain; charset=utf-8

A NameError occurred in application#index:

  uninitialized constant FooController
  /opt/local/lib/ruby/gems/1.8/gems/activesupport-
1.4.2/lib/active_support/dependencies.rb:266:in ➥
'load_missing_constant'
...
```

In production mode, assuming that Action Mailer is configured correctly, an e-mail alert will be sent. The e-mail message will contain this information along with the subsequent backtrace, session, and environment information.

Updating and Removing Plugins

It's important to note that once a plugin is installed, it's essentially locked to the version you installed (unless you use `svn:externals`, which will be discussed shortly). This means that if there are later updates to the plugin source, you'll need to explicitly update the plugin to receive those updates. You can do this using the plugin manager's `update` command. To update the Exception Notification plugin, for example, you would issue the following command:

```
ruby script/plugin update exception_notification
```

Similarly, if you ever wish to uninstall the Exception Notification plugin, or any plugin at all, you can use the `script/plugin remove` command. For more information and extended options, you can always issue the following command to receive the default help message:

```
ruby script/plugin -h
```

RaPT

RaPT, the Rails Plugin Tool, is a more feature-rich replacement for the default Rails plugin manager. Perhaps its most notable addition is the ability to search plugins from the command line. RaPT is available as a gem, and you can install it by issuing the following command:

```
gem install rapt
```

Let's run a search with RaPT. It's very similar to the way that Debian's `apt-get` tools and various other package management tools work:

```
rapt search "gravatar"
Gravatar
    Info: http://agilewebdevelopment.com/plugins/show/689
    Install: svn://rubyforge.org//var/svn/gravatarplugin/plugins/gravatar
Gravatar tag
    Info: http://agilewebdevelopment.com/plugins/show/783
    Install: http://tools.assembla.com/svn/hasham/plugins/gravatar_tag
```

RaPT also has support for *plugin packs*, a term used to describe sets of plugins that are grouped together for ease of installation. You can learn more about plugin packs (including how to build one of your own) at `http://www.lukeredpath.co.uk/2006/7/27/install-your-favorite-rails-plugins-easily-with-rails-plugin-packs`.

The other RaPT commands are analogous to the standard plugin managers, using the same syntax for installing plugins, updating them, and so on. In short, RaPT does everything the stock plugin manager does and then some. More information is available at `http://rapt.rubyforge.org`.

Accessing Documentation and Tests

Documentation and testing are just as important for plugins as they are for any other piece of code. Fortunately, Rails provides a couple of default Rake tasks that deal with running plugin tests and generating documentation for the plugins you have installed. You'll learn about writing tests for our own plugins in Chapter 28.

To find out what Rake-related plugin tasks are available, you can issue the following command:

```
rake -T | grep plugin
```

```
rake doc:clobber_plugins       # Remove plugin documentation
rake doc:plugins               # Generate documentation for all installed plugins
rake test:plugins              # Run the plugin tests in vendor/plugins/**/test ➥
(or specify with PLUGIN=name)
```

Let's generate some documentation for your installed plugins. It's simple:

```
rake doc:plugins
```

You'll see the familiar RDoc output generated. When it completes, the report shows the HTML output statistics, including the number of files, classes, modules, and methods processed for each plugin. The task deposits documentation for all your plugins in the doc/plugins directory. If you navigate there in a browser, you can open the HTML files and browse through the autogenerated API documentation for the plugin, as shown in Figure 1-1.

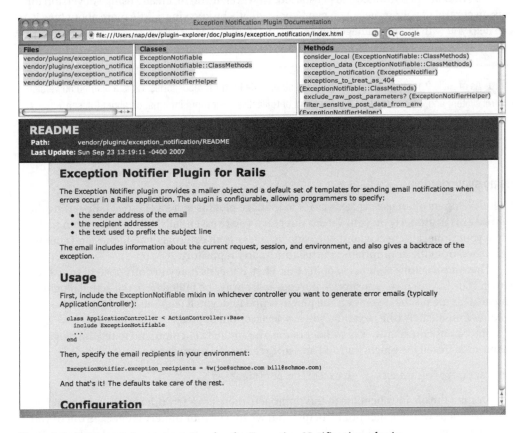

Figure 1-1. *Generated documentation for the Exception Notification plugin*

Running tests for installed plugins should also be familiar to anyone who is used to writing and running unit tests in Rails. To run all the tests that come packaged with your installed plugins, issue the following command:

```
rake test:plugins
```

```
Started
.......
Finished in 0.228314 seconds.

7 tests, 8 assertions, 0 failures, 0 errors
```

If you see this output, it means that everything is installed and working correctly.

Versioning Plugins

We've mentioned that most plugin repositories are really just Subversion repositories, and when you're installing a plugin, you're really just using Subversion to check it out of a remote Subversion repository and into your local source tree. And to be honest, that's really all you need to know about Subversion to get started. However, if you're already using Subversion for version control of your project, you can benefit greatly by knowing a little more about how it can help you with plugin management.

■Tip As of Rails 2.1, plugins can also be installed directly from Git repositories. Git is a distributed version control system and is now used for development of Rails itself. For more information about Git, see http://git.or.cz.

Using svn:externals

Rails developers often use `svn:externals` to manage plugins in a Rails project. By setting the `svn:externals` property on your `vendor` directory, you're essentially telling Subversion that when your project is checked out, the code in `vendor` is an external dependency and should be fetched from the appropriate external third-party repository.

There are a couple benefits to doing this. First, it means that you don't need to store the plugin code in your own repository—the code will always be pulled from the actual plugin source. This means that whenever the plugin is updated, you'll reap the benefits of those new features immediately (the next time you `svn update` your source).

You can use the handy `-x` argument to the `plugin install` command to tell the plugin manager to install the plugin and add an `svn:externals` entry to `vendor/plugins`:

```
ruby script/plugin install -x exception_notification
```

Despite the obvious benefits to this approach, there are a few drawbacks you should be cognizant of as well. We mentioned before that whenever your project is checked out of your Subversion repository or updated, the latest plugin updates will also be pulled down automatically. This is great in a lot of cases, but it can also be problematic if the updated plugin unexpectedly breaks something in your codebase. To overcome this, you can manually add the `-r` argument to specify that you want the revision number locked.

Another drawback is what happens if the third-party repository becomes temporarily unavailable, which is a liability many businesses just can't afford. And of course, if you're working in a team environment, as most of us are, and dealing with a high volume of Subversion updates to keep in sync, you must remember that every time an update is issued, Subversion is checking not only your local repository but also each remote plugin repository for updates.

Oh, and what happens if you decide you need to make a change to some of that plugin code? Smells like trouble.

■**Note** If you insist on using `svn:externals` anyway, note that you can use the `-ignore-externals` option to the `update` command to ignore external repository checking.

Using Piston

Another solution, which has become increasingly popular and is arguably the best of both worlds, is to use the Piston gem to manage your plugins with Subversion. Piston is a Ruby gem that simplifies vendor branch management for plugins. To install it, type this:

```
gem install piston -y
```

Note that your project must be in a working copy of a Subversion repository in order for this to work.

Here's how you would use Piston to install the Annotate Models plugin, rather than using the stock plugin manager for the installation. Note that you can also specify a specific revision to snatch:

```
piston import http://svn.pragprog.com/Public/plugins/annotate_models ➥
vendor/plugins/annotate_models -r 15
```

```
Exported r15 from 'http://svn.pragprog.com/Public/plugins/annotate_models' to ➥
'vendor/plugins/annotate_models'
```

So what does Piston do that makes it so different? Piston essentially copies the current (or specified) revision of the imported plugin into your repository, and keeps track of the revision number and where it came from. You end up with a local copy of the plugin code checked into your repository, which you can modify if necessary. Later, you can choose to update those plugins by issuing a `piston update` command, which will replace that plugin source with a newer version from the vendor, and even manage merging your own modifications into it if necessary. Slick, eh?

```
piston update vendor/plugins/annotate_models/
```

```
Processing 'vendor/plugins/annotate_models/'...
  Fetching remote repository's latest revision and UUID
  Restoring remote repository to known state at r15
  Updating remote repository to r22
  Processing adds/deletes
  Removing temporary files / folders
  Updating Piston properties
  Updated to r22 (3 changes)
```

Piston is extremely easy to use and is the plugin management strategy of choice for a growing number of professional Ruby on Rails developers.

If using Piston sounds good to you, but you have a large number of plugins already installed using `svn:externals`, you'll be pleased to know that Piston can also be used to convert existing plugins with its `convert` command. You can read more about Piston and its features at `http://piston.rubyforge.org`.

Throughout this book, we'll be using the standard plugin manager to install plugins because of its ubiquity and lack of dependence on Subversion. That said, we use Piston in real-world projects ourselves, and we think that you probably should, too.

Discovering Plugins

A commonly asked question is, "How do I find useful new plugins?" Running the `discover` and `list` commands from the plugin manager finds the names of available plugins through known repositories, and RaPT is a great tool to use when searching plugins for a particular keyword. However, there are other resources on the Web that are rich with useful information, allowing you to view lists of plugins by categories and read descriptions and user comments.

The first resource worth mentioning is, of course, the official Ruby on Rails Wiki, which maintains a page on plugins, separating them by category. You can view this page at `http://wiki.rubyonrails.com/rails/pages/Plugins`.

Another useful resource is the Agile Web Development Rails Plugin Directory, created by Ben Curtis, an exhaustive and well-organized directory of plugins. It is divided by categories and fully searchable. Users of the service contribute ratings and comments to each plugin entry, making it easy to filter out the great from the very good. RSS feeds are also available to keep you abreast of current developments. The Plugin Directory can be accessed at `http://agilewebdevelopment.com/plugins`. RailsLodge (`http://railslodge.com`) and RailsPlugins.net (`http://railsplugins.net`) provide similar offerings.

Finally, there is the web site associated with this book, `http://www.railsplugins.com`, which contains source code for the examples found here and supplementary information that you may find useful. You can also find the source code for the examples for this book in the Source Code/Download area of the Apress web site (`http://www.apress.com`).

Summary

Rails plugins put a wealth of powerful, multipurpose extensions at your fingertips. With a uniform installation mechanism, you only need to know how to look for them and employ a simple set of commands to get up and running quickly and easily, adding powerful functionality to your applications. Learning Subversion (or, alternatively, the even more powerful Git distributed version control system) is paramount, and most Rails developers are already using it for source control. If such is the case, learning to use Piston is very little extra work for a lot of extra flexibility in managing your plugins.

This book will demonstrate how you can quickly bring a web application into existence with minimal time spent on the more generic aspects such as login systems, dealing with attachments, user ratings, and such. By leveraging plugins, you can free yourself from these routine tasks and focus on those unique aspects that make your application stand out from the competition.

PART 2

■■■

Model Enhancement

Active Record models represent the first third of the Model-View-Controller (MVC) triad within the Rails framework, and some of the best-known and most generally applicable plugins fall into this category.

Plugins can enhance models in a variety of ways. Some may simply add new validations; others allow you to store different versions of model data so that no data is ever lost during revisions. Plugins can even make adding complex states and state-transition rules relatively straightforward tasks.

In this part of the book, we'll demonstrate how to use plugins that accomplish all of these things, and integrate them into interesting sample applications. You'll also see plugins that allow other resources—such as tags, ratings, and even file attachments—to be easily associated with any Active Record model.

## CHAPTER 2

Web 2.0 Tagging with Acts As Taggable

Tagging is a deceptively simple mechanism by which the users of your web service assign their own categories or keywords (*tags*) to items. This usually has a twofold purpose: it helps users organize their own information, and it makes information easier for others to locate.

Users of popular web services (del.icio.us, Flickr, Gmail, Last.fm, and many others) use tagging to organize information, such as bookmarks, photos, e-mail, and music. By outsourcing the task of classifying information to their user base (which includes content creators and consumers, as well as domain experts), these services are not only relieved from the burden of categorizing resources themselves, but may also achieve more accurate results. The sort of taxonomies generated by this process are often referred to as *folksonomies*, and are at the very heart of Web 2.0.

As an example, consider a web site that lets people share slide show presentations. Users of this application upload their presentations and use text-based tag keywords to help classify them. These tags are basically just ad hoc categories. They can be used to locate the presentation when browsing or to fuel keyword-based search results. Other visitors can expand on the initial set of tags that were assigned to the presentation by adding their own tags. For instance, Alice, the creator of a presentation about search engine optimization, may choose to tag her work with the words marketing, search, seo, and google. Later, Ankit may stumble upon the same presentation when doing some research about web spidering, and find it useful. He may choose to add the tag spidering or crawlers to the presentation for his own reference, and by doing so, help other people with similar interests find it.

As users like Alice and Ankit upload new content and add tags to existing content, they're creating a dense network of keywords and categories that can be used to navigate among related items in the system. This has a number of advantages over traditional categorization and, assuming that you believe in the wisdom of crowds, it makes content discovery easier for consumers than ever before.

Of course, tags can be used in a variety of other ways. Sometimes tags can be assigned only by the creators of an item; sometimes they can be added by only the creators and their "friends"; and other times, anyone can add a tag to an object. In more complex systems, tags can be weighted by the number of people who have assigned them to the same object, thus increasing their relevancy as a search term.

You may choose to implement and leverage tags in any number of ways within your own application. In this chapter, we'll get you started with minimal fuss by using Jonathan Viney's Acts As Taggable (on Steroids) plugin, which allows tags to be easily attributed to any number of models through a simple API. It's based on the original Acts As Taggable plugin implementation written by Rails framework founder David Heinemeier Hansson, but features a number of improvements, including an enhanced tag assignment interface and autogeneration of tag clouds.

Our Task: Enable User-Categorized Content by Adding Tagging Capabilities

One of our clients, Sammy, runs an arcade machine restoration business. Recently, he set up a forum package, and a community has started to form around his site. He has found that community members are constantly trading links to other web sites and resources on the forum, and a lot of the same links are reposted over and over again.

Having observed this, Sammy has decided that he wants to create a resource site for aggregating classic arcade game resources found on the Web. The idea is that community members can add new links to the resource site whenever they find something they want to share with others, rather than starting yet another thread on the forum site. In order to be useful, the site must be able to index a lot of information and make individual resources easy to find over time.

Sammy's first idea was to manually review and categorize each link that is submitted by a user. However, he's a busy man and, although he knows a lot about arcade machine restoration, he doesn't have the appropriate domain knowledge to categorize certain related topics correctly. But what if he could instead leverage the collective knowledge of his user base? Well, that's worth a closer look. His site attracts a lot of knowledgeable hobbyists and professionals, and it turns out that they would be more than happy to help with this task, since it directly benefits them!

To facilitate this categorization of links, we propose the addition of a tagging feature to Sammy's arcade resources site. This way, when users add a new link, they can also (optionally) add any number of tags to it. A set of tags for an arcade game resource might be something like `restoration`, `pac-man`, and `cocktail` for a page that documents step-by-step restoration of a Pac-Man cocktail table arcade system; or `pinball`, `glass`, and `replacement`, for a manufacturer that sells replacement glass for pinball machines. This information will function as notes left by the person creating or visiting the linked resource, as well as provide a way for others to locate the same information.

Building Taggable Arcade Resource Links

To begin, let's create a new Rails project:

```
rails arcadelinks
cd arcadelinks
```

To install the taggable plugin, execute the following command inside the new project directory:

```
ruby script/plugin install ➥
http://svn.viney.net.nz/things/rails/plugins/acts_as_taggable_on_steroids
```

Next, we'll use the taggable migration code generator the plugin provides to create a database migration:

```
ruby script/generate acts_as_taggable_migration
```

```
    exists  db/migrate
    create  db/migrate/001_acts_as_taggable_migration.rb
```

This migration specifies the database tables that are needed to save tags (the tags table) and associate them with the models we'll be creating (the taggings table). To create these tables using the default development database, we just need to run the rake db:migrate task:

```
rake db:migrate
```

```
== 1 ActsAsTaggableMigration: migrating ========================================
-- create_table(:tags)
   -> 0.0033s
-- create_table(:taggings)
   -> 0.0037s
-- add_index(:taggings, :tag_id)
   -> 0.0023s
-- add_index(:taggings, [:taggable_id, :taggable_type])
   -> 0.0256s
== 1 ActsAsTaggableMigration: migrated (0.0356s) ===============================
```

■**Note** As of Rails 2.0.2, the default database configuration for a Rails application is a SQLite version 3 file-based database. Unless the configuration is changed, the database file will be created automatically in db/development.sqlite3. If you wish to change this, edit config/database.yml and set up your database as appropriate. Throughout this book, unless otherwise noted, we'll be using the standard SQLite 3 development database.

Constructing the Arcade Resource Link Model

Before we dive into the implementation of the tagging service itself, we first need a model that represents an arcade resource on the Web (a Link). To get started, let's create a migration for the links table, from which the Link model will inherit its attributes, as shown in Listing 2-1.

Listing 2-1. *Migration for Arcade Resource Link Model (db/migrate/002_create_links.rb)*

```
class CreateLinks < ActiveRecord::Migration
  def self.up
    create_table :links do |t|
      t.string :name
      t.string :url
      t.text   :description
      t.timestamps
    end
  end

  def self.down
    drop_table :links
  end
end
```

Save the migration as db/migrate/002_create_links.rb, and then migrate the database once again using the rake db:migrate task:

```
rake db:migrate
```

```
== 2 CreateLinks: migrating =====================================================
-- create_table(:links)
   -> 0.0044s
== 2 CreateLinks: migrated (0.0045s) ============================================
```

The migration creates three attributes for a Link: a name (probably the name of the linked site), its URL, and a description of the content to be found there. A name and a URL should be required for a Link, but a description may be optional. Furthermore, URLs should be unique in our system so that we don't list a given resource twice under two different names—after all, that would defeat the purpose of adding tags to organize them. These requirements are enforced in the model code, as shown in Listing 2-2. Save it as app/models/link.rb.

Listing 2-2. *Arcade Resource Link Model (app/models/link.rb)*

```
class Link < ActiveRecord::Base
  acts_as_taggable

  validates_presence_of :url, :name
  validates_uniqueness_of :url
end
```

In addition to specifying some validation logic, we've gone ahead and called the special class method acts_as_taggable in our class definition body. This method is provided by the plugin. Adding this single line to the class automatically adds associations to the Tag and Taggings models introduced by the plugin, and also mixes in a number of other useful class and instance-level methods we can use to manipulate those tags. For example, we can now access the tag list (an array of plain-text tags) for a given `Link` model using the `tag_list` instance method, and add and remove tags by calling `tag_list.add` and `tag_list.remove`, respectively. The `tag_counts` class method will calculate the number of tags associated with a certain class of object (`Link.tag_counts`). We can also use a special finder method, `Link.find_tagged_with`, to retrieve objects by tag.

■Tip Many other methods are provided by the Acts As Taggable (on Steroids) plugin. If you're curious, you can generate the plugin's documentation by running the `rake doc:plugins` task. It will place all the documentation in `doc/plugins/acts_as_taggable_on_steroids/index.html`.

To become more familiar with the basics of the tagging system before building our controller, let's test these new model facilities using the Rails console.

Creating Sample Data with the Rails Console

The Rails console can be a handy tool for testing, debugging, reporting, and other infrequent tasks for which it would be difficult or just plain silly to build a proprietary interface. It's really just a wrapper around the Interactive Ruby shell (IRb) that includes access to the current Rails environment. That means that you can directly manipulate the models in your application interactively.

We'll use it now to create two arcade resource links. Then we'll add some tags to those objects. Start the Rails console by typing `script/console` within the project directory, and then type the following commands:

```
>> klov = Link.create!(:name => "Killer List Of Video Games",
        :url => "http://www.klov.com",
        :description => "An authoritative database of coin-operated video games")
>> byoac = Link.create!(:name => "Build Your Own Arcade Controls FAQ",
        :url => "http://arcadecontrols.com/arcade.htm",
        :description => "Build or buy real arcade controls for your PC! " +
          "Instructions and downloads.")
```

■Note To create our links via the Rails console, we've used the `create!` method, which functions much like the normal `create` method, except that it raises an exception if the model-creation task fails for any reason. This allows us to easily see if we've forgotten a required field or made a similar validation error.

Now let's add some tags to our models, using `tag_list` and a few other associated methods that we mentioned earlier:

```
>> klov.tag_list = "arcade, klov, directory"
=> "klov, directory, arcade"
>> klov.save_tags
=> true
>> klov.tag_list.add("coin-op")
=> ["klov", "directory", "arcade", "coin-op"]
>> klov.save_tags
=> true
>> byoac.tag_list.add("coin-op", "diy", "controls", "arcade")
=> ["coin-op", "diy", "controls", "arcade"]
>> byoac.tag_list.remove("coin-op")
=> ["diy", "controls", "arcade"]
>> byoac.save_tags
=> true
>> Link.find_tagged_with("arcade").collect { |link| link.name }
=> ["Killer List Of Video Games", "Build Your Own Arcade Controls FAQ"]
```

This console session illustrates the process of adding tags to our Link models, removing them, and saving them. Note that, although we're making an explicit call to save_tags on the link objects to save the tags we've assigned, the plugin automatically saves associated tags whenever the normal Active Record save method is invoked as well.

The last line of our console session uses the find_tagged_with class method to look up any links that are associated with a given tag. This might be useful if we're browsing or searching for links given a particular tag (or set of tags), for instance.

Adding Tags to the Web Application

We now have a working tags system. The next step is to integrate it into a web application so arcade resource users can work with it. Exposing tags might be useful in a number of places:

- When browsing links, show some of the tags that have been applied to them to help the users decide if they are interested in that resource.

- Allow users to click a tag from a detailed resource information page directly and find other resources that have those tags.

- Show a clickable tag cloud throughout the site, for easy topic/category browse access.

To accomplish these tasks, we'll create two controllers: LinksController and TagsController. They will both be modeled as standard RESTful resources.

The LinksController will be responsible for all things related to links (arcade resources). This means that viewing the list of arcade resources, adding a new resource, and adding tags to resources are all tasks that will need to be handled by actions on this controller.

The TagsController will be used solely for browsing links by tags. When a user requests a list of arcade resources that correspond to a tag, it will be a request made to the show action on the TagsController.

We'll begin by setting up our routes. Listing 2-3 shows the contents of config/routes.rb for this project. Notice that the links resource receives an extra member method, tag, which will be used to assign tags to a specific link.

Listing 2-3. *Routes for the Arcade Resources Project (config/routes.rb)*

```ruby
ActionController::Routing::Routes.draw do |map|
  map.resources :links, :member => { :tag => :post }
  map.resources :tags
end
```

■**Note** As an alternative to adding a tag member method to the links resource, we could optionally nest the tags resource within the links resource and use the nested create action to add new tags to a given link resource. You'll see an example of using nested resources (and more information about RESTful resources in general) in Chapter 11.

Creating Taggable Resources

Aside from the special tag method, the rest of the methods on LinksController are the standard RESTful actions you would expect to find on any resource. The controller code is shown in Listing 2-4. Note that we're omitting the destroy, update, and edit actions for the sake of brevity.

Listing 2-4. *Controller for Arcade Resource Links (app/controllers/links_controller.rb)*

```ruby
class LinksController < ApplicationController
  def index
    @title = "Recently Added Resources"
    @links = Link.find(:all, :order => "created_at DESC")
  end

  def new
    @title = "New Arcade Resource"
    @link = Link.new
  end

  def create
    @link = Link.new(params[:link])
    if @link.save
      redirect_to(:action => 'index')
    else
      render(:action => 'new')
    end
  end
```

```
def show
  @link = Link.find(params[:id])
  @title = @link.name
end

def tag
  @link = Link.find(params[:id])
  @link.tag_list.add(params[:tags].split(','))
  @link.save_tags
  redirect_to(link_path(@link))
end
end
```

There are three views that correspond to the index, new, and show actions of this controller. We'll begin our analysis with the index action and its view, shown in Listing 2-5. Save it as app/views/links/index.html.erb.

Listing 2-5. *Arcade Resource Links Index Template (app/views/links/index.html.erb)*

```
<ul>
  <% @links.each do |link| -%>
    <li><%= link_to(link.name, link_path(link)) %>
      (<%= truncate(link.tag_list.join(', '), 20) %>)</li>
  <% end -%>
</ul>
```

The index action template iterates through each link in the set of all links, provided in the @links instance variable by the controller action, and displays them in the order of most to least recent. For each resource, it renders a list item containing a link to the detailed resource information page for that item, as well as a truncated list of tags that have been applied to the resource (the full list of tags will be displayed on the detailed resource information page after the click-through).

To view this template in a web browser, start the server using ruby script/server and point a web browser at http://localhost:3000/links. Since we already added two arcade resources through the Rails console, you will see a screen that resembles Figure 2-1.

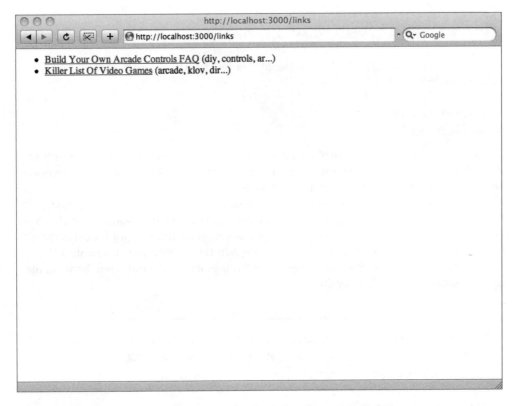

Figure 2-1. *Viewing the list of arcade resources (http://localhost:3000/links)*

Next up is the new action's template. It contains a simple form for creating a new arcade resource link. Save the code shown in Listing 2-6 as app/views/links/new.html.erb.

Listing 2-6. *New Arcade Resource Link Template (app/views/links/new.html.erb)*

```
<%= error_messages_for(:link) %>
<% form_for(:link, :url => links_path) do |f| -%>
  <p><label for="link_name">Name: </label><br/>
  <%= f.text_field(:name) %></p>

  <p><label for="link_url">URL: </label><br/>
  <%= f.text_field(:url) %></p>
```

```
<p><label for="link_description">Description: </label><br/>
<%= f.text_area(:description, :rows => 3) %></p>

<p><label for="link_tag_list">Tags (separated by comma): </label><br/>
<%= f.text_field(:tag_list) %></p>

<%= submit_tag("Create") %>
<% end -%>
```

In addition to the standard attribute fields in the form, this template includes a text field for adding tags directly to a new resource. This works because of the tag_list virtual accessor method that the plugin has added to our Link model.

When the submit button is clicked, the form is submitted to the links_path (/links), which, when combined with the HTTP POST method, indicates that the create action should be called. The create action uses mass assignment to set the attributes of the model to those parameters passed in from params[:link] and then calls save. Not only are the name, URL, and description attributes set in this manner, but any tags specified are also set, thanks to the tag_list setter method added by the plugin.

Tip If multiple tags are entered, they should be separated by commas. To change the delimiter used to parse and present tags, you can set TagList.delimiter. For example, to use spaces as delimiters, just add the following to config/environment.rb:

```
TagList.delimiter = " "
```

Go ahead and load the URL http://localhost:3000/links/new into your browser, and try adding a link. The new link page should look like the screenshot shown in Figure 2-2. After submitting the form, you should be redirected to the index page where the newly created link should appear at the top of the page.

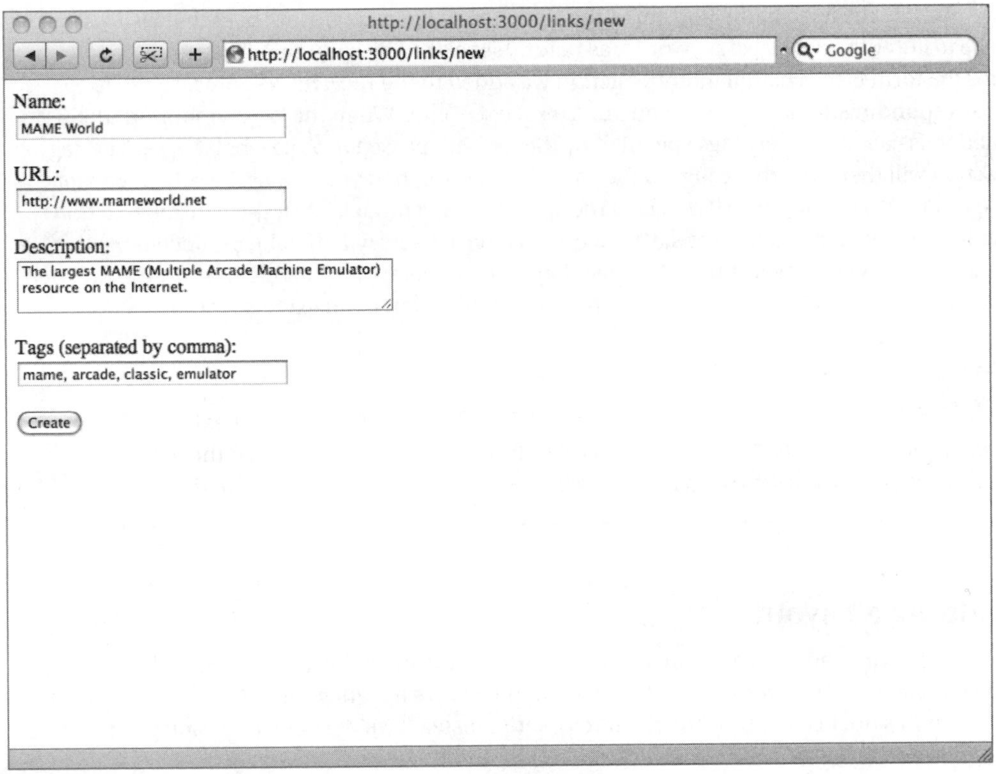

Figure 2-2. *Viewing the new arcade resource link form (http://localhost:3000/links/new)*

Our final template for LinksController, the show action template, is shown in Listing 2-7. It is used to show detailed information about a particular arcade resource link and is also the place where visitors will be able to add new tags to a resource. Save it as app/views/links/show.html.erb.

Listing 2-7. *Arcade Resource Link Show (Detailed Info) Template (app/views/links/show.html.erb)*

```
<p><strong>Link: </strong><%= link_to(@link.url) %></p>
<p><strong>Description:</strong> <%= h(@link.description) %></p>
<p><strong>Tags:</strong> <%= @link.tag_list.join(', ') %></p>
<p>Created <%= time_ago_in_words(@link.created_at) %> ago</p>

<% form_tag(tag_link_path(@link)) do -%>
  <%= text_field_tag(:tags) %>
  <%= submit_tag('Add New Tags') %>
<% end -%>
```

Notice the form at the bottom of the template. It has a single text field that visitors can use to enter the new tags/keywords (as before, separated by commas). The submission URL for the form is the custom member action we added to the RESTful resource, tag_link_path, corresponding to the tag action on our LinksController. When the form is submitted, this action is called, and any tags specified by the user are passed in as params[:tags]. The tag action will then pass those tags to the tag_list.add method you saw earlier in our console session. This will add the new tags to the specified Link model. Next, the controller action calls the save_tags method to save the updated tags. Users will then be redirected back to the show action, which means that the page they were on before is reloaded to show the updated set of tags (we could also do the refresh via Ajax; this is left as an exercise for the reader).

■**Caution** If a user tries to tag a link with a tag that has already been applied, no change will take place because that tag has already been applied to the resource. This simplistic example does not handle multi-user tag weights; it handles only tag frequencies.

Adding a Layout

Before viewing the show template in a browser, let's add an application layout to dress up the display a little. You've most likely noticed that the @title instance variable set in our controller actions has not been appearing in our templates. Instead, we've chosen to display it in the application layout.

A layout is a special kind of template in Rails that is used to wrap the display of any view rendered by a controller action. If present, the template named application.html.erb in the app/views/layouts directory is automatically rendered for any action, unless explicitly instructed otherwise. The code for this layout is shown in Listing 2-8.

Listing 2-8. *Application Layout (app/views/layouts/application.html.erb)*

```
<!DOCTYPE html PUBLIC "-//W3C//DTD XHTML 1.0 Transitional//EN"
       "http://www.w3.org/TR/xhtml1/DTD/xhtml1-transitional.dtd">

<html xmlns="http://www.w3.org/1999/xhtml" xml:lang="en" lang="en">
<head>
  <meta http-equiv="content-type" content="text/html;charset=UTF-8" />
  <title>Classic Video Game Resources</title>
  <style type="text/css">
    form { margin: 0; padding: 0; }
    #left { float: left; width: 65%; }
    #right { float: right; width: 30%; }
    .sidebox { border: 2px solid black; background: #eee;
      padding: 10px; margin-top: 20px; }
```

```
    .cloud1 { font-size: 0.5em; color: blue; }
    .cloud2 { font-size: 0.8em; color: darkblue; }
    .cloud3 { font-size: 1.1em; color: purple; }
    .cloud4 { font-size: 1.4em; color: darkpurple; }
  </style>
</head>
<body>

  <%= link_to('Arcade Resources', links_url) %> |
  <%= link_to('Add New Resource', new_link_url) %>
  <hr/>

  <div id="title">
    <% unless @title.nil? -%>
      <h1><%= h(@title) %></h1>
    <% end -%>
  </div>

  <div id="left">
    <%= yield  %>
  </div>

  <div id="right">
    <!-- TBD -->
  </div>

</body>
</html>
```

This layout defines a number of styles, as well as left and right regions of the screen. We're just concerned with the left region for now. The right region will eventually be used to display a tag cloud, which we'll add later in the chapter. The layout also includes display of the previously mentioned page title (if @title is present) and a minimal top navigation control that can be used to navigate to the main resources listing and to the new link page as well.

You should now be able to refresh our index page and see the page with the updated layout. Click one of the links and view a detailed information page for one of our arcade links (the show template). It should resemble the screen shown in Figure 2-3.

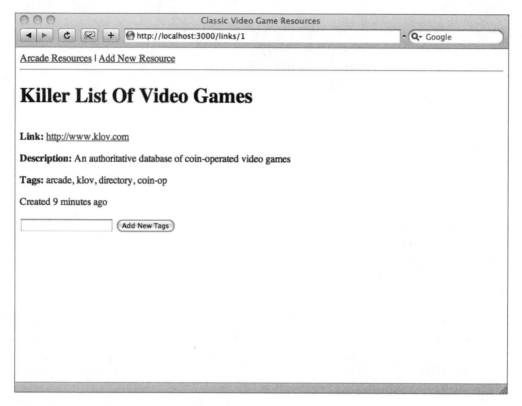

Figure 2-3. *Viewing arcade resource detailed information (http://localhost:3000/links/1)*

Feel free to enter a new set of tags for one of the existing links. The page should be reloaded and the new tag(s) displayed.

Navigating with Tags

At this point, we have a fully functional (albeit minimal) web application for adding arcade resource links and managing tags for those links. This is all well and good, but tags are relatively useless if we don't have any way to use them for browsing the data in our system. Therefore, our next step will be to implement the TagsController, as shown in Listing 2-9. Save it as app/controllers/tags_controller.rb.

Listing 2-9. *Controller for Tag Resources (app/controllers/tags_controller.rb)*

```ruby
class TagsController < ApplicationController
  def show
    @tag = Tag.find(params[:id])
    @title = "Links Tagged With '#{@tag.name}'"
    @links = @tag.taggings.collect { |t| t.taggable }
    render(:template => 'links/index')
  end
end
```

This controller contains a single action, show, which looks up the particular tag that we're inquiring about and displays a list of links that have been branded with that particular tag. It does this by collecting all the taggable objects that are associated with this tag through its taggings. As you've seen, Acts As Taggable uses the Tagging model to associate a tag with any other model object (a taggable) in the system. In our case, all taggable items are Link models, but this doesn't need to be the case—they could be any model at all.

Once we have a list of those links, we place them in the @links instance variable. We wrap things up by making an explicit call to the render method, specifying that it should use the template in app/views/links/index.html.erb. Since we just want to display a list of link results, we can reuse the template we developed earlier for this purpose.

Try loading the URL http://localhost:3000/tags/1 into a web browser. The page displayed should resemble the screen shown in Figure 2-4.

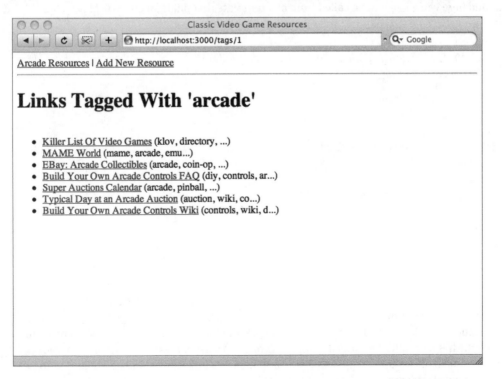

Figure 2-4. *Arcade resources available for a given tag keyword (http://localhost:3000/tags/1)*

What we've done is asked the system to show us all the links that are associated with the first tag saved in our system (the tag with an ID of 1), which happens to be arcade. This, as expected, returns a list of resources relevant to that keyword.

■**Tip** Want to use URLs like /tags/restoration or /tags/super-awesome-game? You can override the to_param method in the Tag model (supplied by the plugin) to alter the way identifiers are represented in URLs. Chapter 11 shows an example of this.

Adding Clickable Tag Links

With this new controller in place, we now need to provide links to the tag listing pages in order to allow visitors to browse to them. We'll do this in two places: on the arcade resource detailed information pages, as described in this section, and in the tag cloud, as described in the next section.

To satisfy our first objective, let's make the tag lists that are shown in the resource detailed information pages clickable. We can accomplish this by implementing a helper method in ApplicationHelper, which we'll call clickable_tag_list.

Save the code shown in Listing 2-10 as app/helpers/application_helper.rb. Since helper methods defined in ApplicationHelper are usable throughout your application, placing this method here will allow it to be called from any template that might need to display a clickable tag list.

Listing 2-10. *ApplicationHelper with Tag Navigation Methods (app/helpers/application_helper.rb)*

```
module ApplicationHelper
  include TagsHelper

  def clickable_tag_list(tag_list)
    out = []
    tag_list.each do |tag|
      out << link_to(tag.name, tag_path(tag))
    end
    out.join(', ')
  end
end
```

The clickable_tag_list method receives an array of tags as a parameter and processes it. For each tag, it generates an HTML anchor tag that contains the tag's name as link text and its tag_path (the page showing a list of links for that tag, such as the one shown in Figure 2-4) as the location to link to. It then joins these tags together into a comma-delimited list. The result is that the helper method returns a string that contains a list of tags, each of which can be clicked to take the visitor to a page that shows a full list of links that have been tagged with that particular keyword.

We'll need to update the LinksController's show template in app/views/links/show.html.erb to use this new helper. The change simply involves replacing the line that displays the (plain-text) tag list with this new line of code that uses our helper method:

```
<p><strong>Tags:</strong> <%= clickable_tag_list(@link.tags) %></p>
```

Now we should be able to reload any detailed resource information page (such as http://localhost:3000/links/1) and use the tag list links to navigate between other articles that bear the same tag. Suddenly, we have a tag-friendly way to navigate through the site! You may want to add this same feature to the main listing (index) page as well.

Building a Tag Cloud

One technique that's often used in conjunction with tagging is the display of *tag clouds*. Tag clouds are a set of related tags with corresponding weights, represented using increased font sizes and other visual clues, such as color. They're a nice, intuitive way to visualize the relevancy of tags as they correspond to some object or set of objects, especially when there are a lot of tags (often 20 or more).

Tag clouds can convey different types of information. A common approach is to use the font size of the tag to represent the number of times the particular tag has been applied to a single item. Another strategy is to use the font size to represent the number of items in the system to which the tag has been applied. We'll implement the latter here, as we want to display an omnipresent tag cloud in our layout that represents the overall occurrences of tags in our resource site, as a navigational device.

■**Tip** It's also common to apply hot/cold colors in tag clouds to indicate some vector of tag relevancy.

When we added our clickable_tag_list helper in Listing 2-10, we also included the TagsHelper in ApplicationHelper. TagsHelper is a helper module provided by the Acts As Taggable plugin. By using the include directive with the name of the module, we are mixing any methods in that module into our ApplicationController, thus making them available in our application's views. TagsHelper actually provides only a single helper method, tag_cloud, but this method is a useful one—it gives us an easy way to create tag clouds right out of the box!

The tag_cloud method takes two parameters and a block. The first parameter should be the list of tag counts (tags with associated frequency information) that we want to represent in the cloud, and the second should be an array of Cascading Style Sheets (CSS) classes that will be used to style the tags rendered within the cloud. In this case, we want the first parameter to be Link.tag_counts, which will return the array of tags that have been applied over the entire set of arcade resource links in our system. Each tag object in this array also has a counts attribute which the helper uses internally to find out how many times the tag has been applied. The CSS classes we need for the second parameter were defined previously in our layout, back in Listing 2-8. We have four classes: cloud1 through cloud4. The higher numbered classes are used to indicate tags that appear more frequently in the system; the font size is larger and the color is darker.

```
.cloud1 { font-size: 0.5em; color: blue; }
.cloud2 { font-size: 0.8em; color: darkblue; }
.cloud3 { font-size: 1.1em; color: purple; }
.cloud4 { font-size: 1.4em; color: darkpurple; }
```

The tag_cloud method automatically assigns the appropriate CSS style to each tag it's passed, based on the weight/frequency of the tag. The block passed to the method will be displayed for each tag. This means we can use it to generate a link for each tag, which we'll wrap up inside a div to display as a cloud. The code in Listing 2-11 does just this.

Listing 2-11. *Tag Cloud Display for Insertion in Layout (app/views/layouts/application.html.erb)*

```
<div id="tagcloud" class="sidebox">
  <% tag_cloud(Link.tag_counts,
     %w(cloud1 cloud2 cloud3 cloud4)) do |tag, css_class| -%>
       <%= link_to(tag.name, tag_path(tag), :class => css_class) %>
  <% end -%>
</div>
```

Insert this code into the application layout (app/views/layouts/application.html.erb) within the div element whose ID is "right". Placing it here will float it to the right of the page content at all times, so there will be an omnipresent tag cloud, no matter where users are within the arcade resources web site.

If you refresh the detailed information view for one of our arcade resources now, you will see a screen similar to the one shown in Figure 2-5. The tag cloud will be present on any page that you visit within the application. Tags in your own application will vary, of course, depending on which links you have added and the frequency of the tags that are present. Make sure to add a number of links with a variety of tags, and watch the tag cloud change as frequently used tags increase in prominence.

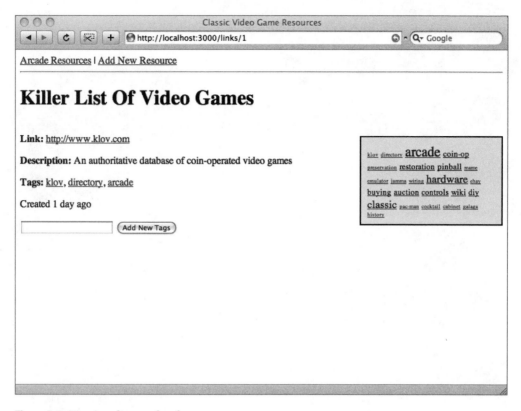

Figure 2-5. *Viewing the tag cloud*

Summary

Tagging is an increasingly common and effective way to help users organize their information and discover new content. In this chapter, we've shown how tagging features can be added to a site and how they can help a community collectively organize and navigate through a large amount of data. Our actual implementation burden was extremely minimal due to our use of Acts As Taggable (on Steroids), a helpful plugin that creates a ready-to-use tagging system that interoperates cleanly with existing models in an application.

You can read more about the Acts As Taggable (on Steroids) plugin at `http://svn.viney.net.nz/things/rails/plugins/acts_as_taggable_on_steroids/README`. It includes a number of interesting features that we haven't covered in this chapter, such as the ability to cache tags. In addition, you can find more information about tag clouds and tag visualization techniques at `http://www.smashingmagazine.com/2007/11/07/` `tag-clouds-gallery-examples-and-good-practices`.

CHAPTER 3

■■■

Uploading Images and Generating Thumbnails with Attachment Fu

Modern web sites thrive on interaction with users. Of course, some static web sites still exist, but the majority of new web startups are founded with user interaction in mind. The forms of user activity range widely—from blogging, to comments, to voting, to tagging—and such activities find homes in places as diverse as new media social networking sites or the virtual home pages of old media vanguards like CNN and BBC. While the exact usage varies, the nature of the interaction remains fairly constant: users are generating content.

This content comes in various forms—not all of it is text. It's common to upload *avatars*, which are small pictures that represent a user. These avatars range from the relatively serious, such as a photo portrait, to the whimsical, such as a cat or a bowling ball. The handling of such images can be complicated, but as Ruby on Rails developers, we have the Attachment Fu plugin to help us.

Attachment Fu can automatically perform a number of actions on images. It can verify the correct file format, set maximum and minimum file sizes, and resize images. It can even resize images to multiple sizes. For example, you could automatically create thumbnail-sized images for previews, a medium size for web browsers, and a full-size image for printing. Attachment Fu makes all of this easy.

Attachment Fu also provides support for files other than images. For example, you can create an Attachment Fu model for PDFs. You can also extend Attachment Fu to perform operations on uploaded files automatically. You could use Antiword (http://www.winfield. demon.nl/) to convert Word document uploads to PDF, or you could use FFmpeg (http:// ffmpeg.mplayerhq.hu/) to convert video uploads into Flash or QuickTime format.

This chapter focuses on the most common use of Attachment Fu: letting users automatically upload images and then resize them. Images can come from a wide variety of sources: cell phones, digital cameras, scanners, and so on. In this example, we'll demonstrate how to manipulate images that come from scanners, but the techniques apply to the other types of images as well.

Our Task: Manage Scanned Images with Attachment Fu

Suppose you are writing an application that manages documents for an accounting firm. The system must track a large number of scanned documents with absolute reliability. These documents are scanned in as PNG images. In addition, some of the firm's audits are for high-profile clients, including one suspected of accounting fraud. The auditors need to assure accuracy and completeness. They also need to eliminate any chance that documents have been illicitly tampered with, which means keeping a complete record of every scan, every day.

But there are also strict deadlines, so the auditors require a system that is efficient and easy to use. For instance, they shouldn't need to print out all of the documents again and fax them. Other functional requirements include a system that automatically resizes images to an appropriate width and height, and has an easy "download as ZIP archive" option, which archives all of the scanned images into a ZIP file.

Before we walk through the creation of the application, let's take a look at what it will look like when we are finished. Download the full application from the Sources/Download section of the Apress web site (http://www.apress.com), and then start the application using the command ruby script/server.

Browse to http://127.0.0.1:3000/documents, and you should see a screen with a few links on it. Click the New Document link, and type any random description in the Description field. Click Browse and pick a random JPEG or PNG to upload to the system. If you don't have one handy, you can download a sample page from http://www.railsplugins.com/examples/ch4_document.png. Once you do so, you should get a confirmation screen. Click Back to return to the index page. Next, move your mouse over the text "#1." A preview of the image should appear on the right. Your page should look similar to Figure 3-1.

You can also download the documents as a ZIP file. Click Today's Documents, open the resulting ZIP file, and you should see a screen similar to Figure 3-2.

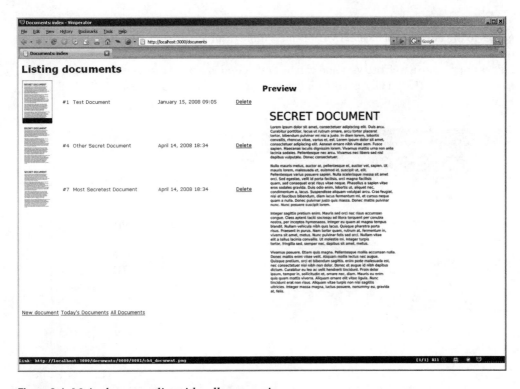

Figure 3-1. *Main document list with rollover preview*

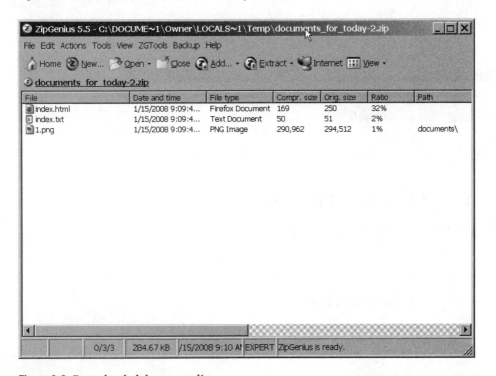

Figure 3-2. *Downloaded document list*

Two index documents—one in HTML format and one in plain text format—serve as guides to the directory of files. HTML format is more flexible, with links for each image; it is quite convenient if you have a great many documents. The text format has the advantage that it does not require a web browser and can be embedded in a plain text e-mail message more easily. Open the HTML index document in a web browser. You should see a screen similar to Figure 3-3.

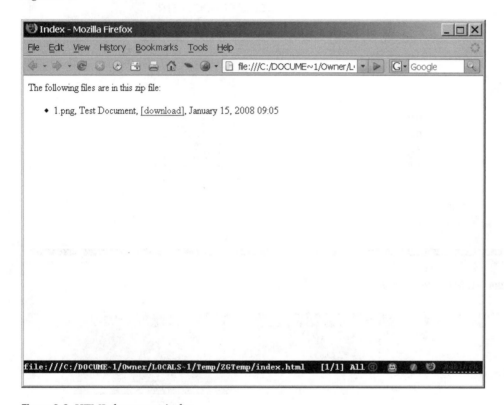

Figure 3-3. *HTML document index*

Now that you've seen a preview of our application, let's get to work creating it.

Creating the Document Manager

Let's get started by creating a new Rails project:

```
rails document_manager
```

Install Attachment Fu by executing the following command inside the new Rails project:

```
ruby script/plugin install attachment_fu
```

```
+ ./CHANGELOG
+ ./README
+ ./Rakefile
+ ./amazon_s3.yml.tpl
+ ./init.rb
+ ./install.rb
+ ./lib/geometry.rb
+ ./lib/technoweenie/attachment_fu/backends/db_file_backend.rb
+ ./lib/technoweenie/attachment_fu/backends/file_system_backend.rb
+ ./lib/technoweenie/attachment_fu/backends/s3_backend.rb
+ ./lib/technoweenie/attachment_fu/processors/image_science_processor.rb
+ ./lib/technoweenie/attachment_fu/processors/mini_magick_processor.rb
+ ./lib/technoweenie/attachment_fu/processors/rmagick_processor.rb
+ ./lib/technoweenie/attachment_fu.rb
+ ./test/amazon_s3.yml
+ ./test/backends/db_file_test.rb
+ ./test/backends/file_system_test.rb
+ ./test/backends/remote/s3_test.rb
+ ./test/base_attachment_tests.rb
+ ./test/basic_test.rb
+ ./test/database.yml
+ ./test/extra_attachment_test.rb
+ ./test/fixtures/attachment.rb
+ ./test/fixtures/files/fake/rails.png
+ ./test/fixtures/files/foo.txt
+ ./test/fixtures/files/rails.png
+ ./test/geometry_test.rb
+ ./test/processors/image_science_test.rb
+ ./test/processors/mini_magick_test.rb
+ ./test/processors/rmagick_test.rb
+ ./test/schema.rb
+ ./test/test_helper.rb
+ ./test/validation_test.rb
attachment-fu
=====================

...snip...
```

Next, you'll need to install RMagick, which is used to resize the thumbnails:

```
gem install -y rmagick
```

RMagick requires either ImageMagick or GraphicsMagick to be installed. You can find out the details on ImageMagick and GraphicsMagick at the following URLs:

```
http://www.imagemagick.org/script/download.php
http://www.graphicsmagick.org/www/download.html
```

Tip Not everyone likes the RMagick library. You can also use the ImageScience library, which has fewer features, but also has a lower memory footprint. You can find this library at `http://seattlerb.rubyforge.org/ImageScience.html`.

Place the code from Listing 3-1 in db/migrations/001_create_documents.rb.

Listing 3-1. *Document Creation Migration (db/migrations/001_create_documents.rb)*

```ruby
class CreateDocuments < ActiveRecord::Migration
  def self.up
    create_table :documents do |t|
      t.string    :description
      t.timestamps

      t.integer   :size
      t.string    :content_type
      t.string    :filename
      t.integer   :height
      t.integer   :width
      t.integer   :parent_id
      t.string    :thumbnail
    end
  end

  def self.down
    drop_table :documents
  end
end
```

Each row in this table will represent one document. Most of the columns are used by Attachment Fu. Only the top two declarations, `t.string :description` and `t.timestamps`, are unique to our application.

Note that we'll be using the rubyzip gem. Issue the following command to install it:

```
gem install rubyzip
```

Using Attachment Fu in the Document Model

The Document model will represent a document uploaded by the user; it stores data in the documents table we just created.

Before we create the model, let's run the migration:

```
rake db:migrate
```

```
== 1 CreateDocuments: migrating ==================================================
-- create_table(:documents)
   -> 0.0150s
== 1 CreateDocuments: migrated (0.0150s) ========================================
```

Let's create a model for our new table. Listing 3-2 shows the code for our model.

Listing 3-2. *Document Model (app/models/document.rb)*

```
class Document < ActiveRecord::Base
  has_attachment :storage => :file_system,
                 :path_prefix => 'public/documents',
                 :content_type => :image,
                 :size => 0..5.megabytes,
                 :resize_to => "800x1100",
                 :thumbnails => {:small=>"80x110",
                                 :medium=> "400x550"}

  validates_as_attachment
  def zip_filename
    filename =~ /\.([^.]*)$/
    extension = $1.downcase
    "#{id}.#{extension}"
  end
end
```

This model has two notable parts: a has_attachment call and a validates_as_attachment call.

The call to has_attachment adds the Attachment Fu functionality to our model. The various options set the allowed size and the permissible document types, as well as control the automatic resizing. In this case, the original image is resized to 800×1100, and then two smaller versions are created: one at 80×110 and one at 400×550.

The sizes of our resized images are specified as strings, but you can also specify sizes as arrays, such as [80,100]. However, the array specifies an exact size. The string specifier has the benefit of specifying a maximum size for each dimension, which ensures that the image's original aspect ratio is preserved. Also, other options are available for the string. For example, the string "80!x100!" resizes to exactly 80 by 100, whereas the string "x100" resizes the height of the image to be exactly 100 pixels—changing the height to maintain the image aspect ratio. You can also use > and < modifiers to change the size only if it's larger or smaller. For example, "80x100>" will resize an 800×1000 image to 80×100, but will leave a 40×50 image as is. This is beneficial if you expect a lot of small images that will lose quality as they're enlarged.

■**Note** The size specifiers are the same ones that ImageMagick uses. You can find out about available options at http://www.imagemagick.org/RMagick/doc/imusage.html.

Our `has_attachment` call specifies `:path_prefix => 'public/documents'`; this is the directory that our files will be stored under; let's create this directory using the following command:

```
mkdir public/documents
```

DIRECTORY PARTITIONING

Why is the path option to the `has_attachment` call named `path_prefix` and not simply `path`? It's because Attachment Fu automatically partitions files into separate directories from each ID. It also partitions ID directories into two groups of four digits, so that in our example, ID 1 is stored in the directory `public/documents/0000/0001`. This partitioning is important for scalability.

Many file systems have an upper limit on the number of files (or subdirectories) in a directory. So if you store all of the images in the same directory, or in subdirectories off of the same directory, you'll run into problems fairly quickly. Ext2, a common Linux file system, has an upper limit of 32,768 files. Microsoft's FAT32 provides a limit of 65,534. That's it. If you need more images, you're stuck. However, by partitioning, you have an upper limit of 9999×9998, which comes out to be 99,980,001. If each file is 20KB, this means filling up the partition with take roughly 1.86TB of space—much more than most applications will use.

And if you even approach the limit, you can override the partitioning to allow more images. For example, the following method, based on the method in `vendor\plugins\attachment_fu\lib\technoweenie\attachment_fu\backends\file_system.rb`, will generate directories in the form `public/documents/0000/0000/0000/0001` for ID 1:

```
def partitioned_path(*args)
  ("%016d" % attachment_path_id).scan(/..../) + args
end
```

This method lets you store 199,900,017,998,600,040 images, which works out to be more than 465 million terabytes of images at 20KB an image. (The size of 20KB per image is probably low, but it's a useful figure for visualizing the power of partitioning.) You can find out more about Ext2 limitations at `http://www.charmed.com/txt/ext2.txt`.

Next, our model calls to `validates_as_attachment`, which adds attachment validation. This means that if the user uploads an image that is too large, Attachment Fu will supply an error message.

Let's try out our new model in the Rails console:

```
ruby script/console
```

```
Loading development environment (Rails 2.0.1)
>> doc = Document.new
=> #<Document id: nil, size: nil, description: nil, content_type: nil, filename:
 nil, height: nil, width: nil, parent_id: nil, thumbnail: nil, created_at: nil,
updated_at: nil>
```

```
>> doc.content_type = 'image/png'
>> doc.filename = 'testpath.png'
>> (doc.temp_data = File.open('/some/path/ch4_document.png').read()); true
>> doc.save
>> doc.public_filename
=> "/documents/0000/0001/testpath.png"
>> doc.public_filename(:thumb)
=> "/documents/0000/0003/testpath_small.png"
>> exit
```

If you look at the public/documents/0000/0001/testpath.png file, you'll see your original image. The preceding code creates a new document; sets its content_type, filename, and temp_data attributes; and saves it. We can call the public_filename method on the document and see its path. We can even pass a thumbnail size, like :thumb, to the public_filename method, which returns an appropriately sized image.

■**Tip** What does the ; true in (doc.temp_data = File.open('/some/path/ch4_document.png').read()); true mean? It's completely unrelated to Attachment Fu. It keeps the Rails console from automatically displaying the results of your operation. If you don't end the line with ; true, Rails will attempt to display the contents of the binary file on your screen. Binary files frequently contain nontextual characters, and the terminal will misread these as control codes. However, if you append ; true, the Rails console will return the last value, true, instead.

Attachment Fu actually created several more files for us behind the scenes. Let's use the console to examine them:

```
ruby script/console
```

```
Loading development environment (Rails 2.0.1)
>> puts YAML.dump(Document.find(:all))
---

- !ruby/object:Document
  attributes:
    content_type: image/png
    updated_at: 2008-01-13 23:16:53
    thumbnail:
    size: "31982"
    id: "1"
    description:
    height:
```

```
      filename: testpath.png
      parent_id:
      created_at: 2008-01-13 23:16:53
      width:
    attributes_cache: {}

- !ruby/object:Document
    attributes:
      content_type: image/png
      updated_at: 2008-01-13 23:16:53
      thumbnail: medium
      size: "31982"
      id: "2"
      description:
      height:
      filename: testpath_medium.png
      parent_id: "1"
      created_at: 2008-01-13 23:16:53
      width:
    attributes_cache: {}

- !ruby/object:Document
    attributes:
      content_type: image/png
      updated_at: 2008-01-13 23:16:53
      thumbnail: small
      size: "31982"
      id: "3"
      description:
      height:
      filename: testpath_small.png
      parent_id: "1"
      created_at: 2008-01-13 23:16:53
      width:
    attributes_cache: {}
```

Saving one attachment produced three records. ID 1 is our original file, and the next two represent our thumbnails. Attachment Fu uses several columns and stores thumbnails in separate rows. As a result, if you want to query the documents table and return only the full-sized images, not thumbnails, you'll need to build a query like WHERE parent_id IS NULL. (The same is true if you would like to get a count of the number of documents; otherwise, you'll end up with triple the number of uploaded documents.)

Let's take a look at our controller code next.

Building the Document Management Controllers

First, let's create some routes. Put the following in `config/routes.rb`:

```
ActionController::Routing::Routes.draw do |map|
  map.resources 'documents'

  map.connect   '/documents_for_today.zip',
                :controller=>'documents',
                :action=>'index',
                :today_only=>true,
                :format=>'zip'

  map.connect ':controller/:action/:id'
  map.connect ':controller/:action/:id.:format'
end
```

This creates a RESTful route for the `documents` resource, which automatically makes create, show, edit, and related routes for our `DocumentsController`. The next line creates a route, `/documents_for_today.zip`, which downloads all of our documents scanned on the current day as a ZIP file.

■Note If you're not familiar with REST, RESTful design and routes are briefly introduced in Chapter 11.

Add the following code to the end of your `config/environment.rb` file:

```
Mime::Type.register "application/zip", :zip

require 'zip/zip'
require 'zip/zipfilesystem'
```

The first line registers the `.zip` extension as the `application/zip` MIME type, so that Rails will let us use the `.zip` extension with a `respond_to` block. The last two lines require the rubyzip gem, as well its `zipfilesystem` library, which allow us to manipulate and create ZIP files using library calls, similar to how we would access a regular file system.

Next, let's begin our `DocumentsController`. The first method for the `DocumentsController`, shown in Listing 3-3, lists all of the documents.

Listing 3-3. *DocumentsController, Part I (app/controller/documents_controller.rb)*

```
class DocumentsController < ApplicationController
  def index
```

```
if params[:today_only]
  @documents = Document.find(:all,
               :conditions=>'parent_id IS NULL AND
                             TO_DAYS(created_at)=
                             TO_DAYS(NOW()) ')
else
  @documents = Document.find(:all, :conditions=>'parent_id IS NULL')
end
```

Note that if the today_only parameter is passed, it returns only documents from today.

Next, our code in Listing 3-4 responds to various format types and then passes the data back in the correct format.

Listing 3-4. *DocumentsController, Part II (app/controller/documents_controller.rb)*

```
respond_to do |format|
  format.html # index.html.erb
  format.xml  { render :xml => @documents }
  format.zip do
    headers['Cache-Control'] = 'no-cache'
```

Our code handles the first two response formats fairly simply. The first passes control to the default view, index.html.erb, and the second renders the @documents array as XML. The third format, zip, is a bit more complicated. Our code first sets the Cache-Control header to 'no-cache', so that subsequent downloads will return updated data. Then we can create the ZIP file, as shown in Listing 3-5.

Listing 3-5. *DocumentsController, Part III (app/controller/documents_controller.rb)*

```
tmp_filename = "#{RAILS_ROOT}/tmp/temp_zip_" <<
               rand (10000) << "_" <<
               Time.now.to_f.to_s << "-" <<
               request.remote_ip <<
               ".zip"

Zip::ZipFile.open(tmp_filename,
                  Zip::ZipFile::CREATE) do |zip|
```

First, we generate a temporary file name. Normally, we would use the Tempfile class to do this, but the rubyzip gem assumes that existing files should be opened instead of overwritten. Therefore, our script uses a hybrid strategy. It generates a random number between 0 and 10000, concatenates it with the current time in fractional seconds, and appends the remote IP address to it. As a result, you would need to have a fairly large number of concurrent requests from the same IP address in order to have a collision.

Next, we start placing files inside the ZIP file, as shown in Listing 3-6.

Listing 3-6. *DocumentsController, Part IV (app/controller/documents_controller.rb)*

```
text = render_to_string :partial=>'zip_index.text.erb',
            :locals=>{:documents=>@documents}

zip.get_output_stream('index.txt') do |zh|
  zh.puts text
end

html = render_to_string :partial=>'zip_index.html.erb',
            :locals=>{:documents=>@documents}

zip.get_output_stream('index.html') do |zh|
  zh.puts html
end
```

The first line uses the `render_to_string` method to retrieve the result of evaluating the `zip_index.text.erb` view. We then write that string to the `index.txt` file. Next, we do the same with the `zip_index.html.erb` view, and write that to `index.html`. This allows users to have either an HTML view with pictures of the documents or a text view without pictures. The HTML view references documents stored in the `documents` directory, so we need to add them, as we do in Listing 3-7.

Listing 3-7. *DocumentsController, Part V (app/controller/documents_controller.rb)*

```
@documents.each do |doc|
  zip.add( "documents/#{doc.zip_filename}",
        doc.full_filename )
end
```

We use the `zip_filename` instance method of the `Document` class; it returns a file name based on the ID number of the document. By default, Attachment Fu sets file names based on the originally uploaded file name, but since the ZIP file will be sent to outside parties, it's preferable to have a uniform naming scheme for all of the documents.

At this point, the ZIP file is created, and it has our two index files and our various documents in it. Let's send the data to the user, as shown in Listing 3-8.

Listing 3-8. *DocumentsController, Part VI (app/controller/documents_controller.rb)*

```
    end

    send_data File.open(tmp_filename,'rb+').read
    File.unlink tmp_filename
  end
 end
end
```

We use the send_data call to read from our temporary file and send the data to the user. Next, we'll examine the show routine, which displays a full view of the document to the user, as shown in Listing 3-9.

Listing 3-9. *DocumentsController, Part VII (app/controller/documents_controller.rb)*

```
def show
  @document = Document.find(params[:id])

  respond_to do |format|
    format.html # show.html.erb
    format.xml  { render :xml => @document }
  end
end
```

This routine is straightforward. It retrieves a document from the database and then displays the appropriate view. Next, Listing 3-10 shows our new method.

Listing 3-10. *DocumentsController, Part IIX (app/controller/documents_controller.rb)*

```
def new
  @document = Document.new

  respond_to do |format|
    format.html # new.html.erb
    format.xml  { render :xml => @document }
  end
end
```

The final method in our controller is the create method, as shown in Listing 3-11.

Listing 3-11. *DocumentsController, Part IX (app/controller/documents_controller.rb)*

```
def create
  @document = Document.new(params[:document])

  respond_to do |format|
    if @document.save
      flash[:notice] = 'Document was successfully created.'
      format.html { redirect_to(@document) }
      format.xml  { render :xml => @document,➡
                           :status => :created,➡
                           :location => @document }
    else
      format.html { render :action => "new" }
```

```
      format.xml  { render :xml => @document.errors,➥
                           :status => :unprocessable_entity }
    end
  end
end

end
```

Note that we don't need to do anything special to save the attached file to our Document model. Even though our class has a number of methods relating to our file—content-type, filename, and temp_data—these are automatically pulled from the form data and set appropriately (assuming our view is constructed appropriately, as you'll see when we discuss the app/views/documents.new.html.erb view in the next section). The rest of the method simply renders a success or failure response in either HTML or XML.

We'll create our views next.

Creating Application Views

First, let's create our index view, /app/views/documents/index.html.erb. The top of the view will include the Prototype JavaScript library, which will be used later to make the image preview rollover effect. It will also give us a header and some style information, as you see in Listing 3-12.

Listing 3-12. *Index HTML View, Part I (app/views/documents/index.html.erb)*

```
<%=javascript_include_tag :defaults%>

<h1>Listing documents</h1>

<style>
  #document_list, #document_preview {
    width:49%; float:left;
  }
  #document_preview {
    margin-left:1%;
  }
  #navigation {
    float:left;
    clear:left;
  }
</style>
```

Normally, we would include this CSS in a separate file, but for the sake of brevity, we've included it in-line here.

Next, let's take a look at the actual list of documents in Listing 3-13.

Listing 3-13. *Index HTML View, Part II (app/views/documents/index.html.erb)*

```
<table id="document_list">

<% for document in @documents %>
  <tr>
    <td><%=link_to image_tag(document.public_filename(:small),
                           :preview_src=>document.public_filename(:medium),
                           :border=>0),
                  document.public_filename  %>
    <td>#<%=document.id%></td>
    <td><%=document.description%></td>
    <td><%=document.created_at.to_s(:long)%></td>
  </tr>
<% end %>
</table>

<div id="document_preview">
  <h2>Preview</h2>
  <img src="" id="preview_picture">
</div>
<br />
```

This code is reasonably straightforward. We loop through all of the documents and display a thumbnail of each with a link to the complete version. We also list the ID, the description, and the time the document was uploaded. It's pretty easy to embed an Attachment Fu thumbnail in a view. Get the file name of the thumbnail you want with `public_filename`, and pass that to `image_tag`.

You may also notice the `:preview_src=>document.public_filename(:medium)` fragment. This sets the `preview_src` attribute to the medium resized version of the document. We'll use this for a rollover preview, and we'll place it in our `#preview_picture` img element. (You can see an example of what it looks like in action in Figure 3-1, shown earlier in the chapter.)

Next, we have a `#navigation` div tag, which will contain our navigation links, as you see in Listing 3-14.

Listing 3-14. *Index HTML View, Part III (app/views/documents/index.html.erb)*

```
<div id="navigation">
  <%= link_to 'New document', new_document_path %>
  <%= link_to 'Today\'s Documents', '/documents_for_today.zip' %>
  <%= link_to 'All Documents', '/documents.zip' %>
</div>
```

The first link uses the named route automatically created by the `map.resources :document` line in our `routes.rb`. The next line links to the ZIP files containing today's uploads only. The last line links to all documents.

Next, let's take a look at our rollover JavaScript, shown in Listing 3-15.

Listing 3-15. *Index HTML View, Part IV (app/views/documents/index.html.erb)*

```
<script>
  $$('#document_list tr td').each(function(elem){
    Event.observe(elem, 'mouseover',function(){

      $('preview_picture').src = $(this.up())➥
                                  .select('img')[0]➥
                                  .readAttribute('preview_src');
  });
});
</script>
```

This code sets up our mouse rollover to display a medium-size preview of the image in the right part of the screen. Specifically, it loops through each td element, which is inside a tr element, which is inside our #document_list table. It adds a mouseover observer to each tr element, which finds the element's parent tr, finds its img tag, reads the preview_src attribute containing the preview image URL, and assigns the preview image URL to our #preview_picture img tag.

Just a few more views are used in our application. Let's examine them briefly.

The first is the app/views/documents.new.html.erb view, shown in Listing 3-16.

Listing 3-16. *New Document View (app/views/documents.new.html.erb)*

```
<h1>New document</h1>

<%= error_messages_for :document %>

<% form_for(@document, :html=>{:multipart=>true} ) do |f| %>
  <p>
    Description: <%=f.text_field 'description'%>
  </p>
  <p>
    File: <%=f.file_field 'uploaded_data'%>
  </p>
  <p>
    <%= f.submit "Create" %>
  </p>

<% end %>

<%= link_to 'Back', documents_path %>
```

The :html hash is notable because it contains the key :multipart=>true. This sets the enctype attribute of our form to multipart, which is required to upload files over HTTP. (Additionally, the HTTP method must be POST, but since Rails forms are POST by default, this requires no additional work.) We use the file_field method to create an HTML control that lets people select files to upload. Note that the field is named uploaded_data. This is important because it's the name Attachment Fu uses to automatically extract the data, content type, and file name. If we use this name, no additional work is required to connect the controller code with our form.

Next, let's take a look at the HTML index for our ZIP files, shown in Listing 3-17.

Listing 3-17. *ZIP File HTML Index (app/views/documents/_zip_index.html.erb)*

```
<html>
  <head>
    <title>Index</title>
  </head>
  <body>

    <p>The following files are in this zip file:</p>
    <ul>
<%documents.each do |doc|
%>    <li><%=doc.zip_filename%>,
        <%=doc.description%>,
        <%=link_to "[download]",
                 "documents/#{doc.zip_filename}"%>,
          <%=doc.created_at.to_s(:long)%></li>
<%end%>
    </ul>
  </body>
</html>
```

This HTML is a partial used by the part of our code that generates ZIP files. It loops through all of the documents and generates an li element with a download link and description. Note that the download link is not a link to the web site. It's a link to a local copy of the document, which assumes that the user has unzipped the entire archive into a directory. However, it doesn't require that the user has an active Internet connection, or even that our application is accessible to the Internet. With this approach, the only connection between your Rails app and the outside world might be manually distributing this ZIP file via e-mail, or even snail mail if security requires it.

The text index is quite similar, as you see in Listing 3-18.

Listing 3-18. *Zip File Text Index (app/views/documents/_zip_index.text.erb)*

```
The following files are in this zip file:

<%documents.each do |doc|
%>  <%=doc.zip_filename%>,  <%=doc.description%>, <%=doc.created_at.to_s(:long)%>
  <%
end%>
```

As before, this code simply loops through all of the documents and lists a brief description. Of course, the text index can't include links to the documents.

Finally, let's take a look at the layout for our `DocumentsController`, which will wrap all of the previous views; you can see it in Listing 3-19.

Listing 3-19. *DocumentsController Layout (app/views/layouts/document.html.erb)*

```
<!DOCTYPE html PUBLIC "-//W3C//DTD XHTML 1.0 Transitional//EN"
      "http://www.w3.org/TR/xhtml1/DTD/xhtml1-transitional.dtd">

<html xmlns="http://www.w3.org/1999/xhtml" xml:lang="en" lang="en">
<head>
  <meta http-equiv="content-type" content="text/html;charset=UTF-8" />
  <title>Documents: <%= controller.action_name %></title>
  <%= stylesheet_link_tag 'scaffold' %>
</head>
<body>

<p style="color: green"><%= flash[:notice] %></p>

<%= yield  %>

</body>
</html>
```

This layout is fairly straightforward. It has a simple header with basic information and a link to our style sheet, and it includes any flash notices the controllers generate.

Summary

In this chapter, we've covered how you can use Attachment Fu to cleanly and easily accept uploads and create conveniently resized versions of them, as well as how you can display image thumbnails and rollover previews. We've even covered how you can zip up those images and offer them as a single file, a neatly indexed archive.

Images are an extremely important part of web sites today, and Attachment Fu lets you easily handle and resize those images, as well as handle file uploads of arbitrary types. Of course, you could write controller code to do it by hand, but Attachment Fu makes this quick and easy—both to create initially and to later maintain.

## CHAPTER 4

Versioning Database Models with Acts As Versioned

From news portals to search engines, the Internet is a powerful tool for spreading information quickly. However, for many applications, it's not enough to see the most recent version of a resource. You need to see the full history of the resource, from its initial creation, through each new change, to its final state.

Many sites use data versioning in order to protect against vandalism. For example, Wikipedia stores old versions of pages, which allow users to revert to previous versions of pages and quickly erase the effects of various malicious activities (yes, Wikipedia is a target of web vandals). However, it's easy to use versioning for many other purposes. You can use versioning to show timestamps for data changes, which can be useful in situations ranging from personal applications to e-commerce sites—whenever a user might be interested in the old data of an object. Or you might use versioning to determine the date when a product shipped. As another example, versioning is useful to find out what a user originally posted in a forum before he edited his post. You can even roll back your objects to an earlier version.

The Acts As Versioned plugin by Rick Olson is a great way to do this. Acts As Versioned creates a new table that is similar to your original table, but it has additional columns that store version information. It also installs callbacks into your model, so that you can use the standard Active Record methods to add new records and update old records. When you change an existing record, the version table will be updated automatically with the new data, so that it always holds a complete record.

In this chapter, we'll demonstrate how to use the Acts As Versioned plugin to store and access historical data using a sales inventory management application as an example.

Our Task: Manage Inventory with Acts As Versioned

Suppose we are writing an application for a used-car dealer to automate the process of keeping track of each vehicle on the lot. Eventually, we will want to create a web-based front end that displays the entire inventory of the lot in real time on the Web. But for now, we want to make a simple system for keeping track of the make, model, and condition of each car, plus some other basic data. We also want to keep track of whenever any data associated with the car is changed, such as when a car is first brought onto the lot, when the buyer initially puts a deposit down on the car, and so forth.

We can use Acts As Versioned to automatically keep track of the history of each car. However, Acts As Versioned stores complete records, not just changes, so we need to use the Riff plugin (`http://tfletcher.com/dev/rails-plugins`) by Tim Fletcher to determine what changed from each version of the record to the next. Let's get started by installing both of those plugins.

Building the Car Lot Inventory System

First, create a blank Rails project for our inventory management system:

```
rails lot_manager
```

Next, install Acts As Versioned by executing the following command inside your Rails project:

```
script/plugin install http://tfletcher.com/svn/rails-plugins/riff/
```

To install the Riff plugin, execute the following command:

```
ruby script/plugin install http://tfletcher.com/svn/rails-plugins/riff/
```

Next, place the code in Listing 4-1 into db/migrations/001_create_cars.rb.

Listing 4-1. *Document Creation Migration (db/migrate/001_create_cars.rb)*

```
class CreateCars < ActiveRecord::Migration
  def self.up
    create_table :cars do |t|
      t.string :make
      t.string :model
      t.integer :year
      t.decimal :price
      t.boolean :is_on_lot
      t.boolean :is_sold
      t.boolean :is_paid_in_full
      t.text :notes

      t.timestamps
    end
    Car.create_versioned_table
  end

  def self.down
    drop_table :cars
    Car.drop_versioned_table
  end
end
```

Note the last line of the `self.up` method, which creates a versioned table for our Car model. It will automatically be named `cars_versions`. This method also adds a `version` column to the table.

Next, run the migration by using the following command:

```
rake db:migrate
```

Using Acts As Versioned in the Model

Before we test out our new plugin, let's create our single model, as shown in Listing 4-2.

Listing 4-2. *Car Model (app/models/car.rb)*

```
class Car < ActiveRecord::Base
  def to_s
    "#{self.year} #{self.make} #{self.model}, Inventory ##{self.id}"
  end
  acts_as_versioned
end
```

The important line of code is the `acts_as_versioned` line, which lets us use the versioning functionality on our model. The `to_s` method, incidentally, will be used by our view. It provides a description of our model instances to our views.

Let's examine exactly what we can do with this model using the Rails console:

```
ruby script/console
>> test_car = Car.create(:make=>'Honda', :model=>'Acura', :year=>'2012')
>> test_car.update_attributes(:notes=>'This is a test note.')
>> test_car.update_attributes(:is_sold=>true)
>> puts YAML.dump(test_car.versions)
```

```
- !ruby/object:Car::Version
  attributes:
    is_paid_in_full:
    updated_at: 2008-01-23 17:00:42
    price:
    id: "5"
    notes:
    car_id: "2"
    version: "1"
    make: Honda
    year: "2012"
    model: Acura
    is_sold:
    is_on_lot:
    created_at: 2008-01-23 17:00:42
  attributes_cache: {}
```

```
- !ruby/object:Car::Version
  attributes:
    is_paid_in_full:
    updated_at: 2008-01-23 17:01:02
    price:
    id: "6"
    notes: This is a test note.
    car_id: "2"
    version: "2"
    make: Honda
    year: "2012"
    model: Acura
    is_sold:
    is_on_lot:
    created_at: 2008-01-23 17:00:42
  attributes_cache: {}
```

As you can see, you can call the versions method on an instance of our model and get an array of older versions. It creates these versions for us automatically when we call update_attributes or create. Any change to our model that's saved to the database will trigger the creation of a new row in our cars_versions table. In fact, we can use completely normal Active Record code. No special handling is necessary to use Acts As Versioned.

Note that our version tables store the full record for each version. They don't store the difference between records. For that, we use the Riff plugin. Let's test that next using the console:

```
>> first_version = test_car.versions[0]; second_version = test_car.versions[1]
>> puts YAML.dump(first_version.diff(second_version))
```

```
:version:
- 1
- 2
:updated_at:
- 2008-01-23 17:00:42 -05:00
- 2008-01-23 17:01:02 -05:00
:notes:
-
- This is a test note.
=> nil
>> exit
```

The diff function on the Car model instances takes another Car instance and returns a hash of differences. The keys are the field names, and each element in the hash is a two-element array. The first element of each array is the value from the model on which you called diff. The second element is the value from model you passed as an argument. Since we called diff on the old value, the first element is the older value, and the second element is the newer value. You can also pass a hash into the diff function, such as a params hash, and it will work in the same way.

Using Acts As Versioned in the Controller

Let's start creating our controller code. First, Listing 4-3 shows our `routes.rb` file.

Listing 4-3. *Routing Configuration (config/routes.rb)*

```ruby
ActionController::Routing::Routes.draw do |map|
  map.resources :cars

  map.connect ':controller/:action/:id'
  map.connect ':controller/:action/:id.:format'
```

Next, let's create our single controller, as shown in Listing 4-4.

Listing 4-4. *Car Controller (app/controllers/cars_controller.rb)*

```ruby
class CarsController < ApplicationController
  def index
    @cars = Car.find(:all)

    respond_to do |format|
      format.html # index.html.erb
      format.xml  { render :xml => @cars }
    end
  end

  def show
    @car = Car.find(params[:id])
    @car_history = @car.versions

    respond_to do |format|
      format.html # show.html.erb
      format.xml  { render :xml => {'current'=>@car,
                                    'history'=>@car_history }}
    end
  end

  def new
    @car = Car.new

    respond_to do |format|
      format.html # new.html.erb
      format.xml  { render :xml => @car }
    end
  end

  def create
    @car = Car.new(params[:car])
```

```ruby
      respond_to do |format|
        if @car.save
          flash[:notice] = 'Car was successfully created.'
          format.html { redirect_to(@car) }
          format.xml  { render :xml => @car, :status => :created, :location => @car }
        else
          format.html { render :action => "new" }
          format.xml  { render :xml => @car.errors, :status => :unprocessable_entity }
        end
      end
    end

    def update
      @car = Car.find(params[:id])

      respond_to do |format|
        if @car.update_attributes(params[:car])
          flash[:notice] = 'Car was successfully updated.'
          format.html { redirect_to(@car) }
          format.xml  { head :ok }
        else
          format.html { render :action => "edit" }
          format.xml  { render :xml => @car.errors, :status => :unprocessable_entity }
        end
      end
    end

    def destroy
      @car = Car.find(params[:id])
      @car.destroy

      respond_to do |format|
        format.html { redirect_to(cars_url) }
        format.xml  { head :ok }
      end
    end
end
```

This is mostly a CRUD (Create Read Update Delete) controller as created by Rails 2.0's resource_scaffold generator. Note that it does not have an edit method. Since you can view data from an edit page as easily as you can from a show page, we've combined the edit and show methods.

Usually, people pass an array of objects to render :xml, which displays the data in XML format. But you can pass multiple objects of varying types in a hash, as we've done with the following line:

```ruby
      format.xml  { render :xml => {'current'=>@car,
                                    'history'=>@car_history }}
```

This creates XML output that looks like this:

```xml
<?xml version="1.0" encoding="UTF-8"?>
<hash>
  <history type="array">
    <history>
      <car-id type="integer">1</car-id>
      <created-at type="datetime">2008-01-21T14:01:33-05:00</created-at>
      <id type="integer">1</id>
      <is-on-lot type="boolean">true</is-on-lot>

      <is-paid-in-full type="boolean">false</is-paid-in-full>
      <is-sold type="boolean">false</is-sold>
      <make>Honda</make>
      <model>Civic</model>
      <notes></notes>
      <price type="decimal">20000.0</price>

      <updated-at type="datetime">2008-01-21T14:01:33-05:00</updated-at>
      <version type="integer">1</version>
      <year type="integer">2008</year>
    </history>
        ...snip...
  </history>
  <current>
    <created-at type="datetime">2008-01-21T14:01:33-05:00</created-at>
    <id type="integer">1</id>

    <is-on-lot type="boolean">true</is-on-lot>
    <is-paid-in-full type="boolean">true</is-paid-in-full>
    <is-sold type="boolean">true</is-sold>
    <make>Honda</make>
    <model>Civic</model>
    <notes>Cleaned up and ready for sale</notes>

    <price type="decimal">20000.0</price>
    <updated-at type="datetime">2008-01-24T10:03:16-05:00</updated-at>
    <version type="integer">6</version>
    <year type="integer">2008</year>
  </current>
</hash>
```

Using Acts As Versioned in the Views

Next, let's take a look at our index.html.erb view, which displays the list of cars. Listing 4-5 shows this view.

Listing 4-5. *Inventory List (app/views/cars/index.html.erb)*

```
<h1>Listing cars</h1>

<table>
  <tr>
    <th>Make</th>
    <th>Model</th>
    <th>Year</th>
    <th>Price</th>
    <th>On lot?</th>
    <th>Sold?</th>
    <th>Paid in full?</th>
    <th>Notes</th>
  </tr>

<% for car in @cars %>
  <tr>
    <td><%=h car.make %></td>
    <td><%=h car.model %></td>
    <td><%=h car.year %></td>
    <td><%=h car.price %></td>
    <td><%=h car.is_on_lot %></td>
    <td><%=h car.is_sold %></td>
    <td><%=h car.is_paid_in_full %></td>
    <td><%=h car.notes %></td>
    <td><%= link_to 'Show', car %></td>
    <td><%= link_to 'Delete', car, :confirm => 'Are you sure?',
                                   :method => :delete %></td>
  </tr>
<% end %>
</table>

<br />

<%= link_to 'New car', new_car_path %>
```

Again, this is a fairly straightforward index view. Aside from some label and link changes, it is identical to what resource_scaffold would create.

However, the new car view has been refactored to more closely follow the Rails DRY (Don't Repeat Yourself) principle. Listing 4-6 shows this view.

Listing 4-6. *New Car View (app/views/cars/new.html.erb)*

```
<h1>New car</h1>

<%= error_messages_for :car %>
<%=render :partial=>'form', :locals=>{'@car'=>@car}%>

<%= link_to 'Back', cars_path %>
```

This uses a partial to hold the actual data-entry form, which is reused by our show action. Listing 4-7 shows the partial.

Listing 4-7. *Car Partial (app/views/cars/_form.html.erb)*

```
<% form_for(@car) do |f| %>
  <p><b>Year</b><br />
    <%= f.text_field :year %> </p>
  <p><b>Make</b><br />
    <%= f.text_field :make %> </p>
  <p><b>Model</b><br />
    <%= f.text_field :model %> </p>

  <p><b>Price</b><br />
    <%= f.text_field :price %></p>

  <p><%= f.check_box :is_on_lot %>
    <b>On lot</b><br /></p>

  <p><%= f.check_box :is_sold %>
    <b>Sold</b></p>

  <p><%= f.check_box :is_paid_in_full %>
    <b>Paid in full</b></p>

  <p><b>Notes</b><br />
    <%= f.text_area :notes %></p>

  <p><%= f.submit "Create" %></p>
<% end %>
```

This is a reasonably straightforward data-entry form. We use three check boxes to determine if the car is on the lot, if the car has been sold, and if the bill for the car has been paid in full. In this case, we have a fairly simple set of Boolean flags that can be used in any combination. This is necessary because car dealers use seemingly illogical combinations of these conditions. For example, a car may be sold before it reaches the lot, perhaps because it was purchased through an auto sales web site.

Tip In some cases, it may be preferable to use a "state" column with a drop-down list or other means to change state. If you have constraints of any kind on transitions, you may also want to consider tracking state information in a state machine. For this, you can use the Acts As State Machine plugin, which is covered in Chapter 6.

Let's examine our show view, which allows the user to edit car data, as well as to view the current and past states. Listing 4-8 shows this view.

Listing 4-8. *Car Show/Edit View (app/views/cars/show.html.erb)*

```erb
<h1><%=@car.to_s%></h1>

<div style="width:50%; float: left;">
  <%=render :partial=>'form', :locals=>{'@car'=>@car}%>
</div>

<div style="width:50%; float: left;">
  <h2>History</h2>
  <ul>
  <%
    last_version = nil
    (@car_history).each do |version|
      %><li><%=version.created_at.to_s(:short)%>: <%
      if last_version.nil?%>
        Initially Created
  <% else %>
    <%ignored_fields = [:updated_at, :version, :id]
    changes = []
      differences = version.diff(last_version)
      differences.each do |field, d|
        next if ignored_fields.include?(field)
        new_value, old_value = *d
        changes << "#{field.to_s.humanize} changed " <<
                   "from '#{old_value}' to '#{new_value}'"
      end
      %><%=h changes.to_sentence%><%
      end
      last_version = version%>
      </li>
    <%
  end%>
</div>
```

```
<p style="clear:left">
  <%= link_to 'Back', cars_path %>
</p>
```

This view is split vertically into two parts. The first shows the form partial—just as the new car view did—which allows the user to make changes. The second half shows the history of the car.

The history of the car is created by looping through all of the versions of the car that have existed. The first version is described simply as "initially created," and each successive version is described by its differences. Specifically, we use the `diff` function to return the differences between the two records. We loop through them and skip the fields that will always change: the timestamps, ID, and version number fields. When finished, we combine all of the changes into a single, timestamped entry on the right side of the screen.

Next, let's briefly examine our layout, shown in Listing 4-9.

Listing 4-9. *Car Controller Layout (app/views/layouts/cars.html.erb)*

```
<!DOCTYPE html PUBLIC "-//W3C//DTD XHTML 1.0 Transitional//EN"
        "http://www.w3.org/TR/xhtml1/DTD/xhtml1-transitional.dtd">

<html xmlns="http://www.w3.org/1999/xhtml" xml:lang="en" lang="en">
<head>
  <meta http-equiv="content-type" content="text/html;charset=UTF-8" />
  <title>Cars: <%= controller.action_name.humanize %></title>
  <%= stylesheet_link_tag 'car' %>
</head>
<body>

<%if flash[:notice]%>
  <p style="color: green"><%= flash[:notice] %></p>
<%end%>

<%= yield  %>

</body>
</html>
```

To go along with this layout is our style sheet, shown in Listing 4-10.

Listing 4-10. *Car Controller Style Sheet (public/stylesheets/car.css)*

```
body { background-color: #fff; color: #333; }

body, p, ol, ul, td {
  font-family: verdana, arial, helvetica, sans-serif;
  font-size:   13px;
  line-height: 18px;
}
```

```
pre {
  background-color: #eee;
  padding: 10px;
  font-size: 11px;
}

a { color: #000; }
a:visited { color: #666; }
a:hover { color: #fff; background-color:#000; }

.fieldWithErrors {
  padding: 2px;
  background-color: red;
  display: table;
}

#errorExplanation {
  width: 400px;
  border: 2px solid red;
  padding: 7px;
  padding-bottom: 12px;
  margin-bottom: 20px;
  background-color: #f0f0f0;
}

#errorExplanation h2 {
  text-align: left;
  font-weight: bold;
  padding: 5px 5px 5px 15px;
  font-size: 12px;
  margin: -7px;
  background-color: #c00;
  color: #fff;
}

#errorExplanation p {
  color: #333;
  margin-bottom: 0;
  padding: 5px;
}
```

```
#errorExplanation ul li {
  font-size: 12px;
  list-style: square;
}

div.uploadStatus {
  margin: 5px;
}

div.progressBar {
  margin: 5px;
}

div.progressBar div.border {
  background-color: #fff;
  border: 1px solid gray;
  width: 100%;
}

div.progressBar div.background {
  background-color: #333;
  height: 18px;
  width: 0%;
}
```

Running the Inventory Application

At this point, we can run the application:

```
ruby script/server
```

Point your web browser to http://localhost:3000/cars. You should see a simple index page with the single car we created earlier using the Rails console. Click View, and you'll see a screen similar to Figure 4-1.

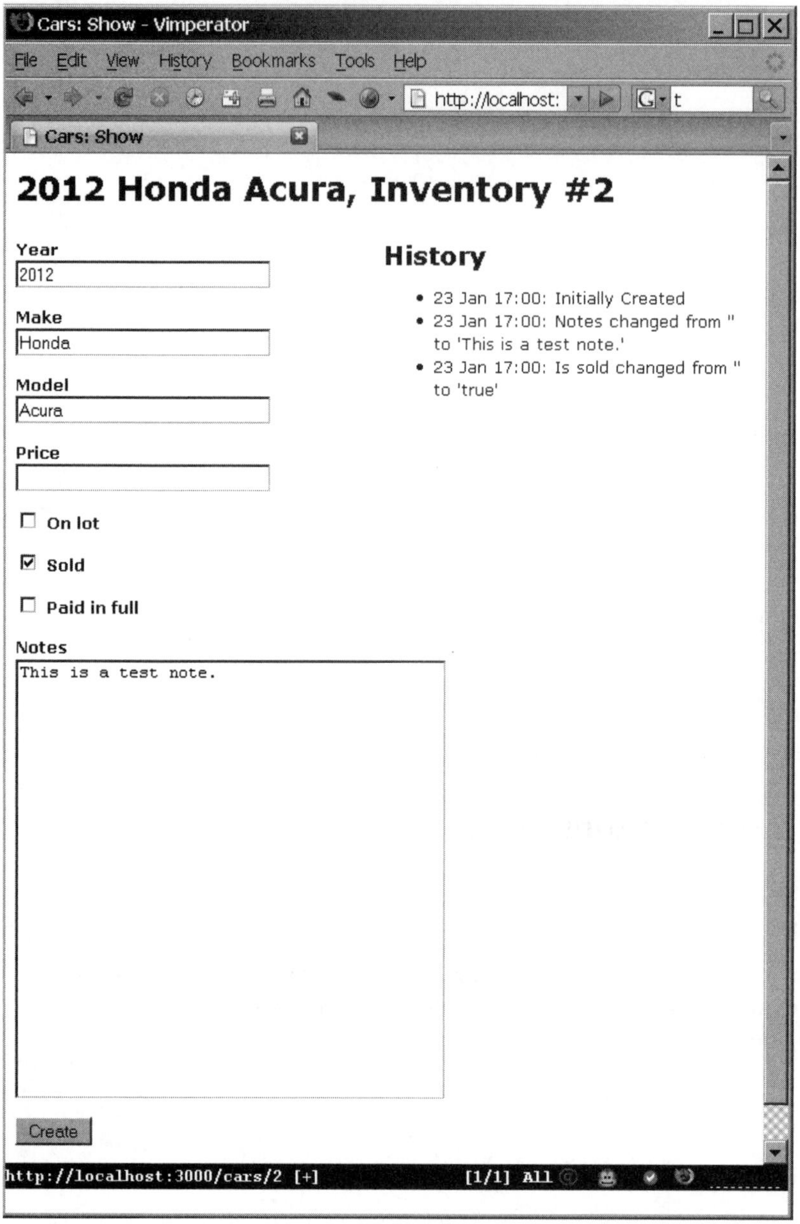

Figure 4-1. *Car view page showing various changes*

Try changing a few fields and then save the changes. You will see the changes reflected in the history on the right side of the screen.

Summary

Storing old versions of data is an easy way to extend a database into the past, so you can view the entire history of a resource on the Web. While we often focus on the current state of an object, the past state may be just as important. Whether you're trying to improve something—like efficiency, sales, or click-throughs—or to reduce something—like fraudulent orders or page defacement—looking at old data can help you use the past to improve the future.

As you've seen, a very easy way to store and access historical data is by using the Acts As Versioned plugin. In fact, you can use the same Active Record code you might use otherwise, and you can even use Riff to .easily summarize it and then present it to your users. See `http://ar-versioned.rubyforge.org` for the Acts As Versioned documentation.

∎∎∎

## CHAPTER 5

Adding a Five-Star Ratings Widget with Ajaxful Rating

User-contributed content has changed the web landscape forever, leveling the field to allow just about anyone to become the star of a hit mini-film, reach the masses with her music, or publish a thought-provoking book or a tasty recipe for others to rave about. However, a clear side effect of the success of everyone rushing to share content is what we call *information overload*. With everyone now empowered as media producers and a global distribution channel, it has become increasingly difficult to decide what's good and what's bad. In fact, without some sort of filtering mechanism, it's completely overwhelming.

One of the services that traditional media outlets—television, radio, and print media—provide to us is a sort of filtering mechanism. They decide what's good enough for the masses. In reality, this is a bit constricting. Our tastes as a society are clearly not "one size fits all," and we would rather make such decisions on our own. The solution, at least for online niche communities, is to allow users to rate and filter this sort of content collaboratively. By allowing users to rank worthwhile content themselves, we rely on the wisdom of the crowd to float the most worthwhile content to the top, thus making it easier to find by casual visitors.

Many sites choose to implement ratings using a five-star ratings widget, a concept which has been used and popularized by the likes of Netflix, Amazon, Yelp, YouTube, and many others. In the Netflix system, illustrated in Figure 5-1, red stars represent average community ratings, and yellow stars are ratings that were personally assigned by the current (logged-in) user. Discriminating between community and personal ratings is a common feature in web ratings systems.

Other sites handle ratings in different ways. Reddit, for instance, provides users the ability to give a thumbs-up or thumbs-down to an article listed in its system. Digg allows you to click a single button to express your interest in something. The exact rating mechanism that you choose for your site depends on the type of content your site indexes.

Fortunately for Rails developers, a number of plugins are devoted to the task of adding ratings to our model objects. Some, such as Acts As Rateable (`http://www.juixe.com/techknow/index.php/2006/07/05/acts-as-rateable-plugin`), are very barebones, leaving implementation of the interface up to you, but providing the basic facilities to associate ratings with any model for maximum flexibility. Others, such as Acts As Voteable (`http://acts_as_voteable.richcollins.net`), tie ratings specifically to user models, which can eliminate extra development for the most common case.

Figure 5-1. *Example of a user-driven five-star ratings widget on Netflix (http://www.netflix.com)*

In this chapter, we'll use a plugin that provides the model behavior we're looking for, along with a nice, easy-to-use view helper that can communicate with a controller action using Ajax to update an attractive five-star ratings widget in place. The Ajaxful Rating plugin (http://docs.mimbles.net/projects/ajaxful_rating), by Edgar J. Suarez Heredia, is a very slick drop-in addition to any Rails project that might benefit from community ratings.

Our Task: Add Community Ratings to an Existing Application

Back in Chapter 2, we created a system for classic arcade game enthusiasts to share links with one another and added tagging features to allow visitors to easily find and classify content. As more links have been added to the system, it has grown increasingly difficult to determine which links are the highest quality. Users of the service have started adding tags like excellent and outdated to links in the system to indicate their rating of the link content. This is smart on their part, but it's also a misuse of the tagging system. So, obviously, we need to give them some way to explicitly rate the quality of the links.

To make it easier for users to find and rate quality resources in the arcade resource links system, we've proposed adding a five-star ratings widget to each resource. This will serve as a familiar interface with which users can rate links, and it will also allow us to prioritize the display of links so that the top-rated resources for any given tag can be displayed first in the results listing. Using the Ajaxful Rating plugin, we can easily add these capabilities to our application.

Adding Ratings to Arcade Resources

Since we'll be extending the existing Rails project from Chapter 2, make sure to switch to that project directory before continuing. Once you're within the arcadelinks project directory, execute the following command to install the Ajaxful Rating plugin:

```
ruby script/plugin install http://svn.mimbles.net/rails/plugins/ajaxful_rating
```

The plugin provides us with a new generator we can use to create the database tables necessary for the ratings. It also installs other files, such as the Rate model itself and the style sheet and images that we'll use later to display the ratings widget in our views. Run the generator now by executing the following command:

```
ruby script/generate ajaxful_rating
```

```
      create  app/models/rate.rb
      exists  db/migrate
      create  db/migrate/003_create_rates.rb
      create  public/images/ajaxful_rating
      create  public/images/ajaxful_rating/star_off.gif
      create  public/images/ajaxful_rating/star_on.gif
      create  public/images/ajaxful_rating/star_hover.gif
      create  public/images/ajaxful_rating/blank.gif
      create  public/stylesheets/ajaxful_rating.css
```

We'll also need to migrate the database at this time by using the familiar rake db:migrate task:

```
rake db:migrate
```

```
== 3 CreateRates: migrating ======================================================
-- create_table(:rates)
   -> 0.0747s
-- add_index(:rates, :user_id)
   -> 0.0033s
-- add_index(:rates, :rateable_id)
   -> 0.0044s
== 3 CreateRates: migrated (0.0829s) =============================================
```

Rating Arcade Links

In order to make our existing Link model rateable, all we need to do is add a single statement to the class: has_ajaxful_rates. By calling this method, made available by the plugin, a relationship with the Rate model is automatically established, and a number of new instance and class-level methods for dealing with ratings are mixed in.

The updated code for the Link model is shown in Listing 5-1, with the modification shown in bold. Save it as app/models/link.rb before continuing.

Listing 5-1. *Updated Link Model with Ratings (app/models/link.rb)*

```
class Link < ActiveRecord::Base
  acts_as_taggable
  has_ajaxful_rates

  validates_presence_of :url, :name
  validates_uniqueness_of :url
end
```

With this in place, our class now has the ability to use the rate instance method to add a new rating to an arcade link. The rate method takes two parameters: the rating to assign to the object, and the rater (discussed in the next section) that assigned it that rating. The rate_average method can also be called to return an average of all ratings on an arcade link object. The total_rates method will return the total number of ratings for the object. A number of class-level finder methods are now available as well. For instance, find_rated_with returns all objects rated with a given number of stars, find_rated_by can be used to find all links rated by a particular rater, and find_most_popular will return the rateable object with the highest average rating.

■**Tip** Ratings, by default, are on a scale from one to five stars. To vary the rating scale available on the object, override the stars class method in your model. For instance, to allow ratings of one to ten stars on arcade resource links, we would create the following method in our Link class:

```
def.self.stars
  10
end
```

Attributing Ratings to a User (Rater)

Because ratings must be attributed to some source, we also need some notion of a "rater." In practice, this rater is usually a user model. We'll talk about proper user models in Chapter 11, but for now, we'll represent a user simply by an IP address. This is a convenient way to allow us to let visitors rate objects without needing to actually log in or establish an account. At the same time, it ensures some level of identity for users. Of course, if a user logs in from a different IP address or shares a single IP with other users (via network address translation), then this system breaks down somewhat, and ratings from different sources can get confused. But this will be good enough for us (and for our classic arcade hobbyist brethren) for now.

Without further ado, let's create the User model and its accompanying database migration. The migration, shown in Listing 5-2, should be saved as db/migrate/ 004_create_users.rb.

Listing 5-2. *Migration for Users Table (db/migrate/004_create_users.rb)*

```
class CreateUsers < ActiveRecord::Migration
  def self.up
    create_table :users do |t|
      t.string :ip_address
      t.timestamps
    end
  end

  def self.down
    drop_table :users
  end
end
```

Migrate the database by once again running rake db:migrate:

```
rake db:migrate
```

```
== 4 CreateUsers: migrating =======================================================
-- create_table(:users)
   -> 0.0976s
== 4 CreateUsers: migrated (0.0977s) ==============================================
```

Now we can define our User model, as shown in Listing 5-3. Save it as app/models/user.rb.

Listing 5-3. *User Model (app/models/user.rb)*

```
class User < ActiveRecord::Base
  is_ajaxful_rater

  validates_presence_of :ip_address
  validates_uniqueness_of :ip_address
end
```

The model's validation logic simply ensures that the IP address is unique, as this is the only characteristic we're using to differentiate between our users. The model definition also includes a call to the plugin's is_ajaxful_rater method, which creates the appropriate association with the Rate class.

Honestly, this is all we need to do to make a model rateable, and many ratings-related plugins stop right here, as this is already substantial functionality. Ajaxful Rating goes one step further by adding view helpers as well, which we'll use momentarily.

Before we get to that, let's take a moment to try out the new ratings-related methods on our model by using the Rails console.

Rating Arcade Links in the Rails Console

Start a Rails console session by issuing the command `script/console` in the project directory. We'll add a number of ratings to a couple different arcade links, and then calculate average ratings for each of them.

```
ruby script/console
```

```
Loading development environment (Rails 2.0.2)
>> link1 = Link.find(:first)
>> link2 = Link.find(:first, :order => "created_at DESC")
>> link1.rates
=> []
>> link1.rate(4, User.find_or_create_by_ip_address('192.168.1.1'))
>> link1.rate(5, User.find_or_create_by_ip_address('192.168.1.2'))
>> link1.total_rates
=> 2
>> link1.rate_average
=> 4.5
>> link2.rate(3, User.find_or_create_by_ip_address('192.168.1.2'))
>> link2.rate_average
=> 3.0
```

This all works pretty much as we would expect. A `User` stands in for the `Rater`, and since we differentiate users solely by IP address, we can use `find_or_create_by_ip_address` to retrieve the correct `User` instance if it exists, or create a new one if it does not.

We've added a number of ratings to two different links using `rate`, and seen how the plugin can automatically calculate the total number of ratings that have been applied to an object and average ratings for those objects.

Next, let's use the class methods provided by the plugin to find all ratings that were made by a particular user and locate the most popular link in our collection of arcade resources:

```
>> Link.find_rated_by(User.find_by_ip_address('192.168.1.1')).collect {
      |link| link.name }
=> ["Killer List Of Video Games"]
>> Link.find_rated_by(User.find_by_ip_address('192.168.1.2')).collect {
      |link| link.name }
=> ["Killer List Of Video Games", "Galaga: History"]
>> link2.rated_by?(User.find_by_ip_address('192.168.1.2'))
=> true
>> Link.find_most_popular.name
=> "Killer List Of Video Games"
```

In this example, we also used the `rated_by?` instance method. This method allows us to easily determine if a given rateable object (in this case, a `Link`) has been rated by a particular rater (`User`). We'll make use of this in our views later on.

Since one of our goals in adding the ratings capability to the arcade resources site is to allow lists of resources to be displayed according to their popularity, let's think for a moment about how we'll achieve that. First, we'll need to look up an existing tag that we know has some number of links, such as arcade, and find those resources associated with it. We've already done this in Chapter 2, in the TagsController. The trick is to collect the taggable items associated with a given Tag (in this case, the taggable items are always Link objects). Once we have that, we can order links by popularity by using the sort_by method on the resultant array, passing it a block that specifies that it should use the rate_average method on each link to determine the sort order, as follows:

```
>> links_with_tag = Tag.find_by_name('arcade').taggings.collect { |t| t.taggable }
>> links_with_tag.sort_by { |link| link.rate_average }.reverse.collect {
     |link| link.name }

=> ["Killer List Of Video Games", "Build Your Own Arcade Controls FAQ",
    "Super Auctions Calendar", "Typical Day at an Arcade Auction",
    "EBay: Arcade Collectibles", "MAME World",
    "Build Your Own Arcade Controls Wiki"]
```

Our call to sort_by does just what we would expect it to do, returning the array of items reordered according to the average rating of those links. We then need to reverse the array so that the links with the highest ratings are first, rather than last. Finally, we use collect to see the names of those items that have the highest ratings.

Building an Ajax-Enabled Star Rating System

Now that you've seen how link ratings work in our system, and thought a bit about how they'll interface with our existing tags to improve our listings, let's implement the necessary changes. This means ordering links returned in the TagsController's show action by their rating/popularity, as shown in the preceding section, and also exposing a five-star rating widget so that our visitors can actually rate links.

Sorting Links by Popularity (Average Ratings)

Let's start by updating the existing TagsController. Modify the links method so that it resembles the code shown in Listing 5-4.

Listing 5-4. *Updated Links Action for TagsController, with Links Sorted by Rating (app/controllers/tags_controller.rb)*

```
class TagsController < ApplicationController
  def show
    @tag = Tag.find(params[:id])
    @title = "Links Tagged With '#{@tag.name}'"
    @links = @tag.taggings.collect { |t| t.taggable }.sort_by {
      |t| t.rate_average }.reverse
    render(:template => 'links/index')
  end
end
```

We've changed only one line of code here, shown in bold, updating it to use the same sort of logic we used in the console to display links by popularity (for a given tag).

If you start the server using `script/server` and view link results for a particular tag, you will see that the links are now ordered according to user ratings. To verify that they're being displayed in the right order, let's edit our index view template to show the numeric average rating for each arcade resource in the list. As you may recall, the `links` action on `TagsController` renders the template in `app/views/links/index.html.erb`. Update that file to resemble the code shown in Listing 5-5.

Listing 5-5. *Updated Links Index View with Numeric Rating Values (app/views/links/index.html.erb)*

```
<ul>
  <% @links.each do |link| -%>
    <li><%= link_to(link.name, link_path(link)) %>
      <strong>[<%= sprintf('%.2f', link.rate_average) %>]</strong>
      (<%= truncate(link.tag_list.join(', '), 20) %>)</li>
  <% end -%>
</ul>
```

If you navigate to the links available for the `arcade` tag in your browser (use the tag cloud), you will see a screen similar to Figure 5-2. Note that the exact number of links displayed depend on what you've added to the arcade resources example.

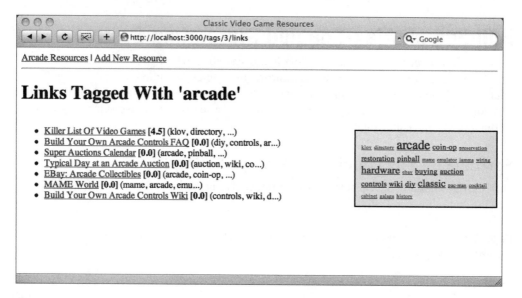

Figure 5-2. *Listing of links with numeric ratings displayed (http://localhost:3000/tags/1/links)*

The links should be displayed according to their ratings, with the most popular (according to average ratings) links shown first. It's possible that you may have links in your system that have not yet received a rating of any kind. In that case, the rating will be displayed as 0.0. Later, as you add more ratings, the links should reorder themselves accordingly. This way, the highest rated links will always appear first whenever a visitor browses to a tagged topic in the system.

■**Note** We will continue to order links shown on the main `LinksController` index page (`/links`) by creation date alone, as it serves primarily as a list of "latest updates" for the front page. You can change this if you prefer another ordering. Also, you may want to consider adding pagination, as demonstrated in Chapter 15.

Adding the Five-Star Ratings Widget

It's nice that link results for a tag are now ordered according to their rating, but that's not of much use to us unless visitors also have some way to add new ratings to the system. After all, our purpose here is to crowdsource content ratings to our visitors, so we need to expose some mechanism through which they can make their voices heard.

To allow users to rate links, we'll add a five-star ratings widget to the detailed arcade link pages (rendered by the `show` action). The users will interact with this widget, clicking some number of stars to register their rating of the current link. When they click, the number of stars they've selected will be sent to a new action in our `LinksController`. This action, available as a method called `rate`, will be called from the ratings widget and will add or update the user's rating of the link. It will then return some data asynchronously to be inserted into the template, rather than re-rendering the entire page.

Since `rate` is not a standard RESTful action, we'll need to update our routes to include it. The `rate` action is triggered by a `POST` to a URL such as `/links/1/rate`, making it a member action that needs to be added to the `links` resource. Edit `config/routes.rb` and modify it to look like the code shown in Listing 5-6.

Listing 5-6. *Updated Routes with Rate Member Action for Links Resource (config/routes.rb)*

```
ActionController::Routing::Routes.draw do |map|
  map.resources :links, :member => { :tag => :post, :rate => :post }
  map.resources :tags
end
```

■**Note** For more information about RESTful resources and custom member actions, see the documentation for `ActionController::Resources` at `http://api.rubyonrails.org/classes/ActionController/Resources.html`.

The actual implementation of the rate method we've referred to is shown in Listing 5-7. Add it to the existing LinksController in app/controllers/links_controller.rb at this time.

Listing 5-7. *Updated LinksController with Rate Action (app/controllers/links_controller.rb)*

```ruby
class LinksController < ApplicationController
  ... snip! ...

  def rate
    @user = User.find_or_create_by_ip_address(request.remote_ip)
    @link = Link.find(params[:id])

    @link.rates.find_by_user_id(@user.id).destroy if @link.rated_by?(@user)
    @link.rate(params[:stars], @user)

    render(:update) do |page|
      page.replace("link_#{@link.id}_rating",
        :partial => "link_with_rating", :object => @link)
    end
  end
end
```

When this action is called, we first set the @user instance variable to the appropriate user, as identified by that user's IP address. If a user account with that IP is found, we'll retrieve it. Otherwise, we'll create a new one.

Next, we retrieve the appropriate Link, based on the parameter found in the URL. Once we have that Link model in the @link instance variable, we can find out if the user has already rated this particular link by using the rated_by? method. If the user has rated the link, we'll use the find_by_user_id dynamic finder method on the rates association to return the Rate object previously recorded by the user and remove it using the destroy method. After all, we don't want a single user to record more than one rating for any object in the system. If users opt to change their rating on an existing link, our implicit assumption is that they're replacing their previous rating, not recording an additional one.

Once the old rating has been removed, adding a new one is straightforward. We just call the rate method, as previously demonstrated, specifying the value of the stars parameter as the rating to assign to it, and the current user as the rater. We can then update the page using the render(:update) method, and instruct it to replace the element link_#_rating (where # is the ID of the Link) with the output generated by rendering the link_with_rating partial template.

Let's take a look at that partial view template. It is shown in Listing 5-8 and should be saved as app/views/links/_link_with_rating.html.erb.

Listing 5-8. *Partial Template to Display Link Ratings (app/views/links/_link_with_rating.html.erb)*

```
<div id="link_<%= link_with_rating.id %>_rating">
  <%= ajaxful_rating_for(link_with_rating,
        rate_link_path(link_with_rating),
        :method => :post) %>
</div>
```

■**Note** The Link model in @link is made available inside the partial template as the variable link_with_rating by passing it to render with the :object parameter. The :object available inside the template is named after the template itself by convention.

This partial defines the div element referenced in the controller action earlier. We've included the div with such an appropriate DOM ID so that it can be easily replaced using the page.replace Prototype (Ajax) helper in the rate action.

Inside the div is a single call to the ajaxful_rating_for method, which is the handy view helper provided by the Ajaxful Rating plugin. Its purpose is to render a five-star ratings widget that shows the current average rating of a particular rateable item, and allow users to hover and click a star to register their own rating. When the rating is registered, it will be communicated asynchronously to the rate action in LinksController.

The helper takes two required parameters and any number of options. The first required parameter is the rateable model itself, in this case our Link model object. The second required parameter is the path to the action that should be called to add or update the model's rating. In this case, that path is available to us using the rate_link_path method, which indicates the rate action for the specific model object. We also pass the :method option to specify that a POST method should be used to access the action. The user-specified rating is sent to the rate action in the stars parameter (params[:stars]), thus allowing our rate method logic to use it for updates.

■**Tip** You can set a conditional to control whether the current user is allowed to select a rating from the widget (keeping it visible but effectively disabling it) by using the :enable_rate option to the ajaxful_rating_for helper. For instance, if you were using the RESTful Authentication system (covered in Chapter 11) in your application and wanted to make sure that users had logged in before allowing them to select a rating, you could use :enable_rate => logged_in?.

In order to make this visible to our users, we need to update the preexisting show action template in app/views/links/show.html.erb to render the partial. We've done this in Listing 5-9.

Listing 5-9. *Updated Show Template with Ratings Partial (app/views/links/show.html.erb)*

```
<p><strong>Link: </strong><%= link_to(@link.url) %></p>
<p><strong>Description:</strong> <%= h(@link.description) %></p>
<p><strong>Tags:</strong> <%= clickable_tag_list(@link.tags) %></p>
<p>Created <%= time_ago_in_words(@link.created_at) %> ago</p>

<%= render(:partial => 'link_with_rating', :object => @link) %>

<% form_tag(tag_link_path(@link)) do -%>
  <%= text_field_tag(:tags) %>
  <%= submit_tag('Add New Tags') %>
<% end -%>
```

Because the helper relies on the Prototype JavaScript library for asynchronous JavaScript communication and some CSS to render the star ratings widget correctly, we also need to reference a style sheet and include the JavaScript library in our document. We can do this by editing the application layout in use, `app/views/layouts/application.html.erb`. We need to add only the following two lines within the `<head>` section of the HTML page found in that file:

```
<%= javascript_include_tag('prototype') %>
<%= stylesheet_link_tag('ajaxful_rating') %>
```

The first line includes the Prototype JavaScript library supplied with Rails. This is used by the plugin helper method we saw earlier to make the asynchronous call to the `rate` action and inject the response that's returned into the user view without requiring a page refresh. This is an example of an Ajax request. Prototype and Rails do a good job of abstracting all the difficult bits away from us, but if you're curious, we invite you to take a look at the generated source in your browser and dig through Prototype's API reference at `http://prototypejs.org`.

The second line includes a style sheet that is supplied with the Ajaxful Rating plugin, which will be used to show the star ratings. It was automatically placed in your `public/stylesheets` directory when you installed the plugin. Without this, the star images won't appear correctly. Feel free to modify this style sheet and the corresponding images if you wish to change the look and feel of the stock ratings system.

With these elements in place, you can test our five-star ratings system by browsing to any arcade detailed resource information page (`show` action page) in a web browser. A link that has yet to receive any ratings should show five dim yellow stars, indicating that no ratings have yet been registered. Hover over the ratings widget to see the state change, and then select your rating for the arcade resource—three stars for this example.

When you click, the helper method provided by the plugin will asynchronously contact the `rate` action, which will add a new rating for that item, and then send back a JavaScript response to tell your browser to replace the part of the page that was used to display the rating. Once updated, it should show three brightly colored stars, followed by two of the dimmer stars from before, thus indicating a rating of three out of five, as shown in Figure 5-3 (the fourth star illustrates the hover state when the mouse is placed over the star for selection). From the end user point of view, things work smoothly, without a page refresh, and you aren't even aware that any asynchronous tasks are happening.

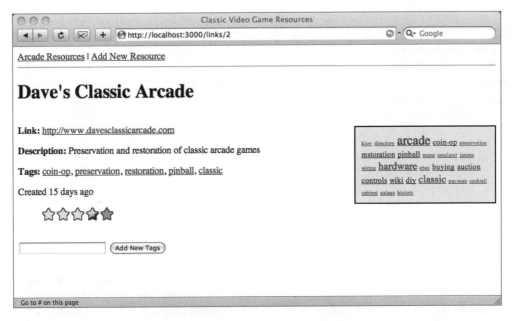

Figure 5-3. *Arcade resource page with a five-star ratings widget (http://localhost:3000/links/2)*

STAR RATINGS SYSTEM VARIANTS

In this example, we are using a three-state star ratings system; that is, we're showing a single star rating widget that represents the average rating of the rateable item. Therefore, when you rate an item that already has ratings (from other users), it will adjust to reflect the new average, rather than your own rating. You might also want to show a separate rating value in the partial to indicate the user's own rating (if available) of that item.

A popular alternative approach is to use a four-state star ratings system. Taking this approach, you would replace the average community rating with the user's own rating, and the stars would be a different color to indicate that the rating the user is seeing is his own.

It's a matter of opinion which option is preferable. The four-state system is certainly a popular technique, used by Netflix as well as many other major web applications. It tends to work best when users form their own opinion of something and cease to care about what everyone else thinks, as is usually the case with film reviews.

Adding the Ratings Widget to the Index View

Many web sites, particularly social news sites like Digg and Reddit, provide a quick way to rate assets or items at a glance, by including a ratings widget next to each list item in a long list of items. Although this is probably more common with yes/no and thumbs-up/thumbs-down rating systems than it is with five-star systems, it's still quite useful in our example, where visitors may already be familiar with the links shown on the main listing screens.

Because we constructed our ratings partial template to use the ID of a `Link` model in the div, this is as easy to do as adding one line of code to our existing link `index` action template, as shown in Listing 5-10.

Listing 5-10. *Updated Index Template to Display Ratings Widgets (app/views/links/index.html.erb)*

```
<ul>
  <% @links.each do |link| -%>
    <li><%= link_to(link.name, link_path(link)) %>
      <strong>[<%= sprintf('%.2f', link.rate_average) %>]</strong>
      (<%= truncate(link.tag_list.join(', '), 20) %>)<br/>
      <%= render(:partial => 'links/link_with_rating', :object => link)➥
 %></li>
  <% end -%>
</ul>
```

This change is almost identical to the one we made in the `show` action template. The only difference is that the `:object` specified this time is the `link` variable, the value of the current element as we iterate over the array. This means that a ratings widget showing the current rating is displayed for each item in the array. Each of these widgets will be coded to contact its particular `rate_link_path`, which will update only the relevant section of the page when a new rating is recorded.

With this in place, you can return to our main page at `http://localhost:3000/links` or visit any tag page index such as `http://localhost:3000/tags/3/links`. Each item from the list will have a ratings widget displayed for it, as shown in Figure 5-4.

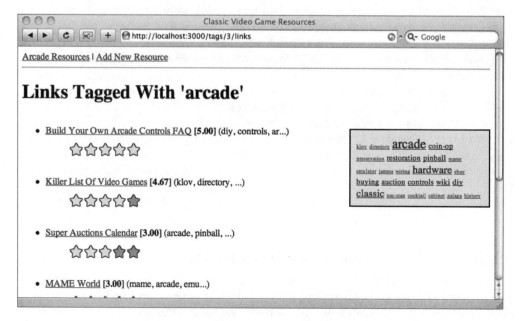

Figure 5-4. *Listing of arcade resources with individual ratings widgets (http://localhost:3000/tags/3/links)*

Go ahead and rate any number of items. You'll notice that their ratings are updated appropriately, but that the list is not reordered. However, the next time that the page is redisplayed (unless it is the main "recent links" page), the link order will be updated to display the highest rated items first.

Improving Performance by Caching Average Ratings

We're actually performing a relatively expensive operation when we ask for a list of links sorted by average ratings. First of all, we're asking Rails to retrieve data from the database and instantiate models for every link in the list. We're also asking it to calculate their average by summing the ratings associated with them and dividing by the total number of rates on each link. Then, once we have that value, we still need to call Ruby's sort_by method to order the list of objects appropriately. To get an idea of the database queries generated by the first part of this process, take a look at the server logs in logs/development.log. You'll notice that two additional SQL queries are generated for each link on behalf of the ratings system: one SUM query and one COUNT query.

The expense of this operation is multiplied when we consider that many users may be asking for the same information over and over again. Not to mention that, in production, we'll be dealing with a larger number of rateable items. Imagine having 100+ links for a page of tag results and trying to determine which has the highest average rating. Clearly, this isn't something we want to calculate on the fly if we can avoid it. Instead, we would prefer to cache the average rating of each link so it can be easily returned and used to sort links.

Ajaxful Rating does much of the hard work for us here. It allows us to cache average ratings on a model instance simply by adding an attribute called rating_average on the rateable (Link) model.

■**Tip** You can choose an alternate name for the cached rating column by specifying it as a symbol parameter to the set_cached_average_column method in your model.

To accomplish this, we need to create a database migration and update the links table once more, adding the appropriate column. Save the code shown in Listing 5-11 as db/migrate/005_create_link_rating_average.rb.

Listing 5-11. *Database Migration to Add Cached Rating Column (db/migrate/005_create_link_rating_average.rb)*

```
class CreateLinkRatingAverage < ActiveRecord::Migration
  def self.up
    add_column :links, :rating_average, :decimal,
      :precision => 3, :scale => 1, :default => nil
    Link.find(:all).each { |link| link.update_cached_average }
  end
```

```
  def self.down
    remove_column :links, :rating_average
  end
end
```

In addition to adding the column, this migration also uses the `update_cached_average` method provided by the plugin to automatically calculate current averages and populate the cached value field at migration time. Run the `rake db:migrate` task now to add this column and populate it.

```
rake db:migrate
```

```
== 5 CreateLinkRatingAverage: migrating ========================================
-- add_column(:links, :rating_average, :decimal, {:precision=>3, :scale=>1, ➥
:default=>nil})
   -> 0.0145s
== 5 CreateLinkRatingAverage: migrated (0.0149s) ===============================
```

With this update in place, the plugin will detect the presence of the cache and make use of it. Whenever a new rating is added or removed from a rateable object, the average rating will be automatically recalculated and cached in the `rating_average` column, accessible as an attribute on the model instance. Then, when the `rate_average` method is called to calculate the average rating for some `Link`, this value will be returned, instead of being calculated on the fly. This results in substantial savings (two SQL queries per arcade link).

Summary

One of the hallmarks of Web 2.0 is user-generated content, and the Web is a better place for it. As important as it is to empower users to generate content and new media for online distribution, it's at least as important to allow them to help rate and filter the large amount of content that is being produced every day by their peers. In practice, this helps users tailor services to their needs and gives them a sense of ownership, as well as making the best content easier to locate by casual visitors.

Ajaxful Rating, Acts As Rateable, Acts As Voteable, and a host of other Rails plugins can help us in this endeavor by easing the implementation burden of adding ratings to model objects. In addition, Ajaxful Rating provides a useful view helper we can use to display an attractive five-star ratings widget.

In this chapter, we demonstrated how to add Ajax-powered ratings widgets to existing arcade resource links and discussed a number of the plugin's features along the way. For more information, see the Ajaxful Rating documentation at `http://docs.mimbles.net/projects/ajaxful_rating`.

CHAPTER 6

■ ■ ■

Modeling State Machines

Although Active Record callbacks and observers can be very useful, they can quickly lead to clutter in your model. If you are using one or more attributes to manage some notion of state in your model and find yourself making excessive use of callbacks or observers, it's possible that you might benefit from modeling your class as a *finite state machine*.

A finite state machine (FSM) is a model of behavior made up of a finite number of states and transitions between those states, with rules that define how and when those transitions happen. Many machines and tasks both inside and outside of computer science follow this model: state machines are used in fields as varied as electronics design, linguistics, biology, and philosophy. Cars, airplanes, and robots all make use of them. The artificial intelligence powering enemy soldiers in your favorite video game may as well.

In our own development projects, we often find ourselves using FSMs if it's possible to identify multiple distinct stages that the model will pass through in its lifetime. Each stage, or state, is used to represent some amount of knowledge about the system, and the actions available at any given point in time are constrained by the rules governing the state. A state transition can occur only to a neighboring state, and those transitions are triggered only when the rules for the state transition are satisfied.

To get a better grasp on how this works, it's often informative to see FSMs represented in a state diagram, where nodes represent the states and edges represent the transitions. Figure 6-1 shows such a diagram for an extremely simple state machine: a light switch.

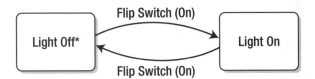

Figure 6-1. *Simple two-state FSM (light switch). Note that the asterisk indicates the initial state.*

In this diagram, we represent two states, on and off. When the light switch is off, you can flip the switch to turn it on, and when the light is on, you can flip the same switch to turn it off. These actions trigger the state transitions. Note that in this case, the same action is called both times, and that only when the action is coupled with knowledge of the preexisting state can the outcome state be determined.

Although this is an extremely simple example, it's helpful for you to begin to grasp the concept of a state machine and how it can simplify representing and implementing certain model behaviors. In this chapter, we'll show you how a state machine can help you model a complex (but practical!) real-world task.

Our Task: Model the Conference Proposal Process

We're working for a committee that is putting together an emerging technologies conference in Metro City, and the name of it is, unsurprisingly, the Metro City Emerging Technologies Conference (MCETC). Our co-organizers are going a bit crazy, organizing a conference being the tough business that it is, so we've offered to create a system to help handle at least one element of the conference: speaker proposals.

MCETC wants to send out a call for presenters next week and have them come to our web site and fill out a form to propose a talk. The talk proposals will all get saved to a database, and someone will have the task of reviewing them and deciding which speakers to invite to the conference.

The tricky part is that there are various parts of the speaker proposal process and various tasks that have to happen at each stage in that process. After a proposal is reviewed, it can be either accepted or denied; if it's accepted, the proposed talk then needs to be scheduled, which means assigning it a time and a room within the convention center. In addition, MCETC obviously wants to keep the speakers updated about the status of their proposals, so organizers would like to have e-mails automatically sent to speakers whenever the status of their proposal is changed.

Without a system to manage this process, it could get unwieldy very quickly. In fact, you might already be a little confused. So to clarify things, let's look at the stages of the speaker sign-up process as a series of states, as shown in the state diagram in Figure 6-2.

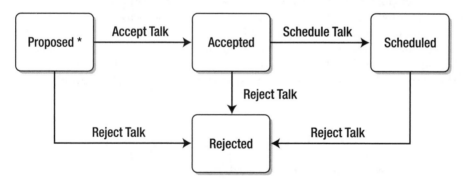

Figure 6-2. *FSM for the ConferenceTalk model. Note that the asterisk indicates the initial state.*

As before, the states are represented by rectangles and the transitions between states represented by arrows. Clearly, this is a more complex example than our light switch diagram in Figure 6-1, but it should be obvious that this task can be modeled quite elegantly as an FSM.

Although we could build an FSM on top of a plain old Active Record model using an instance variable (or a series of Boolean flags) to maintain state and callbacks and observers to make sure the right things happen at the right time, that could become difficult to maintain as complexity is added. On the other hand, we can use Scott Barron's powerful Acts As State

Machine plugin, which will allow us to define states and events in a domain-specific language (DSL) layered on top of our Rails model code. That sounds much cleaner!

Modeling with Multiple States

Let's create a new Rails project for this project. We'll call it confplanner:

```
rails confplanner
cd confplanner
```

To install the Acts As State Machine plugin, execute the following command inside the new project directory:

```
ruby script/plugin install➥
http://elitists.textdriven.com/svn/plugins/acts_as_state_machine/trunk
```

Once installed, you'll be able to give your models the characteristics of an FSM by adding a simple declarative statement and then using the provided DSL to define states and the transitions between them.

We're also going to need to install a set of extensions (overrides), published by Chetan Patil, for the stock Acts As State Machine plugin. These overrides will provide an extra instance method we need in our models to enumerate all state transitions reachable from the current state of the model. You can access the extensions, as well as read about this additional instance method and other benefits, at `http://justbarebones.blogspot.com/2007/11/actsasstatemachine-enhancements.html`. Download the file `acts_as_state_machine_overrides.rb` from that site (or from our own source code repository at `http://www.railsplugins.com`) and place it in the `lib/` directory at this time.

Creating a Conference Talk Model

Part of our task in creating the `ConferenceTalk` model is to represent each of the talk proposal life cycle stages that we discussed earlier and depicted in Figure 6-2.

The basic workflow goes something like this: once a user proposes a talk, it will be automatically set to the `proposed` (initial) state. After conference organizers have had an opportunity to review submissions, they will want to update each talk proposal to either the `accepted` or `rejected` state. Finally, once they've performed that filtering and are a little further along in the process, they will schedule each talk for a particular date/time and room in the conference center. At that point, the state of the model will be updated yet again to note that the talk has been `scheduled`.

Clearly, we'll need some way in our model to store the current state of the proposal. Acts As State Machine expects a special model attribute named `state` to exist for this purpose. In addition to the `state` attribute, our model will need attributes to describe the speaker, the name and abstract of the speaker's proposed talk, and any additional notes about the talk. It will also need a few other attributes to be managed by the conference staff, such as the room and time of the talk once it is scheduled.

Before we can develop the `ConferenceTalk` model itself, we first need to create the underlying database table that makes these attributes available to the model. A Rails migration to do this is shown in Listing 6-1.

Listing 6-1. *Migration for conference_talks (db/migrate/001_create_conference_talks.rb)*

```ruby
class CreateConferenceTalks < ActiveRecord::Migration
  def self.up
    create_table :conference_talks do |t|
      t.string   :speaker_name
      t.string   :speaker_email
      t.text     :speaker_bio
      t.string   :name
      t.text     :abstract
      t.text     :notes
      t.string   :room
      t.datetime :scheduled_at
      t.string   :state
      t.timestamps
    end
  end

  def self.down
    drop_table :conference_talks
  end
end
```

■**Note** By default, Acts As State Machine looks for a column named "state," which it will use to record the current state of the model. However, as this is a common attribute name, you may wish to use something else. Fortunately, this is easily accomplished by passing the `:column` option to the `acts_as_state_machine` method in our model definition.

Save the migration as db/migrate/001_create_conference_talks.rb and then run it using the rake db:migrate task shown here. It should create the required table for us.

```
rake db:migrate
```

```
== 1 CreateConferenceTalks: migrating ============================
-- create_table(:conference_talks)
   -> 0.0069s
== 1 CreateConferenceTalks: migrated (0.0073s) =======================
```

We can now create the model. Save the code shown in Listing 6-2 as app/models/conference_talk.rb. We'll dissect and analyze it in the following paragraphs.

Listing 6-2. *ConferenceTalk Model (app/models/conference_talk.rb)*

```ruby
require 'acts_as_state_machine_overrides'

class ConferenceTalk < ActiveRecord::Base
  validates_presence_of :speaker_name, :speaker_email, :speaker_bio,
                        :name, :abstract

  attr_protected :state # protect from mass assignment
  acts_as_state_machine :initial => :proposed

  state :proposed, :after => Proc.new { |p| ConferenceMailer.deliver_proposed(p) }
  state :accepted, :after => Proc.new { |p| ConferenceMailer.deliver_accepted(p) }
  state :scheduled, :after => Proc.new { |p| ConferenceMailer.deliver_scheduled(p) }
  state :rejected, :after => Proc.new { |p| ConferenceMailer.deliver_rejected(p) }

  event :accept_talk do
    transitions :from => :proposed, :to => :accepted
  end

  event :schedule_talk do
    transitions :from => :accepted, :to => :scheduled, :guard => :scheduled?
  end

  event :reject_talk do
    transitions :from => :proposed, :to => :rejected
    transitions :from => :accepted, :to => :rejected
    transitions :from => :scheduled, :to => :rejected
  end

  def scheduled?
    self.errors.add(:scheduled_at, "must be assigned") if self.scheduled_at.blank?
    self.errors.add(:room, "must be assigned") if self.room.blank?
    !self.scheduled_at.blank? && !self.room.blank?
  end
end
```

First, we set up a simple validation on the model, ensuring that any speaker who wishes to propose a talk includes information in at least the mandatory fields. For real-world usage, we'd probably want to make validation a bit more robust and might also create a separate speaker model. We also declare the state attribute as protected using attr_protected. By doing this, we ensure that the current state cannot be set directly through mass assignment, which we'll be using in our controller to set multiple attributes from form values en masse. (We wouldn't want speakers to be able to supply extra data to set the state of their proposal to accepted or scheduled, for instance!)

The call to `acts_as_state_machine` in our model declares it to be a state machine, which means that it gets access to all the special facilities provided by the plugin we installed. We pass one parameter to this method in order to set the initial state to `proposed`; this will be the first state that any newly saved conference talk proposal will be assigned. Note that we've also added a `require` statement to the top of the file in order to pull in the plugin overrides provided by Chetan Patil's extensions, mentioned earlier.

■**Caution** When the `new` method is called to initialize a new instance of a state machine object, the state is initially `nil`. Only when the object is saved to the database is the initial state actually assigned!

Now that we've done this, we can explicitly define the states and actions (events) that trigger state transitions. The use of a limited DSL here makes it very easy for us to describe our model's logic in a natural way, which translates into rules and methods our application will use to conduct itself.

```
state :proposed, :after => Proc.new { |p| ConferenceMailer.deliver_proposed(p) }
state :accepted, :after => Proc.new { |p| ConferenceMailer.deliver_accepted(p) }
state :scheduled, :after => Proc.new { |p| ConferenceMailer.deliver_scheduled(p) }
state :rejected, :after => Proc.new { |p| ConferenceMailer.deliver_rejected(p) }
```

The four states that we outlined in our diagram are declared here, and we specify an `:after` option for each, meaning that the specified `Proc` will be run immediately after the state is entered. In each case, we make a call to the `ConferenceMailer` class, telling it to deliver one of several messages to the user. These messages are e-mail alerts that inform the conference speaker of the state change. We haven't created the `ConferenceMailer` class yet, but we will shortly.

■**Note** Acts As State Machine also allows you to define `:enter` and `:exit` options on states. The difference between `:enter` and `:after` is that `:enter` actions are called before the state transition occurs, on entry, and `:after` actions are called after the state has already been set. In our case, we use `:after` because we want to report on the current state, which has just changed!

Next, we define a series of events that trigger state transitions from one state to another. Each event declaration takes the name of an action and a block. The block contains one or more transitions, each of which has a `:from` (origin) state and a `:to` (destination) state.

```
event :accept_talk do
  transitions :from => :proposed, :to => :accepted
end
```

```
event :schedule_talk do
  transitions :from => :accepted, :to => :scheduled, :guard => :scheduled?
end

event :reject_talk do
  transitions :from => :proposed, :to => :rejected
  transitions :from => :accepted, :to => :rejected
  transitions :from => :scheduled, :to => :rejected
end
```

These events become available on an object as methods, which we can use to trigger the specified transition if the precondition is met. For instance, when a conference talk is in the proposed state and the reject_talk! method is called, the state transition is run and, based on the rules we've defined, the state is updated to the rejected state. Make sure to note the exclamation point in the dynamically created method name used here; this is a Ruby idiom to indicate that the method modifies its receiver (our model), in this case by changing its state.

The accept_talk! and schedule_talk! methods work in the same manner as reject_talk!. However, note the presence of the :guard option for the schedule_talk event. This option specifies a method that is run to ensure that additional prerequisites are met before the state transition can occur. In this case, it specifies that the scheduled? method should be called to determine whether or not the state is allowed to transition from the accepted state to the scheduled state. In this case a symbol is used to indicate the method name to call, but a Proc can also be used.

```
def scheduled?
  self.errors.add(:scheduled_at, "must be assigned") if self.scheduled_at.nil?
  self.errors.add(:room, "must be assigned") if self.room.nil?
  !self.scheduled_at.nil? && !self.room.nil?
end
```

The scheduled? method simply checks to make sure that a date and time has been scheduled for the talk, and that the talk has been assigned a room in the convention center. If these criteria have not been satisfied, the method will return false, and the guard condition will therefore prevent the state transition from occurring. The scheduled? method also adds messages to the errors object, which will make it convenient for us to display to the conference organizer in a web form later.

Managing Conference E-Mail Updates with ActionMailer

As you may recall, we defined our states in such a way that each status update would notify a user via e-mail when the state was successfully entered. This was accomplished by calling a class method of the ConferenceMailer class, such as deliver_accepted, to tell it to deliver a given e-mail message. The message will presumably be sent to the speaker's e-mail address and will reflect the updated status of his or her proposal.

In order to make this happen, we need to create the ConferenceMailer class, as shown in Listing 6-3, and save it as app/models/conference_mailer.rb.

Listing 6-3. *ActionMailer Class to Handle E-Mail Alerts (app/models/conference_mailer.rb)*

```
class ConferenceMailer < ActionMailer::Base
  def proposed(conference_talk)
    status_update(conference_talk, 'Thanks for your submission')
  end

  def rejected(conference_talk)
    status_update(conference_talk)
  end

  def accepted(conference_talk)
    status_update(conference_talk, 'Your proposal has been accepted!')
  end

  def scheduled(conference_talk)
    status_update(conference_talk, 'Your talk has been scheduled!')
  end

  private

    def status_update(conference_talk, subject = 'Proposal status updated')
      recipients conference_talk.speaker_email
      from       'noreply@mcetc-conference.com'
      sent_on    Time.now
      subject    "[MCETC] #{subject}"
      body       render_message('status', :conference_talk => conference_talk)
    end
end
```

The mailer class inherits from ActionMailer::Base and has one method for each type
of message that needs to be delivered. By following ActionMailer's conventions, when an
instance method named accepted is defined in a class that inherits from ActionMailer::Base,
we automatically gain access to a class method called deliver_accepted, which can be used
to deliver the appropriate e-mail message. The same is true for proposed, rejected, and
scheduled.

Each of the e-mail action methods calls the private status_update method, where most
of the real work happens. It sets the recipient address of the e-mail to the speaker's e-mail
address and specifies the sender address, recipient, subject, and delivery timestamp. The last
thing it does is set up the body of the e-mail message, which uses a template much like controller actions render view templates.

Under normal situations, we'd probably want to have a completely separate template
for each of these actions, which is actually the default behavior of ActionMailer; the template for the accepted e-mail would be in accepted.erb, the template for the rejected
e-mail would be in rejected.erb, and so on. But in this case, for brevity, we've collapsed

all the messages into a single template, status.erb, and instructed status_update to render that for each of the e-mails that needs to be sent.

The template, shown in Listing 6-4, also makes use of the conference_talk value passed in from our model (values passed in from render_message are available as instance variables within the template). Save the template as app/views/conference_mailer/status.erb.

Listing 6-4. *Generic Status Update E-Mail Template (app/views/conference_mailer/status.erb)*

```
Dear <%= @conference_talk.speaker_name %>,

This message refers to your proposed talk for MCETC, "<%= @conference_talk.name %>".
Your talk status is: <%= @conference_talk.state.upcase %>.

<% if @conference_talk.state == "scheduled" -%>
  Room: <%= @conference_talk.room %>
  Time: <%= @conference_talk.scheduled_at %>
<% end -%>

Let us know if you have any questions or concerns.

Thanks,

MCETC Organizers.
```

For more information on ActionMailer, please see the official API documentation at http://api.rubyonrails.org/classes/ActionMailer/Base.html.

Testing the Conference Proposal System

To test our models and the mailer functionality, we'll once again turn to our dear friend the Rails console. We'll also want to periodically refer to the development log to make sure that our application is sending e-mails when appropriate (at each successful state transition). Note that while in the development environment, by default, outgoing e-mails will be displayed in logs/development.log. Therefore, it's useful to tail that log, even if we are not actually configured to send outgoing e-mails.

■**Note** In the development environment, Rails will default to sending e-mail via SMTP. If it fails to contact a mail server running on localhost port 25, the mail will be written to the log anyway, so this usually works fine for development. For the production environment, you'll want to edit your mailer settings. More information on this is available at http://wiki.rubyonrails.org/rails/pages/ HowToSendEmailsWithActionMailer.

Start a console session using `script/console` in the Rails application root directory and enter the following commands:

```
>> ct = ConferenceTalk.create(:name => "Rails Plugin Development",
      :abstract => "How to build plugins for Ruby on Rails",
      :speaker_name => "Mr. Foo Bar",
      :speaker_email => "info@acceleratedrails.com",
      :speaker_bio => "An experienced Ruby developer...")
>> ct.state
=> "proposed"
>> ct.accept_talk!
>> ct.state
=> "accepted"
>> ct.schedule_talk!
>> ct.state
=> "accepted"
>> ct.errors.full_messages
=> ["Room must be assigned", "Scheduled at must be assigned"]
>> ct.room = "112A"
=> "112A"
>> ct.scheduled_at = Time.parse("November 27, 2008 11:00")
=> Fri Jun 27 11:00:00 -0400 2008
>> ct.save
=> true
>> ct.schedule_talk!
>> ct.state
=> "scheduled"
```

As you can see, we have successfully created a conference talk proposal and moved it through the various life cycle states on its way to being accepted and scheduled. Note that the rules we defined for our transitions prevented us from entering the `scheduled` state without first setting the date/time and room for the talk. If you've been keeping an eye on your log file, you will also see that e-mails have been generated for each state change that occurred. Listing 6-5 shows an excerpt from a log trace noting that an e-mail has been sent after the "schedule talk" state change.

Listing 6-5. *E-Mail Delivery Notification Log Excerpt*

```
Sent mail:
Date: Tue, 29 Apr 2008 19:19:58 -0400
From: noreply@mcetc-conference.com
To: info@acceleratedrails.com
Subject: [MCETC] Your talk has been scheduled!
Mime-Version: 1.0
Content-Type: text/plain; charset=utf-8
```

Dear Mr Foo Bar,

This message refers to your proposed talk for MCETC, "Rails Plugin Development".
Your talk status is: SCHEDULED.

  Room: 112A
  Time: Thu Nov 27 11:00:00 -0500 2008

Let us know if you have any questions or concerns.

Thanks,

MCETC Organizers.

Building a Web Interface

Now that we've verified our state machine model and the mailer code, let's build a web front end to allow speakers to submit proposals for the conference. The front end should be simple and will consist of a single controller that MCETC organizers will also be able to use to update the state of a proposal. Of course, we don't want users to be able to update the state of their own proposal or assign themselves a room, so we're going to need some very basic access controls. For simplicity's sake, we've decided that, for now, users will not be able to revisit the web interface to check on the status of their proposal, since they're already receiving e-mail updates. They also won't be able to edit copy, as it's currently under consideration.

First, let's add a route for the proposals resource that we will be creating. Edit your config/routes.rb file to look like the code in Listing 6-6.

Listing 6-6. *Routes for the Proposals Resource (config/routes.rb)*

```
ActionController::Routing::Routes.draw do |map|
  map.resources :proposals
end
```

Next, we'll define the ProposalsController. Save the code in Listing 6-7 as app/controllers/proposals_controller.rb.

Listing 6-7. *Controller for Handling Proposals (app/controllers/proposals_controller.rb)*

```
class ProposalsController < ApplicationController
  before_filter :set_conference_talk, :only => [:show, :edit, :update]
  before_filter :authenticate, :only => [:index, :edit, :update]

  def new
    @conference_talk = ConferenceTalk.new
  end
```

```
def create
  @conference_talk = ConferenceTalk.new(params[:conference_talk])
  if @conference_talk.save
    redirect_to(:action => 'show', :id => @conference_talk.id)
  else
    render(:action => 'new')
  end
end

def index
  @conference_talks = ConferenceTalk.find(:all,
      :conditions => "state != 'rejected'", :order => "scheduled_at ASC")
end

def show; end

def edit; end

def update
  @conference_talk.update_attributes(params[:conference_talk])
  case(params[:state])
    when 'reject_talk':   @conference_talk.reject_talk!
    when 'accept_talk':   @conference_talk.accept_talk!
    when 'schedule_talk': @conference_talk.schedule_talk!
  end
  render(:action => 'edit')
end

private

  def set_conference_talk
    @conference_talk = ConferenceTalk.find(params[:id])
  end

  def authenticate
    authenticate_or_request_with_http_basic do |username, password|
      username == "admin" && password == "secret"
    end
  end
end
```

The new and create actions shown here are essentially boilerplate code; the template for the new proposal template, shown in Listing 6-8, renders a form that is submitted to the create action. Save this listing as app/views/proposals/new.html.erb.

Listing 6-8. *New Proposal Form (app/views/proposals/new.html.erb)*

```
<h1>New Proposal</h1>
<%= error_messages_for(:conference_talk) %>
<% form_for(:conference_talk, :url => proposals_path) do |form| -%>
  <p>Speaker Name:<br/> <%= form.text_field(:speaker_name) %></p>
  <p>Speaker Email:<br/> <%= form.text_field(:speaker_email) %></p>
  <p>Talk Name:<br/> <%= form.text_field(:name) %></p>
  <p>Talk Abstract:<br/> <%= form.text_area(:abstract, :rows => 8) %></p>
  <p>Speaker Bio:<br/> <%= form.text_area(:speaker_bio, :rows => 5) %></p>
  <p>Notes:<br/> <%= form.text_area(:notes, :rows => 3) %></p>
  <%= submit_tag('Submit') %>
<% end -%>
```

The create action uses the parameter values passed into it to instantiate a new
ConferenceTalk model, saves it, and then renders the minimalist show action template, as
shown in Listing 6-9. Save the show template as app/views/proposals/show.html.erb.

Listing 6-9. *Proposal Status (Show) Template (app/views/proposals/show.html.erb)*

```
<h1>Proposal: <%= @conference_talk.name %></h1>
<p>Speaker Name: <%= @conference_talk.speaker_name %></p>
<p>Status: <%= @conference_talk.state.upcase %></p>
```

■**Note** The set_conference_talk method runs as a before_filter prior to the show action being
called, which sets the @conference_talk instance variable to the appropriate model so it can be displayed
in the template. This same filter is also used prior to calling the edit and update actions, in order to keep
our code DRY (Don't Repeat Yourself).

At this point, we can start the application by running script/server within our Rails
application directory and visit http://localhost:3000/proposals/new in a web browser. You
should see a form for creating a new MCETC talk proposal that looks something like the form
in Figure 6-3. Try it out; go ahead and create a new proposal. After the form is submitted, you
should be redirected to the simplistic status page we've created.

We've verified that new and create are working, so we'll move on to developing the management tools our fellow conference organizers will need to review, edit, and schedule
proposals. These tasks will be performed by the edit action.

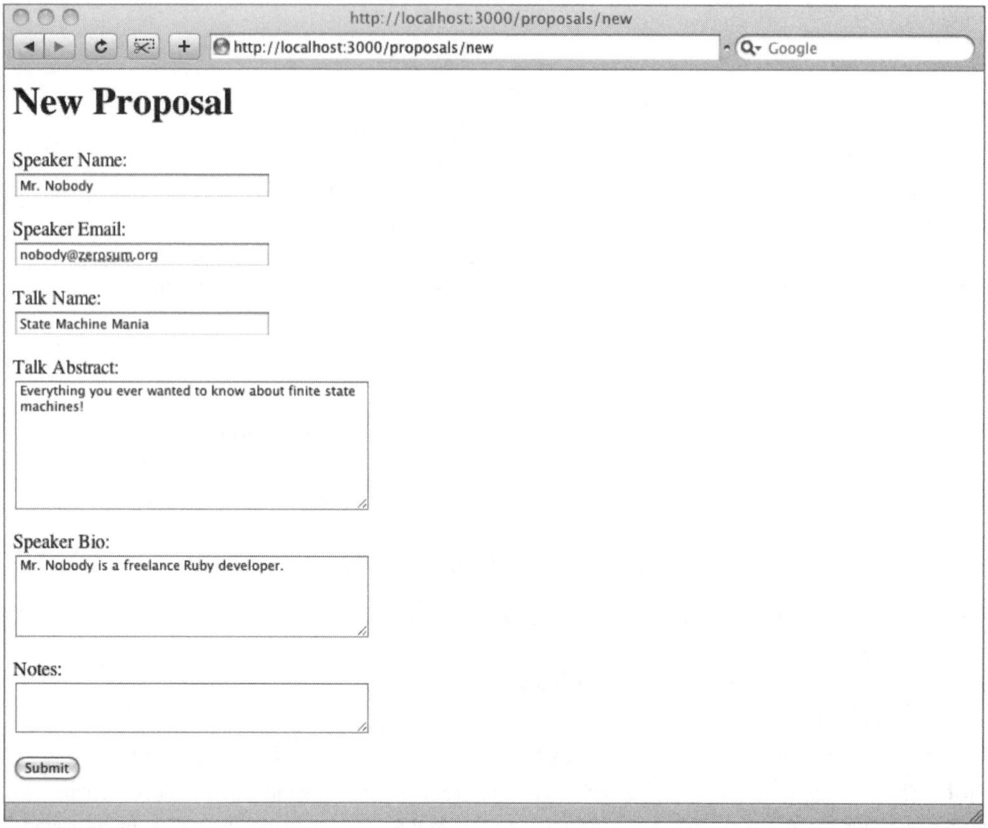

Figure 6-3. *New conference talk proposal form (http://localhost:3000/proposals/new)*

Facilitating State Transitions

Since we want to restrict the list of users authorized to update and change the state of submitted talk proposals, we've implemented a simple `before_filter` in our controller to protect the `edit`, `update`, and `index` actions. This filter references the `authenticate` method, which forces a user to authenticate with basic HTTP authentication in order to access the named actions. This is a simple way to implement basic access controls if all that's needed is a single username/password, as in this case. Organizers will be given a common set of credentials (user: `admin`, pass: `secret`) and can then update the status of proposals as needed. Any other access will be prohibited.

The view template for the proposal editing form is shown in Listing 6-10. Save it as `app/views/proposals/edit.html.erb`.

Listing 6-10. *Proposal Edit Template (app/views/proposals/edit.html.erb)*

```
<h1>Proposal: <%= @conference_talk.name %></h1>
<%= error_messages_for(:conference_talk) %>
<% form_for(:conference_talk, :url => proposal_path(@conference_talk),
        :html => {:method => :put}) do |form| -%>
```

```erb
<p>Speaker Name:<br/> <%= form.text_field(:speaker_name) %></p>
<p>Speaker Email:<br/> <%= form.text_field(:speaker_email) %></p>
<p>Talk Name:<br/> <%= form.text_field(:name) %></p>
<p>Talk Abstract:<br/> <%= form.text_area(:abstract, :rows => 8) %></p>
<p>Speaker Bio:<br/> <%= form.text_area(:speaker_bio, :rows => 5) %></p>
<p>Notes:<br/> <%= form.text_area(:notes, :rows => 3) %></p>
<p>Status: <%= @conference_talk.state.upcase %></p>
<hr/>
<h2>Scheduling</h2>
<p>Room: <br/><%= form.text_field(:room) %></p>
<p>Scheduled At:<br/> <%= form.datetime_select(:scheduled_at) %></p>
<p>Change Status: <%= select_tag(:state, options_for_select(
    @conference_talk.next_events_for_current_state.map { |event|
      [event.to_s.humanize, event]
    }.insert(0, ['No change', 0]), 'No change')) %></p>
  <%= submit_tag('Update') %>
<% end -%>
<%= link_to('Return to Index', proposals_path) %>
```

In addition to the input fields found in the first form, we've added two fields specific to scheduling. A text field has been added for the room attribute, and a datetime_select widget has been added for selection of the date and time. The most notable addition, however, is the select_tag for changing the status of the proposal. The options_for_select helper method is used to populate the status selection widget, and it takes two parameters: an array of [name, value] pairs for the options and a default value.

To construct the array we need, we call the next_events_for_current_state method on the @conference_talk instance variable. This is a special method on state machine models that will return an array of all the state change events that are reachable from the current state, as defined in our model. This method is not included in the base Acts As State Machine plugin, but it is provided by the set of extensions (overrides) published by Chetan Patil. As you may recall, we installed those overrides when we were setting up our project and modified our model to require them. By doing this, we have reopened and extended the ScottBarron::Acts::StateMachine module at runtime, adding a new instance method and a number of other features to it, which can then be used by our Active Record model.

■**Tip** If a plugin doesn't do exactly what you need, don't be afraid to modify or extend it. Plugins are not immutable, after all; they're just code, and we can extend or modify them just as they extend and modify the base Rails framework. We often strive to make changes to plugins outside of the plugins' own code base, as in this case where we're loading another file to patch Acts As State Machine. In other cases, when more drastic changes are required, we may choose to fork the plugin and maintain our own changes to it. The Piston utility, discussed in Chapter 1, can be useful when doing this.

In any case, since we have now retrieved all of the reachable events, we can take the resultant array in our template and use it with the map method to convert it to the [*name, value*] format needed by options_for_select, where *name* is a string formatted for readability (each event name is first converted to a string and then "humanized" using built-in inflection rules) and *value* is the raw event name. We also need to insert a default option in the list with the value "No change." This indicates to the user that no status update should occur when the form is submitted.

When the update action is invoked in ProposalsController, it will call update_attributes on the instance variable to update the model attributes en masse and then use a case statement to determine what to do with the state change parameter. The when clauses in the case statement correspond to every possible event, but the events reachable from the current state of the model are, of course, limited to the set returned by next_events_from_current_state (the form will expose only the event options that are currently applicable). Note also that there is no specific case for the "No change" option and no default case to be handled, so if the user does not change the state selection widget, no state change event will be triggered.

```
case(params[:state])
  when 'reject_talk':   @conference_talk.reject_talk!
  when 'accept_talk':   @conference_talk.accept_talk!
  when 'schedule_talk': @conference_talk.schedule_talk!
end
```

Listing Conference Proposals

At this point, we have all the facilities we need to handle creating and managing the various stages of the conference talk proposal process for MCETC. However, for the sake of completeness, we should also give our fellow organizers some way to navigate through the submitted proposals. This should be handled by the index action and its template, as shown in Listing 6-11. Save the template as app/views/proposals/index.html.erb.

Listing 6-11. *Proposals Index Template (app/views/proposals/index.html.erb)*

```
<h1>Conference Proposals</h1>
<ul>
  <% @conference_talks.each do |proposal| -%>
  <li><%= link_to("[#{proposal.state.upcase}] #{proposal.name}",
    edit_proposal_path(proposal)) %></li>
  <% end -%>
</ul>
```

This view allows conference organizers to see the list of talks that have been scheduled and those that have yet to be reviewed. As specified in the index controller action's find conditions (shown earlier in Listing 6-7), talks that have been rejected are not displayed, and elements are ordered according to their scheduled time/date (assuming they have one). Each proposed talk is a link to the edit page for that talk, and both the status and name of the talk are displayed in the link text for convenience.

With these final changes in place, we can now point a web browser at the URL http://localhost:3000/proposals to review any pending conference proposals in our system. A conference organizer can use this interface to review, update, and schedule the talk proposals. You will be prompted for a username (admin) and password (secret) in order to access these facilities.

Click one of the proposals to edit its status and change it to "accepted." Update it again to mark it as "scheduled." The application should look something like what you see in Figure 6-4. Note that the available status change options change each time, depending on the current state of the proposal, based on the rules we defined in our model. Note also that scheduled proposals require a date/time as well as a room assignment.

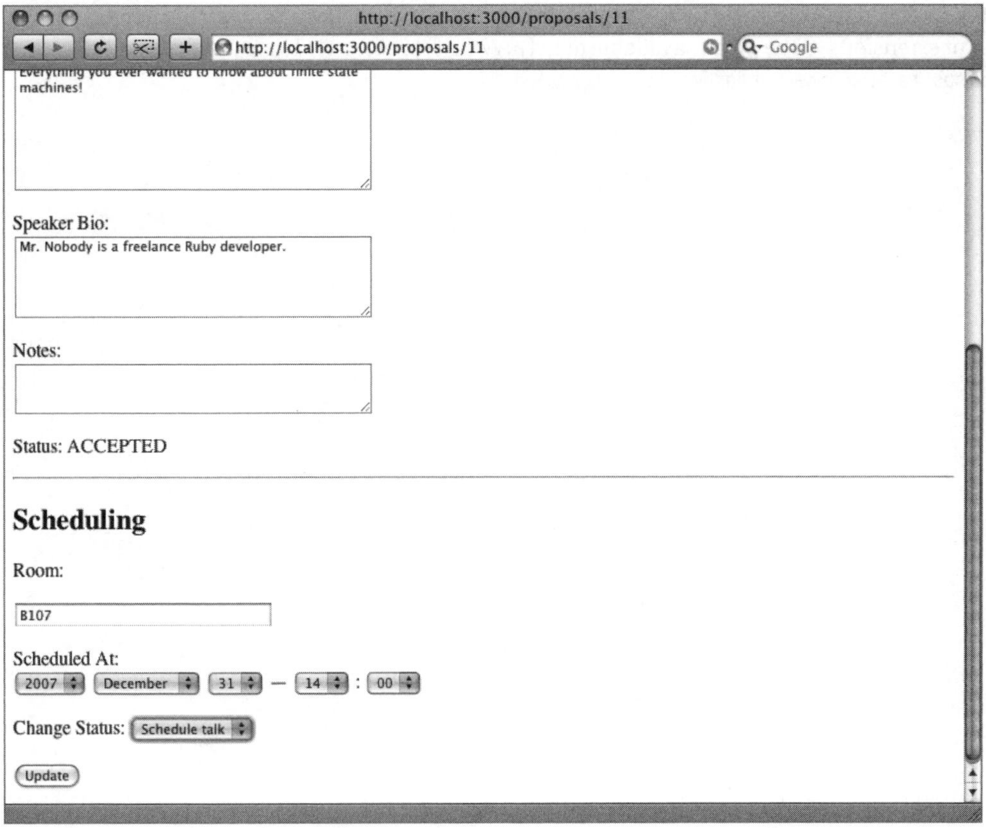

Figure 6-4. *Editing a conference proposal (http://localhost:3000/proposals/1/edit)*

Summary

Many tasks can be effectively (and efficiently!) modeled as FSMs. If it's possible to identify multiple distinct states that your model will pass through in its lifetime, there's a good chance that modeling it as a state machine makes sense. Although some combination of model attributes and Active Record callbacks and observers can also be useful in managing state, they can quickly lead to clutter in your models. Scott Barron's Acts As State Machine plugin is an attractive alternative that allows various states and state-specific events (state transitions) to be defined in a clean manner, as a logical extension to Active Record's already powerful domain-specific language.

In this chapter, we've examined the benefits of this approach, showed how to use Acts As State Machine, and demonstrated how it can be integrated with e-mail notifications and a web-based user interface for simple conference proposal management. As an exercise, think about how you might have implemented this without the plugin; it really does allow for a much cleaner, more maintainable approach!

You can find more information about Acts As State Machine by viewing the plugins README file and its RDocs and examining a number of other simple examples at `http://elitists.textdriven.com/aasm-examples.rb.txt`. Also, don't forget to investigate the set of extensions to the plugin available at `http://justbarebones.blogspot.com/2007/11/actsasstatemachine-enhancements.html`.

■ ■ ■

## CHAPTER 7

Validating Data with Various Plugins

Handling data in some form or another is one of the most important parts of any computer program. Rails—specifically, Active Record—provides an easy way to connect your application to a database as well as to model the data in that database.

The data you store in your database must be valid, or at least reasonably valid, in order to accomplish most tasks you want to perform with that data. The database system your application connects to likely provides simple data validation. For example, you can't store the string "zanzibar" in a MySQL DATETIME column. However, the error messages produced by the database aren't very user-friendly, and it's better to give the user specific feedback as to exactly what's wrong. For that matter, we can often provide more specific validation of our data, such as ensuring that a given string is a telephone number. By providing domain-specific, user-friendly validations, we can make our applications easier to use while at the same time increasing the accuracy of the data we collect.

Some domain-specific validations can be done easily with validations built into Rails. You can use validates_presence_of, for example, to ensure that a given field has been entered before your model is saved. If the field is not present, a human-readable error is created, which you can use in your form. You can find out more about this and the other built-in validations at http://api.rubyonrails.org/classes/ActiveRecord/Validations/ClassMethods.html.

For more complicated validations, a number of plugins are available. In this chapter, we'll focus on the Rails plugins for validating e-mail addresses, web addresses, and phone numbers.

Our Task: Validate a Complex Form Using Rails Plugins

Suppose we want a database that lists the open source projects we are considering adopting in either our professional or our personal projects. We want to store all of the relevant information: what the project is called, who maintains it, and so forth, as well as whether paid technical support is available for that project.

Since we may potentially store a large number of records in this database, and since it's easy to mistype information, we can use various Rails plugins to validate different parts of the record:

- The Validates Email Veracity Of plugin by Carsten Nielsen validates that e-mail addresses are correctly formatted.

- The Validates Url plugin by Timothy Morgan validates URLs.

- The Validates As Phone plugin by Jerrod Blavos validates phone numbers.

A number of other validation plugins are available. For example, Validates Unlike (`http://www.lacaraoscura.com/2006/07/11/validates-unlike-plugin/`) by Edgar González ensures that the field does not match a given regular express, and Validates Child Of (`http://validateschild.rubyforge.org/svn/`) by Carl Mercier ensures that a given record is a child of another record. You can find these and other plugins at the Rails Lodge, which has a comprehensive list of plugins at `http://railslodge.com/plugins`.

Creating the Software Projects Model

First, let's create a new Rails project as follows:

```
rails data_validator
```

Next, let's install the three plugins:

```
ruby script/plugin install ➥
http://svn.savvica.com/public/plugins/validates_email_veracity_of
  ruby script/plugin install http://validates-url.googlecode.com/svn/trunk/
mv vendor/plugins/svn vendor/plugins/validates_as_phone
ruby script/plugin install http://validates-as-phone.googlecode.com/svn/trunk/
```

Next, let's create a migration, as shown in Listing 7-1.

Listing 7-1. *Software Projects Table Migration (db/migrate/001_create_software_projects.rb)*

```
class CreateSoftwareProjects < ActiveRecord::Migration
  def self.up
    create_table :software_projects do |t|
      t.string :name
      t.string :maintainer_name
      t.string :maintainer_email
      t.string :project_url
      t.boolean :commercial_support_available
      t.string :commercial_sales_number
      t.timestamps
    end
  end
end
```

```
  def self.down
    drop_table :software_projects
  end
end
```

Run the migration as follows:

```
rake db:migrate
```

Listing 7-2 shows our single model.

Listing 7-2. *Software Projects Model (app/models/software_project.rb)*

```
class SoftwareProject < ActiveRecord::Base
  validates_http_url :project_url
  validates_presence_of :project_url

  validates_email_veracity_of :maintainer_email
  validates_presence_of :maintainer_email

  validates_as_phone      :commercial_sales_number,
                          :allow_blank=>true
  validates_presence_of :commercial_sales_number,
                          :if=>Proc.new { |p| p.commercial_support_available }

end
```

Note that the last validation is more complicated. The :if parameter specifies you need to enter a phone number only if commercial support is available.

Testing the Plugins

Let's try out our three validation plugins using the Rails console. We'll begin with the Validates Url plugin.

```
ruby script/console
>> new_object = SoftwareProject.new
>> new_object.project_url = 'not_a_valid_url'
>> new_object.errors.on(:project_url)
=> "must be the URL for a website"
>> new_object.project_url='apress.com'
>> new_object.errors.on(:project_url)
=> "must be the URL for a website"
>> new_object.project_url='http://apress.com'
  >> new_object.valid?>> new_object.errors.on(:project_url)
=> nil
```

As you can see from the output, Validates Url correctly rejects the first string `'not_a_valid_url'`, as being an invalid URL. It also correctly rejects the second string, `'apress.com'`, because it does not have a protocol. The last string, `'http://apress.com'`, passes validation. You may have noticed a slight delay on the last call to `new_object.valid?`. This is because Validates Url actually connects to the server via HTTP and verifies that the target URL exists.

■**Caution** The URL validation technique shown here allows visitors to generate arbitrary HTTP requests by inserting records. Conceivably, this facility could be used as part of a denial of service (DoS) attack or present other security problems. We do not recommend using this, or similar plugins, in a public site, but you'll likely be fine using this in an intranet site. (If your company employees are using your site to launch DoS attacks, you have larger problems.) If you need to run something similar to Validates Url on a public site, you can try a URI parse-based approach, such as is found at `http://snippets.dzone.com/posts/show/4532`.

Next, let's test the validation for the maintainer e-mail field:

```
>> new_object.maintainer_email = 'test@not_a_real_domain'
>> new_object.valid?
>> new_object.errors.on(:maintainer_email)
=> "is invalid."
>> new_object.maintainer_email = 'test@berubeconsulting.com'
>> new_object.valid?
>> new_object.errors.on(:maintainer_email)
=> nil
```

The first e-mail is shown to be invalid. The Validates Email Veracity Of plugin uses a somewhat fuzzy algorithm for validating e-mail addresses, which marks `test@not_a_real_domain` as invalid. Technically, `test@not_a_real_domain` is an RFC 2822-compliant address, even though in the real world, almost no top-level domains handle requests directly. Usually, when someone types a domain without a dot in it, it's wrong.

The Validates Email Veracity Of plugin has a handy optional parameter: if you add the `:domain_check=>true`, it will perform a Domain Name System (DNS) record check to ensure that the domain is valid and has an MX (mail exchange) record.

■**Note** You can get an RFC-compliant validation plugin at `http://api.pluginaweek.org/validates_as_email_address/`. However, it lacks the MX checking that the Validates Email Veracity Of plugin can do with an optional parameter.

Finally, let's take a look at our next plugin, Validates As Phone:

```
>> new_object.commercial_support_available=true
>> new_object.commercial_sales_number = 'not a number'
>> new_object.valid?
>> new_object.errors.on(:commercial_sales_number)
=> "is invalid: not a number"
>> new_object.commercial_sales_number = '(555) 555-1212 ext 555'
>> new_object.valid?
>> new_object.errors.on(:commercial_sales_number)
=> "is invalid: (555) 555-1212 ext 555"
>> new_object.commercial_sales_number = '555-555-1212'
>> new_object.valid?
>> new_object.errors.on(:commercial_sales_number)
=> nil
>> new_object.commercial_sales_number = '(555) 555-1212'
>> new_object.valid?
>> new_object.errors.on(:commercial_sales_number)
=> nil
>> new_object.commercial_sales_number = '5555551212'
>> new_object.valid?
>> new_object.errors.on(:commercial_sales_number)
=> nil
>> new_object.commercial_sales_number = '5551212'
>> new_object.valid?
>> new_object.errors.on(:commercial_sales_number)
=> nil
```

As you can see, Validates As Phone supports most common formats for entering phone numbers, both with and without area codes. Note, however, that it does not allow users to enter extensions.

Implementing the Validation Plugins

Now that we've tested the validation plugins, let's create our controller, as shown in Listing 7-3.

Listing 7-3. *Software Projects Controller (app/controllers/software_projects_controller.rb)*

```
class SoftwareProjectController < ApplicationController
  def index
    @software_project = SoftwareProject.new
    if request.post?
      software_project = SoftwareProject.new(params[:software_project])
      if software_project.save
        flash[:notice] = 'Saved!'
```

```
      else
        @software_project = software_project
      end
    end

    @software_projects = SoftwareProject.find(:all)
  end
end
```

Listing 7-4 shows our single view.

Listing 7-4. *Index View for Software Project Controller (views/software_project/index.html.erb)*

```erb
<style>
  form table th { text-align:right; }
</style>
<h1>Create New Software Project</h1>

<%flash.each do |key, msg|%>
  <div class="<%=key%>">
    <%=msg%>
  </div>
<%end%>

<%=error_messages_for 'software_project'%>
<%form_for('software_project') do |f| %>
    <table>      <p>Name:</th>
        <td><%=f.text_field :name%></th></tr>

    <p>Maintainer's Email:</th>
        <td><%=f.text_field :maintainer_email%></p>

    <p>URL:</th>
        <td><%=f.text_field :project_url%></p>

    <p>Commerical Support</th>
        <td><%=f.check_box :commercial_support_available %> Available?</p>

    <p>Commerical Sales Number</th>
        <td><%=f.text_field :commercial_sales_number %></p>

    <p><%=f.submit 'Create'%></p>
<%end%>
```

```
<%
  ignore_columns  = ['id', 'created_at', 'updated_at']
  display_columns = SoftwareProject.columns.map(&:name) -
                    ignore_columns
%>

<%if @software_projects.length>0%>
  <h1>Software Projects List</h1>
  <table>
    <p><%display_columns.each do |c|%>
        <th><%=c.humanize%></th>
      <%end%>
    </tr>

  <%@software_projects.each do |s_p| %>
    <tr>
      <%display_columns.each do |c|%>
        <td><%=s_p.send(c)%></td>
      <%end%>
    </tr>
  <%end%>
  </table>
<%end%>
```

This view includes both a form to insert data and a list of all data that has already been added. In a full application, you would almost certainly have a way to edit and delete old data.

Let's run the project:

```
ruby script/server
```

If you browse to localhost:3000, you should see a form with a number of fields: the name of the project, the project URL, and so forth. Try adding an fake project with an invalid e-mail address, such as test. After you click Create, you should see a message similar to that shown in Figure 7-1.

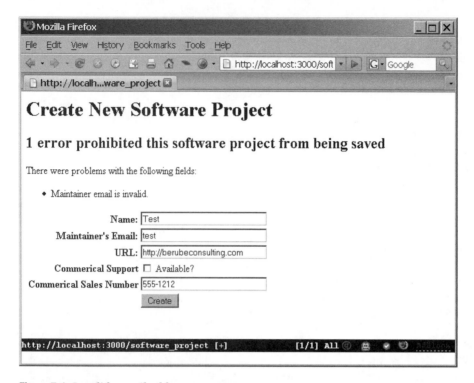

Figure 7-1. *Invalid e-mail address error*

If you correct the error and resubmit the form, you should see it in the list that appears before the form.

Summary

There's a nearly infinite array of data-validation types, and some validations will always require custom code. But you may find just what you need provided by one of the many open source validation plugins available. When they fit your needs, you can quickly and easily use them to implement complicated validations.

PART 3

■■■

Controller Enhancement

Controllers are one of the most important parts of a Rails application, and they certainly have some of the most varied tasks. They respond to user interaction; write to files; handle session data; create, update, and delete records; and sometimes even invoke external utilities.

Just as the tasks controllers perform are varied, so are the plugins we'll cover in this part. Throughout the next three chapters, we'll build sample applications with plugins that provide powerful payment processing and content management capabilities and also see how we can use advanced automated scaffolds to get up and running quickly.

CHAPTER 8

■■■

Easy Production-Ready Ajax Scaffolds with ActiveScaffold

Many web applications are divided into at least two parts. One is the public-facing side, which serves customers, vendors, and others in the public at large. The second is the private, administrative side, which serves a much wider purpose. The administrative side supports changes to the site—content changes, rate changes, inventory changes, and much more. It also serves as an error catchall. If one of the users makes an uncommon mistake, or if a bug in the software causes a misfortune to one of the users of the site, the administrative area allows you to make appropriate changes.

Generally, this second administrative layer must be created by hand, and it often involves a level of duplication. When additional fields are added, for example, you must often enter a reference to the field in two places: one for the public-facing side and one for the administrative side. However, there is an easier way. Rails includes a built-in, albeit limited, facility called *scaffolding*, which can quickly and easily create such administrative interfaces. Even better, these built-in facilities can be extended.

Although the Rails built-in scaffolding facility is limited and unsuited to production use, ActiveScaffold (written by Richard White et al.) is a much more powerful, extensible, and easy-to-use scaffolding interface that can be employed in a wide variety of production environments. For example, if you had a social networking site, you could use ActiveScaffold to perform odd tasks on the back end, like ban users or edit offensive comments. Of course, you can also use ActiveScaffold to enter data, such as inventory data on an e-commerce site or revenue data in an accounting system.

In this chapter, we'll demonstrate using ActiveScaffold to quickly create administrative interfaces.

Our Task: Create an Events Calendar with ActiveScaffold

Let's suppose we're developing a site for a community theater, including all of the events scheduled for the season. The theater group also has a number of guests, such as directors, actors, lecturers, musicians, and so forth. They would like a page listing upcoming events, which can be edited easily and automatically removes events that have already taken place. Often, local guests will book a number of events at once, so the interface should allow adding multiple events to a guest simultaneously without too much work. We could, of course, write such an interface by hand, but it's much easier and faster to use ActiveScaffold to do it.

■Tip A number of other plugins allow you to create administrative interfaces quickly. For example, Streamlined (`http://streamlinedframework.org/`) is a more comprehensive, and more complicated, framework for CRUD (Create Read Update Delete) interfaces.

First, let's create a new Rails project, as follows:

```
rails upcoming_events && cd upcoming_events
```

Next, let's install the ActiveScaffold plugin:

```
ruby script/plugin install ➥
http://activescaffold.googlecode.com/svn/tags/active_scaffold
```

Creating the Models

Let's create a migration. Listing 8-1 shows the code.

Listing 8-1. *Database Schema Migration (db/migrate/001_initial_schema.rb)*

```ruby
class InitialSchema < ActiveRecord::Migration
  def self.up
    create_table :events do |t|
      t.string :title
      t.datetime :occurs_at
      t.timestamps
    end
    create_table :guests do |t|
      t.string :name
      t.string :description
      t.string :href
      t.timestamps
    end
    create_table :events_guests, :id=>false do |t|
      t.integer :event_id
      t.integer :guest_id
    end

  end
```

```
  def self.down
    drop_table :events_guests
    drop_table :guests
    drop_table :events
  end
end
```

We have just three tables, including one join table. Let's run the migration, as follows:

```
rake db:migrate
```

Now create the two models, as shown in Listings 8-2 and 8-3.

Listing 8-2. *Event Model (app/models/event.rb)*

```
class Event < ActiveRecord::Base
  has_and_belongs_to_many :guests
  def self.upcoming_events
    self.find(:all,
              :conditions=>"events.occurs_at  > date('now')",
              :order=>'occurs_at ASC')
  end
end
```

Listing 8-3. *Guest Model (app/models/guest.rb)*

```
class Guest < ActiveRecord::Base
  has_and_belongs_to_many :events
  has_and_belongs_to_many :upcoming_events, :class_name=>'Event',
                          :conditions=>"events.occurs_at  > date('now')"
end
```

Each model has a `has_and_belongs_to_many` relationship with the other model. The first, Event, also has a custom finder, named `upcoming_events`, which returns all of the events that occur in the future. Of course, we could simply use similar code in our controller, but by adding this method, we keep our code in line with the Rails DRY (Don't Repeat Yourself) principle and easy to use. This also has a side benefit of keeping event-specific code in the model, which could be beneficial. For example, if we later added a form to the site allowing guests to request a time slot, we could tentatively add events to our database as "unconfirmed," and then modify the `upcoming_events` finder so that it returns only confirmed events.

The second model has a similar feature, but it's added as a condition of a custom association. We create an association named `upcoming_events`, and use the `:class_name` parameter to modify the class name, so that Rails knows that the model `upcoming_events` is associated with is called simply Event, not `upcoming_events`. Note that because it's a `has_and_belongs_to_many` association, it automatically has a join condition in it. Our `:conditions` parameter adds to the automatically created condition, so that our `upcoming_events` association refers to all of the upcoming events for a given guest. (This is a slight break from the DRY principle, since this relationship and the `upcoming_events` finder in the Event model both contain the knowledge of the condition events.occurs_at > date('now'), but at least it's contained to the two models, as opposed to spread out through various controllers.)

Creating the Controllers

Let's examine our first admin controller, which allows our administrative users to list, add, view, edit, and delete events. Listing 8-4 shows the code.

Listing 8-4. *Events Admin Controller (app/controllers/events_admin_controller.rb)*

```
class EventsAdminController < ApplicationController
  before_filter :authenticate_as_admin
  layout 'admin'

  active_scaffold :events do |config|
   config.list.columns = [:occurs_at, :title, :guests]
  end
end
```

The first line of our controller uses a before filter referencing the authenticate_as_admin method (covered shortly) to ensure that our users have entered a password. Our controller uses the layout command to specify that we should use the admin layout, and then calls active_scaffold to create a scaffold for the Event model. When you pass a block to the active_scaffold method, you can change the configuration of your scaffold. We use it here to specify which columns will be shown in our list of records. We don't change any of the columns displayed in any of the other views, so that columns we don't explicitly include here are included by default. This applies to our timestamp columns as well. There is no compelling reason to show those, so they are removed from our list by our customization. (Note that these columns are removed from the edit and create pages automatically by ActiveScaffold.)

Additionally, notice that one of the columns in our list is not a field from our database: guests, which refers to the Guest model. Since the Event model has a has_many relationship with the Guest model, ActiveScaffold knows that it should handle this by displaying a comma-separated list of guests on our list page. A similar ability to edit related rows in other tables is also found in all of the other views, so you can create a new event and add a guest to it, or delete guests from existing events.

Next, let's look at the admin controller for guests, which allows us to manage our guest list, as shown in Listing 8-5.

Listing 8-5. *Guests Admin Controller (app/controllers/guests_admin_controller.rb)*

```
class GuestsAdminController < ApplicationController
  before_filter :authenticate_as_admin
  layout 'admin'
```

```
    active_scaffold :guest do |config|
      config.list.columns = [:name, :description, :upcoming_events]
      config.create.columns = [:name, :description, :events]
      config.update.columns = [:name, :description, :events]
    end
  end
```

This controller also has an `authenticate_as_admin` before filter and uses our `admin` layout. Notice that our list view includes the `upcoming_events` column. This is an association that refers to the `Event` model, but it includes only the events that haven't occurred yet. After all, it wouldn't be very helpful to view events from the past, so using this technique lets us limit the information displayed to just what's useful.

Next, let's take a look at the application controller, which has two important protected methods. Listing 8-6 shows this controller.

Listing 8-6. *Application Controller (app/controllers/application.rb)*

```
class ApplicationController < ActionController::Base
  helper :all

  protect_from_forgery
  protected

  def self.active_scaffold_controller_for(klass)
    return "#{klass.to_s.pluralize}AdminController".constantize rescue super
  end
  def authenticate_as_admin()
      authenticate_or_request_with_http_basic do |username, password|
          username=='admin' && password=='secret'
      end
  end
end
```

The first protected method, `active_scaffold_controller`, lets us define a new naming convention for ActiveScaffold controllers. ActiveScaffold uses nested forms, and ActiveScaffold needs to know what the other controllers are called in order to use them to display the nested forms. However, the default naming convention is to look for controllers named for the plural of the model followed by the word `Controller`, so that the controller for the `Event` model becomes `EventsController`. But our ActiveScaffold controllers are useful only for the administrators. We may later want to have other controllers named Events and Guests, so here we want to use an alternate method.

The code in the custom `active_scaffold_controller_for` method we define here pluralizes the name of the class, and then adds `AdminController` to it, so that the controller for the `Event` model becomes `EventsAdminController`. You can use a similar method to define any naming convention you like, and if you have just one or two special cases, you can accommodate them.

The second method, `authenticate_as_admin`, is called by our two controllers to ensure that the user is authenticated as an administrator. Basic HTTP authentication with hard-coded passwords, as used here, is a simple, although not ideal, way to do authentication. It requires passwords to be transmitted in unencrypted form over the Internet, and on top of that, every HTTP request results in a retransmittal of the password. See Chapter 11 for a more robust way to do authentication.

Tip Basic HTTP authentication is reasonably secure when used over a Secure Sockets Layer (SSL) connection, so requiring an SSL connection may be very convenient for administrative interfaces. You can find out more about requiring SSL for a controller at `http://www.railsonwave.com/railsonwave/2007/7/10/howto-put-a-controller-under-a-ssl-subdomain`.

Let's take a look at our front page controller, which controls the way data is displayed on the front page of the application. Listing 8-7 shows this code.

Listing 8-7. *Front Page Controller (app/controllers/frontpage_controller.rb)*

```ruby
class FrontpageController < ApplicationController
  def index
    @events  = Event.upcoming_events
  end
end
```

This controller, with just a single action, `index`, grabs the upcoming events and passes them to the view. Listing 8-8 shows the view.

Listing 8-8. *Front Page Index Page (app/views/frontpage/index.html.erb)*

```erb
<style>
  body { font-family: sans-serif; }
  li { list-style-type:none;  }
  li div.calendar_line { background-color: #f4f4f5; padding:0.5em; }
  li div.calendar_description { padding-left: 1em; }
  li div.calendar_description p.guest { padding-left: 1em; }
</style>

<h1>Upcoming Events</h1>

<ul>
  <%@events.each do |event|  %>
    <li>
      <div class="calendar_line">
        <em><%= event.occurs_at.strftime('%D %H:%M %P') %></em>,
            <%= event.title %>
      </div>
```

```
      <div class="calendar_description">
        <p><strong>Featuring:</strong></p>
        <%event.guests.each do |g| %>
          <p class="guest">
              <% if g.href?  %>
                <%= link_to g.name, g.href  %>
              <%else %>
                <%= g.name  %>
              <%end %> &mdash;
              <%= g.description  %>
          </p>
        <%end %>
        <p>Register now - just <%= event.occurs_at.to_date - Date.today  %>
            days to go!</p>
      </div>
    </li>
  <%end %>
</ul>
```

This view loops through all of the events and displays the event data, title, and guest list. If guests have a hyperlink to their web site, they will be used as links. Otherwise, only the guest's name will be displayed. Additionally, note that the current date is subtracted by the occurs_at field and converted to a date. This gives us the number of days until the event occurs.

Our administrative layout will be used for our ActiveScaffold code. Listing 8-9 shows this layout.

Listing 8-9. *Admin Layout (app/views/layouts/admin.html.erb)*

```
<!DOCTYPE html PUBLIC "-//W3C//DTD XHTML 1.0 Transitional//EN"
      "http://www.w3.org/TR/xhtml1/DTD/xhtml1-transitional.dtd">

<html xmlns="http://www.w3.org/1999/xhtml" xml:lang="en" lang="en">
  <head>
    <meta http-equiv="content-type" content="text/html;charset=UTF-8" />
    <title>Calendar Admin</title>
    <%= javascript_include_tag :defaults  %>
    <%= active_scaffold_includes  %>
  </head>
  <body>
    <div>
      <strong>Calendar Adminstration</strong>
          <a href="/admin/events">Events</a>
          <a href="/admin/guests">Guests</a>
    </div>
```

```
    <%= yield   %>

  </body>
</html>
```

The call to `active_scaffold_include` ensures that we include ActiveScaffold's built-in JavaScript and CSS resources. However, it doesn't include Prototype, so we need to include that using the `javascript_include_tag :defaults`. After that, we simply include a basic navigational header for our administration page, and then use `yield` to include the contents of our view.

Finally, let's take a look at our routes, shown in Listing 8-10.

Listing 8-10. *Route Configuration File (config/routes.rb)*

```
ActionController::Routing::Routes.draw do |map|
  map.connect 'admin/events/:action/:id', :controller=>'events_admin'
  map.connect 'admin/guests/:action/:id', :controller=>'guests_admin'

  map.root :controller=>'frontpage'

  map.connect ':controller/:action/:id'
  map.connect ':controller/:action/:id.:format'
end
```

Notice that we put the two administrative actions in a separate path, under /admin. This serves to separate them from regular actions. This approach does not provide much security, since it's not hard to guess, but it's convenient and lets us have a front-end controller with the same name as the administrative controllers. For example, we could have an events controller that displays a list of all current events.

Delete the file `public/index.html`, and you're ready to go.

Running the Events Calendar Application

Now that we've put together all the pieces for our upcoming events calendar, let's run the application:

```
ruby script/server
```

Browse to `http://localhost:3000/admin/events`. You will see a mostly blank display. That's because we don't have any events yet. Click Create New to add a new event. Your form should look similar to Figure 8-1.

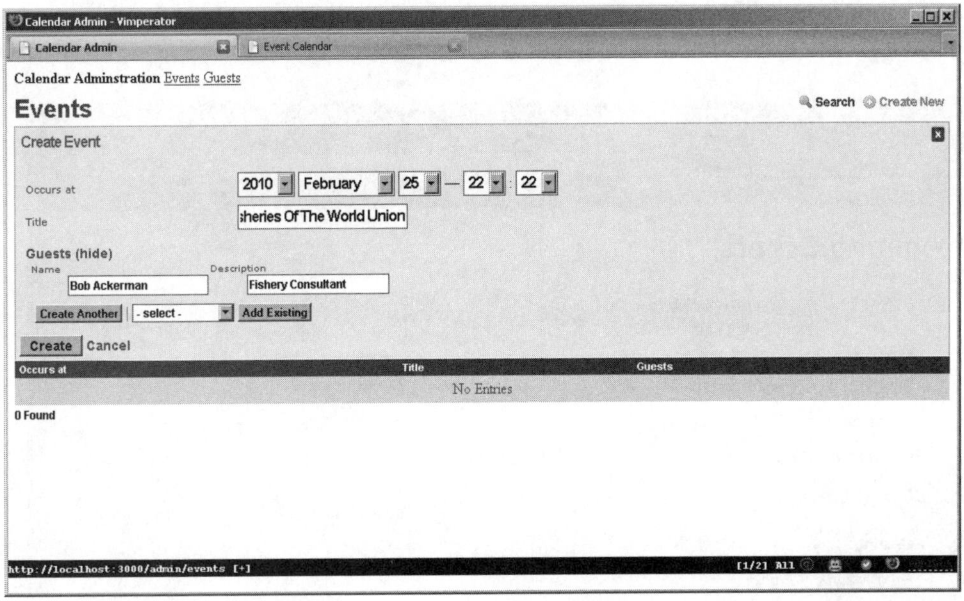

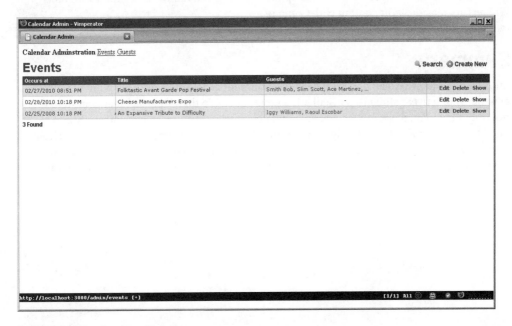

Figure 8-1. *Creating a new event*

Type in any arbitrary title and description. Notice that you can also add guests to the event as you create it. You can add existing guests using the Add Existing button and drop-down list, and you can even add new guests using the Name and Description text boxes. Once you've added an event, it will appear in the list of events. Add a few, and you should see a screen similar to Figure 8-2.

Figure 8-2. *Event list for administrators*

Once you've added at least one event, browse to `http://localhost:3000`. You will see the application's front page, which will look similar to Figure 8-3.

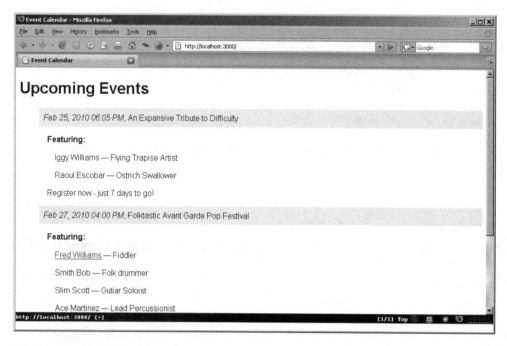

Figure 8-3. *Front page of the application*

In the next chapter, we'll extend this application and add tabbed navigation with Rails Widgets and easy-to-edit content with Comatose.

Summary

Eliminating repetitive drudgery from web development is definitely a strong point of Rails in general, and ActiveScaffold in particular is a great way to do that. You can create a system that not only allows you to search, create, edit, and delete records, but also lets you easily and quickly do the same for subordinate records of your records. Because your knowledge of relationships is already encoded in your models, you don't even need to instruct ActiveScaffold in the particulars of your schema. As a result, it's easy to set up, and a great solution for quickly creating administrative interfaces.

CHAPTER 9

■■■

Content Management and User Navigation with Comatose and Tabnav

In this chapter, we'll take a look at two common web application requirements and integrate them into a single functional solution. One is the capability to edit and maintain external content pages. The other is proper user navigation for these and other pages. Essentially, we'll be talking about how to manage information and how to access it—two inextricably linked activities.

It's extremely common to need to give end users basic content-editing capabilities in an existing web application whose primary purpose isn't publishing. This is usually the domain of content management systems (CMSs) and blogging packages. With Rails, you have many options, including Radiant, Rubricks, Typo, and Mephisto. However, these projects offer a complete, stand-alone solution, and they can be somewhat challenging to integrate into an existing Rails application, depending on your requirements.

Matt McCray's Comatose CMS offers an interesting alternative. It was designed to be small and easily embedded within the context of an existing application, and it's packaged as a Rails plugin. So rather than trying to fit your custom application inside the additional constraints of a full-featured CMS, you can take the opposite approach with Comatose: install the plugin to an existing project, set a mount point for routes, log in to the administrative interface it provides, and start creating hierarchically organized content. The public-facing content pages are published and available to visitors at the mount point you set.

Clearly, this is good news to those of us who have labored over building a web application with a bunch of specific domain logic and just need a simple publishing system to "tack on." It allows us to avoid developing yet another custom piece of software. At the same time, Comatose is flexible enough to do some relatively complex things, thanks to its usage of Liquid templates and drops (explained in more detail in Chapter 22).

Comatose is fantastic at publishing pages, but being lightweight and minimalist also means not dictating the context in which those pages are displayed. We need to provide some way, then, on the public-facing side of things, to navigate between the pages we create. That's where navigation bars, menus, and tabs come into play.

We're all familiar with a number of different navigation techniques. On the Web, it's common to find horizontal main navigation menus at the top of the screen or vertical navigation bars in a column to the left or right of the main content area. Also popular are tabbed navigation schemes, where each tab represents a different top-level section of site. Wherever the navigational controls are positioned and however they are laid out, the concerns are the same: the navigation mechanism must be easy to use, indicate its selected status if the user is visiting that area of the site, and not be too difficult to implement or maintain.

In the world of Rails, we are free to roll our own scheme, use existing libraries and code snippets, or use a plugin. For simple tasks, we recommend SeeSaw's Rails Widgets plugin, which includes the popular and extremely useful Tabnav widget. Tabnav allows us to express navigation menus in a clean, easy-to-maintain sort of domain-specific language (DSL). The Rails Widgets plugin also includes a standard Navigation widget, useful for building vertical and horizontal navigation bars. We'll use both of these widgets in this chapter.

Our Task: Add a Lightweight Content Management Solution and Tabbed Navigation

In Chapter 8, we developed a simple events management system for a community theater. This fit the troupe's needs nicely, allowing administrators to notify the theater's adoring public of upcoming events and add new events with ease. However, since the theater also has a vibrant community and a rich history, the administrators would like to be able to maintain some extra pages on the site that detail the history of the theater and its staff, hours of operation and contact information, and maybe even a simple announcements blog that will be maintained by the theater's director. We can do all this by integrating our existing application with the Comatose micro-CMS and creating a few pages using its administrative interface.

Of course, if we're going to be displaying this information to the public, we also need to give visitors an easy way to navigate through the pages we're creating. After discussing the options with the theater staff, we've decided that the types of information fall into four main categories, each of which will be represented in the tabbed navigation that we'll construct: Upcoming Events (the original events calendar, which will also serve as the default home page), About, Contact, and Blog.

Preparing to Extend the Events Calendar Application

Since we'll be extending the existing Rails project from Chapter 8, make sure to switch to that project directory before continuing. Once you've done that, you'll need to install a number of plugins.

In order for the Comatose plugin to work, we need to supplement it with two other plugins: Acts As List and Acts As Tree. At one point, these plugins were part of the Rails core, but as of Rails 2.0, they've been removed and are available as plugins in the core repository. To install Comatose and its dependencies, issue the following commands:

```
ruby script/plugin install acts_as_tree
ruby script/plugin install acts_as_list
ruby script/plugin install http://comatose-plugin.googlecode.com/svn/trunk/comatose
```

To finish installing Comatose and prepare it for use, we need to generate a migration and execute it to create the database tables that will store our content. Issue the following commands to accomplish this:

```
ruby script/generate comatose_migration
rake db:migrate
```

```
== 2 AddComatoseSupport: migrating =============================================
-- create_table(:comatose_pages)
   -> 0.0041s
Creating the default 'Home Page'...
== 2 AddComatoseSupport: migrated (0.1326s) ===================================
```

You also need to install the Rails Widgets plugin, which contains the Tabnav and Navigation widgets we'll use:

```
ruby script/plugin install http://rails-widgets.googlecode.com/svn/widgets
```

Note that the installation process will also copy a number of files to your public/images and public/javascripts directories.

Adding Content Pages to an Existing Application

To access your new micro-CMS, you need to add the routes shown in bold in Listing 9-1 to config/routes.rb. These routes will establish a mount point for the Comatose administrative interface as well as the user-visible pages we'll be creating.

Listing 9-1. *Updated Routes for the Comatose Micro-CMS Integration (config/routes.rb)*

```
ActionController::Routing::Routes.draw do |map|
  map.connect 'admin/events/:action/:id', :controller => 'events_admin'
  map.connect 'admin/guests/:action/:id', :controller => 'guests_admin'
  map.root :controller => 'frontpage'

  map.comatose_admin 'admin/cms'
  map.comatose_root '', :layout => 'application'
end
```

The routes in bold instruct our application to route all requests for the URL /admin/cms to the Comatose administrative controller, and that any routes that match the path prefix specified as the first parameter to map.comatose_root should be rendered by Comatose as user-visible pages.

In this case, our path prefix is '', which means that those pages are available from the application root (/about, /contact, and so on). Because of this, it's important that the map.comatose_root route declaration be added beneath any custom routes for our application. That way, the Comatose controller will be invoked only for routes that are not already explicitly handled by some other controller.

■**Tip** You can also add multiple mount points with Comatose and use named routes. For instance, adding the route `map.comatose_help 'help', :index => 'help'` specifies that the content page identified as `'help'` will be available at the URL `/help`. It also means that you can refer to the URL within your application as `comatose_help_path`, which can be a useful shortcut.

At this point, start the server using `script/server`. Visit `http://localhost:3000/admin/cms` in a web browser to see a screen similar to the one shown in Figure 9-1. This is the standard Comatose administrative interface. Next, we'll add the child pages for Contact, About, and Blog, as shown in the screenshot.

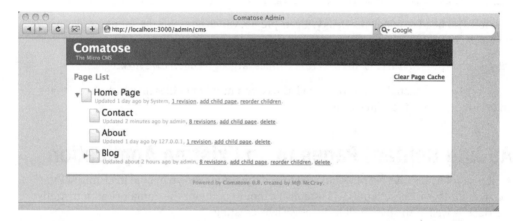

Figure 9-1. *Standard Comatose administrative interface (http://localhost:3000/admin/cms)*

Click the add child page link under the Home Page node. Name the new page `Contact`. If you click the more link next to the title, it will expand to reveal meta-information for the page, such as the URL slug, keywords, and the page parent node. The slug for the page should be `contact`. Enter some text for the body of the new page. You can select an optional markup filter below the text area. Textile is the default text filter, and will translate "human-readable" (non-HTML) markup text to reasonably formatted HTML markup.

■**Note** Textile, along with Markdown and other alternative "human-readable" markup syntaxes, tend to be very useful to most end users, who generally are unfamiliar with HTML but still need to be able to format their entries intelligently. More information about Textile can be found at `http://hobix.com/textile/`.

Once you've entered contact information for the theater company, go ahead and click the Preview button. You will see a preview of the new page in the area below the editing interface. Feel free to edit it some more to your satisfaction (use it as an excuse to experiment with Textile). When you're satisfied, publish the page. Comatose should return to the main administration screen, where the new page is now listed under the Home Page navigation hierarchy.

Repeat this process for the other pages that the theater company wants to set up. Name them About and Blog (their URL slugs should be about and blog). Don't worry too much about their content, but make sure at least some text is visible in each page content area.

When you're finished publishing, visit http://localhost:3000/contact. It will look something like the page shown in Figure 9-2 (but showing whatever content you added instead, of course). The same should be true for the other slugged URL paths.

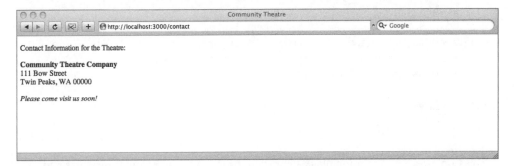

Figure 9-2. *First draft of the published contact page (http://localhost:3000/contact)*

Return to the main Comatose administration screen, update the Contact page, and then refresh the visitor view. The change should be propagated.

You may have noticed that when you returned to the main administration screen after publishing, it now shows two revisions listed beneath the updated node in the hierarchy. If you click the revisions link, you'll be taken to a screen where past revisions of the document can be viewed, compared, and set to the current (displayed) version. This is helpful if numerous people are editing CMS content, or if you wish to maintain a log of changes over time.

■Note Comatose supports page caching. This means that, when running in production mode, it will write out a new static cached copy to the public/ directory when updates are made. If your production hosting environment is configured correctly, your front-end web server, such as nginx or Apache, can then serve this content directly, rather than needing to ask your Rails application to create it each time. This can result in substantial savings if your site receives a large number of page views. If you wish to clear the cache, you can use the clear page cache option in the Comatose administrative interface.

Authenticating Access

Comatose does not provide its own authentication mechanism out of the box. As a micro-CMS, it's intended for integration within a larger preexisting application, so it logically assumes that if you need authentication capabilities, you most likely have already created them. And following that logic, Comatose makes it extremely simple to interoperate with pretty much any existing authentication scheme.

We're going to take the easy route here and just add basic HTTP authentication to protect updates to our Comatose administration screens. Add the code shown in Listing 9-2 to the bottom of `config/environment.rb`.

Listing 9-2. *Comatose Configuration/Authentication (config/environment.rb)*

```
Comatose.configure do |config|
  config.admin_title = "Community Theatre"
  config.admin_sub_title = "Content Management System"
  config.admin_authorization = Proc.new do
    authenticate_or_request_with_http_basic do |username, password|
      username == "admin" && password == "secret"
    end
  config.admin_get_author = Proc.new { "admin" }
  end
end
```

This Comatose configuration block allows you to customize how Comatose works and interoperates with the rest of your environment. Here, we set the following options:

- The `admin_title` and `admin_sub_title` options simply change the default title and sub-title displayed at the top of the Comatose administration screen.

- The `admin_authorization` configuration option tells Comatose that when it authorizes users for access to the administrative interface, it should run the defined `Proc`. The `Proc` uses the basic HTTP authentication mechanism (built into Rails 2.0 and later) to authenticate a user, requiring the username `admin` and the password `secret` in this case.

- The `admin_get_author` configuration option determines the name of the user responsible for publishing and updating new articles. This will be displayed in the mini-blog that we'll be building shortly, and posts will be attributed to this username. If you don't set this option, Comatose will default to displaying the IP address of the visitor who last updated the page as the author.

For more information about these and other Comatose configuration options, see `http://code.google.com/p/comatose-plugin/wiki/ConfigurationSettings`.

At this point, if you restart the server and revisit the Comatose administration screen at `http://localhost:3000/cms/admin`, you'll be prompted with an HTTP basic authentication request. Once you authenticate, you'll see that the title and subtitle of the main administration screen have changed to match our customized settings.

INTEGRATING WITH AN EXISTING AUTHENTICATION SYSTEM

What if you want to interoperate with an existing authentication scheme rather than rolling your own (with HTTP authentication, in our example)? For example, suppose you wanted to integrate with an application using the RESTful Authentication plugin (profiled in Chapter 11). You can simply change your configuration block to read something like the following:

```
Comatose.configure do |config|
  config.admin_includes << :authenticated_system
  config.admin_authorization = :login_required
  config.admin_get_author do
    current_user.login
  end
end
```

This configuration block makes Comatose aware of your authenticated system module and guarantees that the `login_required` filter (a method provided by RESTful Authentication) will be run in order to mandate access to the administration interface. As an added bonus, it also sets the username supplied by RESTful Authentication's `current_user` method as the username responsible for publishing and updating new articles.

Adding Navigation Elements

We've come a long way in a very short amount of time. We've added three new content pages that will be easy for our friends at the theater company to update. However, this content isn't much good if it can't be located by a visitor on the public web site interface. This means that it's time for us to add the appropriate navigation elements to the application layout. We'll add both tabbed navigation and a standard navigation menu.

Adding Tabbed Navigation

To add tabbed navigation to the theater company web site, we'll start by using the generator provided by the Rails Widgets plugin. Enter the following command:

```
ruby script/generate tabnav main
```

This will generate a main Tabnav template in app/views/widgets/_main_tabnav.rhtml. When you open that file and examine it, you'll find that it contains many useful comments that describe how you can alter the template to fit your own situation. We want to modify it so that the contents look like the code in Listing 9-3.

Listing 9-3. *Main Tabnav Partial Template (app/views/widgets/_main_tabnav.rhtml)*

```
<%
render_tabnav :main,
              :generate_css => true do

  add_tab do |t|
    t.named "Upcoming Events"
    t.links_to :controller => "frontpage"
  end

  cms_pages = ["about", "contact", "blog"]
  cms_pages.each do |name|
    add_tab do |t|
      t.named name.camelize
      t.links_to "/#{name}"
      t.highlights_on Proc.new { !params[:page].nil? &&
        params[:page].include?(name) }
    end
  end
end
%>
```

■**Note** As of this writing, the Tabnav widget and Comatose both use Rails 1.*x*-style template-naming schemes, ending with `.rhtml` instead of `.html.erb`. These templates are fully compatible with Rails 2.*x*.

The `render_tabnav` method provided by the plugin takes the name of the `tabnav` to render as a symbol and an option that specifies whether you want CSS for the navigation display to be generated in-line. We'll have it generate CSS for this example, but for a production site, you would most likely want to style the tabbed navigation with your own CSS, assign it an appropriately named CSS class, and keep the styles themselves in a proper style sheet.

The block we pass to `render_tabnav` makes a number of calls to the `add_tab` method, and each `add_tab` method takes a block of its own. Inside that inner block, we specify the name to be displayed on the tab (`t.named`), the URL that it should link to (`t.links_to`), and, optionally, any other conditions under which the tab should stay highlighted/selected (`t.highlights_on`).

■**Note** The syntax used for Tabnav is very much like a DSL for defining navigation elements. Many other options are available in addition to those shown here, such as methods to specify when a tab should be disabled. For more information, see the source in `vendor/plugins/widgets` and Paolo Donà's blog entry at `http://blog.seesaw.it/articles/2007/09/03/what-changes-in-the-new-widgets-tabnav`.

When the tabbed navigation is rendered, we want to add a tab for the upcoming events, which is obviously the main focus of the site. But we'll want to add tabs to the About, Contact, and Blog pages as well. Since we know their URLs will take the form of /#{*name*}, we can safely instruct the tab to link to that page. We'll add an additional instruction to highlight the tab when the page parameter is present and includes the named top-level node (thus indicating that the visitor is on that page at the time). This is quite simple when you are dealing with only top-level pages, but if you want to handle proper section highlighting for pages that are *n*-levels deep within a section, you need to understand a bit about how Comatose's routing works.

Whenever a request is made that matches the comatose_root mapping (in our case, '', so this applies to any request that hasn't already been handled by a route with higher precedence), the Comatose controller's show action is invoked and passed an array of page elements in params[:page]. In the case of a top-level element like our Contact page, params[:page] will contain ['contact']. However, in the case of a page that is a child of one of the top-level elements, like a blog-entry page (which will be a child of the Blog page), that parameter will contain an array of URL slugs like ['blog', 'title-of-blog-entry']. By checking the page parameter array and looking for an identifier that matches your top-level element name, Tabnav can determine if the request being made is for a page that is a child of one of the main sections, and if so, it can highlight the appropriate section tab to indicate to the users which part of the site they're in. This is the job of the Proc we wrote back in Listing 9-3, which is specified as a parameter to the highlights_on method. It will evaluate to either true or false, and the highlight will be set accordingly.

Tip It's also possible to pass a hash to the highlights_on method that will be matched against the current URL. You could, therefore, easily indicate that this tab should highlight for all methods of, say, FooController, by specifying t.highlights_on :controller => 'foo'.

This technique gives you maximum flexibility and would allow you to easily add a subpage to the Contact page, for instance, that would maintain the appropriate top-level section highlight in the tabbed navigation without changing the code that displays the tabs (of course, you would probably want to build a subnavigation element to display within that section as well).

With proper highlighting rules now in place, our next step is to render this tabbed navigation, which means we need to add it to a view somewhere. Since we want it to be universally visible if someone is visiting any part of the site (excluding administrative sections), we'll add it to app/views/layouts/application.html.erb, our default application layout, as shown in Listing 9-4.

Listing 9-4. *Updated Layout with Tabbed Navigation (app/views/layouts/application.html.erb)*

```
<!DOCTYPE html PUBLIC "-//W3C//DTD XHTML 1.0 Transitional//EN"
  "http://www.w3.org/TR/xhtml1/DTD/xhtml1-transitional.dtd">
<html xmlns="http://www.w3.org/1999/xhtml" xml:lang="en" lang="en">
<head>
  <meta http-equiv="content-type" content="text/html;charset=UTF-8" />
  <title>Community Theatre</title>
</head>
<body>
  <% tabnav(:main) do -%>
    <%= yield %>
  <% end -%>
</body>
</html>
```

The Tabnav view helper method used here takes a symbol to specify which `tabnav` to render (there may be many defined within your application, including nested ones), and then passes it a block. Anything in the block will be rendered inside the tabbed navigation box that is displayed. In this case, we `yield` inside the block, which means that the view template for the action that rendered this layout will be displayed there.

Reload `http://localhost:3000/contact` in your web browser. You should see a simple, clean tab navigation system displayed at the top of the page, with page-level content displayed inside it, as shown in Figure 9-3. Go ahead and navigate around the pages we've created.

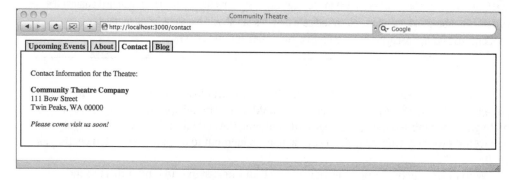

Figure 9-3. *Tabbed navigation for content pages (http://localhost:3000/contact)*

We now have a CMS fully integrated into our existing web application, easily navigable by a visitor and easily updated by the theater company staff.

Adding Another Navigation Option

Tabs work really well for some sites. For other sites, they make relatively little sense, and traditional navigation bars or menus are more desirable. It's also commonplace to find tabbed navigation or a main menu bar supplemented by a minimalist footer menu for easy navigation to static top-level elements.

■**Note** Comatose is designed to be safe for your users and nondestructive to the rest of your application. Therefore, it limits access to potentially destructive Active Record methods, Rails helpers, and your own application helpers within Comatose page content. If you need access to specific application data within the processing context, you can create a `ComatoseDrop`. For more information about this and other advanced Comatose features, see the guide at `http://code.google.com/p/comatose-plugin/wiki/ GettingStartedGuide`.

Save the Blog page with these changes. Then reload the visitor view of the web site and navigate to the Blog tab. You will see something similar to the page shown in Figure 9-4. Notice that a link with content text is rendered for each child of the blog section. You can click the title link to be taken to a full page containing just that article (a permalink). When you do this, you'll see that the tab selection for the section is maintained in the tabbed navigation above.

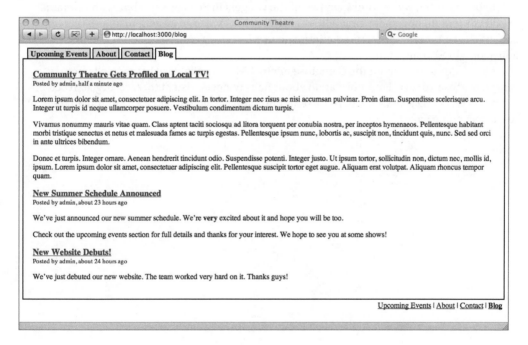

Figure 9-4. *User view of mini-blog (http://localhost:3000/blog)*

■**Tip** Although it's very flexible, Comatose is not intended as a fully functional blog package. It lacks many of the core features present in modern blogs, such as native ability to support RSS feeds and comments. If your requirements are more complex than what we've presented here, you may want to investigate more robust blog and CMS packages, such as Typo (`http://typosphere.org`), Mephisto (`http://mephistoblog.com`), and Radiant (`http://radiantcms.org`), all of which are also powered by Ruby on Rails.

Summary

Adding basic self-publishing capabilities to a larger web application project is a common task. The Comatose plugin allows you to drop this sort of functionality into existing Rails applications easily. Its small size and ease of integration make it ideal for those sorts of projects where content management is not the main focus and yet a flexible solution is still needed. Advanced features, such as altering the administration interface itself, building custom Liquid drops, and rendering Comatose content pages in-line from other parts of your application, are also provided by the plugin.

Another ubiquitous requirement for web site development is good intuitive user navigation facilities. Navigation comes in many flavors, but two popular variants include tabbed navigation and more traditional sidebar-style menus. In both cases, state needs to be maintained when a user navigates throughout a subsection. Fortunately, SeeSaw's Rails Widgets plugin provides a number of navigation helpers that can take care of these tasks for you, as well as providing other useful UI tools such as JavaScript tooltips and show/hide widgets.

In this chapter, we've combined two of the widgets in SeeSaw's toolbox with Comatose to add content management capabilities and a basic navigation system to an existing application. The result is a full-featured micro-site to which new content sections can be easily added or edited at any time.

More information about the Comatose micro-CMS is available at `http://code.google.com/p/comatose-plugin`. For information about Rails Widgets, visit `http://code.google.com/p/rails-widgets`. Discussion groups exist for both projects, and links can be found on their respective home pages.

CHAPTER 10

■ ■ ■

Payment Processing with ActiveMerchant

Electronic commerce is big business. The Internet data-measurement firm comScore estimates that more than $102 billion was spent online during 2006, a 24% increase from the previous year, and this spending shows no sign of slowing down.

Online shopping comes in a variety of flavors: traditional retailers who have decided to augment their existing business/brand by establishing a digital presence, powerhouse "e-tailers" like Amazon.com, and specialty shops that see the Internet as a new medium to sell their wares with very little in the way of up-front costs. Other types of e-commerce include online travel agencies; auction sites like eBay; and numerous companies selling digital goods, services, and access to data. While what they are selling may vary, you can bet that all these organizations have at least one thing in common: they need to handle payments easily and efficiently.

How online businesses deal with payment processing is a bit of a mystery to the average consumer. If you're someone looking to get started selling goods online, understanding how this process works is paramount. In most cases, businesses seek to accept credit card payments online, which usually means working with a third-party payment-processing service (and paying some combination of a fixed monthly fee and a percentage of sales for that service). Payment gateways such as Authorize.Net, Braintree, and LinkPoint are popular options for domestic payments, and are usually coupled with a merchant account where the funds are actually deposited.

Using a third-party service for credit card processing also means integrating with that service's API, a task that can be daunting, especially since every vendor has its own API. This means that if you want to change from provider A to provider B, you likely have a fair amount of work to do. Many web commerce platforms for small business, such as Shopify and Yahoo Merchant Solutions, make this somewhat easier by providing a simple interface that can be configured by a shop owner to support any number of gateways. But shop owners often want features or functionality outside the scope of these systems, requiring the development of custom e-commerce solutions.

In Ruby on Rails, we're lucky enough to have ActiveMerchant (`http://activemerchant.org`), a library written and open-sourced by Tobias Luetke, Cody Fauser, and the fine folks at Shopify. It provides a simple, unified API for access to dozens of different payment gateways. This means that it removes the hard work involved in supporting more than one provider.

Our Task: Allow Quick and Easy Electronic Payments

Cobol Pizza is a local pizzeria. The chefs make killer pies, and they name each of their unique concoctions after a programming language. For example, The Haskell is a nitrate-free pepperoni and mushroom combination; The Lua is a white pizza; and The Perl is covered with olives, red peppers, and anchovies. Our personal favorite is The Ruby, of course, which is a spicy BBQ pizza using only free-range chicken—tasty!

Needless to say, Cobol Pizza is a big hit with the area tech companies and creative firms. Since many of the restaurant's regular customers are of the geeky persuasion, the owner has started thinking seriously about taking orders online. Many customers have asked about this, as it's easier for them. From the proprietor's point of view, it's also more accurate, since each order can be printed directly from the information that the customer supplies online, instead of translated by whoever answered the phone. Plus, it's just another cool gimmick, right?

Well, the owner has decided that she wants to allow online ordering, and she has come to us for help. We need to build a Rails-based web application that receives a pizza order through a form, processes a credit card payment, and then gives the customer an order confirmation. The order process should consist of just two simple steps: customers specify the pizzas they want and their delivery information, and then they confirm their order and enter payment information. In Cobol Pizza's kitchen, a computer monitor will show a constantly updated list of orders coming in from the Web, relayed through a password-protected URL.

Cobol Pizza's owner doesn't know who she wants to use for a payment gateway yet. She tells us that she needs some time to investigate the options and figure out which gateway's fee structure best fits her business model. We say, "No problem."

Because ActiveMerchant gives us access to a unified payment processing API, interaction with any specific gateway is pretty much the same to us. By hiding the implementation details, ActiveMerchant allows us to easily switch between, say, Authorize.Net and PayPal Website Payments Pro (WPP) for payment processing. If we later decide to change to LinkPoint, we can just modify a couple lines of code—no dramatic refactoring is required.

■**Tip** For a full list of all payment gateways supported by ActiveMerchant, including international providers, see `http://activemerchant.rubyforge.org`.

Throughout this chapter, we'll be using the Braintree payment gateway (see `http://braintreepaymentsolutions.com`). Braintree offers a full feature set and secure customer data storage, compliant with Payment Card Industry Data Security Standard (PCI DSS) requirements, as well as many other powerful features, such as recurring billing capabilities. If you wish to use a gateway that you already have credentials with instead, feel free to substitute its class name in place of `BraintreeGateway` throughout this example, and supply your username and password credentials where appropriate. It's really that simple!

PAYMENT CARD INDUSTRY STANDARDS

The Payment Card Industry Data Security Standard (PCI DSS) requires conformance to a strict set of standards, especially if your online business stores persistent credit card information. If possible, it's better to have a third party who is an expert in this realm, such as your payment gateway, deal with storage of credit card numbers. In the example presented in this chapter, we do not store credit card data of any sort, but rather rely on the gateway to perform this function.

Meeting PCI DSS requirements is important for your customers' security, and any business that handles credit cards online needs to be familiar with this standard. If you are not in compliance with PCI DSS, your ability to process cards may be revoked. More information is available at http://en.wikipedia.org/wiki/PCI_DSS.

Preparing to Process Payments

To get started, let's create a new Rails application for the pizzapay project:

```
rails pizzapay
cd pizzapay
```

ActiveMerchant is available both as a Rails plugin and a stand-alone Ruby gem for use in other (non-Rails) Ruby applications. For more information about the library, see the documentation at http://activemerchant.org. To install it in our new application as a Rails plugin, execute the following command:

```
ruby script/plugin install git://github.com/Shopify/active_merchant.git
```

■**Note** Installation from the Git repository, as shown here, is the suggested way to install the plugin. Support to install plugins from Git is only available in Rails 2.1 and later. If you are using an older version of Rails, see http://www.activemerchant.org for other options.

You'll also need to install the Money gem, a flexible library for working with currency amounts and conversions in Ruby applications. You can find more information about the Money library at http://dist.leetsoft.com/api/money. To install it as a gem, execute the following command:

```
gem install money
```

Creating the Pizza and Order Models

Before we can get to the meat of our example (ha!), we need to define data models to represent different types of pizzas and customer orders, as well as a migration to create the appropriate database tables. Start by saving the migration in Listing 10-1 as db/migrate/001_create_orders_pizzas.rb.

Listing 10-1. *Database Migration (db/migrate/001_create_orders_pizzas.rb)*

```ruby
class CreateOrdersPizzas < ActiveRecord::Migration
  def self.up
    create_table :pizzas do |t|
      t.string   :name
      t.text     :description
      t.integer :price, :default => 0
      t.timestamps
    end

    create_table :orders do |t|
      t.string   :customer_name
      t.string   :customer_email
      t.string   :customer_phone
      t.string   :customer_address
      t.string   :customer_city
      t.string   :authorization
      t.boolean :paid, :default => :false
      t.timestamps
    end

    create_table :order_items do |t|
      t.integer :order_id
      t.integer :pizza_id
      t.integer :quantity, :default => 0
    end

    Pizza.create(:name => "The Ruby",
      :description => "Spicy BBQ Chicken", :price => 1400)
    Pizza.create(:name => "The Haskell",
      :description => "Pepperoni & Mushroom", :price => 1400)
    Pizza.create(:name => "The Lua",
      :description => "White Pizza", :price => 1300)
    Pizza.create(:name => "The Perl",
      :description => "Olives, Peppers, Anchovies", :price => 1500)
    Pizza.create(:name => "The Java",
      :description => "Lots of Meat!", :price => 1500)
  end

  def self.down
    drop_table :order_items
    drop_table :orders
    drop_table :pizzas
  end
end
```

This migration specifies three tables, which correspond to the models that we'll describe next. It also explicitly creates five different types of pizzas to get us started. Each has a name, description, and a price (Cobol Pizza is somewhat inflexible; the owner doesn't believe in small/medium/large—it's one size fits all!).

Let's define our `Pizza` model now. It requires a unique name, a description, and a price. Save the code shown in Listing 10-2 as `app/models/pizza.rb`.

Listing 10-2. *Pizza Model (app/models/pizza.rb)*

```
class Pizza < ActiveRecord::Base
  validates_presence_of :name, :description, :price
  validates_uniqueness_of :name

  has_many :order_items
  has_many :orders, :through => :order_items
end
```

Note that the pizza's `price` attribute is stored as an integer. Given this representation, a value of 1 is equal to 1 cent, and 100 equals $1.00. We'll be using US dollars (USD) as the currency in our example, which is the default currency for both ActiveMerchant and the Money gem. ActiveMerchant wants all payment amounts to be described in cents, so that's what we'll use for our database representation as well. If you want, you can use the Money gem to convert this to alternate representations. See the Money library's documentation (`http://dist.leetsoft.com/api/money`) for details.

The `Pizza` model is related to the `Order` model through an `OrderItem` join model. An `OrderItem`, in this case, represents one or more of a particular pizza type. We use a join model and `has_many :through`, instead of a simpler `has_and_belongs_to_many` association, because we need the ability to specify a quantity. An order may contain one or more of any given specialty pizza items. Save the code in Listing 10-3 as `app/models/order_item.rb`.

Listing 10-3. *OrderItem Join Model (app/models/order_item.rb)*

```
class OrderItem < ActiveRecord::Base
  validates_presence_of :order_id, :pizza_id, :quantity
  validates_inclusion_of :quantity, :in => 1..100
  belongs_to :order
  belongs_to :pizza

  def price
    quantity * pizza.price
  end
end
```

The `Order` model, shown in Listing 10-4, should be saved as `app/models/order.rb`. It contains basic information about the customer and delivery address.

Listing 10-4. *Order Model (app/models/order.rb)*

```ruby
class Order < ActiveRecord::Base
  validates_presence_of :customer_name, :customer_email, :customer_phone,
      :customer_address, :customer_city

  has_many :order_items, :dependent => :destroy
  has_many :pizzas, :through => :order_items

  attr_protected :paid, :authorization

  def price
    self.order_items.inject(0) { |sum, item| sum += item.price }
  end

  def reference_number
    "C#{self.created_at.strftime("%w%S")}#{self.id}"
  end

  def complete(gateway_response)
    if gateway_response.success?
      self.paid = true
      self.authorization = gateway_response.authorization
      self.save
    else
      false
    end
  end

  def summary
    self.order_items.collect { |item| "#{item.quantity}x #{item.pizza.name}" }
  end
end
```

The Order model contains a Boolean flag, paid, which indicates whether or not the customer has paid for the order, and an authorization code, which will be returned by the payment gateway and recorded for accounting and record-keeping purposes. These attributes are protected from mass assignment using attr_protected, as we wouldn't want customers to be able to set them through a form.

We define four additional methods on the Order model as well:

- The price method uses Array#inject and the order_item association to sum the cost of all the pizzas that are part of the current order.

- The reference_number method exists so we can give customers a number to refer to their order in case they want to check on its status or cancel it (we *could* just use the primary key as the identifier, but because it's more cosmetically pleasing and future-proof, we use a combination of the formatted creation time and the id).

- The complete method finalizes order details and updates the model. When it's called, it is passed a response from a payment gateway (an ActiveMerchant::Billing::Response object, which we'll talk about in the "Processing the Payment" section later in the chapter) and uses this to mark the order's paid status and set the authorization code.

- The summary method prepares an easy-to-read summary for someone working in the kitchen at Cobol Pizza. It does this by iterating through the order items, collecting the name and quantity of each item. Later, in our index action view, we'll format this information for easy viewing.

We can now run the migration to add the appropriate tables and populate them with the five default pizza types.

```
rake db:migrate
```

```
== 1 CreatePizzasOrders: migrating ==============================================
-- create_table(:pizzas)
   -> 0.0035s
-- create_table(:orders)
   -> 0.0025s
-- create_table(:order_items)
   -> 0.0018s
== 1 CreatePizzasOrders: migrated (0.0085s) =====================================
```

Processing Payments in a Controller

Now that we have the plugin installed and some basic models in place, we can build our OrdersController, which will handle the customer ordering and payment processing. We'll implement two controller methods to accomplish this, new and create, and their associated views. We'll also implement the index action, which will be used by the Cobol Pizza staff to monitor orders that need to be filled. The code for OrdersController is shown in Listing 10-5. Save it as app/controllers/orders_controller.rb.

Listing 10-5. *Orders Controller (app/controllers/orders_controller.rb)*

```
class OrdersController < ApplicationController
  # support a subset of the cards supported by the gateway
  CARD_TYPES = [["Visa", "visa"], ["MasterCard", "master"],
    ["Discover", "discover"]]

  before_filter :authenticate, :only => :index

  def new
    @order = Order.new
    @order_items = Pizza.find(:all).collect { |pizza| OrderItem.new(
        :pizza => pizza, :order => @order, :quantity => 0) }
  end
```

```ruby
def create
  if !params[:confirmed]
    get_payment
  else
    process_payment
  end
end

def index
  @orders = Order.find(:all,
      :conditions => ["created_at >= ? AND paid = 't'", 1.day.ago],
      :order => "created_at DESC")
end

private

  def authenticate
    authenticate_or_request_with_http_basic do |username, password|
      username == "admin" && password == "secret"
    end
  end

  def get_payment
    @order = Order.new(params[:order])
    @order_items = params[:order_items].collect { |oi| OrderItem.new(oi) }
    if @order.save
      @order_items.each { |item| @order.order_items << item if item.quantity > 0 }
      render(:action => 'payment')
    else
      render(:action => 'new')
    end
  end

  def process_payment
    @order = Order.find(params[:order_id])
    @credit_card = ActiveMerchant::Billing::CreditCard.new(params[:credit_card])
    if @credit_card.valid?
      gateway = ActiveMerchant::Billing::BraintreeGateway.new(
        :login => AM_GATEWAY_LOGIN,
        :password => AM_GATEWAY_PASSWORD)
```

```
      response = gateway.purchase(@order.price, @credit_card,
        { :order_id => @order.reference_number })
      if response.success? && @order.complete(response)
        render(:action => 'receipt')
      else
        # report errors
        @order.errors.add_to_base(response.message)
        render(:action => 'payment')
      end
    else
      render(:action => 'payment')
    end
  end
end
```

Tip After familiarizing yourself with ActiveMerchant, you may want to move the bulk of the gateway purchase and response handling to a method on your Order class or to a separate OrderTransaction class. This helps keep your controllers as slim as possible. We've added it to the controller here for demonstrative purposes.

Before we examine these controller actions in depth, we'll first need to add a couple configuration directives to our config/environments/development.rb file. Settings in this file take precedence over those listed in config/environment.rb when the server is running in development mode. We'll use this as a convenient way to add settings specific to our development environment. The lines to add are shown in Listing 10-6.

Listing 10-6. *Additional Development Environment Configuration (config/environments/development.rb)*

```
ActiveMerchant::Billing::Base.mode = :test # required for Braintree test mode
AM_GATEWAY_LOGIN = 'demo'
AM_GATEWAY_PASSWORD = 'password'
```

The first line puts ActiveMerchant into test mode by using ActiveMerchant::Billing::Base.mode, and the subsequent lines set up the Braintree API login and password constants that we'll use to test the payment-processing system (user: demo; password: password).

Before you deploy a production version of an application like this one, you'll need to obtain a set of live gateway credentials so that you can process actual transactions. If you wish to do this, you can sign up at http://developer.getbraintree.com. Place the production credentials you receive in config/environments/production.rb, so that when running in production mode, the server will use the live credentials, and when in development mode, it will use the test credentials.

In order to reach our controller actions, we'll also need to define a resource route. Update your routes in `config/routes.rb` to resemble the code shown in Listing 10-7.

Listing 10-7. *Updated Routes with Orders Resource (config/routes.rb)*

```
ActionController::Routing::Routes.draw do |map|
  map.resources :orders
end
```

With these changes in place, we can now move on to an in-depth examination of the new and create actions and their respective view templates.

Displaying the New Order Form

The first view a customer will visit is the one for the new action, so we'll start there. The new method in OrdersController just sets up a few instance variables for its view:

```
def new
  @order = Order.new
  @order_items = Pizza.find(:all).collect { |pizza| OrderItem.new(
      :pizza => pizza, :order => @order, :quantity => 0) }
end
```

Of particular interest here is the @order_items instance variable, which will contain an item for each pizza type. We're going to construct a simple order form in the view, with one line for each pizza type, where customers specify the desired quantity (the default quantity is 0). There are sexier ways to do this, such as using a traditional shopping cart approach or using JavaScript/Ajax techniques to select a pizza type and a quantity while updating a total in real time, but our goal here is to keep things simple (of course, feel free to implement something more sophisticated on your own). Listing 10-8 shows the view rendered by this action, the new order form. Save it as app/views/orders/new.html.erb.

Listing 10-8. *New Order View (app/views/orders/new.html.erb)*

```
<h1>Cobol Pizza Order Form</h1>
<%= error_messages_for(:order) %>
<% form_for(@order) do |order_form| -%>
  <div style="float: left; width: 50%;">
    <h2>Your Order</h2>
    <% fields_for('order_items[]') do |item_form| -%>
      <table border="1" cellpadding="5" width="90%">
        <tr><th>Pizza Type</th><th>Price</th><th>Quantity</th></tr>
        <% @order_items.each do |item| -%>
          <tr>
            <td><%= h(item.pizza.name) %>
              <%= item_form.hidden_field(:pizza_id, :index => nil,
                :value => item.pizza_id) %><br/>
```

```
            <font size="-1"><%= h(item.pizza.description) %></font></td>
          <td><%= format_money(item.pizza.price) %></td>
          <td><%= item_form.text_field(:quantity, :index => nil,
              :value => item.quantity || 0, :size => 2) %></td>
        </tr>
      <% end -%>
    </table>
  <% end -%>
  <p><%= submit_tag('Next &raquo;') %></p>
</div>
<div style="float: left; width: 50%;">
  <h2>Delivery Information</h2>
  <p>Delivery Name: <br/><%= order_form.text_field(:customer_name) %></p>
  <p>Street Address: <br/><%= order_form.text_field(:customer_address) %></p>
  <p>City: <br/><%= order_form.text_field(:customer_city) %></p>
  <p>Email Address: <br/><%= order_form.text_field(:customer_email) %></p>
  <p>Phone Number: <br/><%= order_form.text_field(:customer_phone) %></p>
</div>
<% end -%>
```

This template uses the variables we set up to display the pizza order form. The `form_for` helper, when passed the `@order` instance variable (a new record), will create a form element that will submit data to the `create` method, which we'll discuss in the next section.

The right-hand `div` within the form captures standard customer delivery and contact information. The left-hand `div` sets up a table from which customers can select the number of pizzas they want to order. We iterate through the `@order_items` instance variable here, adding one row to the table for each pizza type. The default quantity is 0; the `text_field` helper allows customers to change this to the number they want. We use `fields_for('order_items[]')` and specify `:index => nil` in each of the fields, because we want order item data to be sent to our controller in an array.

When displaying the price of a pizza, we call a helper method, `format_money`. Since we're storing all prices as cents for ActiveMerchant, we need a helper to convert it to a friendly format for display to customers. That helper can be found in our `ApplicationHelper` (app/helpers/application_helper.rb), which is shown in Listing 10-9.

Listing 10-9. *ApplicationHelper (app/helpers/application_helper.rb)*

```
module ApplicationHelper
  def format_money(cents)
    sprintf("$%0.2f", cents.to_f / 100)
  end
end
```

Once you've saved these files, you can start your web application by running `ruby script/server`. If you open a web browser and point it to `http://localhost:3000/orders/new`, you will see a form that resembles Figure 10-1.

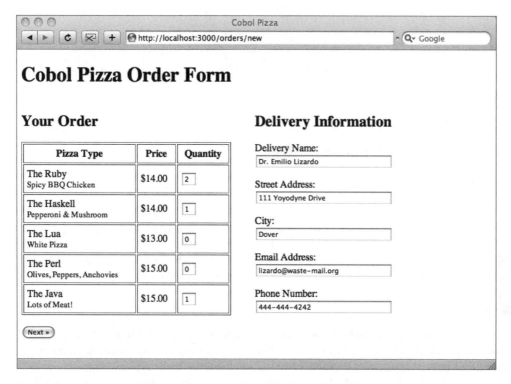

Figure 10-1. *New pizza delivery order form (http://localhost:3000/orders/new)*

Specify quantities and fill in your delivery information, but don't click the Next button yet. First, we need to examine the create action and install the appropriate templates.

Creating an Order

When the form is submitted from the new template, the create method is invoked. This action basically has two modes that correspond to the two order stages that we'll need.

After the submission of an order with delivery information, we need to display an order summary/confirmation page with a total cost, along with a prompt for payment information. This is just good practice in general. In many cases, you'll want to implement a multistage checkout process that also confirms the card to be charged.

Tip If you need a flexible multistage checkout process, you may want to consider modeling your orders as state machines and implementing them using the Acts As State Machine plugin (see Chapter 6). The ActiveMerchant mini-book by Cody Fauser (published by PeepCode Press, http://peepcode.com/products/activemerchant-pdf) includes useful ActiveMerchant production examples that leverage Acts As State Machine.

The second time the form is submitted, we'll have a hidden form element, which will be available in our controller as params[:confirmed], indicating that the private process_payment controller method should be called. This time, however, the parameter is not set, and therefore the get_payment method will be called instead.

```
def get_payment
  @order = Order.new(params[:order])
  @order_items = params[:order_items].collect { |oi| OrderItem.new(oi) }
  if @order.save
    @order_items.each { |item| @order.order_items << item if item.quantity > 0 }
    render(:action => 'payment')
  else
    render(:action => 'new')
  end
end
```

The get_payment method creates a new order from the form parameters POSTed to create, and we add any order items for which a nonzero quantity was specified. We then attempt to save the order, which triggers validation. If the save is successful, we render the payment template for the second stage of the checkout process. If not, we redisplay the previous template with error messages so the user can correct them. The payment template is shown in Listing 10-10. Save it as app/views/orders/payment.html.erb.

Listing 10-10. *Confirmation and Payment View (app/views/orders/payment.html.erb)*

```
<h1>Confirm &amp; Pay</h1>
<%= error_messages_for(:credit_card, :order) %>
<% form_for(:credit_card, :url => orders_url) do |cc_form| -%>
  <div style="float: left; width: 50%;">
    <h2>Order Summary</h2>
    <table border="1" cellpadding="5" width="90%">
      <tr><th>Pizza Type</th><th>Price</th><th>Quantity</th></tr>
      <% @order.order_items.each do |item| -%>
        <tr>
          <td><%= h(item.pizza.name) %><br/>
            <font size="-1"><%= h(item.pizza.description) %></font></td>
          <td><%= format_money(item.pizza.price) %></td>
          <td><%= h(item.quantity) %></td>
        </tr>
      <% end -%>
      <tr>
        <td colspan="3" align="right">Total: <%= format_money(@order.price) %></td>
      </tr>
    </table>
    <p><%= submit_tag("Submit Payment") %></p>
  </div>
```

```
<div style="float: left; width: 50%;">
  <h2>Billing Information</h2>
  <p>First Name: <br/><%= cc_form.text_field(:first_name) %></p>
  <p>Last Name: <br/><%= cc_form.text_field(:last_name) %></p>
  <p>Credit Card Type: <br/>
    <%= cc_form.select(:type, OrdersController::CARD_TYPES) %></p>
  <p>Credit Card Number: <br/><%= cc_form.text_field(:number, :size => 16) %></p>
  <p>Credit Card Expiration: <br/>
    <%= cc_form.text_field(:month, :size => 2) %> /
    <%= cc_form.text_field(:year, :size => 4) %></p>
  <p>Credit Card Verification: <br/>
    <%= cc_form.text_field(:verification_value, :size => 4) %></p>
</div>
<%= hidden_field_tag(:order_id, @order.id) %>
<%= hidden_field_tag(:confirmed, 1) %>
<% end -%>
```

This template shows an order summary in the left-hand div, including a total calculated using the price method on the Order model. In the right-hand div, we display a form to enter credit card information. Our form_for helper takes the :credit_card symbol and explicitly specifies a URL for the POST (the OrdersController create action again) this time. Payment fields include the first name and last name on the credit card, along with the card number, type, expiration date, and CVV2 verification value (the three- or four-digit security code printed on the back of the card). These are all values that the ActiveMerchant::Billing::CreditCard class, supplied by ActiveMerchant, expects to have in order to verify the validity of a card.

Possible card types are specified in a select list and can be any of the options listed in the CARD_TYPES constant in OrdersController. CARD_TYPES is an array that contains any credit cards that Cobol Pizza supports. Each element of the array is itself a two-element array, consisting of a display name and a value like ['MasterCard', 'master']. The complete list of supported cards is returned by the ActiveMerchant::Billing::CreditCardMethods.card_companies method.

Two additional hidden fields are present in this template as well. The confirmed hidden field was already discussed. The order_id field is used to specify the primary key of the order that was saved in the previous step. This will enable us to look up the Order object that is associated with this payment when we resubmit the form to the create method for processing.

Once you've saved this template, click the Next button in your web browser to be taken to this page. You should see something similar to the screen shown in Figure 10-2. Fill out the form using test credit card data. Test transactions can be submitted using the following information:

Visa: 4111111111111111

MasterCard: 5431111111111111

Discover Card: 6011601160116611

American Express: 341111111111111111111

Expiration: 10/2010

Verification: 999

Don't click the Submit Payment button yet though—we still need to implement the final order processing template.

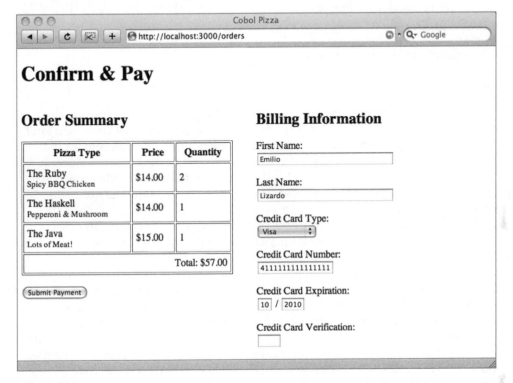

Figure 10-2. *Confirming your order and entering credit card information (http://localhost:3000/ orders/new)*

Processing the Payment

The second time the `create` action is called, the `confirmed` form parameter is set, so we call the private `process_payment` controller method:

```
def process_payment
  @order = Order.find(params[:order_id])
  @credit_card = ActiveMerchant::Billing::CreditCard.new(params[:credit_card])
  if @credit_card.valid?
    gateway = ActiveMerchant::Billing::BraintreeGateway.new(
      :login => API_LOGIN,
      :password => API_PASSWORD)
```

```
        response = gateway.purchase(@order.price, @credit_card,
          { :order_id => @order.reference_number })
        if response.success? && @order.complete(response)
          render(:action => 'receipt')
        else
          # report errors
          @order.errors.add_to_base(response.message)
          render(:action => 'payment')
        end
      else
        render(:action => 'payment')
      end
    end
```

This time, we set the @order instance variable by calling find with the order_id parameter, and we also create a @credit_card instance variable from the set of credit card form data available in our parameters. We then attempt to determine if the credit card is valid. ActiveMerchant employs fairly sophisticated checks to determine the validity of different cards. It performs these checks to ensure that the card is valid before we bother contacting the remote payment gateway to attempt the charge, which saves us time and makes the process less error prone.

If the credit card is not valid, errors will be set on the @credit_card object, just as with an ActiveRecord object, and we'll rerender the payment template. The error_messages_for helper will try to guide customers to correct their mistakes.

If the credit card is valid, we'll attempt to charge the order to it. We'll do this by first initializing a payment gateway variable to communicate with the remote payment service using the supplied API credentials. In this case, our gateway is an instance of BraintreeGateway. However, ActiveMerchant provides clean, easy-to-use wrappers around most popular payment gateways, so there is relatively little code to change if you would like to substitute some other payment gateway. For instance, if we wanted to use Authorize.Net in place of Braintree, we would replace the call to ActiveMerchant::Billing::BraintreeGateway.new with ActiveMerchant::Billing::AuthorizeNetGateway.new, making sure to pass it a :login and a :password that correspond to the appropriate Authorize.Net credentials. (For any other potential differences in gateway API methods, consult the documentation at http:// activemerchant.rubyforge.org.)

Next, we'll call the purchase method on the gateway, passing it the amount of the purchase and the credit card to charge. The purchase method creates an instant, one-time direct payment and communicates it to the gateway. This method takes two required parameters: the price to charge and the credit card to use in the transaction. An optional third parameter is a hash that includes additional information that you want to pass on to the payment gateway. In this case, we're sending it the order_id (the reference number) of the order identified by this transaction. This could be useful, for instance, if we wanted to search the charges in Braintree's administrative interface for this number. Other options that we may wish to pass might include the IP address of the purchaser or purchaser address information, which could then be checked with the Address Verification System (AVS) to help prevent fraud. See the documentation for the `ActiveMerchant::Gateway` base class for a full list of available options (`http://activemerchant.rubyforge.org/classes/ActiveMerchant/Billing/Gateway.html`).

■**Tip** ActiveMerchant also provides facilities to use an authorize/capture workflow as an alternative to instant, direct payment (with the `purchase` method). Using the `authorize` and `capture` methods allows you to place a customer's funds on hold but not actually capture them until a later time. This might be useful, for instance, if you were selling books or other items that occasionally go out of stock. You could authorize the customer credit card to purchase the book, but delay capture until the book became available and ready to ship.

The call to `purchase` returns an `ActiveMerchant::Billing::Response` object. We can query this object to determine whether the charge was successful by calling its `success?` method, and also use it to retrieve the authorization code for this transaction and any status messages that may have been set (which might indicate the reason that the response was unsuccessful). Assuming that `success?` returns true, we want to update our `@order` model to note that the customer has paid. By calling the `complete` method on `@order` and passing it the response returned by the gateway, we mark the order as paid and record the authorization code for the purchase. The `render` method is then called to render the receipt template for our customer. Save the code for the receipt template in Listing 10-11 as `app/views/orders/receipt.html.erb`.

Listing 10-11. *Receipt View (app/views/orders/receipt.html.erb)*

```
<h1>Thank You</h1>
<p>Your order is being processed, and your pizzas should be delivered within the
  next XX minutes.</p>
<p>The reference number for your order is <%= h(@order.reference_number) %>.
  Please call us at XXX-XXX-XXXX if you have any issues.</p>
```

If the response was unsuccessful for whatever reason, we need to handle it gracefully. For development/testing purposes, we'll simply add the message returned in the response to the errors on the `@order` object, so the problem can be communicated to the user in the view when the form is redisplayed.

Go ahead and click the Submit Payment button now. You should see a simple receipt, such as the one shown in Figure 10-3, which thanks you for your order and lists the reference number.

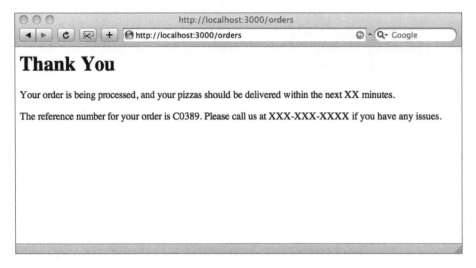

Figure 10-3. *Receipt for purchase (http://localhost:3000/orders/new)*

At this point, the order has been charged to the customer's credit card. Since we're in test mode and using the dummy credentials supplied by our gateway, no transaction has actually taken place (no charges were made against a credit card). However, if we had a live set of credentials with a payment gateway such as Braintree, we could update our credentials and view the result of the test transactions through its administrative interface.

■**Caution** In a production environment, where you're using real credit card numbers, you want to make sure that all credit card transactions occur over a secure connection, instead of over plain-text HTTP. The usual strategy is to obtain an SSL certificate signed by a trusted certificate authority (CA) and use that to conduct transactions over HTTPS. See your web server documentation for more information.

VIEWING PAYMENT GATEWAY TRANSACTION REPORTS

The default Braintree test account we've been using in our sample application (user: demo; password: password) does not have any sort of administrative interface login available to it. In order to see transactions in Braintree's administrative dashboard, sign up for an account at http://getbraintree.com.

When a new account is set up, all transactions will be automatically set to test mode. Go ahead and log in at the URL you received in your welcome e-mail and take a look at the payment processing dashboard and virtual terminal.

To see transactions in your account's administrative interface, just replace the dummy credentials used for the AM_GATEWAY_LOGIN and AM_GATEWAY_PASSWORD constants in your development environment (Listing 10-6) with the real credentials you've been assigned. Then create a new order in the system.

PART 4

■ ■ ■

Login/Security Plugins

Handling user logins and security is one of the most fundamental and important functions of modern web applications. Depending on your specific requirements, it can be a challenging (and time-consuming) task.

Fortunately, basic login systems and access controls are also things that can be generalized and made available as plugins. Using these plugins not only helps you ease your development burden, but also helps to alleviate potential security vulnerabilities, since you are using code that has been scrutinized by an entire community of developers.

Throughout the next three chapters, you'll see plugins that allow you to generate an entire user authentication system, integrate with OpenID, and add support for user roles and access levels within your application.

## CHAPTER 11

Extensible User Authentication

The Web is what it is because of its users. Without people uploading videos, discussing news and pop culture in forums, sharing photos, and gaming together, it just wouldn't be the same place. In order to make these features available and build a sense of community in our web applications, we need a way to attribute content created and shared by our users. This means that we need to provide users with the ability to create and maintain accounts.

User accounts are the cornerstone for personalization, community interaction, and content contribution. Many critical features of social applications—such as content ranking, filtering, media sharing, and profile creation—just aren't possible without the existence of users to attribute them to.

Having user accounts also means having some form of signup facility and an authentication system to verify user credentials so they can log in. Ideally, this system also provides some way to store and query the current (logged-in) user from other controllers and views as well, so the appropriate welcome messages, assets, and personalized screens can be shown to that user. If you're hoping to implement any role-based access controls, then user authentication is also necessary as the foundation for those (we cover authorization in Chapter 12).

Designing and deploying a robust user authentication system can take a bit of thinking and time commitment. Yet, at its core, it's a fairly generic item that's required for a variety of applications. This makes it a great candidate for code generation and reuse, and therefore, a great use of the Rails plugins system.

A variety of authentication plugins are available for Rails. In this chapter, we'll be taking a look at one of them in particular. The plugin we've chosen, RESTful Authentication, is one of the most widely used Rails plugins. It can generate a fully functional user model and authentication system in moments, and can also be extended to suit situations where more extensive customization is desired.

We'll also talk briefly about combating system spam and demonstrate how to implement a CAPTCHA device to verify that sign-ups are initiated by actual human beings.

Our Task: Create a User Wish List System

Everyone in our small development firm really likes using Amazon's wish list facility. We use it to create lists of books and other goods available through Amazon that we would like to receive as gifts. In fact, we use wish lists within our team to thank each other for going above and beyond the call of duty from time to time. If Ian finishes a project vastly ahead of schedule, or if Ty does a fantastic job on that new theme for the company blog, we buy him a little something from his list—it's always a nice morale booster.

One of our clients, visiting the office one afternoon, noticed this system and inquired about it. After we explained how our wish list rewards system works, she remarked that it was a good idea and that she would love to use something like that in her company, but she would rather not be limited to the selection of goods offered by Amazon. "What if people could just copy any old URL into some sort of wish list that they could then publish," she asked, citing examples such as T-shirts from Threadless or geeky office gadgets from ThinkGeek. We agreed that it was a good idea, and decided to build something like it for use in our office.

At its heart, a wish list system is pretty simple. It just needs to allow visitors to sign up for an account and create lists of links (possibly with annotations) associated with that account. In the past, it might have taken us a while to create a user system, but fortunately, Rick Olson's RESTful Authentication plugin (`http://svn.techno-weenie.net/projects/plugins/restful_authentication`) provides a generic user model and authentication controller, with a rich variety of options, right out of the box.

Since we plan on allowing anyone—internal or external to our organization—to create an account, we want some way to verify that the sign-ups are actually performed by human beings, rather than robots whose purpose is to spam our listings with advertisements. A popular way to combat these automated sign-up attempts is to implement a CAPTCHA (Completely Automated Public Turing Test to Tell Computers and Humans Apart) system. CAPTCHAs require users to verify that they are human beings by performing some trivial task that would be difficult for a computer, such as recognizing distorted text in an image. In Rails, we can accomplish this with minimal effort by taking advantage of Sur Max's Simple Captcha plugin (`http://expressica.com/simple_captcha`).

■**Note** CAPTCHAs are found in many applications that permit direct user input to create assets, most commonly blog comment/feedback forms. Our case isn't as obvious as most, but the thinking is that spambots could do something like sign up for numerous accounts, thus spamming the public wish list view, and add products to those wish lists that link to products they are trying to sell or links that they are trying to promote. For more information about the many types of CAPTCHA systems available, see `http://www.captcha.net`.

Using these two plugins, we'll develop a minimalist wish list service that suits our needs and allows arbitrary products to be listed by URL. Any number of users should be able to sign up; create their own lists; and share them with friends, family, and coworkers.

Generating an Authentication System

Let's create a new Rails application for the wish list project:

```
rails wishlist
cd wishlist
```

And then install the RESTful Authentication plugin by executing the following command inside the project directory:

```
ruby script/plugin install ➥
http://svn.techno-weenie.net/projects/plugins/restful_authentication/
```

We'll also install the Simple Captcha plugin at this time. Note that Simple Captcha relies on the RMagick gem in order to generate the images that are used for the Captcha, so we'll need to install that as well.

```
gem install rmagick
ruby script/plugin install ➥
svn://rubyforge.org/var/svn/expressica/plugins/simple_captcha
```

Note As mentioned in Chapter 3, RMagick relies on the ImageMagick package being installed on your system, and will not install properly without it. For more information about installing ImageMagick, see http://www.imagemagick.org/script/download.php.

ARE YOU GETTING ENOUGH REST?

REST stands for Representational State Transfer. If it is a new term for you, suffice to say that for our purposes, REST is a set of useful conventions, as well as a way to structure requests for creating and maintaining resources on the Web. These resources can be just about anything (airline reservations, blog articles, comic books, kittens that are up for adoption, and so on), but in our case, they're going to be users.

By stating that users are RESTful resources, we're implying that there are a number of standard well-known actions available for manipulating user objects at the controller level. These actions include the ability to create new users, show the details of a particular user, edit/update users, destroy users, and list (index) the entire collection of users.

The utility of REST is in its simple language, stressing conventions through a limited set of verbs that operate on a rich set of nouns. Standard URLs, coupled with HTTP's method vocabulary (GET, POST, PUT, and DELETE) are used to specify which operation should be performed, all without the overhead of SOAP, XML-RPC, or other more complicated web service protocols. For instance, the URL /users, coupled with the HTTP GET method, would map to an index action to retrieve the list of users in a system. The same URL, coupled with the POST action, would indicate that a new user should be created using data POSTed to the create action. These conventions give us a number of benefits, including easier to write applications that (to a certain extent) architect themselves at the resource level. No more time spent inventing new action names for routine tasks (although we can certainly add new terms if and when we need them).

The following table shows all the standard REST actions with the method they map to, as well as the routing helper path that can be used to reference them.

HTTP Method	URL	Controller Action	Routing Helper
GET	/users	index	users_path
POST	/users	create	users_path
GET	/users/new	new	new_user_path
GET	/users/1	show	user_path(1)
PUT	/users/1	update	user_path(1)
GET	/users/1/edit	edit	edit_user_path(1)
DELETE	/users/1	destroy	user_path(1)

REST also mandates the separation of resource data from its presentation. In Rails, if you develop your controllers (and their corresponding actions) in a RESTful manner, those resources can be retrieved in a variety of different ways. What a web browser sees is just a different representation (HTML) of the same information available as XML or JSON, for instance. This essentially gives you the ability to create both a web services API and a user-centric web site all at once, with a set of guidelines that lets you easily envision, construct, and maintain the controllers that represent the resources.

Should you build your Rails application in a RESTful way? Well, that's up to you. Your use of REST may vary from project to project or controller to controller; not all controllers need to wrap the notion of a resource (a search controller is a particularly good example of something that doesn't need to be RESTful). That said, REST is a powerful concept and one that is certainly becoming a best practice for building well-structured Rails applications. If you're building a new web application in Rails, we encourage you to read more about the topic and consider embracing it for your next application. See *Practical REST on Rails 2 Projects* by Ben Scofield (Apress, 2008) for more information.

Next, we'll use the code generator provided by the RESTful Authentication plugin to generate a boilerplate user model and authentication system for our wish list application. Running the generator produces the following assets:

- A standard User model that has all of the core features needed for basic operation: a login, e-mail address, encrypted password, and so on. In this case, we don't need extra user data, such as proper first and last names, street address, and so on, so we'll just go with what's provided.

- A UsersController, which manages user resources in our application, including the ability to see a new user sign-up form and create a user. These actions map to the standard REST actions new and create.

- A SessionsController, which is used to manage user sessions in our application. In this case, its new action maps to the login form, and the create action processes the login attempts. The destroy action is used to log a user out of the application. You'll rarely need to modify this resource, other than updating the views to match the design you've chosen. Figure 11-1 shows the default login page.

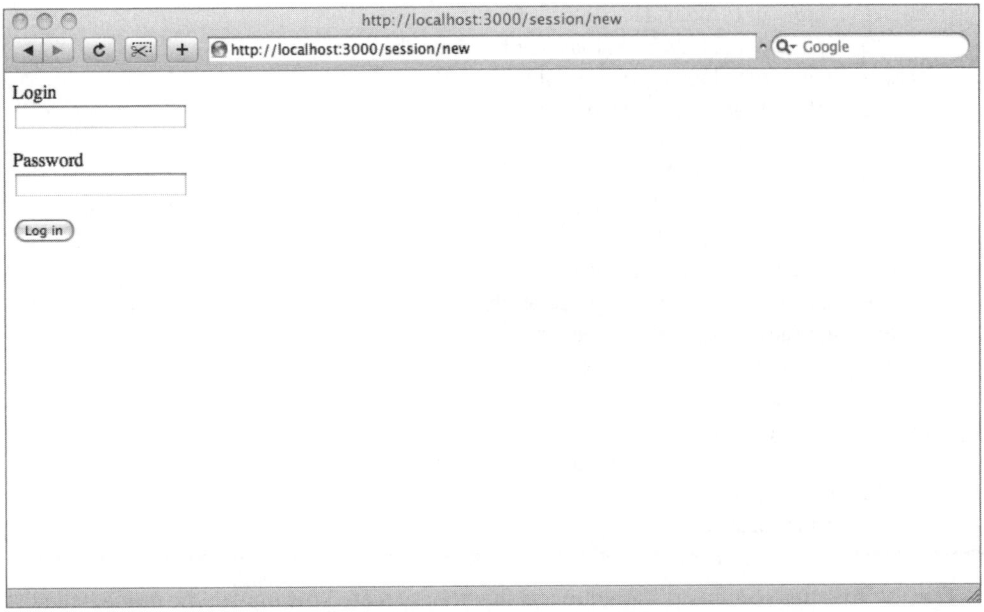

Figure 11-1. *Default login page view (http://localhost:3000/session/new)*

The fact that the models, controllers, and views are *generated* for us is a significant advantage. We can then extend them in any way we want, just as we would any other generated code, adding other features as necessary. If we need to add a publicly viewable list of all active users, for instance, we could implement the index action on the UsersController. If we want to build out user profiles, we might choose to add the show action and its template.

Let's run the generator now. The name of the user model we want to use (and thus the corresponding users controller) and the session management controller name should be specified as parameters:

```
ruby script/generate authenticated user sessions
```

```
...
    exists  app/models/
   exists  app/controllers/
   exists  app/controllers/
   exists  app/helpers/
   create  app/views/sessions
   exists  app/controllers/
   exists  app/helpers/
   create  app/views/users
   exists  test/functional/
   exists  test/functional/
   exists  test/unit/
```

```
create  app/models/user.rb
create  app/controllers/sessions_controller.rb
create  app/controllers/users_controller.rb
create  lib/authenticated_system.rb
create  lib/authenticated_test_helper.rb
create  test/functional/sessions_controller_test.rb
create  test/functional/users_controller_test.rb
create  test/unit/user_test.rb
create  test/fixtures/users.yml
create  app/helpers/sessions_helper.rb
create  app/helpers/users_helper.rb
create  app/views/sessions/new.html.erb
create  app/views/users/new.html.erb
create  db/migrate
create  db/migrate/001_create_users.rb
 route  map.resource :session
 route  map.resources :users
```

Output from this command should reveal that it has created the model, the model's database migration, and the two controllers we've already discussed, as well as boilerplate views for the controllers, helpers, and unit and functional tests. It even automatically adds the two required resource routes to our config/routes.rb file for us.

■**Note** RESTful Authentication, like most good generator-based plugins, also creates a full suite of unit and functional tests for you as it creates your user model and controllers. Since this code is created in your project directory just like any other code, you can run those new tests just like any other tests in your Rails project: by using the command rake test. As you modify your user model and/or controllers, make sure you edit the tests as appropriate and rerun them regularly.

The AuthenticatedSystem module that is created (in lib/authenticated_system.rb) is the heart of RESTful Authentication. It provides the concept of a logged-in (current) user by storing and retrieving a user identifier in the session. At any time, we can query whether the current user is logged in by calling the logged_in? method, and find the particular user model that corresponds to that user using the current_user method.

The AuthenticatedSystem module also provides logic to handle controller action login requirements and what to do if the requirements are not met. A login_required before filter for our controllers allows us to easily mandate access to resources by checking to see if users are logged in. If they are not, they will be redirected to a login form, and, after login, redirected back to the action they were requesting before. You'll see how this works in practice shortly.

These capabilities are afforded to controllers by mixing the `AuthenticatedSystem` module into them. If you open the files containing the `UsersController` and `SessionsController`, you'll see that they already include the module. However, because these are capabilities we want to allow any controller in our application to access, we'll want to mix `AuthenticatedSystem` into `ApplicationController` instead, as shown in Listing 11-1.

Listing 11-1. *ApplicationController Including AuthenticatedSystem (app/controllers/application.rb)*

```
class ApplicationController < ActionController::Base
  include AuthenticatedSystem
  ...snip!...
end
```

Since `ApplicationController` (`app/controllers/application.rb`) is the class from which all our application's controllers inherit, including `AuthenticatedSystem` in that class will make those methods available to every controller in our application. Once we've done this, we can also safely remove the `include` statement from the other controller classes.

Before continuing, we'll also want to run the supplied database migration for the `User` model. We can do this using the following Rake task:

```
rake db:migrate
```

```
== 1 CreateUsers: migrating ======================================================
-- create_table("users", {:force=>true})
   -> 0.0042s
== 1 CreateUsers: migrated (0.0044s) ==============================================
```

We also recommend adding convenience routes in your application's `config/routes.rb` for the sign-up, login, and logout URLs. The plugins `README` suggests the following:

```
map.signup '/signup', :controller => 'users', :action => 'new'
map.login '/login',   :controller => 'sessions', :action => 'new'
map.logout '/logout', :controller => 'sessions', :action => 'destroy'
```

These named routes not only simplify our public-facing URLs, but they also give us convenient named route shortcut paths that we can use in our controllers and views, such as `redirect_to signup_path`.

ADVANCED GENERATOR OPTIONS

Another nice thing the `authenticated` generator provides is the ability to add an activation step to the sign-up process, which sends an e-mail containing an activation code to the address the user enters. If this is enabled, users must click the link or manually enter the code before they are "activated" and allowed to log in. Adding activation with RESTful Authentication is as easy as passing the optional `--include-activation` parameter to the generator.

Activation is a common strategy to guarantee that users provide legitimate e-mail addresses. Additionally, if e-mail addresses are unique in your system, an activation mechanism can be used to make sure that a single human user is not signing up hundreds of times (since hundreds of legitimate e-mail addresses would be required). Activation is also used to make sure that the user is actually a human (rather than a spambot or something of that ilk). Since we'll be demonstrating the use of a CAPTCHA device to verify the humanness of the visitor, and are not that concerned with the validity of e-mail addresses, we will choose to skip over activation in this example.

Some users feel that activation is intrusive and dislike it. Whether you should require user activation depends on the purpose of your application and the temperament of potential users. In particular, casual users may be intolerant of having to wait to receive an e-mail message, especially if certain forms of spam prevention are present, delaying the delivery. On the other hand, for certain applications, this sort of legitimate e-mail verification is absolutely critical.

It's also possible to take this a step further by adding a more robust notion of state to the `User` model. This could be used, for example, to place users in states such as suspended and deleted. You can specify that the `User` model should be stateful by passing the `--stateful` parameter to the generator. More information about this option is available at `http://www.vaporbase.com/postings/stateful_authentication`. For more information about state machines in general, make sure to read Chapter 6.

Adding the User Wish List

Now that our `User` model and authentication system are set up, we'll want to add the concept of wish lists to the system so users can set up and maintain a set of wishes. This means adding a `Wish` model to our system, and then creating a many-to-one relationship between wishes and users; that is, a `User` will have many wishes. The list of all wishes for a particular `User` will be that user's wish list.

Building the Wish Model

The migration and model code for our `Wish` model are shown in Listings 11-2 and 11-3, respectively. Note that a `Wish` has a `user_id` attribute, which relates it to the appropriate `User` model. Other than that, the attributes are as you would expect: a `title` for the wish, a `url` to link to the subject of the wish, and any `notes` that the user wants to make about the wish (such as to specify the color or other variant characteristics, or just to explain why it's desired in the first place!).

Listing 11-2. *Database Migration to Add Wishes Table (db/migrate/002_create_wishes.rb)*

```ruby
class CreateWishes < ActiveRecord::Migration
  def self.up
    create_table :wishes do |t|
      t.integer :user_id
      t.string :title
      t.string :url
      t.string :notes
      t.timestamps
    end
  end

  def self.down
    drop_table :wishes
  end
end
```

Listing 11-3. *Wish Model (app/models/wish.rb)*

```ruby
class Wish < ActiveRecord::Base
  belongs_to :user
  validates_presence_of :title, :url, :user_id
end
```

The Wish model requires a title and a URL for each link, but notes are optional. The user_id is, of course, also a required field. Save these files and make sure to migrate the database in order to add the wishes table to the application:

```
rake db:migrate
```

```
== 2 CreateWishes: migrating ====================================================
-- create_table(:wishes)
   -> 0.0044s
== 2 CreateWishes: migrated (0.0045s) ===========================================
```

We have one last change to make to our models before moving on. We've already established that the Wish belongs_to a User, but we also need to set up the other side of the relationship. Modify the User model to specify the relationship, as shown in Listing 11-4.

Listing 11-4. *User Model with Wish Association (app/models/user.rb)*

```ruby
require 'digest/sha1'
class User < ActiveRecord::Base
  has_many :wishes
...snip!...
end
```

Adding the Wishes Controller

Next, we'll need to add a controller and a set of views in order to allow visitors to manage their wishes. Just like our concept of users, wishes also represent a REST resource in our system. However, we'll always want to scope the wishes that will be displayed to a particular user. This means that we'll be nesting the resources; our new WishesController will be nested within (and therefore scoped to) the UsersController (a user resource). This also needs to be reflected in our updated routes, which are shown in Listing 11-5. Save them as config/routes.rb.

Listing 11-5. *Updated Routes with Nested Wishes Resource (config/routes.rb)*

```
ActionController::Routing::Routes.draw do |map|
  map.resources :users, :has_many => :wishes
  map.resource :session

  map.root :controller => 'users', :action => 'index'
  map.signup '/signup', :controller => 'users', :action => 'new'
  map.login  '/login', :controller => 'sessions', :action => 'new'
  map.logout '/logout', :controller => 'sessions', :action => 'destroy'
end
```

■**Tip** The use of map.resources in our routes specifies a RESTful resource with all the standard action routes we mentioned previously. Note the difference between map.resources for users and map.resource for the session resource. The latter is a singular resource, meaning that there needs to be only one of them, rather than a collection. You can read more about this at http://api.rubyonrails.com/classes/ActionController/Resources.html.

Note that we've also added a root route, so that hitting the root of our application (/) will display the index action on the UsersController, which we'll configure to display a list of users who have wish lists. We'll implement this shortly.

With that in place, we can move on to the implementation of the controller itself. WishesController, as shown in Listing 11-6, features four of the standard REST actions: index, new, create, and delete. The show action is omitted because, with our implementation, we won't ever need to view the particulars of a single wish; we just want to see the list (index) of wishes belonging to a user (we could add show later if desired). The edit and update actions are omitted for brevity; you could add them yourself if desired. Save Listing 11-6 as app/controllers/wishes_controller.rb.

Listing 11-6. *WishesController (app/controller/wishes_controller.rb)*

```
class WishesController < ApplicationController
  before_filter :get_user
  before_filter :ownership_required, :only => [:new, :create, :destroy]

  def index
    @wishes = @user.wishes.find(:all, :order => "created_at")
  end

  def new
    @wish = @user.wishes.build
  end

  def create
    @wish = @user.wishes.build(params[:wish])

    if @wish.save
      flash[:notice] = "Your wish was successfully created."
      redirect_to(user_wishes_url(@user))
    else
      render(:action => "new")
    end
  end

  def destroy
    @wish = @user.wishes.find(params[:id])
    @wish.destroy
    flash[:notice] = "Your wish was removed from the list."
    redirect_to(user_wishes_url(@user))
  end

  protected

  def get_user
    @user = User.find(params[:user_id])
  end

  def ownership_required
    (logged_in? && @user == current_user) || access_denied
  end
end
```

This is a pretty standard CRUD (Create Read Update Delete) controller, with a few interesting characteristics. Notice the before filters specified at the top of the class definition. The first filter method, get_user, retrieves the user who is the author of this particular wish list.

Remember that the `wishes` resource is nested under `users`, for user-facing URLs like /users/
11/wishes. This means that a `user_id` is automatically made available in the parameters hash
for us to use. In the `get_user` method, we use that value to look up the owner of the wish list
(a `User` model) and set the `@user` instance variable. This filter is run before every action in the
controller is processed. It means that, for instance, when the `create` method is called, we can
call `@user.wishes.build` to instantiate a new wish that already has the `user_id` set to the
appropriate value by way of the association proxy. In `destroy`, we use a similar technique
to make sure that the specified wish actually belongs to that user in the first place.

The second filter method, `ownership_required`, is based on the stock `login_required`
method provided by RESTful Authentication. When the `login_required` method is used as
a filter, it mandates that the users must be logged in to the application in order to access
the protected methods. If they're not, it calls the `access_denied` method (found in `lib/
authenticated_system.rb`), which stores the location of the requested resource and redirects
users to a login page, so they can sign in with the proper credentials. Upon successful authentication, the saved address will be pulled out of the session, and the user will be returned to it.

■Note The `access_denied` method always returns false. This means that the `before_filter` that calls
it will also return false, which will halt the filter chain before the controller action is run. `access_denied`
also responds somewhat differently than described here when dealing with XML-based requests. Don't be
afraid to open `lib/authenticated_system.rb` to study the implementation of these techniques. They're
actually quite simple and elegant.

The `ownership_required` method works similarly; in addition to checking whether or not
the user is logged in, it also mandates that the current user must be the owner of this particular collection of wishes. It uses the `current_user` method, provided by `AuthenticatedSystem`,
to this end. If either of these conditions is false, the `access_denied` method is called, which
will redirect them to that same login prompt. This is an easy way to ensure that only the
owner of a wish list may create or destroy a wish list item (note that the filter applies only
to the `new`, `create`, and `destroy` actions).

Creating Wishes View Templates

This controller requires two view templates: one for the `index` action and one for the `new`
action. The `destroy` action and `create` action always result in redirects, so no templates are
required for those actions.

The `index` action template is shown in Listing 11-7. Its job is simply to display each wish
in a given user's wish list, given the `@wishes` instance variable set up in the corresponding controller action. Save it as `app/views/wishes/index.html.erb`.

Listing 11-7. *Wishes Index View Template (app/views/wishes/index.html.erb)*

```
<h1>Wishlist for <%= @user.login %></h1>
<ol>
  <% @wishes.each do |wish| -%>
    <li>
      <p><%= link_to(wish.title, wish.url) %></p>
      <p><%= h(wish.notes) %></p>
      <% if is_current_user?(wish.user) -%>
        <p><%= link_to('Delete', user_wish_url(@user, wish),
           :method => :delete, :confirm => 'Are you sure?') %></p>
      <% end -%>
    </li>
  <% end -%>
  <% if is_current_user?(@user) -%>
    <%= link_to('New Wish', new_user_wish_url(@user)) %>
  <% end -%>
</ol>
```

Note that this template calls the is_current_user? method in order to determine if the logged-in user is the same user whose wish list we are browsing. The first time we see this method, it's used to determine whether the Delete Wish link should be displayed. The second time, it's used to determine if the New Wish link should be displayed. (See Figure 11-2, a little later in this chapter, for an illustration of these links.)

Since this same routine is used more than once within the template, we've extracted it into a helper method. We'll place it in ApplicationHelper so it will be available throughout the application. Save the code in Listing 11-8 as app/helpers/application_helper.rb.

Listing 11-8. *ApplicationHelper With is_current_user? Method (app/helpers/application_helper.rb)*

```
module ApplicationHelper
  def is_current_user?(user)
    logged_in? && (current_user == user)
  end
end
```

Finally, the new action template is shown in Listing 11-9. Its job is just to provide the appropriate fields for creating a new wish and a form with which to submit them to the create action. Save it as app/views/wishes/new.html.erb.

Listing 11-9. *New Wish View Template (app/views/wishes/new.html.erb)*

```
<h1>New Wish</h1>
<% form_for(@wish, :url => user_wishes_url(@user)) do |form| -%>
  <p>Title:<br/><%= form.text_field(:title) %></p>
  <p>URL:<br/><%= form.text_field(:url) %></p>
  <p>Notes:<br/><%= form.text_field(:notes) %></p>
  <%= submit_tag('Save') %>
<% end -%>
```

Adding a List of Users and a Layout

Because we want to be able to navigate through the list of users at the top level of our application, we'll also add a method to the `UsersController` to allow visitors to browse the index of users (and thereby, their wish lists). Listing 11-10 shows the `index` action. Add it to the existing `UsersController` code supplied by RESTful Authentication.

Listing 11-10. *Index Action for UsersController (app/controllers/users_controller.rb)*

```
class UsersController < ApplicationController
  def index
    @users = User.find(:all)
  end

  ...snip!...
end
```

Again, this is a standard (RESTful) index action, which simply retrieves the list of all users for display. The corresponding view template is shown in Listing 11-11. It renders an unordered list with a link for each user in the system. The link will take a visitor to that user's wish list. Save it as `app/views/users/index.html.erb`. Make sure to remove the file in `public/index.html` so that Rails will process the controller action and render the template instead of displaying the static file.

Listing 11-11. *Users Index Action View Template (app/views/users/index.html.erb)*

```
<h1>User Wishlists</h1>
<ul>
  <% @users.each do |user| -%>
    <li><%= link_to(user.login, user_wishes_url(user)) %></li>
  <% end -%>
</ul>
```

Before viewing our work in a browser, let's also add a simple layout so that links to the login and registration pages will be available no matter where our user is in our application. Of course, if users are already logged in, they don't need to see these links. In that case, we'll add a customized welcome message, a logout link, and a link so they can easily navigate to their own wish list from any place in the system. Save the code in Listing 11-12 as app/views/layouts/application.html.erb, and it will automatically be used to wrap the output of each view template.

Listing 11-12. *Application Layout (/app/views/layouts/application.html.erb)*

```
<!DOCTYPE html PUBLIC "-//W3C//DTD XHTML 1.0 Transitional//EN"
        "http://www.w3.org/TR/xhtml1/DTD/xhtml1-transitional.dtd">

<html xmlns="http://www.w3.org/1999/xhtml" xml:lang="en" lang="en">
<head>
  <meta http-equiv="content-type" content="text/html;charset=UTF-8" />
  <title>Wishlist Service</title>
  <style type="text/css">
    .alert { color: blue; border: 1px solid blue; padding: 5px; }
  </style>
</head>
<body>

<% if logged_in? -%>
  Welcome <%= h(current_user.login) %> [<%= link_to('Logout', logout_url) %>] |
  <%= link_to('Your Wishlist', user_wishes_url(current_user)) %>
<% else -%>
  <%= link_to('Log In', login_url) %> |
  <%= link_to('Register', signup_url) %>
<% end -%>
 | <%= link_to('Main', '/') %>
<hr/>

<% if flash[:notice] || flash[:error] -%>
  <div class="alert"><%= flash[:notice] || flash[:error] %></div>
<% end -%>

<%= yield  %>

</body>
</html>
```

With this in place, you should be able to start the server using ruby script/server and visit http://localhost:3000 in a browser to view our work. The root URL would normally show a list of users who have wish lists in the system, but since we haven't yet created any wish lists, you'll see only the links provided in the layout. Click the Register link to create a new user and sign up. You should be automatically logged in and returned to the root URL. You can then follow the link to your own wish list and start adding items to it.

Figure 11-2 shows an example of a wish list display with a couple items in it. Note the presence of the delete and New Wish links, signifying that this is your wish list.

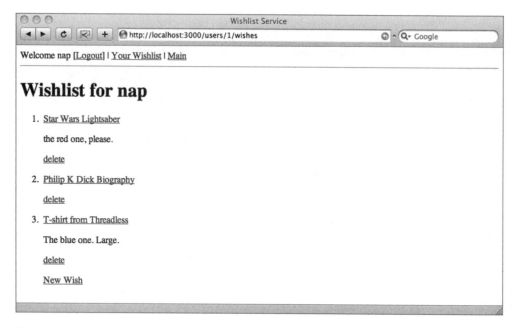

Figure 11-2. *Viewing a user wish list while logged in (http://localhost:3000/users/1/wishes)*

If you log out and view the same wish list, you'll see a display similar to Figure 11-3. Notice that the Delete and New Wish links are no longer present, and that the application invites you to log in or register a new account. In addition, if you try to visit a URL such as /users/1/wishes/new while not logged in (or while logged in as a user other than that user), you will be automatically redirected to the login screen.

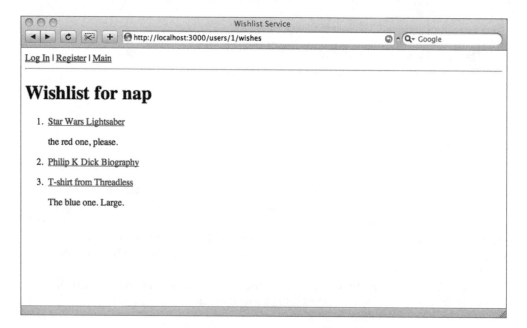

Figure 11-3. *Viewing a user wish list while not logged in (http://localhost:3000/users/1/wishes)*

PRETTY URLS

The URL /users/1/wishes is certainly functional but not exactly pretty. To make it more human-read-able—and search-engine–friendly in the process (!)—you can override the to_param method on the User model. The following implementation will result in URLs like /users/1-myusername/wishes.

```
def to_param
  "#{id}-#{login}"
end
```

You could optionally leave the id out of the parameter representation altogether, in order to use URLs like /users/myusername/wishes. However, this would mean that all calls to User.find within the controllers would need to be replaced with User.find_by_login. The benefit to leaving the id in the representation is that any characters following the id will be truncated automatically and not used in the call to find, thus allowing you to use the default find routine without any changes.

Implementing CAPTCHA

Spambots and other automated sign-up systems can pose various threats to a public service that allows sign-ups like this one. Their purpose is usually to sign up as many times as possible and post advertisements or spam, for marketing and search-engine proliferation purposes. This is not only annoying to users, but can also sometimes overrun a system so badly that it is rendered unusable.

Various techniques are available to combat these nasties. A popular approach is to implement a CAPTCHA system. We've installed the Simple Captcha plugin to make this as painless as possible. Using it, we'll add a visual CAPTCHA device to our new user registration form. In order to create an account, a user will need to identify some distorted text within an image.

The plugin provides a Rake setup task to get things started. Running the following task will create a migration and install a partial template for the CAPTCHA view that we'll need to display:

```
rake simple_captcha:setup
```

Make sure to run the migration before moving on. It will generate the database table necessary to hold CAPTCHA data:

```
rake db:migrate
```

```
== 3 CreateSimpleCaptchaData: migrating =========================================
-- create_table(:simple_captcha_data)
   -> 0.0390s
== 3 CreateSimpleCaptchaData: migrated (0.0392s) ===============================
```

Next, we need to make a small change to our routes file, adding a route specific for Simple Captcha. This route will point to the simple_captcha controller made available through the plugin, whose purpose is to generate the CAPTCHA image (with a little help from RMagick). Add the following line to `config/routes.rb` to add the route now:

```
map.simple_captcha '/simple_captcha/:action', :controller => 'simple_captcha'
```

Since we're using the CAPTCHA as part of the new `User` model validation process, we can use model hooks supplied by the plugin to add two new instance methods on the `User` model: `valid_with_captcha?` and `save_with_captcha`. These are simply variants of the standard Active Record `valid?` and `save` instance methods that also check that CAPTCHA data has been specified and matches a generated image (this information is stored in the database table we created earlier).

To add CAPTCHA validation capabilities to our model, we need to make two small changes to `app/models/user.rb`. The changes are highlighted (in bold) in Listing 11-13.

Listing 11-13. *Updated User Model with CAPTCHA (app/models/user.rb)*

```
require 'digest/sha1'
class User < ActiveRecord::Base
  apply_simple_captcha
  has_many :wishes

  ...snip!...

  # prevents a user from submitting a crafted form that bypasses activation
  # anything else you want your user to change should be added here.
  attr_accessible :login, :email, :password, :password_confirmation,
    :captcha, :captcha_key

  ...snip!...
end
```

The first change is to add the `apply_simple_captcha` method call to the model class. This mixes in new functionality that provides the additional validation and save options we want. The second change is to add the `captcha` and `captcha_key` virtual attributes mixed in by the first step to the list of attributes that can be mass assigned using `attr_accessible`. This is necessary because these attributes will be passed in as parameters from our form during the registration process and should be eligible for mass assignment (for your safety, the `User` model protects any attributes not listed here from mass assignment).

■**Note** The Simple Captcha plugin doesn't have to be used directly in conjunction with a model as we've shown here. However, this is a convenient approach considering that, at the moment, we want to use it only during the sign-up process and validate the CAPTCHA response like any other required field attribute. Alternatively, if you wish to use the controller-level `simple_captcha_valid?` method, make sure to mix the `SimpleCaptcha::ControllerHelpers` module into your controller. See the official home page at `http://expressica.com/simple_captcha` for more information about this as well as other options.

Next, we turn our attention to the UsersController, where one small change is required. We simply need to change the @user.save call to @user.save_with_captcha in order to take advantage of our new model validation capabilities. See the updated code in Listing 11-14.

Listing 11-14. *Updated UsersController with CAPTCHA (app/controllers/users_controller.rb)*

```
class UsersController < ApplicationController
  ...snip!...

  def create
    cookies.delete :auth_token
    @user = User.new(params[:user])
    @user.save_with_captcha
    if @user.errors.empty?
      self.current_user = @user
      redirect_back_or_default('/')
      flash[:notice] = "Thanks for signing up!"
    else
      render :action => 'new'
    end
  end
end
```

Finally, we need to add the CAPTCHA display to our new user registration view template. The show_simple_captcha method added to Action View takes care of rendering the image (by retrieving it from the simple_captcha controller that we added a route for earlier) and entry box for us, and makes sure that they are named appropriately. Listing 11-15 demonstrates the most basic form of this. Save it as app/views/users/new.html.erb.

Listing 11-15. *Updated User Registration Template with CAPTCHA (app/views/users/new.html.erb)*

```
<%= error_messages_for :user %>
<% form_for :user, :url => users_path do |f| -%>
<p><label for="login">Login</label><br/>
<%= f.text_field :login %></p>

<p><label for="email">Email</label><br/>
<%= f.text_field :email %></p>

<p><label for="password">Password</label><br/>
<%= f.password_field :password %></p>
```

```
<p><label for="password_confirmation">Confirm Password</label><br/>
<%= f.password_field :password_confirmation %></p>

<p><%= show_simple_captcha(:object => "user", :image_style => "random") %></p>

<p><%= submit_tag 'Sign up' %></p>
<% end -%>
```

The show_simple_captcha method can also take a variety of options that affect the contents of the CAPTCHA code itself (alphabetic versus numeric), the level of distortion in the displayed text, and the overall style of the image (we've used a random image style in this example, which will showcase the variety of styles that are available). For more information about these options, see http://expressica.com/simple_captcha.

You can view the result of our work by visiting the updated new user registration form at http://localhost:3000/users/new. Attempting to register without specifying the CAPTCHA code or with an incorrect code will generate an error, as shown in Figure 11-4.

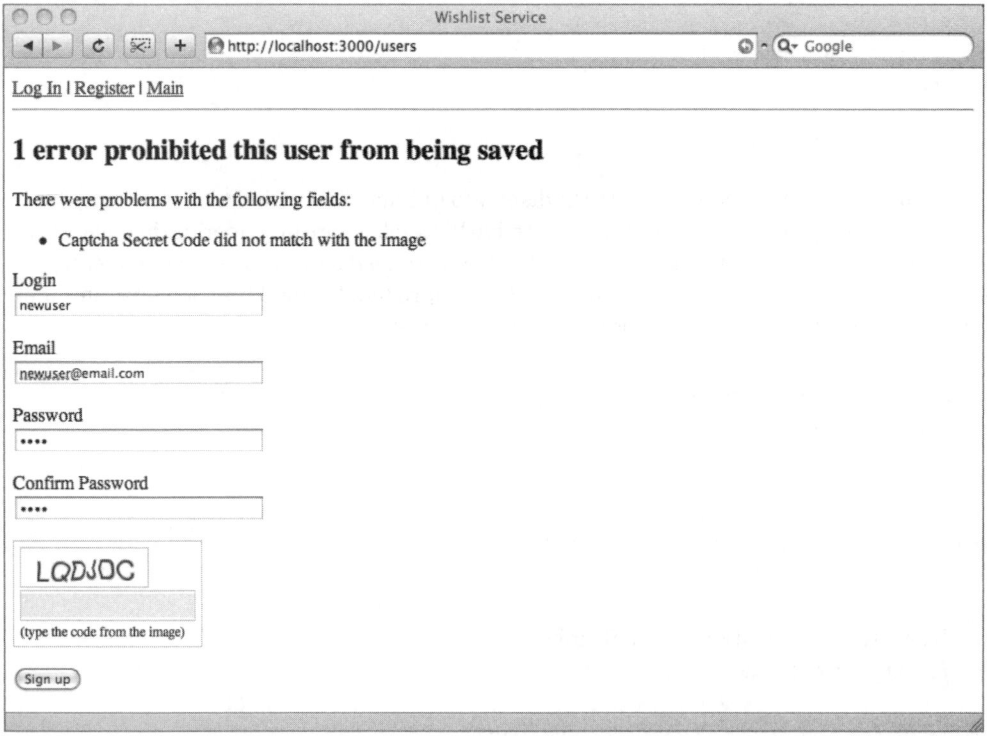

Figure 11-4. *Wish list new user registration form with CAPTCHA (http://localhost:3000/users/new)*

The user will be allowed to sign up only after entering a CAPTCHA code that matches the distorted text shown in the image, thus foiling a large number of spambots or other automated processes trying to create an account with our wish list system.

Summary

The RESTful Authentication plugin provides an easily modified general-purpose authentication system for Rails that lets you bootstrap a basic user model and login facilities in mere moments. In this chapter, we used these facilities in conjunction with custom controller filters and helper methods to create a user wish list system with basic access controls.

We also demonstrated how to add a visual CAPTCHA device to the new user registration form using the Simple Captcha plugin. This is intended to prevent automated sign-ups. Although far from infallible, CAPTCHA systems can significantly cut down on the annoying spam and advertisements created by spambots and other automated processes. Whether you choose to use a CAPTCHA, activation e-mail (as provided by RESTful Authentication), or some other technique, we encourage you to be cognizant of the potential abuses that can accompany all the good things that come with user-generated content. CAPTCHA is no substitute for diligence, but it can be a powerful aid.

For more information about RESTful Authentication, see the README file at http:// svn.techno-weenie.net/projects/plugins/restful_authentication/README. To learn more about the features and options of Simple Captcha, visit http://expressica.com/ simple_captcha.

◼◼◼

## CHAPTER 12

Supporting OpenID Authentication

If you're like most netizens, you have dozens of different user accounts with dozens of different web sites, service providers, and applications. It can be frustrating to keep track of this many different accounts and remember which username/password combination you used where. Even if you try to use the same username and password everywhere, you may find that your username of choice has already been taken on one site, or that another site has different security standards for passwords that prevent you from using your usual credentials (not to mention that using the same password across sites is a dangerous idea to begin with!). If you're as tired of this as we are, OpenID may be the solution you're looking for.

So what, exactly, is OpenID? It's an open, decentralized protocol that provides single sign-on and portable identity profiles to any web applications that choose to support it. This means that users of OpenID have a single set of credentials that allows them to log in to any OpenID-enabled site, resulting in fewer passwords to remember and better management tools for their digital identity.

Sites that support OpenID authentication prompt users to enter an identifier—an OpenID URL—in place of a traditional username and password. You authenticate to the site essentially by proving that you own the URL in question.

Consider Anna, a user who wants to log in to an online photo-sharing site using her OpenID. Anna enters her identity URL, `anna.example-id-provider.com`, and submits the form on the photo site. The photo site, an OpenID *consumer*, retrieves the document at `http://anna.example-id-provider.com` and uses that document's contents to determine the OpenID *provider* that it needs to authenticate against to verify Anna's identity. The consumer site then establishes a shared secret with the provider, and redirects Anna's browser to the provider, where she authenticates with the single username and password she has (some other means of authentication, such as a client certificate, is also possible). Once this is done, the provider redirects her browser back to the photo site with an appropriate OpenID response ("successful"). The photo site verifies the response with the established secret and logs her in.

◼**Note** Our example represents a common scenario, simplified to make OpenID easy to understand. For full details, we encourage you to investigate the OpenID 2.0 specification, available online at `http://openid.net/specs/openid-authentication-2_0.html`.

Although it may seem somewhat complicated at first glance, from a user experience point of view, OpenID's workflow isn't much more difficult than using a traditional username and password. And the ability to have only one set of universal credentials for many sites that you visit is an enormous boon for those who are frustrated with the fractured state of their digital identities. OpenIDs also have the benefit of being globally unique, allowing users to have a portable identity among sites. This means they carry a single user identifier and its associated reputation (and optional profile data) with them anywhere they go.

Of course, OpenID is useful only if web developers enable an OpenID login option in their sites. Fortunately, this practice seems to be gaining in popularity, and many well-known web sites and applications have embraced it. LiveJournal, Jyte, DZone, Zooomr, and Ma.gnolia are just a few of the thousands of sites that support the protocol, and many more can be found in the directory at `http://openiddirectory.com`. Although this recent uptake is encouraging, OpenID adoption still has a long way to go before reaching ubiquity.

The good news is that you can help by OpenID-enabling your own applications! It's easier than you might think. In this chapter, we'll demonstrate how to add your web site or application to the list of OpenID proponents, by integrating a new OpenID authentication option into an existing login system. As you may have suspected, there are Rails plugins that can help us with this.

Since our goal is to add support to an existing authentication system, we'll use the OpenID Authentication plugin for Rails, developed by framework founder David Heinemeier Hansson (`http://svn.rubyonrails.org/rails/plugins/open_id_authentication/README`). It's a relatively simple plugin that provides a Rails-specific wrapper around JanRain's Ruby OpenID library. Other users who don't already have a preexisting user model and authentication system may want to consider EastMedia's RESTful Open ID Authentication plugin (available at `http://identity.eastmedia.com`) as an alternative.

Our Task: OpenID-Enable Our Wish List Application

The wish list application we built in Chapter 11 has been a hit with our friends and coworkers. Everyone in our office is using it, and some friends at other local companies have started spreading it throughout their workplaces as well. It's a simple application, but a useful one, and we would like to make it even more useful before the holiday shopping season begins.

To this end, we've solicited feedback from current users. Most of the feedback is what we would expect: people want a richer user interface, the ability to see what the most popular gifts are, and so on. However, a surprisingly large number of people don't want to use the application at all, simply because it requires them to create yet another user account and have yet another set of credentials. This is further complicated if we choose to implement some of the more advanced features people have asked for, such as building user and gift-giving profiles. This would mean that users would need to reenter even more profile data that they've already entered elsewhere. Wouldn't it be nice if they could establish a single identity and profile that could be used to log in to many different sites, including ours?

Fortunately, OpenID delivers the ability to do something about this right now. Since a growing number of Internet users already have OpenID accounts, using it allows us to lower the barrier to entry a bit. Additionally, through the (optional) Simple Registration extension (SREG) that we'll use, we can sync our local version of a profile with the version that users choose to make available through their OpenID provider. We've run this thought past a few people, and everyone seems to agree that it's a good idea. Thankfully, it's not difficult to do with the OpenID Authentication Plugin for Rails.

Setting Up for OpenID

Before we update our wish list application to integrate OpenID, we need to install the plugin and a couple of libraries, and run a database migration. Also, if you don't have an OpenID account already, you'll want to obtain one before we continue, in order to test our work.

Installing the Plugin and Libraries

To install the OpenID Authentication plugin, execute the following command inside your Rails project:

```
ruby script/plugin install ➥
http://svn.rubyonrails.org/rails/plugins/open_id_authentication
```

As mentioned, the plugin is basically a thin veneer around JanRain's OpenID 2.0 library, so you'll need to install it before you can proceed. You can do this using the Ruby gems system with the following command:

```
gem install ruby-openid
```

Since the OpenID Authentication plugin stores the necessary authentication associations and nonces used by OpenID in the database, we'll need to create the appropriate tables before we can use it. This task is neatly wrapped up in a Rake target provided by the plugin, so all you need to do is execute the following command within your Rails project:

```
rake open_id_authentication:db:create
```

This creates a new migration, which can be run using the rake db:migrate command. But before we do that, we need to make one small change to it: we want to add an openid_url column to our users table. We'll use this new column to store the OpenID identity URL for our users, which will allow them to log in without a username and password through an OpenID provider. Update the code in the generated migration to look like Listing 12-1. The modified lines are shown in bold.

Listing 12-1. *OpenID Auth Migration (db/migrate/004_add_open_id_authentication_tables.rb)*

```
class AddOpenIdAuthenticationTables < ActiveRecord::Migration
  def self.up
    create_table "open_id_authentication_associations", :force => true do |t|
      t.integer :issued, :lifetime
      t.string :handle, :assoc_type
      t.binary :server_url, :secret
    end
```

```
    create_table "open_id_authentication_nonces", :force => true do |t|
      t.integer :timestamp, :null => false
      t.string :server_url, :null => true
      t.string :salt, :null => false
    end

    add_column :users, :openid_url, :string
  end

  def self.down
    remove_column :users, :openid_url
    drop_table "open_id_authentication_associations"
    drop_table "open_id_authentication_nonces"
  end
end
```

Once the changes have been made, run the migration:

```
rake db:migrate
```

```
== 4 AddOpenIdAuthenticationTables: migrating ===================================
-- create_table(:open_id_authentication_associations, {:force=>true})
   -> 0.0044s
-- create_table(:open_id_authentication_nonces, {:force=>true})
   -> 0.0040s
-- add_column(:users, :openid_url, :string)
   -> 0.0108s
== 4 AddOpenIdAuthenticationTables: migrated (0.0197s) =========================
```

Obtaining an OpenID Account

You can obtain a free OpenID account from many OpenID providers. Any OpenID account can be used with any OpenID-enabled consumer application, so your choice of a provider really comes down to the security features offered, the profile management capabilities and extensions supported, and whose name you trust. If you don't trust anyone, you can always run your own provider, too.

■**Tip** It's actually quite likely that you already have an OpenID account and don't even know it! If you have a LiveJournal account, for example, the URL of your LiveJournal doubles as an OpenID you can use to iden-tify yourself. AOL Instant Messenger (AIM), WordPress.com, and Wikitravel also provide OpenIDs to registered users in the same manner.

If you don't already have an account, getting set up with one is extremely easy. We recommend using JanRain's MyOpenID service. You can get started by visiting `http://www.myopenid.com/signup`. During the sign-up process, you'll need to enter a username, a password, and an e-mail address. MyOpenID will provide you with an OpenID, which will be in the form `username.myopenid.com`. The service will also send you an activation e-mail with a link you'll need to click in order to verify your e-mail address and activate the account. Once you've done this, you'll be able to log in.

Make sure to create a persona with the service before continuing. We'll be using the profile registration data to allow users to register with our wish list service without filling out any additional site-specific information. In order for users to sign up, their OpenID provider must be configured to provide a minimum of a user nickname (a login) and an e-mail address.

To establish a MyOpenID persona, click Account Settings and select Registration Personas (if you already have an account, you may wish to use the Add a Persona option). You should see a form similar to the one in Figure 12-1.

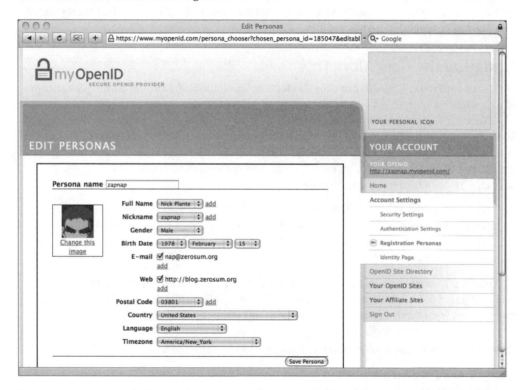

Figure 12-1. *Creating an OpenID persona with MyOpenID (http://www.myopenid.com/signup)*

MyOpenID allows you to maintain many different personas, which are really just an easy way to manage Simple Registration and Attribute Exchange data (extensions to the core OpenID implementation). When you sign in to a consumer site using OpenID, MyOpenID will ask you to choose a persona that you would like to expose. Depending on the site, you may wish to expose a persona that contains only minimal information, or you may choose a persona that contains full profile details. It's up to you.

Note More information about Simple Registration can be found at `http://openid.net/specs/`
`openid-simple-registration-extension-1_0.html`.

At this point, you can now use your OpenID to log in to any of the numerous web applications that support it. Try Jyte (`http://jyte.com`) or DZone (`http://www.dzone.com`) to get started. Next, we'll start work on enabling our own application for OpenID authentication.

Updating Our Application for OpenID

We'll need to make a number of small changes to our wish list application in order to allow users to sign up and log in with OpenIDs. Changes will be required to our `User` model and our `SessionsController`, as well as the view templates for login and registration. Our routes will also need to be amended ever so slightly.

Updating the User Model

We'll start with the changes to our `User` model. They are minimal. Nothing about our concept of a user has really changed—we're just giving our users an extra way to authenticate.

Since we've already added a new attribute, `openid_url`, to the `User` model (by running our latest database migration), we just need to let the model know that it's legitimate to sign on without a password when using an OpenID URL. This change is trivial, as our `User` model already has conditional validation that mandates use of a password only if the `password_required?` method returns true.

```
validates_presence_of      :password,                    :if => :password_required?
validates_presence_of      :password_confirmation,       :if => :password_required?
validates_length_of        :password, :within => 4..40,  :if => :password_required?
validates_confirmation_of  :password,                    :if => :password_required?
```

We simply need to update the logic that the `password_required?` method uses to determine if a password is required. We'll modify the method to look like the code in Listing 12-2 and add a new method, `has_openid?`, to make things more modular and easier to read.

Listing 12-2. *Changes to the User Model to Support OpenID (app/models/user.rb)*

```
def password_required?
    !has_openid? && (crypted_password.blank? || !password.blank?)
end

def has_openid?
  !openid_url.blank?
end
```

Clearly, we want to allow a User model with a missing password only if OpenID is handling the user authentication for that particular user. Otherwise, we want to enforce the original constraints for users logging in with username/password credentials. Save these changes to the User model in app/models/user.rb before moving on.

Updating the Sessions Controller

The single largest change required to OpenID-enable our application will be in the controller that handles user sessions. As you may recall, SessionsController handles the login and logout functions, so we'll be extending it to deal with OpenID authentication as well.

Before we can do that though, we'll need to make a small change to our routes so that the OpenID login process can proceed (the reason for this will be made clear shortly). The necessary modifications are shown in Listing 12-3. Just add the bolded line and save the updated file as config/routes.rb.

Listing 12-3. *Routes Modifications for OpenID Authentication (config/routes.rb)*

```
ActionController::Routing::Routes.draw do |map|
  map.resources :users, :has_many => :wishes

  map.open_id_complete '/session', :controller => 'sessions', :action => ➥
'create', :method => :get
  map.resource :session

  map.root :controller => 'users', :action => 'index'
  map.signup '/signup', :controller => 'users', :action => 'new'
  map.login  '/login', :controller => 'sessions', :action => 'new'
  map.logout '/logout', :controller => 'sessions', :action => 'destroy'

  map.simple_captcha '/simple_captcha/:action', :controller => 'simple_captcha'
end
```

The code shown in Listing 12-4 is a modified version of the OpenID plugin sample code (found in the plugin README file), for integration with our existing User model and the RESTful Authentication system. Change your SessionsController so it looks like the updated code.

Listing 12-4. *OpenID-Friendly Sessions Controller (app/controllers/sessions_controller.rb)*

```
class SessionsController < ApplicationController
  OPEN_ID_REQUIRED = [:nickname, :email]
  OPEN_ID_OPTIONAL = [] # [:fullname]

  # render new.rhtml
  def new
  end
```

```ruby
  def create
    if using_open_id?
      open_id_authentication(params[:openid_url])
    else
      password_authentication(params[:login], params[:password])
    end
  end

  def destroy
    self.current_user.forget_me if logged_in?
    cookies.delete :auth_token
    reset_session
    flash[:notice] = "You have been logged out."
    redirect_back_or_default('/')
  end

  protected

    def password_authentication(login, password)
      if self.current_user = User.authenticate(login, password)
        successful_login
      else
        failed_login("Incorrect username or password")
      end
    end

    def open_id_authentication(openid_url)
      authenticate_with_open_id(openid_url,
          :required => OPEN_ID_REQUIRED,
          :optional => OPEN_ID_OPTIONAL.empty? ?
            nil : OPEN_ID_OPTIONAL) do |result, openid_url, registration|
        if result.successful?
          # look up the user by their openid_url attribute
          # if not found, create a new account
          if openid_user = User.find_or_create_by_openid_url(openid_url)
            # use OpenID profile information to obtain required fields
            assign_registration_attributes!(openid_user, registration)
            if openid_user.save
              # if successful, log the user in
              self.current_user = openid_user
              successful_login
            else
              failed_login("Profile registration failed: " +
                openid_user.errors.full_messages.to_sentence)
            end
```

```
        else
          failed_login("Sorry, no user with that OpenID URL exists in our system")
        end
      else
        failed_login(result.message)
      end
    end
  end

  # map OpenID sreg fields to the fields in our user model
  def assign_registration_attributes!(openid_user, registration)
    model_to_registration_mapping.each do |model_attr, registration_attr|
      unless registration[registration_attr].blank?
        openid_user.send("#{model_attr}=", registration[registration_attr])
      end
    end
  end

  def model_to_registration_mapping
    { :login => 'nickname', :email => 'email' }
  end

  private

  def successful_login
    flash[:message] = "Logged in successfully"
    redirect_to(root_url)
  end

  def failed_login(message)
    flash[:error] = message
    redirect_to(new_session_url)
  end
end
```

The new and destroy methods have not changed at all from their previous incarnation. The form is still displayed as before, and sessions are still terminated in the same way (users are logged out and their login information is removed from the session). We'll focus on the implementation of the create method in the following analysis.

Examining the create Method

As you can see, create handles two different cases: password authentication and OpenID authentication. If we determine that the user has asked to perform OpenID-based authentication (using_open_id? checks for the presence of the appropriately named form element in our parameters), we'll call the open_id_authentication method. Otherwise, we'll call the password_authentication method, which is just a refactored version of the same facility that RESTful Authentication generated for us back in Chapter 11.

If we're dealing with OpenID authentication, authenticate_with_open_id is invoked. We pass it a request parameter that holds the user's identity URL and also set some options to tell it that we want registration profile (SREG) data returned. We *require* that the user's nickname and e-mail address be provided, and we can also specify optional information, if we want to create a more robust profile. A block is passed in as well; within that block, we handle the result of the authentication call that is made. It's important to observe that the create method will actually be called *twice* during the OpenID authentication process, and the block here will behave differently depending on which phase of the process we're in.

Authenticating with OpenID (Plugin Internals)

To understand what's really happening here, let's take a look at the plugin code itself, in vendor/plugins/open_id_authentication/lib/open_id_authentication.rb.

```
def authenticate_with_open_id(identity_url = params[:openid_url], options = {}, ➡
&block) #:doc:
  if params[:open_id_complete].nil?
    begin_open_id_authentication(normalize_url(identity_url), options, &block)
  else
    complete_open_id_authentication(&block)
  end
end
```

When a user initially attempts to log in with his OpenID, the authenticate_with_open_id method first makes a call to the begin_open_id_authentication method defined by the plugin, as follows:

```
def begin_open_id_authentication(identity_url, fields = {})
  return_to = options.delete(:return_to)
  open_id_request = open_id_consumer.begin(identity_url)
  add_simple_registration_fields(open_id_request, options)
  redirect_to(open_id_redirect_url(open_id_request, return_to))
rescue OpenID::OpenIDError, Timeout::Error => e
  logger.error("[OPENID] #{e}")
  yield Result[:missing], identity_url, nil
end
```

This method is a wrapper around the JanRain library's OpenID::Consumer.begin method, which starts the authentication process by contacting the OpenID provider and obtaining an object that allows us to construct a redirect URL to the server. We use this information to build the authentication request and redirect the user to a login screen at the OpenID provider.

■**Note** For more details about the OpenID::Consumer module and the rest of JanRain's excellent OpenID library, see the documentation at http://openidenabled.com/files/ruby-openid/repos/generated/doc.

Once users complete the login process with the provider, select their persona, and authorize the wish list application's access to that information, the provider returns them to our site, for the second pass through the create action. This time, the open_id_complete request parameter is set to indicate the progress. Therefore, the complete_open_id_ authentication method is invoked. This method wraps the OpenID::Consumer.complete method, and will verify and complete the login process using authentication information provided by the OpenID provider (see the OpenID specification for more information). A status code will be returned that represents the outcome. Simple Registration extension data is also made available to us at this point.

```
def complete_open_id_authentication
  params_with_path = params.reject { |key, value| request.path_parameters[key] }
  params_with_path.delete(:format)
  open_id_response = timeout_protection_from_identity_server {
    open_id_consumer.complete(params_with_path, requested_url) }
  identity_url = normalize_url(
    open_id_response.endpoint.claimed_id) if open_id_response.endpoint.claimed_id

  case open_id_response.status
  when OpenID::Consumer::SUCCESS
    yield Result[:successful], identity_url,
      OpenID::SReg::Response.from_success_response(open_id_response)
  when OpenID::Consumer::CANCEL
    yield Result[:canceled], identity_url, nil
  when OpenID::Consumer::FAILURE
    yield Result[:failed], identity_url, nil
  when OpenID::Consumer::SETUP_NEEDED
    yield Result[:setup_needed], open_id_response.setup_url, nil
  end
end
```

The twofold nature of the create action described here, coupled with the fact that the *complete* portion of the authentication process is retrieved using a GET request (rather than a POST) was what necessitated our earlier routing rule update in Listing 12-3. Usually, a RESTful request to the /session URL, a singular resource in our application, would be handled by the show action. However, in this case, we needed to override this so the request is handled by the create action instead.

Processing the User Login

Back in our controller code (Listing 12-4), we continue by checking to see if the response from the plugin authentication operation was successful (indicating that the two-stage authentication process is complete). If it was, we'll attempt to look up the user account with an OpenID URL that matches the one that we just authenticated. The find_or_create_by_openid_url method will return the matching User record, or create one if it's not found.

```
if result.successful?
  # look up the user by their openid_url attribute
  # if not found, create a new account
  if openid_user = User.find_or_create_by_openid_url(openid_url)
    # use OpenID profile information to obtain required fields
    assign_registration_attributes!(openid_user, registration)
    if openid_user.save
      # if successful, log the user in
      self.current_user = openid_user
      successful_login
  else
    failed_login("Profile registration failed: " +
      openid_user.errors.full_messages.to_sentence)
  end
```

Either way, the next step will be to retrieve the registration persona data that we requested and update our current user. The `assign_registration_attributes!` method, from the plugin sample code, handles the mapping of Simple Registration data to our local `User` model naming conventions. It simply iterates through the list of mapped attributes and calls the appropriately named attribute setter method for each.

Note that we assign the registration attributes each time users log in via OpenID, regardless of whether or not it is their first time visiting the site. This allows us to automatically update profile data from the OpenID provider every time a user logs in—an easy way to add value and make sure that user profile details are in sync.

```
# map OpenID sreg fields to the fields in our user model
def assign_registration_attributes!(openid_user, registration)
  model_to_registration_mapping.each do |model_attr, registration_attr|
    unless registration[registration_attr].blank?
      openid_user.send("#{model_attr}=", registration[registration_attr])
    end
  end
end

def model_to_registration_mapping
  { :login => 'nickname', :email => 'email' }
end
```

After the profile fields have been mapped, we attempt to save the record. If all the validations we set up previously on the `User` model pass and the record is saved, we log in the user by setting `current_user` (a convention introduced by RESTful Authentication). We then call the `successful_login` method. If validation fails because we're lacking crucial information, or the authentication operation fails for any other reason, we call the `failed_login` method instead. These methods simply set a notice or error message in the flash and redirect to an appropriate URL—either the application root or the login page.

Adding OpenID Login Views

In order to complete the OpenID integration, we need to add text fields to both our login and registration views. The updated login form is shown in Listing 12-5. Save it as app/views/sessions/new.html.erb.

Listing 12-5. *User Login Form for OpenID (app/views/sessions/new.html.erb)*

```
<% form_tag session_path do -%>
  <p><label for="login">Login</label><br/>
  <%= text_field_tag("login") %></p>

  <p><label for="password">Password</label><br/>
  <%= password_field_tag("password") %></p>

  <p>Alternatively, you can use OpenID to login:</p>

  <p><label for="openid_url">OpenID</label><br/>
  <%= text_field_tag("openid_url") %></p>

  <p><%= submit_tag("Log in") %></p>
<% end -%>
```

All we've done here is to add an extra text field that allows the user to enter an OpenID URL. This, along with our username and password fields, is submitted to the create action of SessionsController. As you saw in the controller code analysis, if an OpenID URL value is present, OpenID authentication is attempted in place of standard password-based authentication.

The updated registration form is shown in Listing 12-6 and should be saved as app/views/users/new.html.erb. Note that we've added an entirely different form to handle OpenID registration this time, instead of just adding an extra text field element to the existing form, as with the login form.

Listing 12-6. *User Registration Form for OpenID (app/views/users/new.html.erb)*

```
<%= error_messages_for(:user) %>
<% form_for(:user, :url => users_path) do |f| -%>
  <p><label for="login">Login</label><br/>
  <%= f.text_field(:login) %></p>

  <p><label for="email">Email</label><br/>
  <%= f.text_field(:email) %></p>

  <p><label for="password">Password</label><br/>
  <%= f.password_field(:password) %></p>
```

```
  <p><label for="password_confirmation">Confirm Password</label><br/>
  <%= f.password_field(:password_confirmation) %></p>


  <p><%= show_simple_captcha(:object => "user", :image_style => "random") %></p>


  <p><%= submit_tag('Sign up') %></p>
<% end -%>


<% form_tag(session_path) do -%>
  <p>Or use OpenID!</p>


  <p><label for="openid_url">OpenID</label><br/>
  <%= text_field_tag("openid_url") %></p>


  <p><%= submit_tag('Sign up with OpenID') %></p>
<% end -%>
```

Unlike the standard user registration form, the OpenID-enabled form doesn't submit any data to the UsersController at all. It submits the OpenID URL to the same place that the login form does: the create action of SessionsController. Since we're using find_or_create_by_ openid_url in the create action handler, both the OpenID login and registration tasks are the same from our application's point of view.

Although we can easily imagine sites where the registration process requires extra steps, this strategy works nicely for a large number of simple web applications and services. And it's not difficult to amend it for more complicated scenarios. However, if you wish to require extra information to associate with a user account at sign-up time, you may want to separate these processes.

Logging In with OpenID

With the final changes in place, we can now point a web browser at http://localhost:3000/ login to see our brand-new OpenID-enabled login form, as shown in Figure 12-2.

Enter your OpenID identity URL in the text field and click Log In. You should be redirected to your OpenID provider's web presence. In the case of MyOpenID, you'll be shown a page that asks you to authenticate with a username and password. After entering that information, you'll be asked to verify that you want to authenticate to the wish list site and given the choice of which persona to send. This should look similar to Figure 12-3 (but with your own persona data, of course).

■Tip It's possible to use your own blog or web site address (such as blog.zerosum.org) as an identity URL, and still use a third-party provider like MyOpenID to handle OpenID authentication. This has the dual benefit of being a familiar, memorable identity and allowing you to switch OpenID providers without changing your identity URL! This feature is called *OpenID delegation*, and configuring it is as simple as adding a couple lines of HTML to your web site. To learn how to set this up, see http://wiki.openid.net/ Delegation.

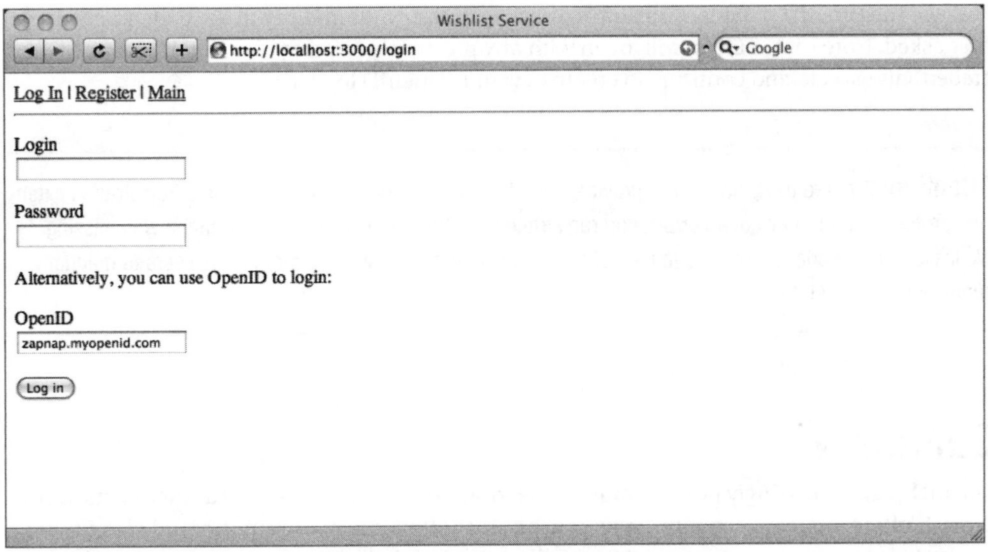

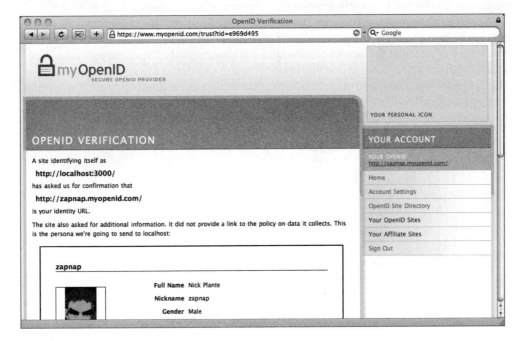

Figure 12-2. *OpenID-enabled login form (http://localhost:3000/login)*

Figure 12-3. *MyOpenID persona selection and verification*

You can select whether you want to allow authentication with this persona once or allow it forever. Clicking Allow Once will redirect you back to the root of the wish list site, where you'll find that you are now automatically logged in to your new account. If you choose Allow

Forever, the OpenID provider will automatically confirm your identity to the consumer whenever asked. Note that you can still log in with any previously existing username/password credentials as well (and continue to create new non-OpenID logins, too).

■**Caution** If you're using an OpenID provider that does not support the optional Simple Registration extension profile data you may get an error upon registration because some required information was missing. We leave it as a reader exercise to implement a modification to this scheme that allows users to manually supply the required information.

Summary

OpenID is an increasingly popular alternative to standard login/password authentication systems. It offers numerous benefits to your users, including single sign-on, simplified login credential management, portable data profiles, and a globally unique ID that carries with it an implicit reputation. Furthermore, unlike other web-based identity protocols, OpenID is open, distributed, and owned by no one. Anyone can implement his own provider.

As we've shown, integrating OpenID with an existing Ruby on Rails application can be a fairly simple task, thanks to the power of Rails plugins and the Ruby OpenID gem. You can find more information about the Open ID Authentication plugin at `http://svn.rubyonrails.org/rails/plugins/open_id_authentication/README`. We also recommend `http://openid.net`, `http://spreadopenid.org`, and `http://dataportability.org` as excellent resources for learning more about OpenID and a gateway to interest in other open identity and data portability efforts such as Attention Profiling Markup Language (APML), OAuth, and microformats.

■ ■ ■

Enforcing Privilege Separation with an Authorization DSL

For some systems, all users are roughly equivalent—everyone accesses the system in the same way. In other cases, completely different types of users must share the same system. In those cases, you need some way to differentiate the user types.

For example, suppose you ran an online message board service, with different forums and subforums. Some members may be moderators, who have the authority to moderate a given subforum, while others may be supermoderators, who can moderate all forums and even create new forums. Other members may have no special privileges, and they can only post new messages; some may even be temporarily put on probation, so that they can't post new messages for a certain number of days. In this example, you have a sort of pyramid structure of authority: the very top has the most authority and the fewest users, and there are more users with less authority as you move down.

On the other hand, rather than a complex hierarchy of user types, many systems simply require a certain number of administrative users and a bunch of "regular" users.

The Rails Authorization plugin, created by Lawrence Pit, allows you to easily control which features of your application can be used by each individual user. You can use this plugin for complex levels of authority, as well as simple administrator/user situations. In this chapter, we'll examine how to use the Rails Authorization plugin in a simple example.

Our Task: Create a Job Interview Framework with Access Controls

Let's suppose we are creating a job interview system. A number of job applicants need to schedule interviews, so we want to create a system that allows them to choose from available time slots. Since some job interviews will almost certainly be scheduled (and rescheduled) over the phone or as a result of applicants handing in forms in person, we also need to set up a system to allow interviewers to manually set appointments.

The interviewers need to be able to update and delete appointments, whereas the interviewees should not have those functions available. To distinguish the users and give them the appropriate access, we'll use the RESTful Authentication plugin and the Rails Authorization plugin.

Preparing for the Authorization Example

First, let's create a new Rails application for our interview scheduler:

```
rails interview_scheduler
cd interview_scheduler
```

Now we need to install the RESTful Authentication plugin (discussed in Chapter 11) and Rails Authorization plugin:

```
ruby script/plugin install \
git://github.com/technoweenie/restful-authentication.git
ruby script/plugin install \
git://github.com/DocSavage/rails-authorization-plugin.git
```

■**Note** Support for installing plugins from Git in this way was not added to Rails until version 2.1. If you are using an older Rails version, you can install older versions of the plugins using their Subversion URLs: `http://svn.techno-weenie.net/projects/plugins/restful_authentication/` and `http://rails-authorization-plugin.googlecode.com/svn/trunk/authorization`. Alternatively, if you have Git installed, you can clone the Git URLs for these plugins to `vendor/plugins` and run their `init/install.rb` scripts manually.

Building the Interview Scheduler Application

To begin, we need to generate a model for our user, a controller for our login sessions, and a model for our roles. Do so with the following commands:

```
ruby script/generate authenticated user sessions
ruby script/generate role_model Role
```

These generators are available thanks to the RESTful Authentication and Rails Authorization plugins, respectively.

Next, let's create a `timeslots` migration. This table will be used to hold the various interview times that applicants can choose from, the position they are applying for, and the associated interviewer and interviewee IDs. Listing 13-1 shows this migration.

Listing 13-1. *Create Timeslot Migration (db/migrate/003_create_timeslots.rb)*

```
class CreateTimeslots < ActiveRecord::Migration
  def self.up
    create_table :timeslots do |t|
      t.datetime :interview_at
      t.string :position
      t.string :time
```

```
      t.integer :interviewer_id
      t.integer :interviewee_id
      t.timestamps
    end
  end

  def self.down
    drop_table :timeslots
  end
end
```

Then run the migration:

```
rake db:migrate
```

Next, create the `Timeslot` model, as shown in Listing 13-2.

Listing 13-2. *Timeslot Model (app/models/timeslot.rb)*

```
class Timeslot < ActiveRecord::Base
  belongs_to :interviewer, :class_name=>'User',
             :foreign_key=>'interviewer_id'
  belongs_to :interviewee, :class_name=>'User',
             :foreign_key=>'interviewee_id'
end
```

The first `belongs_to` call in this model creates a relationship called `interviewer`, which is a relationship with the model `User`, and it has a foreign key of `interviewer_id`. The second `belongs_to` call is similar, but it's called `interviewee` and references the `interviewee_id` field.

The next step is to open the `User` model that we generated earlier and add our authorization and association methods. Listing 13-3 shows the additions to this model highlighted in bold.

Listing 13-3. *User Model (app/models/user.rb)*

```
require 'digest/sha1'
class User < ActiveRecord::Base
  acts_as_authorized_user
  acts_as_authorizable

  has_many :interviewer_timeslots, :class_name=>'Timeslot',
                                   :foreign_key=>:interviewer_id
  has_many :interviewee_timeslots, :class_name=>'Timeslot',
                                   :foreign_key=>:interviewee_id

...snip...
```

The rest of the model is created by the RESTful Authentication plugin, which is discussed in Chapter 11.

Defining Roles

As you may have noticed, our application has two kinds of users: interviewers and interviewees. We will define these as roles and use them to permit different levels of access to our
application. Let's use the Rails console to create those roles, and then create some test users
and time slots to try them out. From the root of our application, run `ruby script/console`,
and enter the following commands:

```
interviewer_role = Role.create(:name=>'interviewer')
interviewee_role = Role.create(:name=>'interviewee')

steve = User.create!(:name=>'Steven Boisvert',
                     :role=>interviewee_role,
                     :login=>'steve', :password=>'test123',
                     :password_confirmation=>'test123',
                     :email=>'test@example.com')

steve.has_role('interviewer')
steve.has_role?('interviewer')
steve.has_role?('interviewee')

mr_iggles = User.create!(:name=>'M R Iggles', :role=>interviewer_role,
                         :login=>'mriggles', :password=>'test123',
                         :password_confirmation=>'test123',
                         :email=>'mr_iggles@example.com')

mr_iggles.has_role('interviewee')

gg_tamborine = User.create!(:name=>'G G Tamborine',
                            :role=>interviewer_role,
                            :login=>'ggtambo', :password=>'test123',
                            :password_confirmation=>'test123',
                            :email=>'gg_tamborine@example.com')

require 'time'

cur_time = Time.parse('8:00am')
10.times do
  t = Timeslot.create(:interview_at=>cur_time,
                      :position=> 'Jr Salesperson')
  cur_time = cur_time + 15.minutes
end
```

```
cur_time = Time.parse('3:00pm')
10.times do
  t = Timeslot.create!(:interview_at=>cur_time,
                        :position=> 'Sr Salesperson')
  cur_time = cur_time + 15.minutes
end

cur_time = Time.parse('8:00am') + 1.day
30.times do
  t = Timeslot.create!(:interview_at=>cur_time,
                        :position=> 'Jr Henchman')
  cur_time = cur_time + 15.minutes
end
```

Creating the Controller and Views

Now that we have models and a database with some sample data, let's create a controller to let
our visitors manipulate that data. Exit the Rails console and create the timeslots controller, as
shown in Listing 13-4.

Listing 13-4. *Timeslots Controller (app/controllers/timeslots_controller.rb)*

```
class TimeslotsController < ApplicationController
  include AuthenticatedSystem
  before_filter :login_required

  # GET /timeslots
  # GET /timeslots.xml
  def index
    conditions = nil
    unless current_user.has_role?('interviewer')
      conditions = ['interviewee_id IS NULL OR interviewee_id = ?',
                  current_user.id]
    end

    @timeslots = Timeslot.find(:all,
                               :conditions=>conditions,
                               :order=>'interview_at asc, position')

    respond_to do |format|
      format.html # index.html.erb
      format.xml  { render :xml => @timeslots }
    end   end
```

```ruby
# GET /timeslots/new
# GET /timeslots/new.xml
def new
  permit 'interviewer' do
    @timeslot = Timeslot.new

    respond_to do |format|
      format.html # new.html.erb
      format.xml  { render :xml => @timeslot }
    end
  end
end

# GET /timeslots/1/edit
def edit
  permit 'interviewer' do
    @timeslot = Timeslot.find(params[:id])
  end
end

# POST /timeslots/1/schedule
def schedule
  permit 'interviewee' do
    @timeslot = Timeslot.find(params[:id])
    @timeslot.interviewee = current_user

    respond_to do |format|
      if @timeslot.save
        flash[:notice] = 'Interview was successfully scheduled!'
        format.html { redirect_to(timeslots_path) }
        format.xml  { render :xml => @timeslot, :status => :created,
                             :location => @timeslot }
      else
        format.html { render :action => "new" }
        format.xml  { render :xml => @timeslot.errors,
                             :status => :unprocessable_entity }
      end
    end
  end
end

# POST /timeslots
# POST /timeslots.xml
def create
  permit 'interviewer' do
    @timeslot = Timeslot.new(params[:timeslot])
```

```ruby
      respond_to do |format|
        if @timeslot.save
          flash[:notice] = 'Timeslot was successfully created.'
          format.html { redirect_to(timeslots_path) }
          format.xml  { render :xml => @timeslot, :status => :created,
                                :location => @timeslot }
        else
          format.html { render :action => "new" }
          format.xml  { render :xml => @timeslot.errors,
                                :status => :unprocessable_entity }
        end
      end
    end
  end
end

# PUT /timeslots/1
# PUT /timeslots/1.xml
def update
  permit 'interviewer' do
    @timeslot = Timeslot.find(params[:id])

    respond_to do |format|
      if @timeslot.update_attributes(params[:timeslot])
        flash[:notice] = 'Timeslot was successfully updated.'
        format.html { redirect_to(timeslots_path) }
        format.xml  { head :ok }
      else
        format.html { render :action => "edit" }
        format.xml  { render :xml => @timeslot.errors,
                              :status => :unprocessable_entity }
      end
    end
  end
end

# DELETE /timeslots/1
# DELETE /timeslots/1.xml
def destroy
  permit 'interviewer' do
    @timeslot = Timeslot.find(params[:id])
    @timeslot.destroy
```

```
    respond_to do |format|
      format.html { redirect_to(timeslots_path) }
      format.xml  { head :ok }
    end
  end
 end
end
```

Each action, other than the `index` action, has a `permit` block. If the user doesn't match the given role, he won't be allowed to perform the action and will be redirected back to the last authorized action. The `create`, `update`, `edit`, and `delete` actions can be accessed only by interviewers, and they allow the interviewers to update time slots.

Tip In this example, we're assuming there are a relatively small number of interviewers, and that they can each be trusted to edit all of the data at will. In a larger system, you would likely want to add a third role, `administrator`, which can edit all records, and then restrict regular interviewers so that they can edit only time slots assigned to them. All of this is possible with the Rails Authorization plugin. See `http://code.google.com/p/rails-authorization-plugin` for details.

Note that `permit` blocks aren't the only way to control access. You can also use a `permit?` predicate, which returns true if the user is authorized; otherwise, it returns false. Unlike the `permit` block, this predicate does not do any redirection, so you can use `permit?` to create fine-grained control. For example, you could use it to limit which fields can be updated on an action. If you wanted even more fine-grained control, you could have role-based control based on particular models or even particular instances of a model. See the Rails Authorization home page (`http://code.google.com/p/rails-authorization-plugin/`) for details.

In the `index` action, we're using the `has_role?` method to check for the `interviewer` role, and if it is not present, we limit the time slots to only those assigned to the `interviewee` role, or to no one.

The `schedule` action is the only action that interviewees can take, and it assigns that time slot to the user. This prevents the interviewee from taking any more time slots, and also prevents any other interviewee from taking that time slot as well. (If you're interested, you can try modifying the example so that each interviewee can take multiple interview time slots, but only one per position.)

Next, let's take a look at the `index` view for the timeslots controller, as shown in Listing 13-5.

Listing 13-5. *Timeslots Controller Index View (app/views/timeslots/index.html.erb)*

```
<style>
.scheduled_interview { background-color: #ffffde; }
  tr td, tr th { padding: 0.5em; }
</style>
```

```
<h1>Available Interview Timeslots</h1>
<%= link_to 'Logout', { :controller=>:session }, { :method=>:delete} %>

<% if current_user.has_role?('interviewer') %>
  <%= link_to 'New timeslot', new_timeslot_path %>
<% end %>

<table cellspacing="0" cellpadding="0">
  <% last_day = nil; last_position = nil %>
  <% @timeslots.each do |timeslot| %>
    <% scheduled =  current_user.interviewee_timeslots.include?(timeslot) %>
    <tr<%= ' class="scheduled_interview"' if scheduled %>>

      <% if last_day != timeslot.interview_at.strftime("%D") %>
        <% last_day = timeslot.interview_at.strftime("%D") %>
        <th><%= last_day %></th>
      <% else %>
        <td></td>
      <% end %>

      <% if last_position != timeslot.position %>
        <% last_position = timeslot.position %>
        <th><%= last_position %></th>
      <% else %>
        <td></td>
      <%end%>

      <td></td>
      <th><%=timeslot.interview_at.strftime('%I:%M%P')%></th>

      <% if current_user.has_role?('interviewer')%>
        <td>
          <%= timeslot.interviewer.name if timeslot.interviewer %>
          <%= timeslot.interviewee.name if timeslot.interviewee %>
        </td>
        <td><%= link_to 'Edit', edit_timeslot_path(timeslot) %></td>
        <td><%= link_to 'Delete',
                        timeslot,
                        :confirm => 'Are you sure?',
                        :method => :delete %></td>
      <% end %>
```

```
    <% if current_user.has_role?('interviewee') %>
      <% if current_user.interviewee_timeslots.length==0 %>
        <td><%= link_to 'Choose This Time',
                        schedule_timeslot_path(timeslot),
                        :method=> :post %></td>
    <% end %>
    <% if scheduled %>
        <td>You're scheduled for an interview at this time;
            please show up promptly at our location at
            33 New Wikitia Avenue, New Wikitia.
            Black tie optional.</td>
    <% end %>
      <% end %>
    </tr>
  <% end %>
</table>
```

Although it has a lot of branching paths, most of what's done in our view is pretty straight-forward. It prints each row, but it prints each date and position only once, which makes the page easier to read.

It then varies the output a bit. It uses the has_role? method of user to see if each user is an interviewee or an interviewer. (Note that each user can have multiple roles, although this ability isn't used in this particular application.) If the user is an interviewer, the name of the interviewer and interviewee, if any, are displayed for each time slot. If the user is an interviewee and has not already chosen a time slot, a link to select a given time is displayed. Once the interviewee has selected a time slot, a "You're scheduled for an interview . . ." message is displayed.

The form for editing a time slot is fairly standard, as shown in Listing 13-6.

Listing 13-6. *Edit Time Slot View (app/views/timeslots/edit.html.erb)*

```
<h1>Editing timeslot</h1>

<%= error_messages_for :timeslot %>

<% form_for(@timeslot) do |f| %>
  <p>
    Interview at:
    <%=f.datetime_select 'interview_at'%>
  </p>
  <p>
    Interviewee:
    <%= f.select 'interviewee_id',
                 User.find(:all).map{ |u| [u.name, u.id] },
                 :include_blank=>true %>
  </p>
```

```
<p>
  Interviewer:
  <%= f.select 'interviewer_id',
                User.find(:all).map{ |u| [u.name, u.id] },
                :include_blank=>true  %>
</p>

<p>
  <%= f.submit "Update" %>
</p>
<% end %>

<%= link_to 'Back', timeslots_path %>
```

Note that we use the include_blank option, so that users can select "no interviewee" or "no interviewer" if desired. (The new time slot form is nearly identical; its code is available with the rest of the downloadable code for this book.)

Next, let's take a look at the new session (login) form, as shown in Listing 13-7.

Listing 13-7. *New Session View (app/views/sessions/new.html.erb)*

```
<h1>Access to this site requires an account</h1>
<%=button_to 'New Account', new_user_url%></p>

<% form_tag session_path do -%>
<p><label for="login">Login</label><br/>
<%= text_field_tag 'login' %></p>

<p><label for="password">Password</label><br/>
<%= password_field_tag 'password' %></p>

<p><%= submit_tag 'Log in' %> </p>
<% end -%>
```

This has been changed slightly from the original form created by the RESTful Authentication plugin. In particular, we added a new header and a button that allows users to create a new account.

■**Tip** If you don't want users to be able to create a new account, you can remove the New Account button. Then you should also either remove the new and create actions from the users controller or add the desired role(s), and wrap those actions in permit blocks similar to the ones we've already used.

The users controller is shown in Listing 13-8.

Listing 13-8. *Users Controller (app/controllers/users_controller.rb)*

```ruby
class UsersController < ApplicationController
  include AuthenticatedSystem


  # render new.rhtml
  def new
  end

  def create
    cookies.delete :auth_token
    @user = User.new(params[:user])
    @user.save
    @user.has_role('interviewee')
    if @user.errors.empty?
      self.current_user = @user
      redirect_back_or_default('/')
      flash[:notice] = "Thanks for signing up!"
    else
      render :action => 'new'
    end
  end
end
```

This is very similar to the stock controller generated by the RESTful Authentication plugin. The big change is the bolded line, which assigns the role of interviewee to all new sign-ups.

Next, let's take a look at our routes. Listing 13-9 shows the route configuration file.

Listing 13-9. *Route Configuration (config/routes.rb)*

```ruby
ActionController::Routing::Routes.draw do |map|
  map.resources :timeslots, :member=>{:schedule=>:post}
  map.root :controller=>'timeslots', :action=>'index'

  map.resources :users
  map.resource :session

  # Install the default routes as the lowest priority.
  map.connect ':controller/:action/:id'
  map.connect ':controller/:action/:id.:format'
end
```

Notice that we've specified the root URL of our application to be the index action of the timeslots controller. The rest of the routes are the normal RESTful Authentication plugin and default Rails entries.

Finally, let's take a look at our layout for the timeslots controller, as shown in Listing 13-10.

Listing 13-10. *Timeslots Layout (app/views/layouts/timeslots.html.erb)*

```
<!DOCTYPE html PUBLIC "-//W3C//DTD XHTML 1.0 Transitional//EN"
      "http://www.w3.org/TR/xhtml1/DTD/xhtml1-transitional.dtd">

<html xmlns="http://www.w3.org/1999/xhtml" xml:lang="en" lang="en">
<head>
  <meta http-equiv="content-type" content="text/html;charset=UTF-8" />
  <title>Available Audition Timeslots</title>
  <%= stylesheet_link_tag 'scaffold' %>
</head>
<body>

<% if flash[:notice]%>
    <p style="color: green"><%= flash[:notice] %></p>
<%end%>

<%= yield  %>

</body>
</html>
```

This is a reasonably straightforward layout. Note that, unlike the scaffold layout this was originally built from, we display the flash notice only if it is present.

Running the Application

Run the application using `ruby script/server`. After deleting `public/index.html`, you should be able to view the application by browsing to `http://localhost:3000/`. You will see a page like the one shown in Figure 13-1.

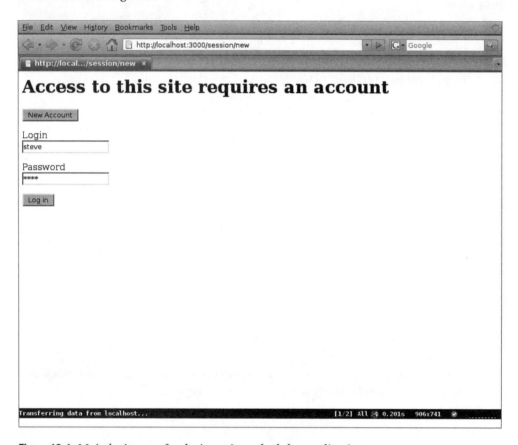

Figure 13-1. *Main login page for the interview scheduler application*

Using the test username `mriggles` and password `test123`, you can log in as an interviewee. Choose a time slot at random, and you should see a page like the one shown in Figure 13-2.

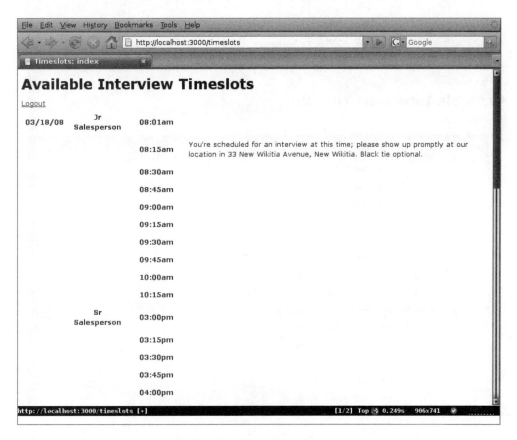

Figure 13-2. *The interviewee page after choosing a time slot*

If you log out and log in again as an interviewer—using username `steve` and password `test123`, you will see the page with Edit and Delete links, as shown in Figure 13-3.

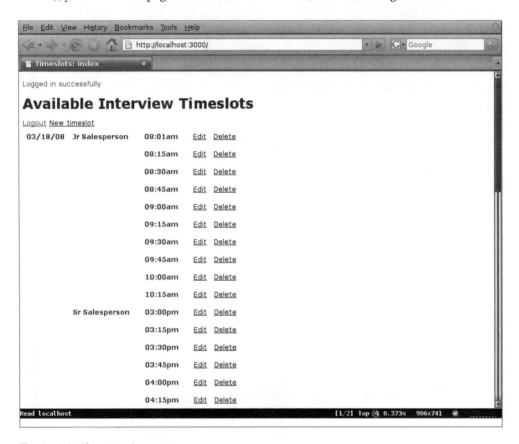

Figure 13-3. *The interviewer page*

Finally, if you try to visit one of the administrative URLs while logged in as `mriggles`, you should see a page like the one shown in Figure 13-4.

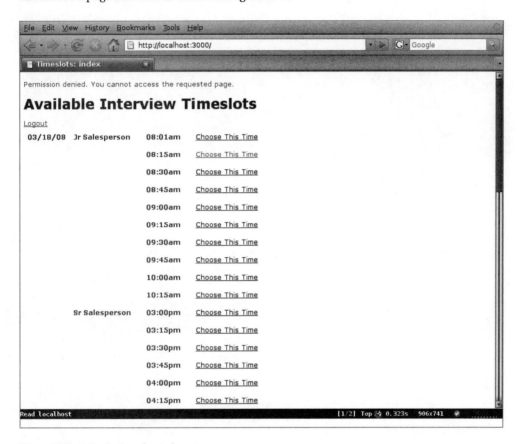

Figure 13-4. *Permission denied message*

Summary

Authentication is just one part of the puzzle; it tells you that users are who they say they are, but it doesn't help you to control which users can use which features of your application. Authorization is the puzzle piece that allows you to control access. The Rails Authorization plugin lets you carefully and easily control which features of your application can be used by each individual user, ranging from entire actions to individual pieces of the view.

PART 5

■ ■ ■

Search and Query Plugins

Many web sites and applications are really just warehouses of certain types of information, especially (but not exclusively) those that deal with user-generated content. Consider product-review sites, movie-rental services, and recipe-sharing applications, for example. When enough data is present in any one of these systems, how we browse and search for relevant data become very important.

Many plugins are available to enhance how we find and access data within our Rails applications. Included in this category are plugins that help us search for specific textual information in database records, plugins that help us find information that is spatially relevant to us, and even plugins that perform the most basic of functions like pagination of results. We'll cover each of these topics in the next three chapters.

CHAPTER 14

■■■

Mapping and Geocoding with the YM4R and GeoKit Plugins

Geocoding is the process of assigning geographic identifiers to different types of location-sensitive data. Although at first this may sound extremely specialized, in practice, it has many useful applications.

Combined with JavaScript mapping APIs like Google Maps and Yahoo Maps Building Blocks, geocoding can be used to place a street address on a map, pinpoint the exact physical location where a picture was taken, or locate the origin point of a visitor's IP address and zoom in to show a satellite view of homes for sale in her neighborhood. These techniques are used in a lot of other interesting ways as well, particularly in web mashups. Flickr, for example, in conjunction with the Yahoo Maps API (`http://flickr.com/map`), lets you search with keywords like "Great Wall China" and see a map marked with various thumbnails, which you can click to see different sections of the Great Wall. Twittervision (`http://www.twittervision.com`), a popular mashup site, merges the Twitter microblogging service with Google Maps, updating in real time to show where the latest user updates are coming from on a world map.

A common version of geocoding works by querying third-party web services that map known street addresses, ZIP codes, or other named places to a geographic coordinate space. In the case of street addresses, different segments of the street are assigned to different spaces, so 111 East Broadway maps to a different location than, say, 1206 East Broadway. A number of public geocoding services exist that do just this sort of thing, free of charge (at least for low-volume usage). For example, Geocoder.us (`http://geocoder.us`) allows you to find the latitude and longitude of any US address through a web interface. Fortunately, these services also have APIs that can be leveraged by your web applications.

In this chapter, we'll use Rails plugins to manipulate Google Maps and Google's Geocoding service for the purpose of pinpointing a location on a map. We'll also make some distance calculations and plot points of interest on the map, given a search radius from the starting location. To assist us with the Google Maps integration, we'll use the YM4R/GM (Google Maps) plugin by Guilhem Vellut, part of the YM4R project (`http://ym4r.rubyforge.org`). For the geocoding and distance calculations, we'll use the GeoKit plugin, written by Andre Lewis and Bill Eisenhauer (`http://geokit.rubyforge.org`). This plugin extends Active Record's finders to allow for distance-based finds, supports geocoding from multiple providers (Google, Yahoo, Geocoder.us, and Geocoder.ca), and provides a unified interface for querying them. It also provides facilities for IP-based location lookups.

Our Task: Locate Nearby Hiking Trails

The editors of MaineHikingJournal.com, a hiking journal for the great state of Maine, have asked us to add a new feature to their web site. The feature will allow users to type in a ZIP code or address and find trails within a certain distance of that starting location, plotted on a map.

They've pointed us to the US Geological Survey (USGS) Graphic Names Information System (GNIS) dataset, which includes more than 200 trails in Maine, and suggested that we use this data for our trail-location system. The GNIS database contains information about physical (summits, islands, swamps, and so on) and cultural (libraries, churches, post offices, and so on) geographic features of all types in the United States. Each feature has a federally recognized name. The database includes geographic coordinates, along with the class of the feature and optional historical and descriptive information.

Fueled with this data, the YM4R/GM (Google Maps) plugin, and the GeoKit plugin, we'll build a Rails application to satisfy the hiking journal's requirements.

Preparing the Trail Finder Application

Let's create a new Rails application for our trail finder application:

```
rails trailfinder
cd trailfinder
```

Next, we'll install the plugins we need for the project. The YM4R/GM (Google Maps) plugin can be installed by using the following command:

```
ruby script/plugin install svn://rubyforge.org/var/svn/ym4r/Plugins/GM/trunk/ym4r_gm
```

■**Note** The YM4R project's stated purpose is to ease the use of a number of different mapping package APIs (Google Maps, Yahoo Maps, and Mapstraction) from within Ruby and Rails. The project itself consists of a suite of libraries, some plugins, and some gems, each focusing on a different part of this task. In this chapter, we'll use only the Google Maps plugin, but you may want to investigate the other YM4R packages as well. They're listed at http://ym4r.rubyforge.org.

We'll need the GeoKit plugin as well. Install it now:

```
ruby script/plugin install svn://rubyforge.org/var/svn/geokit/trunk
```

Note that GeoKit does *not* work with the SQLite database, as SQLite lacks the necessary database-level geometry functions for distance calculations. Therefore, we'll be using a MySQL database in this example. To create the database, issue the following command:

```
mysqladmin -u root -p root_password create trailfinder
```

Then alter the configuration in config/database.yml file to use this database, as follows:

```
development:
  adapter: mysql
  database: trailfinder
  username: your_mysql_username
  password: your_mysql_password
```

Modeling Hiking Trail Data

Before we take a look at implementing location-based search and mapping, we'll need to retrieve the USGS GNIS dataset and use it to construct the Trail models we'll store in our database.

Obtaining USGS Trail Data

Begin by visiting http://geonames.usgs.gov/domestic/download_data.htm. To download data for the state of Maine in pipe-delimited format, select Maine from the state selection list. The download should begin automatically.

When the download is finished, unzip the archive. It contains the text file named ME_DECI.txt. Place it in the db/ directory of your trailfinder Rails project.

The ME_DECI.txt file contains a number of fields, which are named in the first line of the file (the header). Some of these fields are optional. The ones we care about for this project are feature_name, feature_id, class (we'll be working with only features whose class is Trail), state_alpha, county, primary_latitude, and primary_longitude. Note that two different representations of latitude and longitude values are included in the dataset: degrees-minutes-seconds (DMS) and decimal degrees (DEC). For this example, we will use DEC, as this format is most widely used in web service mapping APIs.

Creating the Trail Model

Next, we want to parse the geographic feature data and store it in our database. In order to do this, we'll need to create a migration and an Active Record model to represent a trail. Save the migration specified in Listing 14-1 as db/migrate/001_create_trails.rb.

Listing 14-1. *Migration for Trails (db/migrate/001_create_trails.rb)*

```
class CreateTrails < ActiveRecord::Migration
  def self.up
    create_table :trails do |t|
      t.string  :name
      t.integer :usgs_id
      t.string  :state
      t.string  :county
      t.decimal :latitude, :precision => 15, :scale => 10
```

```
      t.decimal :longitude, :precision => 15, :scale => 10
      t.timestamps
    end
  end

  def self.down
    drop_table :trails
  end
end
```

Now we can migrate the MySQL database using the rake db:migrate task:

rake db:migrate

```
== 1 CreateTrails: migrating =======================================================
-- create_table(:trails)
   -> 0.0335s
== 1 CreateTrails: migrated (0.0337s) =============================================
```

The Trail model, shown in Listing 14-2, inherits its attributes from the trails database table and needs no additional methods for our purposes. Save it as app/models/trail.rb.

■**Tip** The USGS GNIS dataset provides the location of many other physical and cultural features that may be of interest. You may want to consider building an application that deals with more than one feature class. If you do, consider using Single Table Inheritance (STI) and an STI base class (GeographicFeature), sub-classing it to represent different features such as parks, libraries, and so on. For more information about STI and its usage in the Rails API, see http://wiki.rubyonrails.org/rails/pages/ SingleTableInheritance.

Listing 14-2. *Trail Model (app/models/trail.rb)*

```
class Trail < ActiveRecord::Base
  validates_presence_of :name, :usgs_id, :latitude, :longitude
  validates_uniqueness_of :name, :usgs_id
end
```

Validation is present on the Trail model to ensure that a feature with the same USGS ID isn't entered twice, as the IDs are guaranteed to be unique within the dataset. The same is true of the feature names assigned by the USGS. In addition, every feature is required to have a latitude and longitude in order to be useful to us.

Parsing and Importing USGS Data

With our model created and ready for some data, the next step is to parse the file you down-loaded from the USGS and import it into your application. Save the code in Listing 14-3 as lib/usgs_reader.rb.

Listing 14-3. *Script to Parse and Import Geographic Feature Data (lib/usgs_reader.rb)*

```ruby
class USGSReader
  FEATURE_MAP = {
    'Feature_ID' => 'usgs_id',
    'Feature_Name' => 'name',
    'Class' => 'type',
    'State_Alpha' => 'state',
    'County' => 'county',
    'Primary_lat_DEC' => 'latitude',
    'Primary_lon_DEC' => 'longitude'
  }

  def self.import(io)
    first_line = true
    columns = []
    io.each_line do |line|
      if first_line
        columns = line.split('|')
        first_line = false
      else
        feature_data = map_features(columns, line.split('|'))
        if feature_data.delete('type') == 'Trail'
          # skip geographic features that are not trails
          trail = Trail.new(feature_data)
          puts("Saved trail: #{trail.name}") if trail.save
        end
      end
    end
  end

  private

    def self.map_features(columns, features)
      mapped = {}
      features.each_with_index do |value, i|
        column_name = columns[i]
        mapped_name = FEATURE_MAP[column_name]
        mapped[mapped_name] = value unless mapped_name.nil?
      end
      mapped
    end
end
```

The `USGSReader` class contains two class methods. When the `import` class method is called, it's passed an `IO` object—in this case, the USGS data source. Since the first line of the data contains column names delineated by pipe characters (`|`), we have a special case for the first line that splits it into an array of column names, which we'll store and reference later.

Subsequent lines are read in, split into arrays, and fed to the `map_features` method along with the column names we saved earlier. The job of `map_features` is to map the columns from the current line to the appropriate attribute names in our model according to the mappings defined in the `FEATURE_MAP` hash constant.

Back in the `import` method, we check to see if the class of the feature on the current line is a `Trail` by calling the `delete` method on the newly minted `feature_data` Hash. This removes the named key from the `Hash` and also returns its value for use in our comparison. If it turns out that the current line does represent trail data, we'll create a new `Trail` model, mass-assigning its attributes with the values in the mapped `Hash`, and save it to the database. Otherwise, we'll just ignore it and continue to the next line of the file. We parse the entire file in this manner until we're finished, and print a notice for each new model that is created.

We can use the Rails script runner facility (`script/runner`) to run this task within our project's environment, thus allowing it to access our Active Record models and other Rails facilities. Use the following command to bulk-import our dataset. It should display a line to standard output for each trail that it imports

```
ruby script/runner "USGSReader.import(File.read('db/ME_DECI.txt'))"
```

Plotting Trails with Google Maps and YM4R

By running the `import` method with the USGS dataset, we've imported more than 200 trails into our system. Our next step is to whip up an interface to allow us to see those trails on a map and, eventually, allow users to find trail heads that are within a certain distance from a given location.

Normally, we would need to write some JavaScript to interface with the Google Maps API to do this, but the YM4R plugin does most of the heavy lifting for us. It allows us to perform most basic location plotting tasks directly in Ruby, without having to write any JavaScript at all!

■**Tip** We've intentionally skipped over many details regarding the internals of the Google Maps service. For more details about integrating Google Maps with your Rails application, make sure to pick up *Beginning Google Maps Applications with Rails and Ajax* by Andre Lewis et al. (Apress, 2007) or see the service's API documentation at `http://code.google.com/apis/maps`.

We'll need to create a controller action and a view template to display the map. But first, we'll need to add a route to it by replacing the contents of `config/routes.rb` with the code in Listing 14-4.

Listing 14-4. *Routes for the Trail Finder Application (config/routes.rb)*

```
ActionController::Routing::Routes.draw do |map|
  map.trailmaps '/trailmaps', :controller => 'maps', :action => 'show'
end
```

Save the code for the controller, shown in Listing 14-5, as app/controllers/
maps_controller.rb.

Listing 14-5. *MapsController (app/controllers/maps_controller.rb)*

```
class MapsController < ApplicationController
  def show
    @map = GMap.new("map_div")
    @map.control_init(:large_map => true, :map_type => true)

    start = [44.540, -68.427]
    @map.center_zoom_init(start, 8)

    Trail.find(:all).each do |trail|
      @map.overlay_init(GMarker.new([trail.latitude, trail.longitude],
          :title => trail.name,
          :info_window => trail.name))
    end
  end
end
```

The show method of the MapsController is the only action we need to implement for this
example. As you can see, the YM4R plugin makes plotting our hiking trail data points on a
Google map extremely simple.

First, we create a new @map instance variable, setting it equal to a newly instantiated GMap
object (a class supplied by the plugin). The parameter to new is the name of the div element
that will be created in the view. Next, we initialize the map controls, including a large zoom
slider and map-type selector. We also pick a center point for the map display, which we've
decided to hard-code to the area around Ellsworth, Maine, and then instruct the map to zoom
in and center itself around this location using the center_zoom_init method.

To plot markers for each hiking trail on the map, we iterate through all the Trail models
in our system, and for each, we create a new GMarker. In the view, this means that there will be
a number of markers present, each placed at the location of a hiking trail. The parameters we
pass to the GMarker determine the latitude and longitude for that marker, as well as its tooltip
(which appears when the user hovers the mouse over the marker) and info box (which
appears when the user clicks the marker).

Before you can see the results of our work, you need to create a view template for this
action. Let's do that now. Save the code in Listing 14-6 as app/views/maps/show.html.erb.

Listing 14-6. *Maps Show Template (app/views/maps/show.html.erb)*

```
<!DOCTYPE html PUBLIC "-//W3C//DTD XHTML 1.0 Transitional//EN"
        "http://www.w3.org/TR/xhtml1/DTD/xhtml1-transitional.dtd">
<html xmlns="http://www.w3.org/1999/xhtml" xml:lang="en" lang="en">
<head>
  <title>Trails in Maine</title>
  <%= GMap.header %>
  <%= @map.to_html %>
</head>
<body>
  <%= @map.div(:width => 600, :height => 400) %>
</body>
</html>
```

Two calls made in the head section of the HTML document are important here. The first, `GMap.header`, includes the Google Maps API JavaScript code and the helper functions used by YM4R/GM. The second, `@map.to_html`, initializes the view for the map we created in our controller and plots the markers we added to it. As long as we've remembered to do these things in the head section, we can display the map itself in the body of the document by calling `@map.div` and setting the width and height of the map to be displayed.

At this point, you can start your server using `script/server` and view the results. Open a browser and enter the address `http://localhost:3000/trailmaps`. You will see a map similar to the one depicted in Figure 14-1, with a marker present for each of the trails found in the database. You can use the standard Google Maps controls to zoom and pan the display and switch to satellite and hybrid map types.

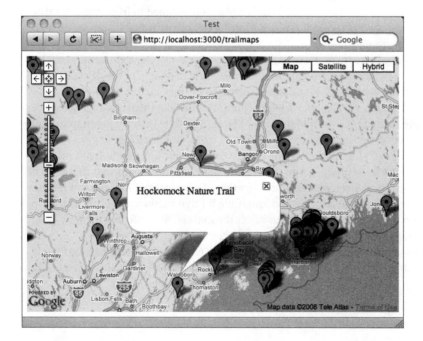

Figure 14-1. *Map of Maine hiking trails (http://localhost:3000/trailmaps)*

Our next task is to extend the application so that users can enter their current location and see only hiking trails that are available within a specified radius from that location. We also want to show the distance to those trails in the info boxes for map markers (which pop up when the marker is clicked).

Geocoding and Distance Calculations with GeoKit

YM4R is an extremely useful library, and along with its ability to manipulate the Google Maps API, it also allows you to use Google for direct geocoding queries. However, for more heavy-weight geocoding applications, we turn to the GeoKit plugin, which offers advanced features such as distance-based finds and other location calculations.

■**Tip** Another geocoding plugin with advanced features is Acts As Geocodable. More information about it is available at `http://opensoul.org/2007/2/13/geocoding-as-easy-as-1-2`.

Geocoder Configuration

When you installed the GeoKit plugin earlier in the chapter, it automatically appended a configuration template to your environment configuration in `config/environment.rb`. You can adjust these configuration settings to control how the plugin works and which geocoders it uses. GeoKit offers a number of options for third-party geocoding services, including Google, Yahoo, and Geocoder.us. Since we're already using Google Maps, and because the YM4R plugin has already provided us with a development API key to work with, we'll use Google for geocoding. GeoKit defaults to using Google first, so we don't need to modify the default search order of geocoding services. We just need to modify our environment to use the API key provided by the YM4R plugin. In `config/environment.rb`, find the line that reads:

```
GeoKit::Geocoders::google = 'REPLACE_WITH_YOUR_GOOGLE_KEY'
```

Replace it with the following code snippet, which will read the API key in from the YAML key file provided by YM4R:

```
GeoKit::Geocoders::google = YAML.load_file(RAILS_ROOT +
  '/config/gmaps_api_key.yml')[RAILS_ENV]
```

■**Note** For production use, you'll want to obtain your own Google API key. See `http://code.google.com/apis/maps/signup.html` for details. Once you've done this you should update your `config/gmaps_api_key.yml` file.

In order to allow us to use the additional finder options and distance-calculation methods provided by GeoKit, we need to make a small change to the `Trail` model we created earlier. All we have to do is declare the model to be `acts_as_mappable`, as shown in Listing 14-7.

Listing 14-7. *Updated Trail Model (app/models/trail.rb)*

```ruby
class Trail < ActiveRecord::Base
  acts_as_mappable :lat_column_name => 'latitude', :lng_column_name => 'longitude'

  validates_presence_of :name, :usgs_id, :latitude, :longitude
  validates_uniqueness_of :name, :usgs_id
end
```

Pinpointing User Location and Distance Calculations

Since we want to allow the user to specify their current location (the user's "home location") as well as the trail search radius, we'll need to add a form to our view. The home location and search radius values will be posted to our lone controller action from the view and available as params[:location] and params[:radius], respectively. We'll use these to center the viewport around the user's location, put a flag there (one that looks different from the standard markers symbolizing a trail location), and then display only the hikes that are within the specified radius, using the standard GMarkers from before.

Update the MapsController that we created earlier to match the code shown in Listing 14-8.

Listing 14-8. *Updated MapsController (app/controllers/maps_controller.rb)*

```ruby
class MapsController < ApplicationController
  include GeoKit::Geocoders

  def show
    @location = params[:location]
    @radius = params[:radius]
    start = [44.540, -68.427]
    finder_options = {}

    @map = GMap.new("map_div")
    @map.control_init(:large_map => true, :map_type => true)

    if @location
      geohome = MultiGeocoder.geocode(@location)
      start = [geohome.lat, geohome.lng]
      finder_options[:origin] = start
      finder_options[:within] = @radius if @radius

      startico = GIcon.new(
          :image => "http://www.google.com/mapfiles/dd-start.png",
          :icon_size => GSize.new(20, 34),
          :icon_anchor => GPoint.new(10, 34),
          :info_window_anchor => GPoint.new(10, 0))
```

```
      @map.overlay_init(GMarker.new(start,
          :icon => startico,
          :title => "Home",
          :info_window => "Home<br/>#{@location}"))
    end

    @map.center_zoom_init(start, 8)

    Trail.find(:all, finder_options).each do |trail|
      @map.overlay_init(GMarker.new(
          [trail.latitude, trail.longitude],
          :title => trail.name,
          :info_window => "#{trail.name}<br/>Distance: " +
            "#{trail.distance_to(start).to_i} Miles"))
    end
  end
end
```

The first change in the updated code listing is to include the GeoKit::Geocoders module in the class. This gives us access to the geocoding routines that we'll need to look up the address that the user enters and retrieve the latitude and longitude for it.

Within the show method, we set our instance variables to the parameter values passed in from the form, and, if the @location variable is not nil, we'll use the MultiGeocoder.geocode method to look up the geocoded location value for the address string entered by the user. The latitude and longitude values returned by the service we're using (Google in this case) are placed in the start variable.

Note   The geocoding address lookup can actually be done by the YM4R/GM plugin without the use of GeoKit or any other plugin, using syntax like geohome = Geocoding::get(@location). However, as mentioned, YM4R lacks many of the more advanced features of GeoKit, which is why we've decided to use it here. Another advantage of GeoKit is that the MultiGeocoder.geocode method can use a variety of service providers, including failover among providers in the order specified in config/environment.rb.

The Hash we create, finder_options, is used to specify optional finder options to pass to the Trail.find call to find trail locations. If a starting location is specified, we'll set an :origin option, and if a radius is specified, we'll set the :within option to that radius. Note that these aren't standard Active Record finder options, but the fact that we've declared our model to be acts_as_mappable extends its finder to support distance-based finds.

If the location is set, we'll also create a new icon, different from the standard map marker icon, and use it to mark the user's home location on the map. For now, we'll hot-link the trip-start image (dd-start.png) from Google Maps, but for any serious use, you should consider downloading it or another icon, and saving it to your local public/images directory so it can be served locally.

For each trail found by our modified finder call, we'll also add some extra information to the info box that appears when a user clicks the marker. This info box is often used for display-ing details about the location, but since we don't have any extra descriptive information from the standard USGS data, we'll simply include the distance from the user's starting location. That distance is calculated by calling the `distance_to` method on the `Trail` model instance and passing the starting location as a parameter. This is another useful method we gain by adding the `acts_as_mappable` declaration to our model.

That's really all that is needed to add this extra functionality to our controller. Of course, we'll also need to update our view, as shown in Listing 14-9, to provide the form for starting location and search radius entry.

Listing 14-9. *Updated Map View (app/views/maps/show.html.erb)*

```
<!DOCTYPE html PUBLIC "-//W3C//DTD XHTML 1.0 Transitional//EN"
        "http://www.w3.org/TR/xhtml1/DTD/xhtml1-transitional.dtd">
<html xmlns="http://www.w3.org/1999/xhtml" xml:lang="en" lang="en">
<head>
  <title>Trails in Maine</title>
  <%= GMap.header %>
  <%= @map.to_html %>
</head>
<body>
  <%= @map.div(:width => 600, :height => 400) %>
  <% form_tag do -%>
    <label for="location">My Location:</label>
     <%= text_field_tag(:location, @location) %><br/>

    <label for="radius">Search Radius:</label>
    <%= select_tag(:radius, options_for_select([10, 20, 50, 100, 200, 500, 1000],
      @radius.to_i)) %> Miles<br/>

    <%= submit_tag('Submit') %>
  <% end -%>
</body>
</html>
```

Running the Updated Application

To see our updated application, reload the URL http://localhost:3000/trailmaps in a web browser. Try entering a ZIP code (such as 04970, in the town of Rangeley, Maine) or an address (such as 65 Commercial Street, Portland, Maine) in the My Location text box. Then select a search radius (such as 50 or 100 miles) for hiking trails. Assuming that you are connected to the Internet so the remote geocoder service can be contacted, the results will be similar to the map shown in Figure 14-2.

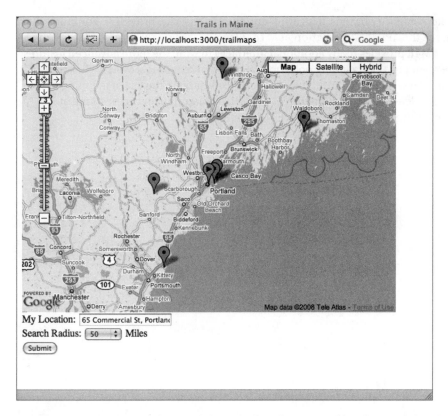

Figure 14-2. *Updated map of Maine hiking trails, reflecting trails within 50 miles of an address in Portland, Maine (http://localhost:3000/trailmaps)*

Summary

The plugins that we've demonstrated in this chapter streamline the process of integrating geocoding and mapping functionality into Rails-based applications and mashups. They abstract away the details of interacting with the various geocoding web services and JavaScript mapping APIs, thereby allowing you to spend your valuable time focusing on what makes your use of them unique.

The example we presented, an interactive map of hiking trail locations, involved geocoding a user-supplied address and using USGS GNIS data to find trails within a given radius. Results were plotted on a map using YM4R's Google Maps integration.

The features we used here are really just the tip of the proverbial iceberg. GeoKit provides many other powerful capabilities, including multiprovider geocoding with failover and IP-based lookups. The latter could be used, for instance, to show a listing of nearby hikes automatically, without the user entering any data at all (of course, the preciseness of

IP-based lookups can vary based on location and Internet service provider). For more information, see the API documentation at `http://geokit.rubyforge.org/api/index.html`.

Similarly, YM4R provides many additional interfaces to wrap the more advanced features of the Google Mapping API, including polygon drawing, marker groups, overlay clustering, and GeoRSS overlays—all very cool features that can really jazz up the use of mapping in your application. Complete documentation for YM4R's Google Maps plugin can be found at `http://ym4r.rubyforge.org/ym4r_gm-doc`.

CHAPTER 15

■ ■ ■

Paginating Active Record Data

Pagination is one of those key requirements that people tend to ignore yet can be extremely important. If the project you're working on needs pagination and it's missing (or just poorly implemented), the problem is a glaring one, and it might make your application unusable. Consider these examples: a forum package that lacks the ability to break up long message threads by page or an online address book, organized alphabetically, that doesn't allow you to jump ahead ten pages to find someone whose last name starts with "M." Clearly, the inability to easily navigate between pages of data is frustrating at very least, and the alternative of putting all that data on a single page is usually not an option.

Search results, such as those you would get from a typical Google or Yahoo! search, are perhaps the canonical example for pagination. The paginator used at Digg (http://www.digg.com), a social news popularity index, is also often cited as a nice-looking, functional example of pagination "done right." Figure 15-1 shows the Digg paginator.

Figure 15-1. *Pagination example as used on Digg*

Pagination impacts not only the user interface but also resource utilization. We don't want to retrieve more information from the database than we have to at any given time or initialize more objects than we absolutely require in order to display the current page of information. Proper use of pagination helps us in both of these areas and makes our interface snappy and intuitive.

Fortunately, pagination is also something that can be generalized and made available as a reusable component. In Rails, we have several options, all available as plugins:

- *Classic Pagination*: Until recently, Classic Pagination was actually part of the framework core. It was removed from the core in Rails 2.0, and a plugin was created. It's currently unmaintained and is available only for the sake of backward compatibility. You can find this plugin at `svn://errtheblog.com/svn/plugins/classic_pagination`.

- *Will Paginate*: This plugin serves as a robust replacement for Classic Pagination (including view helpers) with a wholly different API by Mislav Marohnić and PJ Hyett. Our examples in this chapter use their plugin. More information is available at `http://github.com/mislav/will_paginate`.

- *Paginating Find*: This plugin provides a simple, minimalist approach to pagination by Alex Wolfe, extending Active Record's `find` method to allow pages of data to be defined and returned. No extras, no cruft (and, unlike Will Paginate, no view helpers). You can learn more about Paginating Find at `http://cardboardrocket.com/pages/paginating_find`.

Other ways to do pagination in a Rails project exist as well, including the Paginator gem (`http://paginator.rubyforge.org`), which can be used in any stand-alone Ruby project.

In this chapter, we'll demonstrate how to add pagination to your own application using a simple feed aggregator application as an example.

Our Task: Aggregate (and Paginate!) News Feeds

Like most web developers, we read our fair share of blogs. Most modern blogs, and many other news and informational sites, syndicate their content via RSS or Atom feeds, which means that we don't have to actually read an article or news item on the site where it was published. Instead, we can subscribe to a blog's feed and read it in our favorite feed reader application. This could be a desktop application like NetNewsWire or a web-based application like Google Reader or Bloglines.

Feeds are used in lots of other creative ways. One technique is to republish feed information to a public news aggregator, which might index a number of feeds that are important to a given community. This would allow users to read important news in, say, the Ruby community, without having to have their own feed reader and set of subscriptions. An example of this is the PlanetRubyOnRails web site (`http://www.planetrubyonrails.com`), which indexes a number of popular Ruby blogs. MXNA, available at `http://weblogs.macromedia.com/mxna`, is a similar news aggregator for the Adobe Flash/ActionScript developer community.

We've decided to build our own community news aggregator. Maybe we'll link it from our blog to allow people to see the news we've been following, or maybe we'll use it in a company to aggregate the personal blogs of all our employees in one centralized place. Maybe we'll eventually take the same data and expose it in a blog sidebar (if you're so inclined, it should be simple to modify the sidebar recipe presented in Chapter 24 to do this), but for now we want to make it a wholly separate site.

Of course, if we track any significant number of blogs for an extended period of time, it's clear that we'll need to have some form of pagination to allow users to browse through the archives of news items. We want to give them the ability to move through the pages one page at a time or skip much further ahead, and we want to present pagination in a clean, easily navigable way. Using the Will Paginate plugin, we'll show you how this can be done with just a few lines of code and some CSS to make it visually appealing.

Preparing the Feed Aggregator Application

Let's create a new Rails application for the feed aggregator project:

```
rails myfeeds
cd myfeeds
```

Next, install the Will Paginate plugin by executing the following command inside the new directory:

```
ruby script/plugin install git://github.com/mislav/will_paginate.git
```

■**Note** Installation from the Git repository, as shown here, is the suggested way to install the plugin. Support to install plugins from Git is only available in Rails 2.1 and later. If you are using an older version of Rails, we suggest that you install Will Paginate as a Ruby gem (installation from a legacy Subversion repository is also available). For more information, see `http://github.com/mislav/will_paginate/wikis/` `installation`.

We will also be making use of a preexisting feed processing library to retrieve and process RSS/Atom feeds. Many Ruby libraries do just this, and we encourage you to browse through `http://www.rubyforge.org` to see your options; for this particular project, we've chosen the FeedTools gem. FeedTools is stable and full-featured, and treats both RSS and Atom feeds identically, which means that we don't have to worry about the specific format that each blog uses to syndicate its feed.

To install FeedTools, issue the following command:

```
gem install feedtools
```

Before we show you how the Will Paginate plugin can solve pagination problems, we first need some data to paginate. In this case, that data comes in the form of feed items, and, fortunately for us, adding news items from just a handful of our favorite blogs will provide us with a wealth of data. The more data we have to work with, the more obvious the benefits of good pagination will be.

Creating the FeedItem Model

Out first task is to create a `FeedItem` model and the associated database table it will use to store archived news/feed items, as shown in Listing 15-1.

Listing 15-1. *Feed Item Migration (db/migrate/001_create_feed_items.rb)*

```
class CreateFeedItems < ActiveRecord::Migration
  def self.up
    create_table :feed_items do |t|
      t.string   :feed
      t.string   :title
      t.string   :link
      t.text     :content
      t.datetime :published_at
    end
  end

  def self.down
    drop_table :feed_items
  end
end
```

Save the code in Listing 15-1 as db/migrate/001_create_feed_items.rb. We can then migrate the development database by using the rake db:migrate task:

```
rake db:migrate
```

```
== 1 CreateFeedItems: migrating ================================================
-- create_table(:feed_items)
   -> 0.0023s
== 1 CreateFeedItems: migrated (0.0024s) =======================================
```

Our model is a simple one; it just needs to wrap the database table and provide a few basic validations. The code for the FeedItem model is shown in Listing 15-2. Save it as app/models/feed_item.rb. Note that a feed item's link should be unique: if we have two items with the same link, we have duplication, which we want to avoid. We've enforced this in the model using the appropriate Active Record validations.

Listing 15-2. *FeedItem Model (app/models/feed_item.rb)*

```
class FeedItem < ActiveRecord::Base
  validates_presence_of :feed, :title, :link, :published_at
  validates_uniqueness_of :link
end
```

Obtaining Feed Item Data

Next, we need to obtain the actual feed data. We could use FeedTools to contact each remote feed source in a given list every time a controller action is invoked, but that seems awfully wasteful. Blogs are often updated irregularly, and the nature of our application isn't such that real-time information is required. Requesting and parsing feeds from these remote sources every time a user makes a request would generate a lot of unnecessary traffic and also result in a longer response delay for our user. As a result, our application won't scale well when we add new feeds (or attract more visitors, for that matter!). Instead, we'll create a script that we can run periodically to poll the feed URLs and archive them to the local database. Then, when a user makes a request, we'll just retrieve the relevant data locally.

To script this periodic poll and import process, write a FeedAggregator class, as shown in Listing 15-3, and save it as lib/feed_aggregator.rb.

Listing 15-3. *Script to Retrieve Updated Feed Items from Remote Sources (lib/feed_aggregator.rb)*

```
require 'feed_tools'

class FeedAggregator
  FEED_URLS = ["http://brainspl.at", "http://hackety.org",
    "http://weblog.jamisbuck.org", "http://rubyinside.com",
    "http://blog.zerosum.org"]

  def self.update
    count = 0
    puts("Updating feeds...")
    FEED_URLS.each do |feed_url|
      FeedTools::Feed.open(feed_url).items.each do |item|
        unless FeedItem.find_by_link(item.link)
          FeedItem.create({
            :title => item.title,
            :feed  => item.feed.url,
            :link  => item.link,
            # strip html tags and newlines
            :content => item.content.gsub(/<[^>]*>|\n/, ''),
            :published_at => item.published
          })
          puts("- #{item.link}")
          count += 1
        end
      end
    end
    puts("Retrieved #{count} feed items")
  end
end
```

The FeedAggregator class contains a constant, FEED_URLS, and a lone class method. The FEED_URLS constant contains an array of the URLs for all the blog feeds that we want to aggregate. You can replace these URLs with those of your own favorite blogs.

The update class method is used to iterate through the array, and for each item we retrieve the remote feed and process it. The actual retrieval and parsing of the feed is handled by calling Feed.open, which is provided by the FeedTools library (note that FeedTools is required at the top of the file, thus making it available to us).

For each item in the `items` array that `open` returns, we first check to see whether a feed item with that link already exists. If it doesn't, we create a new `FeedItem` model, saving it to the database. Note that the `gsub` method is used with a regular expression to strip HTML tags and line breaks out of the content that is returned before saving it, so we can truncate the text for a display preview. We also use `puts` to generate a log of the feed items we're retrieving. Since we're going to use the UNIX cron facility to schedule this task, we may want to have it save the log output to a file on the system or e-mail us output whenever the process runs.

The `FeedAggregator.update` method must be run within the context of our Rails application, as it needs to be able to access our database configuration and `FeedItem` model. We can accomplish this by either running it through the Rails `script/runner` facility (`ruby script/runner "FeedAggregator.update"`) or writing a Rake task that has a dependency on the Rails environment. We generally prefer the latter approach in a case like this where the same action will need to be performed repeatedly or perhaps invoked manually by an administrator if an instant update needs to be forced.

Creating a Rake Task for Scripting Updates

Writing a Rake task to run within your Rails project is very straightforward. Any tasks that are created and saved to the `lib/tasks` directory are automatically included in the default list of tasks available for that application. That is, if we define a task named `feeds:update` in `lib/tasks/myfeeds.rake`, we'll be able to execute it by typing `rake feeds:update` from the application root. The code for our Rake task is shown in Listing 15-4.

Listing 15-4. *Rake Task for Updating Feeds (lib/tasks/myfeeds.rake)*

```
namespace :feeds do
  desc "Update from aggregator feed sources"
  task :update => [:environment] do |t|
    require 'lib/feed_aggregator.rb'
    FeedAggregator.update
  end
end
```

Note that the `:update` task is nested within the `:feeds` namespace and has a dependency on the `:environment` symbol, which means that it will run within the context of our application with full access to any models and other facilities we've established. We can now call our Rake task by executing the `rake feeds:update` command. Run it now in order to populate the database with some sample data for pagination.

```
rake feeds:update
```

```
Updating feeds...
- http://brainspl.at/articles/2008/01/14/on-the-road-to-merb-1-0
- http://hackety.org/2008/01/18/theLecturingOfDrPlainstonesTrilby.html
- http://weblog.jamisbuck.org/2008/1/11/advanced-rails-recipes-and-capistrano
...snip!...
Retrieved 85 feed items
```

We can schedule this task to run at a regular interval on a UNIX system by creating a system cron job (usually placed in `/etc/crontab`, but this can vary by distribution). An example cron entry for a task that runs every hour at 53 minutes after the hour might look like this:

```
53 * * * *   user    cd /path/to/your/app; rake feeds:update
```

■Tip You can specify the environment for a given Rake task to run within by specifying `RAILS_ENV=`*environment* after the name of the task to execute, where *environment* is development, test, or production. By default, tasks run in the development environment, unless you instruct them to do otherwise.

Displaying Feed Items with Pagination

Now that we have some feed items archived in our local application, we'll need to display them to the user by creating a controller and a corresponding view. Within this controller, we'll use the `paginate` class method that the Will Paginate plugin adds to `ActiveRecord::Base` to retrieve only enough feed items to display on a single page. The `paginate` method works just like the default `find(:all)` method, except it doesn't actually retrieve all the records. Instead, it takes `:page` and `:per_page` options (the latter of which defaults to 30 if not explicitly specified) to indicate the selection and number of elements to return.

The collection returned by the `paginate` method functions just like a normal `ActiveRecord` collection. However, it has a few extra methods on it that can be used to construct the view helper: `page_count`, `next_page`, `previous_page`, and so on. See the plugin documentation at `http://rock.errtheblog.com/will_paginate/classes/WillPaginate/Collection.html` for more information.

■Tip As an alternative to specifying a `:per_page` option to the `paginate` method, it's possible to allow the model to define the number of items that should be displayed on a given page. You can do this by implementing a method named `per_page` in your model.

The code for the `FeedItemsController` is shown in Listing 15-5, which we save as `app/controllers/feed_items_controller.rb`. This controller contains a single action, `index`, which sets the `@feed_items` instance variable so the appropriate feed items can be displayed in the view template.

Listing 15-5. *FeedItemsController (app/controllers/feed_items_controller.rb)*

```
class FeedItemsController < ApplicationController
  def index
    @feed_items = FeedItem.paginate(
      :order => "published_at DESC",
      :page => params[:page],
      :per_page => 10)
  end
end
```

Feed items are retrieved in order, with most recent items first, and we limit the display to ten items per page by specifying the :per_page option. The :page option is set to the params[:page] request parameter, which indicates the number of the current page of results to be displayed. This parameter is passed through the URL, for example, /feeds/?page=3. The links that the pagination view helper creates will use these parameters to specify the page that the user has requested.

Of course, in order to access this action from a browser, we need to establish our routing rules. We'll update config/routes.rb to reflect the code in Listing 15-6. This will map the /feeds URL to the controller action we just created.

Listing 15-6. *Routes for the Feed Aggregator Application (config/routes.rb)*

```
ActionController::Routing::Routes.draw do |map|
  map.feeds '/feeds', :controller => 'feed_items', :action => 'index'
end
```

USING PAGINATION WITH RAILS PAGE CACHING

Since this example describes a system that is updated at regular intervals by a server-side task and not dynamically altered by users, we could further optimize it by using page caches. Rails page caching allows us to write out a static HTML file to be cached and served directly by the front-end web server (Apache, nginx, etc.). We can turn on page caching for a particular controller action by specifying it at the top of the controller class definition using the caches_page class method:

```
class FeedItemsController < ApplicationController
  caches_page :index
  ...
end
```

However, by default, page caching won't work with our page parameter, because it's specified as a query string parameter (following the question mark) instead of as part of the query string. To use page caching, any component of the parameter used to render the cached response must precede the question mark. Therefore, we'd have to modify our routes to make the page parameter part of the proper query string, like this:

```
map.feeds '/feeds/:page', :controller => 'feed_items', :action => 'index',
  :page => nil
```

This would provide us with URLs like /feeds/1 and /feeds/2 instead of /feeds?page=1 and /feeds?page=2 (which are arguably more attractive anyway). The cached pages are then stored in our public directory as public/feeds/1.html and public/feeds/2.html, allowing them to be served directly by the web server. We should also modify our FeedAggregator class to remove any cached aggregator pages when the feeds are updated. Otherwise, the new pages will never be generated.

Note that by default, page caching is only enabled in the Rails production environment. If you'd like to turn it on to test it in development, open config/environments/development.rb and set the following configuration variable:

```
config.action_controller.perform_caching = true
```

See http://ap.rubyonrails.com/classes/ActionController/Caching/Pages.html for more information about page caching in Rails.

Finally, we also need to add a view to be rendered by the index action. That view should live in app/views/feed_items/index.html.erb, and the code for it is shown in Listing 15-7.

Listing 15-7. *Index View Template for Feed Items (app/views/feed_items/index.html.erb)*

```
<h1>My Reading List</h1>
<ul>
  <% @feed_items.each do |item| -%>
    <li>
      <h4><%= link_to(item.title, item.link) %></h4>
      <div><%= truncate(item.content, 250) %></div>
      <p>lifted from <%= link_to(item.feed, item.feed) %>,
        <%= time_ago_in_words(item.published_at) %> ago</p>
    </li>
  <% end -%>
</ul>

<%= will_paginate(@feed_items) %>
```

This template code simply loops through all the feed items set up by our controller action and displays the title of the item as a link to the full article, along with a truncated version of the article content and the date it was published. At the bottom of the page, the will_paginate view helper renders an unstyled paginator that resembles what you see in Figure 15-2.

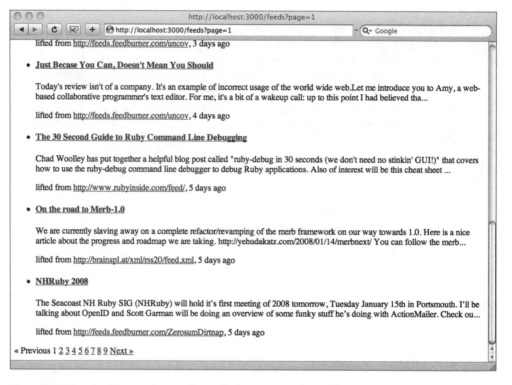

Figure 15-2. *Our feed items view and unstyled paginator (http://localhost:3000/feeds)*

Styling the Paginator

Styling the paginator can be accomplished completely in CSS or with minor adjustments to the surrounding HTML. Using the CSS shown in Listing 15-8 and a tiny bit of added HTML, we can adjust the existing view to resemble the pagination used by designer Steve Dennis on his Subcide CSS layout tutorial at `http://www.subcide.com/tutorials/csslayout`. In your own project, you'd probably want to put this CSS in a proper style sheet and link that style sheet from your application's layout. However, for demonstration purposes here, we can simply add the CSS to the top of our `index.html.erb` template.

Listing 15-8. *Updated View Template with Styled Pagination (app/views/feed_items/index.html.erb)*

```
<style type="text/css">
html, body {
  background-color: #313131;
  color: #cccccc;
  margin: 0;
  padding: 0;
}
```

```
h1 {
  padding: 10px 20px;
  background-color: #3e3e3e;
}
a {
  color: #ec5210;
}
.bottom {
  background-color: #3e3e3e;
  clear: both;
}
.pagination {
  background: #3e3e3e;
  margin: 0 10px;
  font-size: 0.8em;
  font-family: Tahoma, Arial, Helvetica, Sans-serif;
}
.pagination a, .pagination span {
  display: block;
  float: left;
  padding: 0.3em 0.5em;
  margin-right: 0.1em;
  text-decoration: none;
  background: #3e3e3e;
  color: #fff;
}
.pagination span {
  color: #868686;
}
.pagination a:hover {
  background: #ec5210;
}
.pagination span.current {
  font-weight: bold;
  background: #313131;
}
.pagination span.disabled {
  color: #868686;
}
</style>
```

```
<h1>My Reading List</h1>
<ul>
  <% @feed_items.each do |item| -%>
    <li>
      <h4><%= link_to(item.title, item.link) %></h4>
      <div><%= truncate(item.content, 250) %></div>
      <p>lifted from <%= link_to(item.feed, item.feed) %>,
        <%= time_ago_in_words(item.published_at) %> ago</p>
    </li>
  <% end -%>
</ul>

<div class="bottom">
  <%= will_paginate(@feed_items) %>
  <br style="clear:both;" />
</div>
```

Save the updated code listing and visit `http://localhost:3000/feeds` in a web browser to view the results, which should resemble what you see in Figure 15-3.

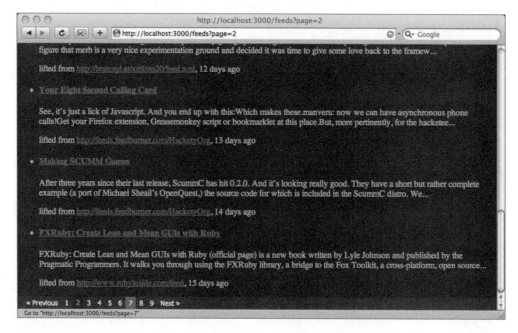

Figure 15-3. *Our feed items view with CSS-styled paginator (http://localhost:3000/feeds)*

Summary

Pagination is a common and important feature of information-centric web sites and applications. Fortunately for us, as Rails developers, we have excellent plugins like Will Paginate and Paginating Find to make adding pagination to our projects far easier than it would otherwise be.

You can find more information about the Will Paginate plugin at `http://github.com/mislav/will_paginate/wikis`. You'll also want to check out the excellent article on pagination best practices at `http://www.smashingmagazine.com/2007/11/16/pagination-gallery-examples-and-good-practices/`, which features a useful gallery of examples.

## CHAPTER 16

Full Text Search with Sphinx

Data is only as valuable as it is available, but having all the data in the world at your fingertips is worthless if you have no way to find anything meaningful in it. On the Web, search engines often serve as our primary interface to the wealth of data that the Internet has to offer. Google, Yahoo!, and Ask.com are some of the most recognizable Internet brands in existence, and rightly so; without them, the Web as we know it would be a very different place, and information would be much more difficult to find.

A lot goes into the heuristics for searching the Internet, and a thorough discussion of this could easily fill an entire book. However, access to powerful search facilities is also important when we're talking about a constrained set of data that we own and wish to make available to our users. Many web sites act as repositories of particular types of information, such as product reviews, open source software libraries, books, local business services, user profile information. If your web property houses a significant amount of data, there's a good chance you or your users will need to be able to search through it.

You can implement many types of searching to accomplish these goals. Often, keyword searching is enough. In Chapter 2, we discussed tagging, which can be used by users to define ad hoc keywords for browsing and category search. This gives us a quick-and-dirty way to return relevant results, powered by the crowd. In the example we'll discuss in this chapter, we don't have the luxury of keywords to help us, but we do have an awful lot of raw text. In cases like this, full text search is what we need.

Searching large amounts of text for particular word or phrase matches doesn't have to be difficult, thanks to a number of powerful and freely available full text search engines. Popular open source solutions include Apache Lucene, Solr, Ferret (a Ruby port of Lucene), and Sphinx. In this chapter, we'll focus on using Sphinx, as it was designed specifically for indexing database content, making it ideal for our situation. Combining this search engine with Evan Weaver's Ultrasphinx plugin (`http://github.com/fauna/ultrasphinx`) for Ruby on Rails provides an easy way to add full text searching to your web application with minimal development work.

Our Task: Create a Searchable Archive of Movie Goofs

Our friend Ty runs a local movie rental store, RebelRebel Video. With competition from national chains like Blockbuster and online goliaths like Netflix, local stores like his are a dying breed. To survive, these stores have to rely on the qualities that make them unique, and Rebel-Rebel Video keeps customers coming back by specializing in the fun, the weird, and the hard to find, and by hosting lots of movie events and contests.

One of their most popular events is the Goof-Off, a weekly event where locals gather at the store to watch a completely random movie. The movie is chosen from a list of movies, each with some particular goof, or flaw: for instance, a scene where a character that is supposed to be deceased coughs or where the shadow of the cameraman can clearly be seen reflected in the sunglasses of a cold-blooded serial killer. While watching the chosen film, participants have to shout out as soon as they see a goof to get points. At the end of the night, the contestant with the most points gets two free movie passes.

Up to this point, the staff of RebelRebel Video has been picking movies somewhat randomly and using the web interface of the Internet Movie Database (IMDb) to find out if those movies had any good goofs in them. They'd like to make this a little easier on themselves and maybe a little more fun for customers, so they've asked us if we can help. They want to build a searchable interface to a database of goofs that they can put on their web site, which they would also use to pick the movie to play each week. RebelRebel Video staffers will ask audience members to suggest search terms, plug them into the web site, and choose one of the movies that comes up.

Obviously, it'd be nice if we had a set of hand-pruned goof data to search through. Fortunately, web users have spent a lot of time entering just this kind of information into IMDb. The powers that be at IMDb have also been gracious enough to provide the database for download, thus allowing us to import it into our own application.

Since IMDb's goof data is usually recorded (without keywords) in a rich description associated with each movie, we'll need to do full text searching to find matches for a couple user-entered keywords. We'll create a data model for movie goofs, parse and import the IMDb goof data, and then whip up a simple searchable interface to this model data using the Sphinx full text search engine and the slick Ultrasphinx Rails plugin interface.

Preparing the Movie Goofs Database

Let's create a new Rails application for the movie goofs database project:

```
rails goofdb
cd goofdb
```

Next, we'll need to download and install Sphinx, which operates as a stand-alone search engine (with built-in data sources to support fetching data directly from popular open source databases such as MySQL and PostgreSQL). Sphinx will run as a separate process on our system and will interoperate with our Rails application. You can download the Sphinx source code and build it yourself or fetch the appropriate Windows binary version at http:// sphinxsearch.com/downloads.html. Note that the version of Sphinx used in the development of this example was v0.9.8 (rc2). The version of Ultrasphinx we'll be using is v1.11, which is incompatible with older versions of Sphinx (make sure to check the Ultrasphinx changelog for latest compatibility requirements).

■**Note** If you have trouble building or installing Sphinx, the support forums on the Sphinx web site (`http://www.sphinxsearch.com`) can be an invaluable resource. Visit them at `http://sphinxsearch.com/forum/forum.html?id=1`.

We'll also need Chronic, a natural language date/time parser library required by the Ultrasphinx plugin. To find out more about Chronic, you can visit the RubyForge page at `http://chronic.rubyforge.org`. To install it as a gem, we issue the following command:

```
gem install chronic
```

Once these prerequisites are installed, the Ultrasphinx plugin can be added to your Rails application. Ultrasphinx, along with a growing number of Rails plugins, is now hosted at Github. Install it using the following command from within your Rails project directory if you are using Rails 2.1 or newer:

```
ruby script/plugin install git://github.com/fauna/ultrasphinx.git
```

■**Note** Plugin support for Git repositories was introduced in Rails 2.1. If you are using Rails 2.0.x, you can visit `http://github.com/fauna/ultrasphinx`, download the package as a tarball, and extract its contents into `vendor/plugins/ultrasphinx`.

Create a subdirectory named `ultrasphinx` in your `config/` directory, and copy the `default.base` file from `vendor/plugins/ultrasphinx/examples` to it. This is the configuration file for the Ultrasphinx plugin; it will be used to generate the Sphinx configuration file (which in turn controls the Sphinx daemon options) later on in the chapter. It can be modified if you want to change the Sphinx host, the port that it runs on, or the index location.

Obtaining Goof Data from IMDb

Before we take a look at implementing search with Ultrasphinx, we'll need some data to search. As mentioned, IMDb provides a large amount of its data in downloadable text file format, so we can obtain our list of movie goofs from this text.

To retrieve this data, visit `http://www.imdb.com/interfaces`. Choose the plain text data files option and select one of the mirror sites. The file you want is called `goofs.list.gz`. Download the file and extract the `goofs.list` file to the `db/` directory of your Rails project using `gunzip` or your favorite compression/archiving tool.

Following is a typical entry from the text file. As you can see, the title of the movie is always preceded with a hash mark (#), with the year following it in parentheses. Subsequent lines preceded by a hyphen (-) represent a goof found in that movie. First the type of goof is listed (CREW indicates a crew error, and CONT indicates a continuity error), followed by an in-depth description of the goof. A goof description may span many lines or can be as short as a single line, but either way, the description will always be terminated by an empty line.

```
# RoboCop (1987)
- CREW: The camera car is reflected in the driver's door of Clarence's
  car in the final chase.

- CONT: Shutters on the door of the van reappear after it is
  abandoned.
```

These formatting conventions are important, as they provide us with the ability to parse the file appropriately. We'll return to that topic in a moment, but first we'll need to create models to represent these movie goofs locally in our application.

Creating Our Movie and Goof Models

We need to create two ActiveRecord models, one to represent a movie (Movie) and another to represent a movie goof (Goof). We'll also need a migration to create the underlying database tables. Save the migration specified in Listing 16-1 as db/migrate/001_create_movie_goofs.rb.

Listing 16-1. *Movie and Goof Migration (db/migrate/001_create_movie_goofs.rb)*

```
class CreateMovieGoofs < ActiveRecord::Migration
  def self.up
    create_table :movies do |t|
      t.string :name
      t.string :year
    end

    create_table :goofs do |t|
      t.integer :movie_id
      t.string :goof_type
      t.text :description
    end
  end

  def self.down
    drop_table :goofs
    drop_table :movies
  end
end
```

Our Movie model, shown in Listing 16-2, has a name and a year. These fields reflect the information that is available to us in the text file. Note that we are purposefully omitting any optional episode information for brevity (IMDb indexes TV shows as well as movies). The Goof model, shown in Listing 16-3, has a goof type and a description, as well as a foreign key referencing the movies table. A movie may have one or more goofs, and a goof always belongs to a movie.

Listing 16-2. *Movie Model (app/models/movie.rb)*

```
class Movie < ActiveRecord::Base
  has_many :goofs
  validates_presence_of :name
end
```

Listing 16-3. *Goof Model (app/models/goof.rb)*

```
class Goof < ActiveRecord::Base
  belongs_to :movie
  validates_presence_of :description
  is_indexed :fields => ['goof_type', 'description']
end
```

Note that the Goof model shown here makes a call to the is_indexed method. This method, provided by the Ultrasphinx plugin, configures the model for indexing by the search engine, thus making it searchable. is_indexed supports a complex set of options for customizing the database fields that are indexed, requiring specific conditions, scoping associations to a parent model, and so on. More information about these and other options can be found at http://blog.evanweaver.com/files/doc/fauna/ultrasphinx/files/README.html or in the comments in our local copy of vendor/plugins/ultrasphinx/lib/ultrasphinx/is_indexed.rb.

Since our example is relatively simple, we won't worry about any of the more advanced options here. We also won't worry too much about model validation, other than noting that a Movie requires a name to be present and a Goof requires a description. Save the two models as app/models/movie.rb and app/models/goof.rb, respectively.

SPHINX DATABASE OPTIONS: MYSQL, POSTGRESQL

Since Sphinx interoperates with both MySQL and PostgreSQL, we'll need to set up a database using one of these packages and change our database.yml file to allow us to connect to it. By default, Rails 2.0.2 uses a SQLite version 3 database for development mode; this is convenient but unsupported by the Sphinx engine, which is intended for searching large production databases.

Either MySQL or PostgreSQL is fine, but we'll use MySQL 5.0 as an example here and throughout the rest of the chapter. If you want to use PostgreSQL, make sure that you're using a version of the Sphinx engine compiled with PostgreSQL support (use --with-postgres as a ./configure flag).

To install the MySQL library, if you haven't already, run the command gem install mysql. Next, start your MySQL server if it isn't already running and use the command mysqladmin –u root -p create goofdb to create a new database named goofdb. You will also need to edit your project's config/database.yml file:

```
development:
  adapter: mysql
  database: goofdb
  user: your_mysql_user
  password: your_mysql_user_password (this should not be blank)
```

We can then migrate the development database by using the `rake db:migrate` task:

```
rake db:migrate
== 1 CreateMovieGoofs: migrating ============================================
-- create_table(:movies)
   -> 0.0022s
-- create_table(:goofs)
   -> 0.0116s
== 1 CreateMovieGoofs: migrated (0.0142s) ===================================
```

Parsing Movie Goof Data

With our models created and ready to go, our next step is to parse the IMDb data and import it into our database. Save the code in Listing 16-4 as `lib/goof_reader.rb`.

Listing 16-4. *Script to Parse and Import Movie Goofs from IMDb Text File (lib/goof_reader.rb)*

```ruby
class GoofReader
  MOVIE_LINE = /^# (.*) \(((\d+)\)$/
  GOOF_LINE = /^- (.*): (.*)$/
  GOOF_EXT_LINE = /(\w+.*)$/
  BLANK_LINE = /^\s*$/

  def self.import(io)
    movie = nil
    goof = nil
    io.each_line do |line|
      if matches = MOVIE_LINE.match(line)
        movie = Movie.find_by_name_and_year(matches[1], matches[2])
        if movie.nil?
          movie = Movie.create(:name => matches[1],
                               :year => matches[2])
        end
      elsif !movie.nil? && matches = GOOF_LINE.match(line)
        goof = movie.goofs.build(:goof_type => matches[1],
                                 :description => matches[2])
      elsif !goof.nil? && matches = GOOF_EXT_LINE.match(line)
        goof.description = "#{goof.description} #{matches[1]}"
      elsif !goof.nil? && matches = BLANK_LINE.match(line)
        goof.save
        puts("Saved goof #{goof.id} for: #{goof.movie.name} (#{goof.movie.year})")
        goof = nil
      else
        movie = nil
      end
    end
  end
end
```

The GoofReader class contains three regular expression constants and a lone class method. The import class method is invoked with an IO object as a parameter. This method iterates through each line of the IMDb data and parses it into usable Movie and Goof objects using the regular expressions we've defined to determine whether a line declares a new movie, declares a new goof, or is extended goof description data.

■**Tip** Regular expressions can be complicated, esoteric, and somewhat daunting for new users. For more information, please see the tutorial and reference materials available at http:// www.regular-expressions.info.

The Regexp.match method returns either nil or a MatchResult object. If the match is good, the [] operator can then be used to access each matched portion of the regular expression (those groupings defined with parentheses in the Regexp constants). In the case of the MOVIE_LINE expression, for instance, the first grouping, matches[1], will hold the name of the movie. The second grouping, matches[2], will contain the year of the movie's release. matches[0] will always contain the fully matched string.

If the line matches a GOOF_LINE, it's the beginning of a goof description for the current movie, so we'll use the Regexp match data to extract the type of the goof and the first line of the description. The description will most often contain multiple lines, in which case those additional lines will match the GOOF_EXT_LINE expression. The next line upon which we encounter a blank line indicates that we've reached the end of a goof description, so we save it and move on to the next line, which may be another goof for the current movie or data for an entirely new movie.

■**Note** IMDb records goof data for television episodes and miniseries alongside movie goof data in this same file. However, our regular expression only matches movie titles so that other data is skipped. If you'd like to build a repository of this information as well, you'll have to tweak the regular expression and will probably want to make the data model more robust.

You'll recall that in Chapter 15 we wrote a Rake task to automate the process of parsing remote feeds. Although we could take that same approach here, in this case we'll just use the Rails script/runner facility, since we're likely to run this task much less frequently (probably just once for the initial import).

```
ruby script/runner "GoofReader.import(File.read('db/goofs.list'))"
```

By invoking the preceding command, we are instructing our Rails project to execute this line of code within the context of its environment. Do this now to see the script in action. It should print a line of output to the display for each movie goof imported from the IMDb text file. This may take a few minutes, as the amount of data is substantial.

Building a Searchable Interface

Now that we've imported the bulk of the IMDb movie goof data, we need to make it searchable by users. To do this, we'll implement a simplistic search controller and add a named route to it by replacing the content of config/routes.rb with the code shown in Listing 16-5.

Listing 16-5. *Routes for the Goof DB Search System (config/routes.rb)*

```
ActionController::Routing::Routes.draw do |map|
  map.search '/search', :controller => 'search', :action => 'show'
end
```

We've only added a single route here, which maps requests for the URL '/search' to the show method of our SearchController. This action, as defined in our controller, will handle both the display of the search entry form as well as the results listings. Both requests will be received as GET requests rather than POST requests. Searches are usually implemented in this manner, as GETs are used for repeatable queries that don't make any change to the state of the server, whereas POSTs modify the state of the server-side data in some way. Search engine requests don't actually change anything; they simply retrieve a set of relevant, repeatable results. Therefore, GET is appropriate.

In any case, save the code for the search controller and its show method, shown in Listing 16-6, as app/controllers/search_controller.rb.

Listing 16-6. *SearchController (app/controllers/search_controller.rb)*

```
class SearchController < ApplicationController
  def show
    @search = params[:query]
    if !@search.nil? && !@search.blank?
      @time_for_search = Benchmark.realtime do
        @results = Ultrasphinx::Search.new(:query => @search).run.results
      end
      render(:action => 'show')
    else
      render(:action => '_form')
    end
  end
end
```

When the show action is called, any search query parameters are placed in the @search instance variable. If the query is empty, the user has yet to make a request. Therefore, only the search request form is displayed. That form is stored in a partial template, shown in Listing 16-7. We use a partial template because we'll also want to redisplay the form at the top of the results listing page, so a user of the service can perform another search quickly and easily without returning to the original page. Save the partial template as app/views/search/_form.html.erb.

Listing 16-7. *Partial Template for the Search Form (app/views/search/_form.html.erb)*

```
<h2>Search for Goofs:</h2>
<% form_tag({:action => 'show'}, :method => :get) do -%>
  <div><%= text_field_tag(:query, @search) %><%= submit_tag('Search!') %></div>
<% end -%>
```

On the other hand, if we have a valid query parameter, our code will retrieve a list of valid search results and place them in the @results instance variable. The process to do this is very simple: we create a new search by calling the new method of Ultrasphinx::Search with the user's query, run the search, and then retrieve the results, all in a single line.

■**Tip** Want to paginate those search results? Ultrasphinx has baked-in support for Will Paginate–style pagination. Simply pass the optional :page and :per_page parameters to Ultrasphinx::Search.new like this:

```
@results = Ultrasphinx::Search.new(:query => @search,
  :page => params[:page] || 1).run.results
```

You can then install the Will Paginate plugin (see Chapter 15) and add pagination to your views with a single line of code. By default, Ultrasphinx shows the first 20 results.

Since we'd like to be able to report how long the search took, we can wrap this call up in a block passed to Benchmark.realtime, which will return the time that elapsed while executing the block. We record that value in the instance variable @time_for_search so we can display it in our show action template, which is shown in Listing 16-8. Save it as app/views/search/show.html.erb.

Listing 16-8. *Show Template to Display Search Results (app/views/search/show.html.erb)*

```
<style type="text/css">
  .search_result { margin-bottom: 10px; width: 400px; }
  .movie_name { font-size: 120%; font-weight: bold; }
  .description { font-size: 90%; }
</style>

<%= render(:partial => 'form') %>
<% if @results.length < 1 -%>
  <h3>No matches found</h3>
<% else -%>
  <h3>Your search took <%= '%02.04f' % @time_for_search %> seconds
    and returned the following results:</h3>
```

```
<ul>
<% @results.each do |result| -%>
  <li class="search_result">
    <div class="movie_name"><%= h(result.movie.name) %>
      (<%= h(result.movie.year) %>)</div>
    <div class="description"><%= h(result.description) %></div>
  </li>
<% end -%>
</ul>
<% end -%>
```

This template loops through each search result returned by the Sphinx search and displays the movie name, year, and a description of the goof that matched the user's query. In addition to displaying the results, the template also renders the new search template as a partial within itself. This makes it easy for users to start a new search and is standard with most web-based search interfaces.

Running with Sphinx's Search Daemon

At this point, all of our code is written, but we still have a couple steps to complete before we can try a live query. First, we need to create our configuration for the Sphinx search daemon. The Ultrasphinx plugin takes care of this for us by autogenerating this configuration file. All we have to do is run the Rake task that's been provided:

```
rake ultrasphinx:configure
```

```
Rebuilding configurations for development environment
Available models are Goof
Generating SQL
```

Edit the file that task produced, `config/ultrasphinx/development.conf`, and check to see whether it includes a `sql_user` key that matches the database user for the application. If it does not, add the following line to the source configuration section (`source goofs`):

```
sql_user = your_mysql_username
```

With that done, we can now have Sphinx create the actual search indexes by running another Rake task supplied by the plugin:

```
rake ultrasphinx:index
```

```
Indexer --config '/path/to/your/project/goofdb/config/ultrasphinx/ ➡
development.conf' complete
Sphinx 0.9.7
Copyright (c) 2001-2007, Andrew Aksyonoff

using config file '/path/to/your/project/goofdb/config/ultrasphinx/➡
development.conf'...
indexing index 'complete'...
collected 67787 docs, 13.1 MB
sorted 2.5 Mhits, 100.0% done
total 67787 docs, 13119689 bytes
total 24.556 sec, 534269.88 bytes/sec, 2760.47 docs/sec
```

This tells us that the index operation was successful and that we're indexing almost 70,000 documents (movie goofs, in this case). Now we just have to start the Sphinx daemon process running:

```
rake ultrasphinx:daemon:start
```

```
Sphinx 0.9.8-rc2 (r1234)
Copyright (c) 2001-2008, Andrew Aksyonoff

using config file '/path/to/your/project/goofdb/config/ultrasphinx/➡
development.conf'...
Started successfully
```

Note You can stop the daemon by issuing the `rake ultrasphinx:daemon:stop` command.

At this point, the daemon is running, and we can test our application by pointing a web browser at `http://localhost:3000/search` and entering a query string. The query string can contain Boolean operators like AND, OR, and NOT, and supports phrases as well, as long as they are enclosed in double quotes (""). Let's try the following string: `"camera man" and car`. Pressing the Search button should return a set of results, as shown in Figure 16-1. It will also tell us how long the request took to process.

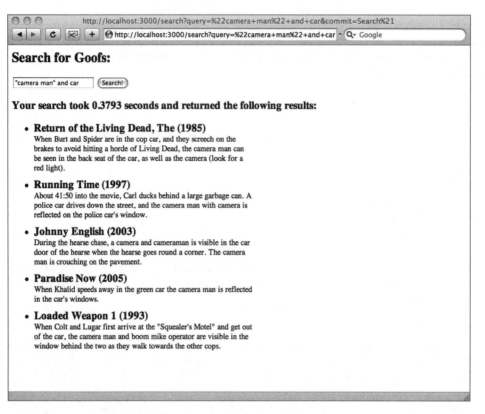

Figure 16-1. *Movie goofs search result (http://localhost:3000/search)*

Sphinx Advantages—Flexible and Fast

Of course, we didn't need to use Sphinx to search our goofs database. We could have written a simple query with find_by_sql to make the request directly on the MySQL database. The advantages to Sphinx are in its flexibility and speed. It is optimized for exactly this sort of task.

Let's run an experiment to measure speed comparisons; we'll compare Sphinx result retrievals against those obtained using the standard SQL search queries. Open up a Rails console (ruby script/console) and enter the following:

```
times = []
100.times do
  times << Benchmark.realtime do
    results = Goof.find_by_sql("select * from goofs where " +
      "description like '%camera man%' and description like '%shadow%'")
  end
end
times.sum / times.length
```

This code computes the average time MySQL takes to return the set of search results we're looking for, natively, using standard SQL syntax. In our trials, it averaged around 2.5 seconds.

MySQL also supports a special mechanism for optimized full text search that can boost this performance significantly. To make use of it, we first have to convert our table to use the MyISAM table format (assuming it uses the InnoDB format by default) and add a full text index on the description field. Bring up your MySQL console (`mysql-u mysql_user-p goofdb`) and enter the following:

```
mysql> ALTER TABLE goofs ENGINE=MyISAM;
mysql> ALTER TABLE goofs ADD FULLTEXT(description);
```

This may take a moment to complete. Once it finishes, we can return to the Rails console and try this altered version of the experiment using the full text `MATCH/AGAINST` syntax:

```
times = []
100.times do
  times << Benchmark.realtime do
    results = Goof.find_by_sql("select * from goofs where " +
      "(MATCH(description) AGAINST ('camera man')) AND " +
      "(MATCH(description) AGAINST ('shadow'))")
  end
end
times.sum / times.length
```

Note For more information on MySQL full text search options, check out `http://dev.mysql.com/doc/refman/5.0/en/fulltext-search.html`.

The query response this time averaged around 0.4 seconds. This is clearly much faster and preferable to the first option, assuming that we don't mind using MyISAM tables and MySQL-specific syntax.

However, using Sphinx is even faster and doesn't require this level of lock-in. The same query run through Sphinx on our dataset, using the Ultrasphinx plugin, takes approximately 0.1 seconds to complete on average. Here is the code for this test:

```
times = []
100.times do
  times << Benchmark.realtime do
    results = Ultrasphinx::Search.new(
      :query => "\"camera man\" and shadow").run.results
  end
end
times.sum / times.length
```

It's also important to note that the Ultrasphinx search returns more results than the comparable MySQL full text match search. This is because when you use the phrase search capabilities of `MATCH/AGAINST` as we've done here, it will only match literal strings. Therefore, descriptions containing words like "camera man's" will not be matched. Sphinx defaults to returning these results as well, which is usually what the user is looking for.

Obviously, results will vary based on the combination of keywords and options that are used. Both MySQL and Sphinx support an array of options, including ANDing, ORing, and negating terms; phrase matching; and more complex options such as weighting results.

Summary

Search isn't synonymous with web crawling. Although the most visible examples of web search are Google, Yahoo!, and the like, search engines are also important for indexing smaller niche collections of documents and data objects, such as the kind that might be the basis of your own web application.

Fortunately, implementing full text search in your application doesn't have to be difficult. The Sphinx search engine, coupled with MySQL and the Ultrasphinx plugin, means that adding powerful full text search to your Ruby on Rails application can be accomplished with minimal fuss and in a database-agnostic fashion.

Sphinx clearly has some speed advantages over using the stock MySQL search capabilities as well; it is specifically optimized for indexing and full text searching, after all. It's also very flexible. Ultrasphinx searches can take a variety of options, allowing you to weight results that are returned and order them by relevancy (`:weight`), support pagination (`:page` and `:per_page`), and search over numerous database tables instead of being limited to just one. When using Ultrasphinx in your project, you can even spell-check user queries with `raspell`.

For more information on these options, make sure to refer to the plugin documentation available at `http://blog.evanweaver.com/files/doc/fauna/ultrasphinx/files/README.html`.

PART 6

■■■

Performance Optimization Plugins

Rails applications all help someone do something—whether it's connecting people with their friends and relatives or helping them do accounting for their small business. In fact, the utility of a web application could be measured by how much it helps people. However, unless an application is scalable, you're fundamentally limited as to how many people can take advantage of your application, which limits its utility.

Fortunately, plugins can help you make complicated applications run faster and be more scalable. In this part, we'll cover two of those plugins: Cache Fu, which can reduce the load on your database server, and Workling, which, in combination with a queue server, can help you manage long background processes easily and quickly.

CHAPTER 17

■ ■ ■

Enhancing Web Site Performance with Cache Fu

The speed at which your web site responds to requests can be extremely important. As a site grows larger, you inevitably need to purchase more hardware. But it is the speed of your application that determines at what point you need to scale your hardware.

You can take a number of approaches to increase an application's speed. Often, optimizing your database-access strategy is a good idea. Rails makes it easy to have hundreds or thousands of database queries per page view, and adding a few eager loading associations (or similar refactoring clauses) can turn many queries into just a few, thus saving huge amounts of execution time. You can also pursue strategies like fragment and page caching, which can allow you to serve cached copies of HTML resources very quickly.

However, in some cases, you can't rely wholly on such strategies. Some database queries can be difficult or impossible to fully optimize, and fragment and page caching can cache only a chunk of output. Fragment and page caching helps less if your performance problems are related to expensive database queries. Additionally, scaling databases efficiently can be hard, and the more you can do with fewer database servers, the better. If you can minimize your load on the database server, you can do more with less. Fortunately, Cache Fu can help you do just that.

The Cache Fu plugin, by Chris Wanstrath, lets you easily and transparently cache queries. This means that once a particular query has been encountered, it will be stored in memory, rather than being recomputed from the database, which can speed up complicated queries significantly. Cache Fu likely won't be your first optimization, and it probably won't be your only caching strategy, but it can be an invaluable way to increase the efficiency of a site more than what you can do with Rails built-in capabilities.

Specifically, Cache Fu uses memcached, which is a distributed system designed for just this kind of caching. Memcached was originally developed for LiveJournal, which was one of the earliest popular blogging communities. Reportedly, the newly developed memcached was able to decrease the site's database load to "nearly nothing" using only existing hardware (see http://www.linuxjournal.com/article/7451). At the time, LiveJournal handled more than 20 million page views a day and had over a million different users, so that decrease was significant. Slashdot and Wikipedia use memcached as well, and both are extremely popular.

■**Tip** Memcached can be used in non–Cache Fu contexts. Rails has built-in support for fragment and session storage via memcached (see `http://wiki.rubyonrails.org/rails/pages/MemCached`). Additionally, most popular languages have a memcached client, so if part of your architecture is written in, say, Java or Python, you can still use memcached to optimize it.

Why is memcached faster than your database? And if it's faster, why wouldn't you store all of your data in memcached? It's faster because it's a completely separate architecture that is designed for caching. There's no permanent disk storage involved. You can think of memcached as a gigantic, fast hash object. However, you can only set values, retrieve values, and delete keys. You can't enumerate over all of the keys in the server, and even if you could, it would be slow, since memcached is not a database server. However, for caching the results of queries, memcached works beautifully. Cache Fu lets you use the model finder requests as keys to the memcached store, and rather than constantly retrieving the same data from the database, you can quickly pull it from the less capable but much faster memcached store.

Our Task: Benchmark a Music Preferences Project

For the example in this chapter, let's suppose we are working on a site that aims to allow users to easily log an entry into the web site every time they listened to a song on their computer. Much as Digg allows users to share web-browsing finds, this site allows users to share musical tastes. As with Last.fm and similar sites, to complete this example, we would need to create a desktop client that recorded the information, but for now, let's focus on the web side.

Let's further suppose that we're concerned about the scalability of our site, since even a casual music listener plays dozens or hundreds of tracks per day. Even a moderate amount of traffic can add up to a tremendous number of records very quickly.

Let's mock up a very simple version of what such a web page might look like, and we'll benchmark the speeds both with and without Cache Fu. This should show us exactly what kind of speed advantage we get by using Cache Fu.

QUERY OPTIMIZATION

Of course, caching a result of a query with Cache Fu helps only on subsequent database hits. The first time a query is encountered, it won't run any faster. For this reason, you need to ensure that your database design and data-access strategy are up to par. You may also need to perform optimizations like eager loading associations, creating indexes, caching counts and function calls, and so forth.

For association counts, Rails can maintain the cache for you. For function calls—like commonly used MySQL built-in functions inside conditions—neither Rails nor MySQL can help you, since, unlike some other databases, MySQL can't create indexes that use function calls. You can, however, create a MySQL trigger that updates a cache column. For example, if you were caching the result of `LCASE(name)`, you might create a trigger that updates `cache_lcase_name` to the result of `LCASE(name)` whenever the table in question was changed. You can find out more about MySQL triggers at `http://dev.mysql.com/doc/refman/5.0/en/create-trigger.html`.

There are many ways you might optimize a MySQL query. A great place to start might be the Query Analyzer plugin. This plugin lets you use MySQL's built-in EXPLAIN facility to determine why queries are slow. Using that information, you can take steps to correct the issues. You can find out more about the Query Analyzer plugin at `http://svn.umesd.k12.or.us/plugins/query_analyzer/README`.

Preparing for the Cache Fu Example

Before we get started, you need to install memcached. You can get a Windows version of memcached at `http://jehiah.com/projects/memcached-win32/`, but using the Windows memcached server for production applications is not recommended. So, in this chapter, we'll assume you're running a Linux, FreeBSD, or Mac OS X computer. You can install memcached on these systems as follows:

- For Debian Linux and related distributions, including Ubuntu Linux, install memcached with this command:

  ```
  sudo apt-get install memcache
  ```

- If you're using Red Hat or CentOS, you can install memcached as follows:

  ```
  yum install memcached
  ```

- If you're on FreeBSD, you can install memcached as follows:

  ```
  cd /usr/ports/databases/memcached/
  make configure && make install
  ```

- If you're on OS X and have MacPorts installed, you can install it as follows:

  ```
  port install memcached
  ```

- For OS X or other Linux distributions, you can also download a binary from the memcached home page: `http://www.danga.com/memcached/`.

You'll also need to install the Memcache Client gem:

```
gem install memcache-client
```

Memcache Client is a Ruby library for accessing memcached servers. You won't need to use Memcache Client directly when you use Cache Fu, since Cache Fu takes care of dealing with the memcached server for you.

Next, let's create a Rails application:

```
rails cache_fu_example
cd cache_fu_example
```

Then install the Cache Fu plugin, as follows:

```
ruby script/plugin install git://github.com/defunkt/cache_fu.git
```

```
removing: /home/dave/cache_fu_example/vendor/plugins/cache_fu/.git
Initialized empty Git repository in ➥
/home/dave/cache_fu_example/vendor/plugins/cache_fu/.git/
remote: Counting objects: 38, done.
Compressing objects: 100% (34/34), done.)
Indexing 38 objects...
remote: Total 38 (delta 2), reused 36 (delta 2)
 100% (38/38) done
Resolving 2 deltas...
 100% (2/2) done


** Checking for memcached in path...
** Checking for memcache-client gem...
** Trying to copy memcached.yml.default to ./config/memcached.yml...
** Trying to copy memcached_ctl.default to ./script/memcached_ctl...

** acts_as_cached installed with no errors. ➥
Please edit the memcached.yml file to your liking.
** Now would be a good time to check out the README. Enjoy your day.
```

As you see, the plugin installation output mentions that you should edit the config/
memcached.yml file. Open that file in your text editor and examine it now. An annotated version
of the sample configuration is shown in Listing 17-1.

Listing 17-1. *Cache Fu Memcached Configuration File (config/memcached.yml)*

```
defaults:
  # The following key controls the default expiration time for stored
  # data:
  ttl: 1800
  readonly: false
  urlencode: false
  c_threshold: 10000
  compression: true
  debug: false
  # This key can be used to have multiple separate
  # apps on the same memcached servers:
  namespace: app
  # Set the next key to true to use Memcached for sessions:
  sessions: false
  session_servers: false
```

```
  # Set the next key to true to use Memcached for fragment storage:
  fragments: false
  memory: 64
  servers: localhost:11211
  benchmarking: true
  raise_errors: true
  fast_hash: false
  fastest_hash: false

development:
  sessions: false
  fragments: false
  servers: localhost:11211

# turn off caching
test:
  disabled: true

production:
  memory: 256
  benchmarking: false
  servers:
    - 192.185.254.121:11211
    - 192.185.254.138:11211
    - 192.185.254.160:11211
```

Note that the production environment has three servers listed. In production, you can spread out a memcached setup into as many servers as you have available. Since application servers are not typically limited by memory, often memcached is set up on application servers alongside their primary function.

Additionally, note that Cache Fu can also handle your session and fragment storage through memcached. Set the appropriate keys in the configuration file shown in Listing 17-1 to easily and quickly cache sessions and fragments as well.

The servers shown in Listing 17-1 are only sample entries. For this chapter's example, delete the last three lines, and replace them with the following line:

```
    - localhost:11211
```

This will cause Cache Fu to look for memcached on your current server while in production mode.

Building the Benchmarking Application

With the Cache Fu plugin installed and configured, you're ready to build the benchmarking application. We'll create the application, load some test data, and run some benchmarks.

Generating the Models

Let's generate our two models: User and TrackListen.

ruby script/generate model user

```
exists   app/models/
exists   test/unit/
exists   test/fixtures/
create   app/models/user.rb
create   test/unit/user_test.rb
create   test/fixtures/users.yml
exists   db/migrate
create   db/migrate/001_create_users.rb
```

ruby script/generate model track_listen

```
exists   app/models/
exists   test/unit/
exists   test/fixtures/
create   app/models/track_listen.rb
create   test/unit/track_listen_test.rb
create   test/fixtures/track_listens.yml
create   db/migrate
create   db/migrate/002_create_track_listens.rb
```

Next, we create the first migration for the users table, as shown in Listing 17-2.

Listing 17-2. *Create Users Migration (db/migrate/001_create_users.rb)*

```ruby
class CreateUsers < ActiveRecord::Migration
  def self.up
    create_table :users do |t|
      t.string :name
      t.string :login
      t.timestamps
    end
  end

  def self.down
    drop_table :users
  end
end
```

This is deliberately oversimplified. For a full system, you would need more than just a username and login, but for our purposes, this should be fine.

Next, let's create the migration for our TrackListen model, which records each individual time a track is played, as shown in Listing 17-3.

Listing 17-3. *Create Track Listens Migration (db/migrate/002_create_track_listens.rb)*

```ruby
class CreateTrackListens < ActiveRecord::Migration
  def self.up
    create_table :track_listens do |t|
      t.integer :user_id
      t.string :track_name
      t.timestamps
    end
  end

  def self.down
    drop_table :track_listens
  end
end
```

Of course, in a typical production environment, you would likely have a separate table for tracks. In this particular example, that could get tricky. You would almost certainly have a myriad of misspellings and alternate spellings for track names, as many people still type in track names by hand when ripping CDs. Also, track names are often slightly different on albums that have been rereleased or when they are part of a "greatest hits" or other collection. Again, this simplified schema is intended only for demonstration purposes.

Now you're ready to run the two migrations:

```
rake db:migrate
```

Next, let's examine our two models. Listing 17-4 shows the TrackListen model.

Listing 17-4. *Track Listen Model (app/models/track_listen.rb)*

```ruby
class TrackListen < ActiveRecord::Base
  belongs_to :user

  def self.most_recent_listens
    TrackListen.find(:all, :order=>'created_at DESC', :limit=>10)
  end
end
```

The TrackListen model has a custom finder. The most_recent_listens class method returns the last ten songs listened to by users on our system. In a real implementation, you would likely have many more types of queries that return different kinds of data. However, one slow query is enough for us to see how much Cache Fu can speed up queries.

As you can see in Listing 17-5, the User model is simple.

Listing 17-5. *User Model (app/models/user.rb)*

```
class User < ActiveRecord::Base
  has_many :track_listens
end
```

The User model has just one relationship. It doesn't contain any custom methods.

Loading Test Data into the Database

We need some test data for our database. We'll use the script shown in Listing 17-6 to load
some sample data.

Listing 17-6. *Load Data Script (load_data.rb)*

```
User.destroy_all
TrackListen.destroy_all

1.upto(5) do |number|
  puts "Creating User ##{number}"
  u = User.create!(:name=>"Test User #{number}", :login=>"user_#{number}")
  total = 20000
  total.times do |i|
     puts "#{i} of #{total} TrackListens  created" if (i % 4000 == 0)
     u.track_listens.create!(:track_name=>"Test Song #{rand(300)}")
  end
end
```

This script first deletes any data present in the database, since you wouldn't dump hundreds of thousands of test records into a database with valuable data. Next, it creates five
users, with 20,000 track listens per user, and it prints out a brief status message every 1,000
records created.

■**Tip** A more comprehensive system for tracking a script's progress is provided by the ProgressBar gem,
which creates a small ASCII progress bar on the terminal. It's a small, easy-to-use gem, so it's a great way
to track long-running processes. You can find out more about the ProgressBar gem at http://0xcc.net/
ruby-progressbar/index.html.en.

You can run the data loader as follows:

```
ruby script/runner load_data.rb
```

This will take a few minutes, so if you prefer, you can download the data from the Source
Code/Download section of the Apress web site (http://apress.com). It's named development.
sqlite3.

Mocking Up a Simple Test Controller

Now that we have two models and two tables with data in them, let's take a look at mocking up a simple controller. The homepage controller for this example is shown in Listing 17-7.

Listing 17-7. *Homepage Controller (app/controllers/homepage_controller.rb)*

```
class HomepageController < ApplicationController
  def index
    @most_recent_listens = TrackListen.most_recent_listens
    render :text=>''
  end
end
```

This controller has just a single action, which renders a blank string. We're not returning a full web page because it would unnecessarily skew our results. We're looking at how much Cache Fu affects database query speed, not at how much time is consumed downloading data from the controller.

■**Note** If you're looking at optimizing an existing system, you typically profile your application in order to figure out which part is causing the slowdown. However, when you are explicitly comparing two techniques, you should isolate them as much as possible.

At this point, the application should be ready to test. Let's set up our test script, as shown in Listing 17-8.

Listing 17-8. *Application Benchmark Script (time_tester.rb)*

```
require 'benchmark'

Benchmark.bm do |b|
  b.report do
    tries = 1000
    tries.times do |i|
      puts "#{i} of #{tries}" if (i % 10) == 0
      `curl http://localhost:3000/homepage 2>&1 > /dev/null`
    end
  end
end
```

Start the web server with ruby script/server. Now we're ready to run some tests.

Running the Benchmarks

It's time to run our benchmarking program and see how much time our query takes.

ruby time_tester.rb

```
0 of 2000 TrackListens created
 ...snip...
user      system    total      real
0.070000  0.340000  6.120000 ( 55.205992)
```

The important number is the last one, 55 seconds. The other numbers aren't very large because only the last time entry reflects the total delay. The other figures show the time spent by the benchmarking program, which isn't the process doing the actual database work; the server process is doing that.

Let's see if we can speed things up using Cache Fu. To do that, we need to enable acts_as_cached for our model. Open app/models/track_listen.rb and add the following line after class TrackListen < ActiveRecord::Base:

  acts_as_cached

This method lets us add caching support to our model.

Tip You can pass an optional :ttl parameter to the acts_as_cached method. The :ttl parameter sets the expiration time on the cache. For example, if you used acts_as_cache :ttl=>10.minutes, results would be cached for 10 minutes before being re-retrieved from the database and reset in the cache.

Open app/controllers/homepage_controller.rb and change the following line:

@most_recent_listens = TrackListen.most_recent_listens

to this:

@most_recent_listens = TrackListen.cached(:most_recent_listens)

We pass the name of our custom finder, most_recent_listens, to the cached method provided by Cache Fu. When the answer isn't present in the cache, it will call our custom finder; otherwise, it uses whatever data is stored in the memcached store. We can still use other methods of TrackListen, of course, but they won't be cached.

The idea is that you take the most commonly used, expensive operations—those that gain the most benefit by being cached—turn them into a custom finder on your model, like our most_recent_listens finder, and cache them. In our case, it was already a custom finder. Many Rails developers feel that most, if not all, complex calls to Find should be turned into a custom finder. If you develop in that style, you can just pass your existing finders to cached.

Although we didn't use them in our example, you can pass additional parameters to the cached method, and they will be passed to the finder. For example, if we refactored most_recent_listens to take an argument specifying the number of songs to return, we could call it like this:

```
@last_twenty_songs = TrackListen.cached(:most_recent_listens, 20)
```

As you can imagine, arbitrarily complex queries can be cached this way.

Incidentally, the cached method is just one of two primary ways you use Cache Fu on your models. You can also pass an ID, or more than one ID, to the get_cache method, like this:

```
a_value = TrackListen.get_cache(1)
some_values = TrackListen.get_cache(1,2,3)
```

These two lines are essentially cached versions of the following two lines:

```
a_value = TrackListen.find(1)
some_values  = TrackListen.find([1,2,3])
```

Next, let's start memcached:

```
ruby script/memcached_ctl start
```

At this point, you can verify that memcached is running using the following command:

```
ps aux | grep memcache
```

```
your_username    12727  0.6  0.5  46676 41112 ? ➥
Ss   16:47   0:00 /usr/bin/memcached -d -m 128 -l 192.168.x.y -p 11211
```

The exact values will vary. The important thing is that you have a line with /usr/bin/memcached in it.

Stop the web server, and then restart it using the following command:

```
ruby script/server -e production
```

Let's run our benchmarking program again:

```
ruby time_tester.rb
```

```
user       system     total      real
0.060000   0.160000   4.300000 (  7.384402)
```

That's about 7.5 times faster—a very significant increase.

■Note We ran this benchmark on a 3.0 GHz Core 2 Duo processor with 8GB of RAM. For your tests, you may want to adjust the number of runs in `time_tester.rb` to be a bit lower. However, if you adjust the number of trial runs to be too low, you may get inaccurate results. In this case, because the differential is so high, that doesn't seem likely, but often you may find yourself testing code with a much smaller difference between optimized and unoptimized. In those cases, if you find that your optimized and optimized bench-marking times are close together, you should increase the number of runs to make sure you're not looking at an anomalous result.

Of course, not all Rails applications will be as dependent on database access. Small applications may benefit more from careful analysis of their database access and better hardware. For large-scale applications, memcached and Cache Fu can be very valuable.

Summary

Performance is an extremely important issue, and caching strategies are a very important part of increasing performance. Of course, other issues can affect performance. You must have sufficient hardware, and you should have a reasonable database design, with carefully chosen keys and, if necessary, automatically maintained denormalization, such as counter caches and function call caches. But at some point, further efficiency is unlikely. When you get there, using Cache Fu is an excellent and relatively easy way to further increase performance.

CHAPTER 18

■ ■ ■

Managing Complex Background Processes with Workling and Starling

As the web applications you develop become more complex, you're likely to encounter situations where you must deal with long-running or computationally expensive tasks. By default, these requests are handled within the normal HTTP request/response cycle, which can be a problem if tasks take a long time to process. For instance, what if the web browser times out? How do we show progress updates to the user? How do we deal with a lot of this sort of activity occurring simultaneously (since a Rails instance blocks while the action is being performed)?

All of these questions lead us to one conclusion: for long-running requests, we need to find some way to off-load tasks so they run outside the request cycle, asynchronously. We can accomplish this in many different ways, ranging from using the simplest spawning servers to far more complex message brokers like Amazon Simple Queue Service (SQS).

On the simple side of things, Spawn (`http://rubyforge.org/projects/spawn`) is a Rails plugin that allows you to fork or thread long-running processes. It's a very minimalist solution to the problem, and it's easy to set up. However, Spawn does not give us as much control over the processes as we might like, or make any guarantees that the tasks are performed at all. Spawn is best for performing simple tasks that do not need any user monitoring or reporting, or where the state of an operation is managed internally, and periodic database polling is implemented. For instance, Spawn would be suitable if you just needed to send system announcements to a list of e-mail addresses.

On the other side of the aisle are heavyweight job and scheduling servers like BackgrounDRb (`http://backgroundrb.rubyforge.org`), and reliable asynchronous message queuing services such as Apache ActiveMQ (`http://activemq.apache.org`) and Amazon's hosted SQS platform. In Ruby, a number of libraries are available to interface with these queues. ActiveMessaging (`http://code.google.com/p/activemessaging/wiki/ActiveMessaging`) is one such library, providing interfaces to either Apache ActiveMQ or Amazon SQS.

■Tip Many other solutions exist for dealing with long-running or computationally intensive tasks. The Async Observer plugin (`http://async-observer.rubyforge.org`), for instance, works with Beanstalkd, an in-memory queue service. BackgroundJob (BJ), BackgroundFu, and AP4R are other options you may want to investigate. Each offers unique advantages and disadvantages. You should spend some time to find the one that best fits your particular situation.

In this chapter, we'll take a look at Starling (`http://rubyforge.org/projects/starling`), a lightweight persistent queue server written entirely in Ruby, by Blaine Cook and the team at Twitter. To interface with Starling, we'll use Workling (`http://playtype.net/past/2008/2/6`), a Rails plugin developed by Rany Keddo and Björn Wolf of Play/Type GmbH. Workling is runner-agnostic, meaning it can interface and run jobs through either Starling or Spawn.

We'll use this combination of technologies to handle long-running processes outside the Rails request/response cycle—in this case, for transcoding video uploads.

Our Task: Transcode Video Uploads for Flash Media Playback

We've been asked by a client to build a system for sharing do-it-yourself style "how-to" screencasts. The content will be largely user-generated, so visitors will need to be able to upload videos. Since Flash Video (FLV) is the format of choice for web video playback (due to the Flash virtual machine's ubiquity and excellent video playback capabilities), we'll want to display all the videos in a nice, skinnable Flash media component.

However, we don't want to restrict our users to uploading FLV files. Instead, we would like to allow them to upload just about any media type, without having to worry that it fits our particular format, size, and bit rate specifications. Therefore, part of our task will be transcoding whatever files users upload to a size and format acceptable for playback within our web application.

Transcoding videos may take some time. If this operation were handled synchronously, the Rails process would block, possibly denying resources to other visitors, and the user's request could time out. To avoid these consequences, and in order to display some sort of progress indicator while the video is being converted, we'll use a message queue, Starling, and the Workling plugin. This approach will allow us to do this work in the background, asynchronously. We could also use it to distribute these transcoding jobs across many different machines as the service becomes increasingly popular.

■Note Using a message queue isn't the only way to handle a system for converting formats. We could also store transcode requests to a database table and periodically poll for new conversion jobs. This isn't quite as robust as a message queue–based approach, but it is simpler and may work for you.

We'll also use a Flash video player component to display the video to visitors once it is encoded to the proper (FLV) format. The plugin we'll use for this is Flash Player Helper (`http://www.jroller.com/abstractScope/entry/flash_mp3_imageslideshow_media_player`), by Farooq Ali. In addition to video playback, this plugin can also be used to handle Flash-based audio playback and image slide shows, making it a good choice for many media-centric applications.

Creating a Video Transcoding Service

Let's create a new Rails application for the how-to video project:

```
rails howtotube
cd howtotube
```

We'll need Starling, as discussed, which is available as a Ruby gem. Starling makes use of memcached (discussed in Chapter 17), so we'll also need to get the Memcache Client gem at this time. To install both of them, issue the following command:

```
gem install memcache-client starling
```

Workling, our interface to the message queue server for running background jobs, is available as a Rails plugin. It also needs to be installed at this point:

```
ruby script/plugin install http://svn.playtype.net/plugins/workling
```

We'll need a tool to do the actual transcoding, too. For this, we'll employ FFmpeg, a powerful command-line utility for converting between various video formats. Instructions for downloading and compiling FFmpeg sources can be found at `http://ffmpeg.mplayerhq.hu/download.html`. Binary versions may be provided through the package management system of your operating system. Alternatively, if you are on a Windows platform and desire a binary version, the links provided at `http://www.videohelp.com/tools/ffmpeg` should prove helpful.

■**Note** Certain compression algorithms used by FFmpeg may be patent-encumbered in some countries. For more information, see `http://ffmpeg.mplayerhq.hu/legal.html`.

Finally, in order to play back the videos we'll be transcoding in the client's browser, we'll want to install the Flash Player Helper plugin. Issue the following command to do that now:

```
ruby script/plugin install svn://rubyforge.org/var/svn/flashplayrhelpr
```

Creating the Video Model

Before we can demonstrate how to handle transcoding asynchronously, we need to prepare a basic model to represent the video resources in our system and allow users to upload a new video.

We'll start by creating a migration for the model, shown in Listing 18-1. It defines a simple videos table with fields for name and description, the actual file name of the file, the (original) file extension, and a status flag to indicate whether it has finished being converted (transcoded). Save the code shown in Listing 18-1 as db/migrate/001_create_videos.rb.

Listing 18-1. *Videos Migration (db/migrate/001_create_videos.rb)*

```
class CreateVideos < ActiveRecord::Migration
  def self.up
    create_table :videos do |t|
      t.string   :file_name
      t.string   :file_ext
      t.string   :name
      t.text     :description
      t.boolean :converted
      t.timestamps
    end
  end

  def self.down
    drop_table :videos
  end
end
```

Next, migrate the project's database using the standard rake db:migrate task:

```
rake db:migrate
```

```
== 1 CreateVideos: migrating ====================================================
– create_table(:videos)
   -> 0.0037s
== 1 CreateVideos: migrated (0.0038s) ===========================================
```

Our Video model will need a number of custom methods in addition to its automatically inherited attribute accessors. The necessary code is shown in Listing 18-2. Save it as app/models/video.rb.

Listing 18-2. *Video Model (app/models/video.rb)*

```
class Video < ActiveRecord::Base
  UPLOAD_DIR = "#{RAILS_ROOT}/public/tmp"
  VIDEO_DIR  = "#{RAILS_ROOT}/public/videos"

  validates_presence_of :name, :file_name, :file_ext
  attr_protected :converted
  before_create :save_uploaded_file
```

```ruby
  def data=(file)
    @tmp_file = file

    timestr = Time.now.strftime('%Y%m%d%H%M%S')
    self.file_name = "#{timestr}-#{file.original_filename.sub(/.\w+$/, '')}"
    self.file_ext = file.original_filename.split('.').last

    # optional: check file.content_type
  end

  def tmp_path
    "#{UPLOAD_DIR}/#{file_name}.#{file_ext}"
  end

  def path
    "#{VIDEO_DIR}/#{file_name}.flv"
  end

  def public_filename
    "/videos/#{file_name}.flv"
  end

  private

    def save_uploaded_file
      Dir.mkdir(UPLOAD_DIR) unless File.exist?(UPLOAD_DIR)
      Dir.mkdir(VIDEO_DIR) unless File.exist?(VIDEO_DIR)

      File.open(tmp_path, "wb") do |f|
        f.write(@tmp_file.read)
      end
    end
end
```

■**Tip** We could implement various safeguards and optimizations here, including checking the file's
content_type to make sure it is an actual video file. This is left as a task for the reader. You may also want
to consider using a more robust file upload/attachment-handling plugin, such as Attachment Fu here; see
Chapter 3 for more information.

In order to allow us to assign an uploaded file to the model from a controller, we've added a
data setter method to the Video model. When this method is called, the file_name and file_ext
attributes are set to the appropriate values using the file's original_filename method, and the
file itself is copied into a @tmp_file instance variable. Notice that the filename that we set up
here includes a timestamp. This is used to ensure some level of uniqueness. Clearly we could

take more accurate measures, but for our purposes it's highly unlikely that two users will upload files with the same name at the exact same second.

The contents of `@tmp_file` are written out to disk in the private `save_uploaded_file` method. This method is run automatically before a new record is saved for the first time because it is specified as a `before_create` filter. The file itself is placed in the temporary file path, returned by the `tmp_path` method. This method, along with the `path` and `public_filename` methods, makes use of the `file_name` and `file_ext` attribute values to construct paths and publicly accessible URLs to the video assets. For convenience, we store all uploaded files in the `UPLOAD_DIR` directory and the finished, converted file in the `VIDEO_DIR` directory.

Creating the Videos Controller

Our next step is to create a videos controller and a new video form in order to allow users to upload their media. We'll also need to add a route to reach this controller and its actions. We'll use a standard resource route for this. The updated `config/routes.rb` file is shown in Listing 18-3.

Listing 18-3. *Video Resource Route (config/routes.rb)*

```
ActionController::Routing::Routes.draw do |map|
  map.resources :videos
end
```

The code for the first version of our `VideosController` is shown in Listing 18-4. At this point, it's just a standard CRUD controller responsible for handling user uploads, transcoding the video in-line (synchronously), and accessing the video resources. None of the work is being handled asynchronously yet—we'll get to that shortly. In the meantime, save the code in Listing 18-4 as `app/controllers/videos_controller.rb`.

Listing 18-4. *Videos Controller (app/controllers/videos_controller.rb)*

```
class VideosController < ApplicationController
  def index
    @videos = Video.find(:all, :conditions => "converted IS NOT NULL")
  end

  def show
    @video = Video.find(params[:id])
  end

  def new
    @video = Video.new
  end

  def create
    @video = Video.new(params[:video])
    if @video.save
      flash[:notice] = "Thanks for uploading your video."
```

```
      cmd = "ffmpeg -i #{@video.tmp_path} -y -ar 22050 -ab 32 -f flv -s 320x240 " +
        @video.path
      system(cmd)

      @video.update_attribute(:converted, true)

      redirect_to(video_path(@video))
    else
      flash[:error] = "Unable to save the video. Please check the form for errors."
      render(:action => 'new')
    end
  end
end
```

Notice the `ffmpeg` options shown in the `create` action. They instruct the command-line utility to take a file of arbitrary format as input; alter the audio sampling rate, audio bit rate, and frame size to the specified values (appropriate for display in our web application); and force the output format to FLV. We use Ruby's `system` method to execute this command in a subshell, and use the paths defined in our model, so it knows where to expect the input file to exist and where it should write output.

Once FFmpeg finishes converting the file, we set the `converted` Boolean flag on the model and save it using Active Record's `update_attribute` method.

■**Tip** For more information about FFmpeg and its rich set of features and options, see `http://ffmpeg.mplayerhq.hu/ffmpeg-doc.html`.

Three views are associated with this controller: one each for the `index`, `show`, and `new` actions. The `index` action template, predictably, just lists all videos that currently exist in the system and provides links to show the videos. It is shown in Listing 18-5 and should be saved as `app/views/videos/index.html.erb`.

Listing 18-5. *Videos Index Template View (app/views/videos/index.html.erb)*

```
<h1>Howto Videos</h1>
<ul>
<% @videos.each do |video| -%>
  <li><%= link_to(video.name, video_path(video)) %></li>
<% end -%>
</ul>

<p><%= link_to('New Video', new_video_path) %></p>
```

The `new` action template, shown in Listing 18-6, is also fairly stock. Save it as `app/views/videos/new.html.erb`. The template contains a basic form that prompts the user for the name and description of the video, and provides a file field used for specifying the video file itself. Note that the multipart option of form_for is required to enable file uploads. When clicked, the Upload button will submit the form to the create action.

Listing 18-6. *New Video Template View (app/views/videos/new.html.erb)*

```
<h1>New Video</h1>
<% form_for(:video, :url => videos_path, :html => { :multipart => true }) do |f| -%>
  <p>Name:<br/>
  <%= f.text_field(:name) %></p>

  <p>Description:<br/>
  <%= f.text_area(:description) %></p>

  <p><%= f.file_field(:data) %></p>

  <%= submit_tag('Upload') %>
<% end -%>
```

We'll update the show action template later to make it a bit more sophisticated. But for now, our needs are pretty simple. We just want to display the video with a basic set of controls, so we'll use the code shown in Listing 18-7. Save it as app/views/videos/show.html.erb.

Listing 18-7. *Show Video Template View (app/views/videos/show.html.erb)*

```
<h1><%= h(@video.name) %></h1>
<p><%= h(@video.description) %></p>
<%= flv_player(:file => @video.public_filename) if @video.converted? %>

<p><%= link_to("Return to Index", videos_path) %></p>
```

The call to flv_player in this template references the helper method provided by Farooq Ali's plugin. It renders a Flash video player component and automatically loads the appropriate file into it for playback (the uploaded movie, after conversion).

■**Tip** The Flash Player Helper plugin supports a variety of options, as well as different players to support MP3 playback, image galleries, and mixed media. For more information about it, see http://www.jroller.com/abstractScope/entry/flash_mp3_imageslideshow_media_player.

In order for it to work correctly, the media player helper plugin requires that we add an extra JavaScript include (`javascript_include_tag 'ufo'`) to our views. Since we also want to add a place where our notice and error messages will be displayed for all the views in our application, we'll create an application layout and include it there.

Save the code in Listing 18-8 as `app/views/layouts/application.html.erb`. This application layout will automatically be used to wrap any views that have not explicitly specified an alternate layout.

Listing 18-8. *Application Layout (app/views/layouts/application.html.erb)*

```
<!DOCTYPE html PUBLIC "-//W3C//DTD XHTML 1.0 Transitional//EN"
        "http://www.w3.org/TR/xhtml1/DTD/xhtml1-transitional.dtd">

<html xmlns="http://www.w3.org/1999/xhtml" xml:lang="en" lang="en">
<head>
  <meta http-equiv="content-type" content="text/html;charset=UTF-8" />
  <title>HowtoTube</title>
  <style type="text/css">
    .alert { color: blue; border: 1px solid blue; padding: 5px; }
  </style>
  <%= javascript_include_tag(:defaults, 'ufo') %>
</head>
<body>

<% if flash[:notice] || flash[:error] -%>
  <div class="alert"><%= flash[:notice] || flash[:error] %></div>
<% end -%>

<%= yield  %>

</body>
</html>
```

Notice that we've also included the default Prototype JavaScript library in the layout; we'll be making use of them shortly.

Testing Synchronous Transcodes

Before we get around to implementing the asynchronous transcoding, let's try out our current application as is, with video transcoding handled synchronously. Start the Rails server using `script/server` and visit `http://localhost:3000/videos/new` in a web browser. The browser should display a form similar to the one shown in Figure 18-1.

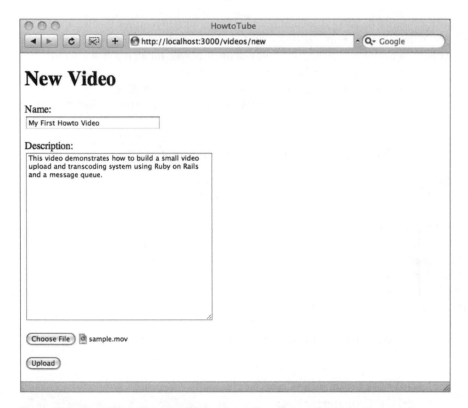

Figure 18-1. *New video file upload form (http://localhost:3000/videos/new)*

Specify the new video's name and description, and select a small QuickTime movie file to be uploaded and reencoded to Flash video. Make sure the file is small, but not too small—anything between 10MB and 20MB should do nicely. Alternatively, you can use the sample movie located at http://railsplugins.com/files/sample.mp4.

When you submit the form, the file will be uploaded and handed off to the create action. Assuming that you've filled in all the fields, the create action should create the model, save the file to your local temp directory, and use the FFmpeg tool to convert it to our chosen output format. When the conversion is finished, it will redirect you to the show action view, and you'll be able to watch the video using the slick Flash video player component provided by the Flash Player Helper plugin. You should see something like the screen in Figure 18-2.

Figure 18-2. *Converted video playback (http://localhost:3000/videos/1)*

You'll no doubt notice a slight delay as FFmpeg converts the video to the desired format. In fact, if you were watching the server output in a console (or tailing the log file in log/ development.log), you would see the output of the command as it ran, in-line with the rest of the server log trace. Although the delay experienced may be acceptable for a small movie, larger files will take far, far longer. And keep in mind that if you're deploying a web service that may receive moderate to heavy usage, there's a good chance you'll have several uploads and transcoding operations going on simultaneously.

Our client is expecting (hoping!) that a large number of people are going to want to use his web site to upload how-to screencasts and share them with others. Therefore, system performance and the ability to handle load are of the utmost concern. We need to make sure that the application is responsive, that it doesn't block when unnecessary (we have a limited number of server instances, after all), and that the request doesn't time out on the user.

■**Tip** A Rails server instance will also block while the file itself is being uploaded, of course. If your real-world application is handling any volume of file uploads, we encourage you to consider using a lightweight file upload handler to supplement Rails. Merb (http://merbivore.com) is a popular framework option for this kind of task.

Asynchronous Transcoding

Clearly, it makes sense to hand off the task of transcoding to another background process. That way, we divorce the transcoding process from the request cycle.

We'll want to modify our existing application to remove the in-line video conversion process that currently exists in the create action. Instead, after the file has finished uploading, we'll immediately redirect the user to our show action. It will be the responsibility of show to check whether the video has been converted. If it hasn't, we'll want to fire off a task to asynchronously convert the video. This means putting a message in our queue that signifies that there is some work to be done. A *runner* (worker process) will poll the queue and convert videos as they arrive or as resources become available. This process is illustrated in Figure 18-3.

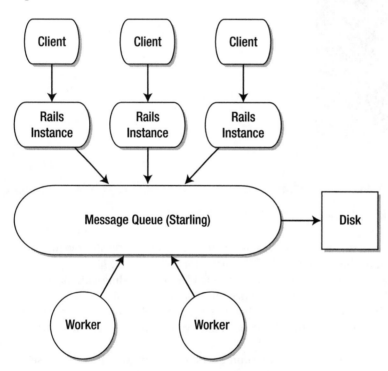

Figure 18-3. *Asynchronous transcoding service workflow*

In the meantime, while we wait for the transcode request to be serviced, the users will be shown a status indicator. Their browser will check in periodically using an Ajax technique to see if the file conversion has finished, and when it has, the video will be displayed.

We'll use Workling to make all this happen without needing to worry too much about the behind-the-scenes implementation details.

Setting Up Asynchronous Workers

In order to use Workling, we first need to specify which runner will be used to process jobs that are in the queue. We can do this in our config/environment.rb file, or, because it's a bit cleaner, we can create a `workling.rb` file in our `config/initializers` directory. Initializer scripts located in this directory are run automatically when the server is started up.

Workling ships with support for both Starling and the far simpler Spawn runner. It's also possible to add your own runners, as Workling itself functions in a server/queue-agnostic fashion. In this case, we'll be using Starling as our message queue. Therefore, we want to use the `StarlingRunner` to process the messages. Save the code shown in Listing 18-9 as `config/initializers/workling.rb`.

Listing 18-9. *Workling Configuration (config/initializers/workling.rb)*

```
Workling::Remote.dispatcher = Workling::Remote::Runners::StarlingRunner.new
```

■Tip If the line in Listing 18-9 is commented out, all asynchronous calls we make in our application will become synchronous, which can be useful for debugging.

Workling mandates that any asynchronous work be done within a `Worker` class. All workers reside in the `app/workers` directory and inherit from `Workling::Base`. They can define any number of operations that are to be performed asynchronously. Once defined, a worker method can be called asynchronously from anywhere in our application, using syntax like the following:

```
TranscodeWorker.asynch_convert_video(:video_id => 1)
```

In this example, `convert_video` is the name of the method being called in the `TranscodeWorker` class. The `asynch_` part of the method name is automatically prepended by convention and used to illustrate that this method is being called asynchronously.

Since our video conversion process is straightforward, our worker does not need to be complex. It's simply going to transcode the video for us using the FFmpeg utility, and then update the model to indicate that the conversion is complete. `TranscodeWorker` encapsulates these actions within a single method, `convert_video`. The entirety of our worker class is shown in Listing 18-10. Save it as `app/workers/transcode_worker.rb`.

Listing 18-10. *TranscodeWorker (app/workers/transcode_worker.rb)*

```
class TranscodeWorker < Workling::Base
  # usage: TranscodeWorker.asynch_convert_video(:video_id => id)
  def convert_video(options = {})
    video = Video.find_by_id(options[:video_id])
    unless video.nil?
      cmd = "ffmpeg -i #{video.tmp_path} -y -ar 22050 -ab 32 -f flv -s 320x240 " +
        video.path
      system(cmd)
```

```
        video.update_attribute(:converted, true)
      end
    end
end
```

All Workling worker methods must accept an `options` hash, and our `convert_video` method is no exception. The `options` hash is automatically populated with a unique identifier for the current job (which is not something the end user has to worry about) and other environmental necessities. Any additional parameters should be passed as named parameters within the hash. In this case, we need to pass the ID of the video we want to convert by specifying the `video_id` in that hash.

■Note We pass an identifier (`video_id`) instead of a `Video` model object directly because the worker runs in a separate process. Certain facilities, such as the model's database connection, would not be available to the process if the model object were passed directly. Instead, we use the ID to look up a fresh instance of the object.

Workling and the `StarlingRunner` take care of most of the hard work for us here. For example, message queue names are mapped to worker methods automatically; that is, our `TranscodeWorker.convert_video` method is automatically mapped to the appropriate message queue. If we had more than one type of asynchronous worker event, we could easily maintain separate queues without giving a second thought to its implementation or job routing.

From our point of view, all we need to know is that once we start the provided client daemon, it will wait for messages and, upon receiving them, will immediately dispatch them to workers responsible for processing them. All of this happens without any help from us! You'll see this in action shortly, but first, we need to finish updating our example by modifying our controller.

Updating the Controller

Now that we have the capability to transcode video asynchronously using Workling and the `StarlingRunner`, we need to update our controller to take advantage of this functionality. We'll remove the explicit in-line conversion from the `create` method and put code in the `show` method to test whether a video has been converted. If it has, we'll just show the template. If it hasn't, we'll kick off the asynchronous transcode process and show a template that has a progress ("working") animation.

The `show` action template will then use an Ajax routine in the form of the Rails Prototype helper, `periodically_call_remote`, to poll our controller action via JavaScript every few seconds to see if the video has finished the conversion process. Since the action's response should differ depending on whether the client asked for an HTML page or a JavaScript status update, we'll use `respond_to` in the controller method to detect the content type that has been requested—HTML or JavaScript—and respond accordingly.

The updated controller `show` and `create` methods are shown in Listing 18-11. Modify your copy of `app/controllers/videos_controller.rb` to reflect these changes.

Listing 18-11. *Updated Show and Create Actions for VideosController (app/controllers/ videos_controller.rb)*

```ruby
def show
  @video = Video.find(params[:id])
  respond_to do |format|
    if @video.converted?
      format.html # render show.html.erb
      format.js { render(:partial => "player.html.erb") }
    else
      format.html do
        TranscodeWorker.asynch_convert_video(:video_id => @video.id)
        # render show.html.erb
      end
      # no content (unsupported), working
      format.js { render(:nothing => true, :status => 415) }
    end
  end
end

def create
  @video = Video.new(params[:video])
  if @video.save
    flash[:notice] = "Thanks for uploading your video."
    redirect_to(video_path(@video))
  else
    flash[:error] = "Unable to save the video. Please check the form for errors."
    render(:action => 'new')
  end
end
```

We'll also need to make some changes to the show action template, as mentioned earlier. Our updated code is shown in Listing 18-12. Save it as app/views/videos/show.html.erb.

Listing 18-12. *Updated Show Video Template (app/views/videos/show.html.erb)*

```erb
<h1><%= h(@video.name) %></h1>
<p><%= h(@video.description) %></p>

<div id="player">
  <% if @video.converted? -%>
    <%= flv_player(:file => @video.public_filename) %>
  <% else -%>
    <script language="javascript">var check_status = true;</script>
    <%= periodically_call_remote(:url => video_path(@video), :method => :get,
        :update => { :success => "player" }, :condition => "check_status" )
    %>
```

```
        <div style="width:260px; border:1px solid blue; padding:20px; background:#eee;">
            <p align="center"><%= image_tag('progress.gif') %></p>
            <p align="center">Please wait. Converting video.</p>
        </div>
    <% end -%>
</div>

<p><%= link_to("Return to Index", videos_path) %></p>
```

This view template should show the FLV video player only if the video has been converted. Otherwise, it will display a different region in the page that shows a "please wait" message and a spinning progress animation (the `progress.gif` file can be downloaded with the rest of the source code for this project, or you can substitute your own animation here).

If the video has yet to be converted, we'll also define a client-side JavaScript variable, `check_status`, that will be used with the `:condition` option of `periodically_call_remote` to determine whether we should poll the server for transcode status updates. We'll set its initial value in the template, and as long as it evaluates to true, we'll continue to make periodic requests to the action using the default duration (10 seconds) and the URL and method specified. It will be the responsibility of the controller to turn off this check once the video has been transcoded, thus halting further polling requests.

■**Note** Since we're using FFmpeg in this example, it would be tricky to measure actual progress in real time. Therefore, we just display the progress animation until we receive a message that the conversion has finished. However, Workling is also capable of asking a job for its current progress and can report this data back to the client, so we could render a real status bar if the situation called for it. For more information about accurate progress indicators and return stores, see the documentation at in the plugin's README file (`vendor/plugins/workling/README`).

As seen in the controller code, the `show` method will respond to requests whose content type is JavaScript in one of two ways. If the video has not yet finished transcoding, it will return a 415 (unsupported media type) status code, and the client will ignore the response. On the other hand, if the video has now finished the conversion process, the partial template `_player.html.erb` will be rendered and returned to the client with a response code of 200 (success). When the status code is in the 200 family, `periodically_call_remote` has been instructed to update the region marked with the DOM ID "player" (the enclosing `div`), replacing its contents with the newly rendered template. That template, `app/views/videos/_player.html.erb`, is shown in Listing 18-13.

Listing 18-13. *Video Player Partial Template (app/views/videos/_player.html.erb)*

```
<script language="javascript">check_status = false;</script>
<%= flv_player(:file => @video.public_filename) %>
```

As you can see, not only does the partial template contain instructions to render the Flash video player, but also the JavaScript that will be evaluated on the client and used to set the `check_status` variable to false, thus halting further attempts to poll the remote service.

The net result is a service that, from the users' point of view, accepts their upload, shows them a progress indicator while the system is transcoding, and then plays the video when the transcoding is complete, without requiring a page reload. Users don't need to be constantly connected to the server while this process is ongoing, and we don't need to worry about them timing out or blocking other users from performing tasks. For the users, it means smooth workflow; for the operators, it means the reduction of unnecessary load and improved system resource utilization.

Testing Asynchronous Transcodes

To see this all in action, we need to start the Starling server and the runner task that polls it for new jobs to execute. By default, Starling runs on localhost port 22122. This can be altered using command-line options (use `starling –help` to see these options). If you do choose to run Starling on a different server or a different port, you need to let Workling know about it. The `starling.yml` file, which was placed in the `config` directory automatically during the plugin installation process, is the place to specify the host and port for contacting the Starling server.

Since we're running in development mode at the moment, we'll assume that the defaults will be fine. The Starling server will be running on localhost and listening on port 22122. Start it up in a terminal window by using the following command:

```
starling
```

■**Note** Starling needs to create a spool file on the disk to write to, in order to persist messages. By default, it uses `/var/spool/starling`. You will most likely need to create this directory by hand (as the root user on a Unix system) and assign the proper permissions to the user that will be running the Starling daemon before starting it. Otherwise, it will fail to initialize. Once you know things are working properly, you can use the `-d` command-line switch to run Starling as a daemonized process.

Next, we'll need to start the Workling Starling client. A script to do this was placed in `script/workling_starling_client` when the plugin was installed. You can manage this process in the background by using the `start` and `stop` parameters, or you can have it run interactively in the current terminal window using the `run` parameter. To see what's happening in real time during development, and for debugging, we prefer the latter for now:

```
ruby script/workling_starling_client run
```

We'll also want to make sure that our Rails application is running. If it hasn't already been started, start it now using `script/server` in a new terminal window.

At this point, you should be able to visit `http://localhost:3000/videos/new` in a browser and submit another video for transcoding. It will be uploaded and, as before, you'll be taken to the video resource page to view the result. However, this time, the transcoding operation will be happening in the background while the animated progress animation is displayed. Figure 18-4 shows an example.

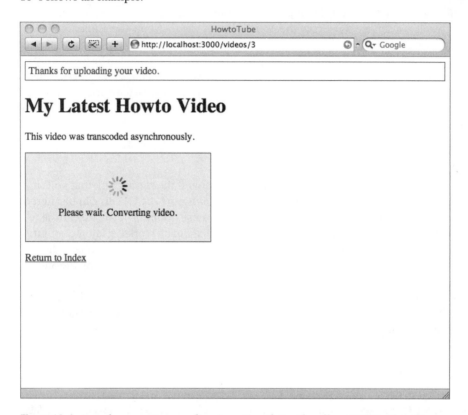

Figure 18-4. *Asynchronous transcoding in action (http://localhost:3000/videos/2)*

If you are running the Workling Starling client in the foreground as suggested, you can watch in real time as it polls the message queue and performs the transcoding task with FFmpeg:

```
starting Workling::Starling::Poller.
lean back. somebody is doing your work for you.
FFmpeg version CVS, Copyright (c) 2000-2004 Fabrice Bellard
Mac OSX universal build for ffmpegX
  configuration: –enable-memalign-hack –enable-mp3lame –enable-gpl ➡
–disable-vhook –disable-ffplay –disable-ffserver –enable-a52 –enable-xvid ➡
–enable-faac –enable-faad –enable-amr_nb –enable-amr_wb –enable-pthreads ➡
–enable-x264
  libavutil version: 49.0.0
  libavcodec version: 51.9.0
  libavformat version: 50.4.0
  built on Apr 15 2006 04:58:19, gcc: 4.0.1 (Apple Computer, Inc. build 5250)
```

```
Input #0, mov,mp4,m4a,3gp,3g2,mj2, from '/Users/nap/dev/plugins- ➥
book/prp_examples/trunk/workling/howtotube/public/tmp/20080423144930-sample.mov':
  Duration: 00:01:25.5, start: 0.000000, bitrate: 307 kb/s
  Stream #0.0(eng), 25.00 fps(r): Video: mpeg4, yuv420p, 640x480
  Stream #0.1(eng): Audio: aac, 32000 Hz, stereo
Output #0, flv, to '/Users/nap/dev/plugins- ➥
book/prp_examples/trunk/workling/howtotube/public/videos/20080423144930-sample.flv':
  Stream #0.0, 25.00 fps(c): Video: flv, yuv420p, 320x240, q=2-31, 200 kb/s
  Stream #0.1: Audio: mp3, 22050 Hz, stereo, 32 kb/s
Stream mapping:
  Stream #0.0 -> #0.0
  Stream #0.1 -> #0.1
Press [q] to stop encoding
frame= 2136 q=4.4 Lsize=    2850kB time=85.4 bitrate= 273.3kbits/s
video:845kB audio:334kB global headers:0kB muxing overhead 141.616599%
```

The browser will periodically check in with the server via Ajax calls to find out if the conversion is complete. When it is, the view will be updated and the Flash video player component will be shown as before.

■**Tip** If you want to start multiple runner instances, set the `:multiple` option to `true` in `script/ workling_starling_runner`. This script also contains other options that can be used to control the behavior of the runners that are spawned.

Summary

If your application involves dealing with potentially long-running or computationally intensive tasks, consider handing those tasks off to a background process. Handling these types of requests in-line forces the Rails server instance to block and can also cause request timeouts. Dealing with them asynchronously eliminates these potential problems and has workflow advantages as well, including the ability to show updatable indications of job progress.

Thanks to a number of freely available open source message queue servers and easy-to-use Rails job processing plugins to interface with them, off-loading tasks doesn't have to be as difficult as it might seem. The Workling plugin that we demonstrated in this chapter takes the complexity out of asynchronous processing work and makes it easy to integrate these functions into your project.

Although we chose to cover Workling and Starling in this chapter, you have many other options for running background processes in your Rails applications as well (including a number of alternative message queue servers). Each has unique characteristics that make it ideal for certain types of tasks. Some solutions are in-memory only; others may store messages in a database; and yet others may rely on hosted third-party infrastructure. The official Rails Wiki maintains a page on this topic that contains descriptions and links to many of the more well-known options. See `http://wiki.rubyonrails.org/rails/pages/ HowToRunBackgroundJobsInRails` for details.

PART 7

■■■

View/UI Enhancement

The job of a user interface (UI) is to allow users to manipulate a system (input) and provide a means for that system to communicate the results of some operation to the user (output). In Rails, our UIs are usually constructed with Action View and ERB templates, which use a mix of HTML and embedded Ruby to produce results viewable in your browser.

By using view plugins, you can change the way that data is presented and make it easier for the developer to create complex UI elements. For example, using the Lightbox Helper plugin makes it easy to automatically generate graphical lightbox effects.

A number of the plugins that we'll discuss can make outputting certain types of views easier and expand your range of output options (to include CSS and Flash-based graphs, as well as PDF documents). We'll also look at plugins that provide alternative templating languages, such as Liquid and Haml.

CHAPTER 19

■■■

Creating Lightbox Image Galleries with the Lightbox Helper and Flickraw

Lightbox is a popular JavaScript effect that allows users to magnify and focus on images with a single click. With this effect, the background is grayed out, so that the image becomes the most prominent object on the screen. You can see an example of the lightbox effect in Figure 19-1, which shows a sample from the Lightbox 2 home page.

Figure 19-1. *The lightbox effect (http://www.lokeshdhakar.com/projects/lightbox2)*

Note Although the term *lightbox* is often used generically to mean any effect that darkens a background to show an image in the center of the page, Lightbox is actually a specific system used to achieve this effect. The original script uses the Prototype JavaScript library, which ships with Rails.

There is also a Lightbox Helper plugin written by Davide D'Agostino (`http://rails.lipsiasoft.com/wiki/lightbox`), which is what we will examine in this chapter. With the helper plugin, it becomes even easier to integrate lightbox-style effects into your Rails application, which can be useful for things like online photo galleries, detailed product images, and more.

Our Task: Create a Lightbox-Enabled Image Gallery

Let's suppose we are tasked with building a portfolio site for a photographer. The photographer was previously using Flickr Pro, the online photo-sharing service, to hawk his services, but has decided that he wants to display a gallery on his own site, for branding and professionalism reasons.

Since all of his photos are already online with Flickr Pro, we can use the Flickr API to pull the image URLs from Flickr, thereby freeing us from having to create a separate administrative interface, and allowing the photographer to keep his photos where they are. Flickr has great tools for managing your photos, after all, and we wouldn't want to try to compete with that! Instead, the photographer would prefer that we focus on presenting his photos in an attractive way.

Fortunately, we can make use of a Ruby gem called Flickraw to retrieve the photographer's images from Flickr with minimal work. Flickraw is a great example of an easy-to-use web service interface. It's also a great example of Ruby dynamic programming, because it automatically creates its own interface based on the responses from the Flickr web services. In other words, if Flickr adds a new field, you can easily add code that accesses that new field without downloading a new version of Flickraw.

Flickraw gives us the ability to leverage the photographer's images on Flickr, but to display them, we want to implement a fancy lightbox effect. Our client wants to show a gallery of thumbnails and allow the user to click to see a more detailed image. To accomplish this, we will use the Lightbox Helper plugin for Rails. This plugin makes it easy to add some pizzazz to an image gallery, without having to write any JavaScript at all.

LIGHTBOX ALTERNATIVES

A number of other powerful JavaScript solutions offer functionality similar to the Lightbox system. Many of them offer features that the Lightbox script does not support, such as including arbitrary text and HTML elements in a pop-up window, external content, support for media playback, data entry via forms, and content served through Ajax.

Perhaps the best known of the Lightbox imitators is ThickBox by Cody Lindley (`http://jquery.com/demo/thickbox`), which offers a number of impressive features and is based on the jQuery JavaScript library. (jQuery is the preferred JavaScript library of both of the authors of this book.)

You may also want to investigate the Lightwindow plugin, also by Davide D'Agostino, which is hosted at the same site as the Lightbox Helper plugin (`http://rails.lipsiasoft.com/wiki/lightwindow`). The Lightwindow plugin is based on the Lightwindow JavaScript by Kevin Miller (`http://www.stickmanlabs.com/lightwindow`), and includes features such as the ability to embed multiple media types, external content, and forms. Another solution is Craig Ambrose's Red Box (`http://www.craigambrose.com/projects/redbox`), which was inspired by both Lightbox and ThickBox. Both of these solutions have the advantage of Rails helpers available through the plugin system, which makes them even easier to use within your project if you're unfamiliar with JavaScript.

Of course, if you have experience with JavaScript, jQuery, or Prototype, you really don't need a Rails plugin to take advantage of this functionality within your Rails project. In many cases, especially those where extensive customization is necessary, it makes more sense to work with JavaScript by hand to achieve these effects. With jQuery (`http://jquery.com`), it's particularly easy to write nice, unobtrusive JavaScript code that will not pollute your view templates with in-line JavaScript.

Creating the Photo Gallery

First, let's create a new Rails project for the photo gallery application:

```
rails photobox
cd photobox
```

Next, we'll need to install Flickraw and the Lightbox Helper plugin. Flickraw is available as a gem, allowing you to use it in any number of Ruby-based projects. For more information about its rich set of features, see `http://flickraw.rubyforge.org`. Install the gem as follows:

```
gem install flickraw
```

Before you can continue, you'll need to adjust your project's environment a bit in order to access Flickraw's facilities. Add the following line to the end of `config/environment.rb` to accomplish this:

```
require 'flickraw'
```

The Lightbox Helper plugin installation is next. It's based on the original Lightbox 2 JavaScript and includes everything you need. Install it by running the following command:

```
ruby script/plugin install git://github.com/Lipsiasoft/lightbox.git
```

■**Note:** Installation from the Git repository, as shown here, is the suggested way to install the plugin. Support for installing plugins from Git is available only in Rails 2.1 and later, however. If you're still on Rails 2.0.2, you can download a ZIP archive or tarball from `http://github.com/Lipsiasoft/lightbox` and extract it into your `vendor/plugins` directory. Rename the resulting directory to `lightbox`, and then, from within that new directory, run the install hook by hand: `ruby install.rb`. Alternatively, you could use this as an excuse to upgrade your project to Rails 2.1!

More information about the plugin is available at `http://rails.lipsiasoft.com/wiki/lightbox`.

Now, we're ready to display some images, so let's get to it!

Retrieving Photos from Flickr with Flickraw

We'll need to create a single controller, `HomepageController`, to display our gallery. It will contain only a single action, `index`, whose job will be to retrieve the appropriate images using Flickraw and set an instance variable, so we can display the images in the corresponding view template. The code for this controller is shown in Listing 19-1. Save it as `app/controllers/homepage_controller.rb`.

Listing 19-1. *Homepage Controller (app/controllers/homepage_controller.rb)*

```
class HomepageController < ApplicationController
  def index
    @photos = flickr.photos.search(:user_id => 'INSERT_YOUR_USER_ID_HERE',
      :per_page => 20)
  end
end
```

You should insert your Flickr user ID into the code listing where appropriate. Note that your user ID is not the same as your Flickr username—it's a separate alphanumeric string that uniquely identifies your account. The easiest way to retrieve this ID is by using the idGettr utility, available from `http://idgettr.com`.

If you don't have a Flickr account, you can sign up for a free one now at `http://flickr.com`. If you do this, make sure to add a few images. Alternatively, you can enter the Flickr user ID of another user. To do so, visit Flickr's home page and click the random photo that appears in the upper-left corner. Then take the URL for that user's photostream (of the form `http://flickr.com/photos/username`) and plug it into idGettr to retrieve that user's ID. You can then use this value in the code listing.

■**Caution** Use of other Flickr users' images is governed by the license with which they've made their work available. Many users choose to make their work available under a Creative Commons license. For more information, see `http://www.flickr.com/creativecommons`.

One of the unusual elements of Flickraw's interface is that it adds a `flickr` method to Ruby's `Object` class. That is how our code can make an unqualified reference to this method, as shown in Listing 19-1. Calling the `flickr` method returns a default instance of the `Flickr` class, and on that instance, we call `photos` to return a `Photos` object. Finally, we call the `search` method on the `Photos` object to specify that we want to search and return photos belonging to a particular user. The `search` method supports a variety of options, including the `:per_page` option, which we use to limit the number of images returned in the first page of results.

FLICKRAW FEATURES AND CREDENTIALS

Our use of Flickraw for this example is very basic. The Flickraw library maps exactly all of the API methods found in the official Flickr API documentation, allowing you to upload new photos and add comments, tags, and other meta-information to your photos, as well as use all the other facilities that Flickr provides. For more information, see the official documentation at `http://flickraw.rubyforge.org`. Note that many of these tasks require authentication, meaning that you must supply credentials to `Flickr.new`.

Flickraw comes with a default API key that can be used for development and testing purposes, but if you want to use it in a commercial application, Flickr requires that you obtain your own API key. See `http://www.flickr.com/services/api/keys` for details. Flickraw lets you specify a custom API key by adding the following lines to your environment:

```
flickr.api_key = 'my_api_key'
flickr.shared_secret = 'super_secret_shared_secret_from_flickr'
```

Adding a Lightbox Effect to View Templates

With our controller code complete, we next need to construct a single view template for the `index` action. Save the code in Listing 19-2 as `app/views/homepage/index.html.erb`.

Listing 19-2. *View Template with Lightbox Helper (app/views/homepage/index.html.erb)*

```
<%= javascript_include_tag :defaults %>
<%= stylesheet_link_tag 'lightbox' %>

<style type="text/css">
  a img { border: 0; }
</style>

<h1>Photo Gallery</h1>

<% @photos.each do |photo| -%>
  <%= lightbox_image_tag make_flickr_url(photo, 's'),
      make_flickr_url(photo, 'm'),
      {},
      {:title => photo.title} %>
<% end -%>
```

First, notice that we've included a javascript_include_tag and a stylesheet_link_tag at the top of the template in order to make the JavaScript and CSS styles for the Lightbox Helper plugin available in this template. (The JavaScript libraries included are just the default Prototype libraries supplied by Rails; these are required by the plugin.) Normally, you would include these elements in an application layout, but we've included them here for convenience.

The remainder of the template instructs the server to loop through each image in our @photos instance variable, and use the lightbox_image_tag helper provided by the plugin to display each one as an image with a lightbox-enabled link. The first argument to this helper method is the thumbnail URL. This URL is retrieved using the make_flickr_url function, which we will examine in a moment. We pass it our Flickr photo object, along with a size: 's' for small. The next argument is the full image URL, which will be displayed with a lightbox effect when the user clicks the thumbnail. We use the medium size ('m') for that image.

Finally, two HTML option hashes are also passed to the lightbox_image_tag helper. The first specifies the options for the anchor (a) tag (no options, in our case), and the section specifies the options for the image (img) tag itself. Note that the title option specified for the image tag affects only the tooltip that most modern browsers display when you move your mouse over an image; no reference to the title is made when the dialog box pops up.

Next, let's take a look at the ApplicationHelper, which is where we'll define the make_flickr_url method used in the template. Save the code shown in Listing 19-3 as app/helpers/application_helper.rb.

Listing 19-3. *Application Helper (app/helpers/application_helper.rb)*

```
module ApplicationHelper
  def make_flickr_url(r, size = 't')
    "http://farm#{r.farm}.static.flickr.com/" <<
      "#{r.server}/#{r.id}_#{r.secret}_#{size}.jpg"
  end
end
```

The make_flickr_url helper constructs the URL for the appropriate Flickr photo. It uses various pieces of data returned by Flickr, such as the appropriate farm (cluster of machines), server name, photo ID number, and so forth. The image size can be included as well; this is optional and will default to thumbnail size if unspecified.

Tip If you're curious, you can find more information about creating Flickr photo source URLs (and their component parts) at http://www.flickr.com/services/api/misc.urls.html.

At this point, you should be able to start your server using ruby script/server and examine the lightbox-enabled photo gallery by visiting http://localhost:3000/homepage in a browser. You can also optionally remove the public/index.html file and edit routes to make the gallery available at the server root URL. To do this, replace your application routes in config/routes.rb with the code shown in Listing 19-4.

Listing 19-4. *Routes for the Homepage (config/routes.rb)*

```
ActionController::Routing::Routes.draw do |map|
  map.root :controller=>'homepage', :action=>'index'
  map.connect ':controller/:action/:id'
  map.connect ':controller/:action/:id.:format'
end
```

As you can see, we've added a new route (shown in bold) to the default routes, mapping the root of our application to the homepage controller. With this modification in place, you can start the application and point your web browser to http://localhost:3000. You should see a page similar to Figure 19-2 (with the images found in the specified Flickr user photostream, of course).

Figure 19-2. *Photo gallery index page (http://localhost:3000)*

Click one of the images. The page should go dark, except for the close-up of the selected image, as shown in Figure 19-3. If you hover over the left or right side of the image, a previous or next button, respectively, will appear. You can click these to quickly and easily navigate through the medium-sized images within the lightbox view. You can click the close button image in the bottom right of the lightbox view to close the image box and return to viewing the gallery. Clicking anywhere but within the image itself should achieve the same effect.

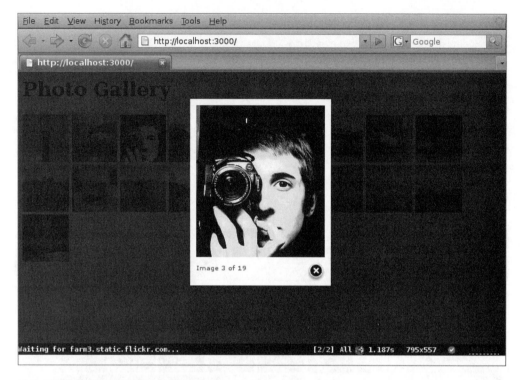

Figure 19-3. *Photo gallery lightbox effect in action*

As you can see, the effect is both useful and attractive, and adding it was a truly simple task, thanks to the Rails Lightbox Helper plugin.

Summary

Lightboxing is a visually attractive way to let users focus on one large image at a time, and clients who need some sort of photo gallery or the ability to preview product images often request lightboxing specifically during project definition. If you want lightboxing support in your project, the Lightbox Helper plugin is a fast and easy way to add it to your application, and it's a great tool to have in your bag of Rails view plugin tricks.

It's similarly easy to take advantage of the more customizable Red Box and Lightwindow plugins in your Rails project, which you can use when you need something more complicated than simple image data. No JavaScript knowledge is required to use these plugins.

Other JavaScript libraries that provide similar functionality, such as ThickBox and Facebox, both based on the jQuery library, do not provide Rails plugins, but can be added to your application with just a minimal amount of JavaScript know-how. If you're not already adept with JavaScript, we encourage you to familiarize yourself with it and learn how to use some of the popular libraries such as jQuery and Prototype. A solid grasp of these techniques is critical when you need something that's a little more outside the box (pun intended!).

## CHAPTER 20

Beautifying HTML Templates with Haml and Sass

In upcoming chapters, we'll cover a couple special-purpose templating systems for Rails: Liquid (Chapter 22) and RTex (Chapter 24). There are many others we would have liked to include in this book, such as Markaby, MasterView, and the faster embedded Ruby (ERb) replacement Erubis, but with so many great plugins to talk about, we simply ran out of room. However, we didn't feel that we could write a book about plugins without devoting a chapter to Hampton Catlin's Haml/Sass plugin.

Unlike RTex, which renders a particular type of view that's unsupported natively in Rails, Haml is general purpose. Haml (the acronym stands for HTML Abstraction Markup Language) provides an alternative markup language to describe HTML without in-line code snippets and is an outright replacement for traditional RHTML/ERb templates. Catlin has stated that he developed Haml because he was disgusted with the ugliness of stock templates, and he wanted to replace them with templates that felt more natural to write and were easier on the eyes.

Sass (for Syntactically Awesome StyleSheets) is packaged along with Haml and does for Cascading Style Sheets (CSS) what Haml does for HTML templates. It's a sort of shorthand way of writing CSS that can really help clean up complex style sheets and also make them easier to maintain. This helps us get even closer to the core Rails DRY (Don't Repeat Yourself) principle. Because Sass is processed and generates standard CSS, just as Haml generates standard HTML output, it's also possible to use variables and simple arithmetic in Sass to cut down even further on unnecessary repetition. Haml and Sass can be used independently of one another or together for maximum effect.

In this chapter, we'll start by examining basic Haml syntax and demonstrating how it can be used in place of HTML and ERb in your view templates. Then we will demonstrate how to translate a more complicated web site layout to Haml. Next, we'll do the same with Sass, reviewing its basic usage and then demonstrating how to translate a preexisting style sheet to Sass.

Our Task: "Haml-ize" a Layout and DRY Up CSS

To implement a small web site quickly, without the aid of a designer, web developers often look to existing web site templates to get started. You can purchase premade web site templates from a variety of sources, and many templates are also freely available as open source options.

Open Source Web Design (OSWD), at http://www.oswd.org, hosts a number of attractive, free-to-use templates, which you can download and use for any number of projects. For this chapter's example, we'll select an attractive CSS-based layout, and then demonstrate how easy it is to translate it to Haml.

We'll also take the template's style sheet and translate it to Sass. Having it represented in Sass will allow us to easily modify it. We'll demonstrate how you can change colors and sizes of elements in the style sheet—modifications that, without Sass, would require changes in numerous places in a very un-DRY fashion.

Preparing for the Template Project

Let's create a new Rails application for the Haml template project:

```
rails hamltpl
cd hamltpl
```

You can install the Haml plugin by using the standard plugin manager. However, Haml is also available as a stand-alone gem, which you can make use of in other Ruby projects. The gem includes its own tool for installing Haml plugin support to your Rails application. Let's do something a little different this time around and use that approach to get up and running:

```
gem install haml
haml --rails .
```

The command haml --rails . adds the plugin to your Rails project (the . specifies your current working directory as the location of the Rails project). If you check your vendor/ plugins directory, you'll find that it now contains a haml directory, just as if you had used the standard plugin manager approach. However, that directory contains only a single init.rb file, used to make the Haml gem's facilities available to us in our current application.

Note For more information about installation options, and for full documentation, tutorials, and more, we encourage you to visit Haml's home on the Web at http://haml.hamptoncatlin.com.

Since we'll need to create sample text within our template, let's install a simple "lorem ipsum" dummy text generator as well. We could easily generate this text at a site like http:// lipsum.com, but John Nunemaker has implemented this same capability in a Ruby gem (more information is available at http://lorem.rubyforge.org), which is even easier to use. Install it as follows:

```
gem install lorem
```

Tip You can try out Haml and Sass rendering directly in a browser before installing them by visiting http://lab.hamptoncatlin.com. This can be useful while you're learning syntax basics.

We'll also be integrating and converting a CSS web site template developed by Andreas Viklund. The template can be previewed online and downloaded from `http://www.oswd.org/design/information/id/2427`. Unzip the file to reveal an `index.html` file and an associated style sheet named `andreas08.css`. Place the style sheet in your `public/stylesheets` directory, and put the HTML file in your `public` directory.

If you want to preview the output locally before starting on the conversion and integration process, you'll need to update the HTML so it looks for the style sheet in the new location. Replace the occurrence of `andreas08.css` with `/stylesheets/andreas08.css`. You can then start the server using `ruby script/server` and point a web browser at `http://localhost:3000` to view the local version of the web site template. It should resemble the screenshot shown in Figure 20-1. Note that at this point, the index file is being served directly to your browser as a static file, rather than being dynamically generated.

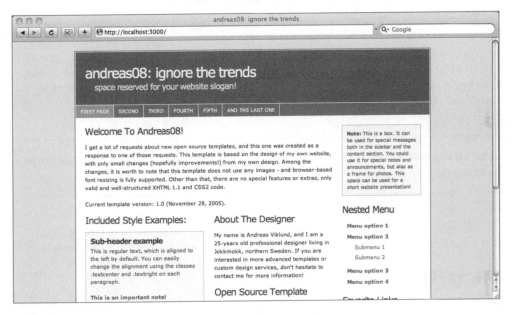

Figure 20-1. *OSWD web site template (http://localhost:3000)*

Later, we'll be turning this static file into a layout to wrap dynamic content generated by a controller, and rewriting it using Haml. We'll also DRY up the CSS file using Sass. But first, we need to go over the basics of Haml syntax. We'll start by working on a simple view template.

Haml: The Basics

Normally, when developing a Rails application, we would create a controller and a set of corresponding views, and mix in the view HTML, probably supplied by our designer, with ERb. Haml is a little different, as you'll see. The controller/view relationship remains the same, however, so we'll need to create a `ContentController` before we can start experimenting with view templates. Save the code in Listing 20-1 as `app/controllers/content_controller.rb`.

Listing 20-1. *Content Controller (app/controllers/content_controller.rb)*

```ruby
require 'lorem'

class ContentController < ApplicationController
  def index
    @title = "Haml is Markup Haiku"
    @author = "Sandra Willoughby"
    @author_website = "http://www.apress.com"
    @published_at = Time.now
    @content = []
    4.times do
      @content << Lorem::Base.new('paragraphs', 1).output
    end
  end
end
```

All we're really doing here is setting up a number of instance variables so we can display them in the view. We're also using the lorem ipsum generator to generate four paragraphs of sample text, and stuffing them into an array that we'll refer to as @content.

Tip You may want to consider moving the require statement to your environment.rb file, where you can list the gem as a dependency for your project.

A simple view for the index action of the ContentController is shown in Listing 20-2. This listing illustrates how we might render the view using a stock RHTML/ERb template.

Listing 20-2. *Content View with ERb*

```erb
<div class="article">
  <h1><%= @title %></h1>
  <div class="author">By <%= link_to(@author, @author_website) %></div>

  <% @content.each_with_index do |paragraph, index| %>
    <p class="copy" id="paragraph-<%= index %>"><%= paragraph %></p>
  <% end %>

  <div class="published_at">
    Published <%= time_ago_in_words(@published_at) %> ago
  </div>
  <hr/>
</div>
<div class="copyright">
  &copy; <%= @published_at.strftime("%Y") %>
  <%= link_to(@author, @author_website) %>
</div>
```

The Haml equivalent is shown in Listing 20-3. Save it as `app/views/content/`
`index.html.haml`. Make sure to specify the suffix of the file as `.html.haml`, not the usual
`.html.erb`. In Rails 2.0 and later, two suffixes are used for view templates by convention; the
first specifies the output content type to be presented to the browser (HTML), and the second
specifies the processor used to render the template (ERb or Haml).

Listing 20-3. *Content View with Haml (app/views/content/index.html.haml)*

```
%div{:class => "article"}
  %h1= @title
  %div{:class => "author"}= "By #{link_to(@author, @author_website)}"

  - @content.each_with_index do |paragraph, index|
    %p{:class => "copy", :id => "paragraph-#{index}"}= paragraph

  .published_at= "Published #{time_ago_in_words(@published_at)} ago"
  %hr
.copyright
  = "&copy; #{@published_at.strftime("%Y")}"
  = link_to(@author, @author_website)
```

You can see that the syntax is clearly quite different, and it may look somewhat daunting
at first. But you can also immediately sense that Haml is much denser and easier to read.

Losing the HTML Tags

The first thing that should be obvious in Listing 20-3 is that all the HTML tags have dis-
appeared. Stock tags, such as `<h1>`, are replaced in this representation by a percent sign
followed by the tag name, such as `%h1`. When the Haml view is processed, these elements
are converted to their HTML representation and delivered to the browser as HTML, but
using this shorthand makes a few things easier for us. Perhaps most important, it means
that we don't need closing tags, which are not only ugly and extra unnecessary typing, but
are also easy to forget—and when you forget to include a closing tag in HTML, you end up
creating documents that don't render correctly or validate.

Closing tags aren't necessary in Haml because it relies on whitespace indentation to
define the nesting. For example, all elements rendered in this particular view are inside an
enclosing `div` element, except for the copyright notice at the very bottom. You can see this
clearly in the code by noting that the indentation levels for these two elements are the same.
Every other element that follows the first `div` declaration is indented appropriately (two
spaces for each indentation level).

`class` and `id` attributes, along with any other tag attributes, can be added to a tag by
specifying them as name/value pairs in brackets following the tag name. So `%div{:class =>`
`"article"}` specifies that a `div` element should be inserted, and that its class name should
be `"article"`. (This syntax should look familiar to Ruby users, as it closely resembles Ruby's
Hash syntax.) The HTML output of this would look like `<div class="article">` ... `</div>`.
Any content that follows the tag becomes content for that tag. Content on other lines can
also be nested within this tag, if the lines are indented. Otherwise, if the next line has the
same indentation level, the tag is automatically closed for you. That sure is nice, right?

Embedding Ruby in Haml

So what about embedding Ruby code? Well, the equal sign following %h1 in Listing 20-3 tells Haml to evaluate anything to the right and print out the return value. The return value of that code—in this case, a string representing the title of the article—becomes the content of the tag.

Similarly, the hyphen character means that the following Ruby code should be run but no output should be rendered. We use this to work with control statements like if and else and, in this case, to iterate through each element of the @content array. For each array element, we create a paragraph (p) tag that contains its value content. We specify both a class and an id attribute for these paragraphs. Note that using a dynamic attribute id is clean and easy with string interpolation ("paragraph-#{index}").

Reducing Clutter

After displaying the paragraphs, we want to print the date that the article was published, and here you see the first line that breaks from the %tag convention. Since div elements are by and large the most common element in most HTML documents, Haml assumes that if we omit an explicit tag, we probably want to render a div. It also allows us to use CSS-style shortcuts to specify the class name and ID of an element, using the period (.) and hash (#), respectively. Therefore, .published_at refers to a div element whose class name is "published_at". Similarly, #my-id.my-class would refer to a div whose ID was "my-id" that belonged to the CSS class "my-class". This is the same as using %div#my-id.my-class.

■**Tip** You can also chain class names together with periods. %span.class1.class2 indicates a span element that belongs to two classes: class1 and class2. For more information about this and other features of Haml, see http://haml.hamptoncatlin.com/docs/rdoc/classes/Haml.html.

In general, we like to use this shorthand when possible, as it's clean and easy to read; however, in some situations, using the longhand syntax is unavoidable. For instance, this applies when we need to render an ID for an element based on a dynamic value supplied by our controller. This is exactly the case within the paragraph display loop we examined earlier, where we wanted to set the IDs of elements to values like "paragraph-1", "paragraph-2", and so on.

■**Tip** Haml also allows you to use square bracket [ ] notation with a Ruby object to automatically set the ID and class of the tag to the ID and class of the Ruby object. This can be particularly useful with Active Record model objects in Rails. For example, %p[@model]= @model.name could be used to produce something like <p class="widget" id="100">widget name</p>.

To view the result of our newfound Haml proficiency in a browser, visit `http://localhost:3000/content`. It will resemble the screen shown in Figure 20-2.

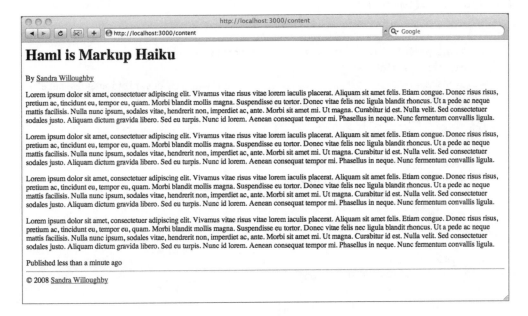

Figure 20-2. *Basic Haml view template output (http://localhost:3000/content)*

Use the "view source" option in your browser to see the HTML source that was generated. There you'll find another benefit of using Haml for view templating: the generated HTML output is generally much cleaner than the corresponding ERb output. Haml takes care of making sure that the correct quotes are used and that the HTML structure is formatted with the proper indentation. This makes the output easy to read and troubleshooting document structure much more bearable.

Porting a Web Site Template to Haml

Now that we have reviewed the basic Haml syntax, we can move on to building a more complicated web site layout with it. We want something that can be used to house our current content view and be shared by any controller actions that we might create later. We've located a nice template for our current project using OSWD, and placed the style sheet in the correct directory. We've also replaced the `index.html` file in our public directory, so we can use it for reference purposes if necessary (view it in a browser by visiting `http://localhost:3000`).

We'll place the Rails view template that we're going to create for our application layout in the `app/views/layouts` directory and name it `application.html.haml`. This way, following Rails conventions, it will be automatically applied to all views unless otherwise instructed; that is, the rendered output of the individual actions will be stuffed inside the layout where `yield` is called. Note that we've taken a few liberties in this process, removing many elements from the template that we don't need right now. Listing 20-4 shows the complete template, which you should save as `app/views/layouts/application.html.haml`.

Listing 20-4. *Haml Web Site Layout (app/views/layouts/application.html.haml)*

```
!!! Transitional
%html{html_attrs('en-en')}
  %head
    %title= @title
    %meta{"http-equiv" => "content-type",:content => ➥
"text/html; charset=iso-8859-1"}
    %meta{:name => "description", :content => "Your website description goes here"}
    %meta{:name => "keywords", :content => "your,keywords,go,here"}
    = stylesheet_link_tag('andreas08')
  %body
    #container
      #header
        %h1= @site_title || "Your New Website"
        %h2= @site_subtitle || "Tasty Morsels of Software Goodness"

      #navigation
        %ul
          %li.selected
            %a{:href => "#"}First page
          %li
            %a{:href => "#"}Second
          %li
            %a{:href => "#"}Third
          %li
            %a{:href => "#"}Fourth
          %li
            %a{:href => "#"}Fifth
          %li
            %a{:href => "#"}And the last one

      #content
        %h2= @title
        = yield

      #subcontent
        %h2 Nested Menu
        %ul.menublock
          %li
            %a{:href => "#"} Menu option 1
          %li
            %a{:href => "#"} Menu option 2
            %ul
              %li
                %a{:href => "#"} Submenu 1
              %li
                %a{:href => "#"} Submenu 2
```

```
    %li
      %a{:href => "#"} Menu option 3
    %li
      %a{:href => "#"} Menu option 4

  %h2 Favorite Links
  %ul.menublock
    %li
      %a{:href => "http://andreasviklund.com/templates"} Free web templates
    %li
      %a{:href => "http://openwebdesign.org"} Open Web Design
    %li
      %a{:href => "http://oswd.org"} OSWD.org
    %li
      %a{:href => "http://rubyonrails.org"} Ruby on Rails
    %li
      %a{:href => "http://haml.hamptoncatlin.com"} Haml and Sass

#footer
  %p
    &copy; 2005-2006
    %a{:href => "#"}= @author
    | Design by
    %a{:href => "http://andreasviklund.com"} Andreas Viklund
```

Caution Most beginner troubles with Haml seem to stem from improperly nested elements, so make sure to pay careful attention to these when developing with Haml. Remember that indentation is very important, given the nature of how Haml handles tag nesting.

Translating a template such as this to Haml is a relatively straightforward task. If you take a quick look at the source of the original HTML template, you'll see that the Haml representation of the HTML alone is clearly much easier to read. And the benefits are even more obvious when you consider that a fair bit of embedded Ruby would need to be rendered into it to convert the same straight HTML template into an ERb representation.

You'll notice a few new Haml conventions in this template (highlighted in bold), which we'll look at before we move on.

A Few More Haml Conventions

The first two lines of the template in Listing 20-4 are used to set up the HTML document type and declare the starting <html> tag with the appropriate language and namespace. Adding these elements to a layout is critical to creating HTML code that can be validated. Different options can be used here, too. For example, by specifying !!! Strict instead of !!! Transitional (which is the default), we could instruct it to use the XHTML 1.0 Strict

document type. Haml also allows you to generate XML prologs. See `http://haml.`
`hamptoncatlin.com/docs/rdoc/classes/Haml.html` for more information about these features. (We'll discuss a plugin that automatically validates HTML output as part of the testing
process in Chapter 27.)

You might also have noticed the line that renders the output of the `stylesheet_link_tag`
helper. No element directly precedes the equal sign on that line (the same is true of the `yield`
statement). In this case, the familiar helper method is called, and its result—here, a line that
instructs the browser where to find the style sheet for the document—is rendered directly to
the output. This works just as it always has, pointing the user's browser to the existing CSS file
that we downloaded and placed in `public/stylesheets`.

In just a moment, you'll see how this style sheet can be converted to Sass, but you might
choose not to do this. Haml and Sass can be used independently of each other, and there are
many cases where you might wish to use one but not the other.

Updating the Index Action Template

Before viewing our work in a browser, let's make a small modification to our `index` action's
view template. We'll remove the title's display in the view template—it's redundant now that
we're displaying a page title in the layout. We'll also move the publication date up with the
author name (under the title) and shrink it using the `<small>` tag, as shown in Listing 20-5.

Listing 20-5. *Updated Index Action Template (app/views/content/index.html.haml)*

```
.article
  %p.small
    = "Written by #{link_to(@author, @author_website)}"
    = "#{time_ago_in_words(@published_at)} ago"

  - @content.each_with_index do |paragraph, index|
    %p{:class => "copy", :id => "paragraph-#{index}"}= paragraph
```

At this point, you can point your web browser at `http://localhost:3000/content` and
see the translated template, with our action-specific result rendered within it, as shown in
Figure 20-3.

■**Note** Haml does render slightly slower than standard Rails templates, by about 25% in our tests. This
may or may not be a big deal for you. As always, we encourage developers to cache as much information as
possible.

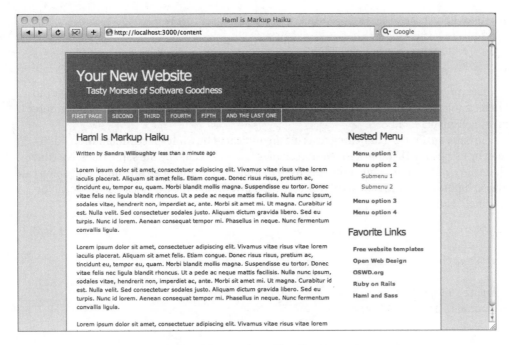

Figure 20-3. *Content view with Haml layout (http://localhost:3000/content)*

Sass: The Basics

We've already cleaned up our views significantly at this point, making them easier to read and extend in the future. However, the layout and view that we've rewritten in Haml are still applying styles from an existing CSS style sheet. This may be just fine. In fact, the style sheet for this particular web site template is rather clean. However, it certainly wouldn't hurt to remove unnecessary redundancy from the style sheet and to make it easier to later change, say, colors or dependent element sizing. This is where Sass can really help us.

Cleaning Up Nested Styles

If you've done any amount of CSS work, you know that nested element selectors for deeply nested styles can get ugly quickly. Consider something like this:

```
#content {
  color: black;
  text-decoration: none;
}
#content p.note, #content p.infotext {
  border: 1px solid black;
  padding: 5px;
  font-weight: bold;
}
```

```
#content p.note a, #content p.infotext a {
  color: red;
  text-decoration: underline;
}
```

Sass provides another way of writing CSS, just like Haml provides an alternative way to build templates out of HTML and ERb code. The basic Sass syntax offers a few extra features missing from plain old CSS.

In Sass, attributes that belong to a rule are indicated by whitespace indentation, rather than by using non-DRY brackets. Nested elements are indicated by the same rules. Newline characters, rather than semicolons, are used to indicate the end of an attribute, and colons are placed before attribute names. Following these conventions, the previous CSS rules can be specified with the following:

```
#content
  :color black
  :text-decoration none

  p.note, p.infotext
    :border 1px solid black
    :padding 5px
    :font-weight bold

  a
    :color red
    :text-decoration underline
```

Using Constant Values

Sass offers other benefits as well. You can define and use constant values in Sass. This can be useful, for instance, when you have a specific color that you want to use repeatedly throughout your style sheet. This way, if you want to change that color to make it a shade or two darker, you don't need to search and replace each occurrence of it!

You can define constants by referencing them with an exclamation point. When the file is processed, Sass will substitute the values into their appropriate places. For example, the following code snippet declares a custom color, iceblue, which can then be used throughout the rest of the style sheet. Note that when you want to use a constant's value like this in an attribute, it must be specified to the right of an equal sign, as shown here.

```
!iceblue = #74bbfb
#header
  background-color= !iceblue
```

Since Sass must process the document to output CSS, it also allows you to perform simple arithmetic functions to calculate items like color values or margin distances. For example, you could set the background color of a subheader region to a slightly darker shade of iceblue by subtracting a hex color value like this:

```
#subheader
  background-color= !iceblue - #222222
```

Porting a Style Sheet to Sass

We'll use the dynamic colors technique discussed in the previous section in our own reimplementation of the andreas08 style sheet, as shown in Listing 20-6 (note that certain styles that are not being used have been removed for the sake of brevity).

Sass styles are saved separately from the traditional style sheet and processed outside the normal Rails request cycle. When you place a `.sass` file in the `public/stylesheets/sass` directory, it is automatically converted to the standard CSS representation—there is no difference at all in the files that are served to the end user's web browser. Therefore, when you save the code in Listing 20-6 as `public/stylesheets/sass/andreas08.sass`, Sass will auto-generate updated CSS the next time a request is made for the style sheet at `/andreas08.css`. When this happens, it will replace the previous version (unless the server is running in production mode—in which case, Sass generates new CSS files only on startup).

■**Note** Since Sass processes style sheets only at startup when in production mode, there is no performance degradation involved in using Sass.

Listing 20-6. *Sass Style Sheet for the Web Site Template (public/stylesheets/sass/andreas08.sass)*

```
!color1 = #467aa7
!color2 = #ffffff

*
  :margin 0
  :padding 0

body
  :font 76% Verdana,Tahoma,Arial,sans-serif
  :line-height 1.4em
  :text-align center
  :color #303030
  :background #e8eaec

a
  :color= !color1
  :font-weight bold
  :text-decoration none
  :background-color inherit

  &:hover
    :color= !color1 - #1c201d
    :text-decoration underline

p
  :padding 0 0 1.6em 0
```

```
#container
  :width 760px
  :margin 20px auto
  :padding 1px 0
  :text-align left
  :background= !color2
  :color #303030
  :border 2px solid #a0a0a0

#header
  :height 110px
  :width 758px
  :margin 0 1px 1px 1px
  :background= !color1
  :color= !color2

  h1
    :padding 35px 0 0 20px
    :font-size 2.4em
    :background-color inherit
    :color= !color2
    :letter-spacing -2px
    :font-weight normal

  h2
    :margin 10px 0 0 40px
    :font-size 1.4em
    :background-color inherit
    :color !color1 - #0f0d0b
    :letter-spacing -1px
    :font-weight normal

#navigation
  :height 2.2em
  :line-height 2.2em
  :width 758px
  :margin 0 1px
  :background= !color1 + #111111
  :color= !color2

  li
    :float left
    :list-style-type none
    :border-right= 1px solid !color2
    :white-space nowrap
```

```
    a
      :display block
      :padding 0 10px
      :font-size 0.8em
      :font-weight normal
      :text-transform uppercase
      :text-decoration none
      :background-color inherit
      :color= !color2

  .selected, a:hover
    :background= !color1 + #3a3633
    :color= !color2
    :text-decoration none

#content
  :float left
  :width 530px
  :font-size 0.9em
  :padding 20px 0 0 20px

  h2
    :display block
    :margin 0 0 16px 0
    :font-size 1.7em
    :font-weight normal
    :letter-spacing -1px
    :color #505050
    :background-color inherit

  h3
    :margin 0 0 5px 0
    :font-size 1.4em
    :letter-spacing -1px

#subcontent
  :float right
  :width 170px
  :padding 20px 20px 10px 0
  :line-height 1.4em
```

```
h2
  :display block
  :margin 0 0 15px 0
  :font-size 1.6em
  :font-weight normal
  :text-align left
  :letter-spacing -1px
  :color #505050
  :background-color inherit

p
  :margin 0 0 16px 0
  :font-size 0.9em

.menublock
  :margin 0 0 20px 8px
  :font-size 0.9em

  li
    :list-style none
    :display block
    :padding 2px
    :margin-bottom 2px

    a
      :font-weight bold

    ul
      :margin 3px 0 3px 15px
      :font-size 1em
      :font-weight normal

      li
        :margin-bottom 0

      a
        :font-weight normal

#footer
  :clear both
  :width 758px
  :padding 5px 0
  :margin 0 1px
  :font-size 0.9em
  :color= !color2 - #0f0f0f
  :background= !color1
```

```
p
  :padding 0
  :margin 0
  :text-align center

a
  :color= !color2 - #0f0f0f
  :background-color inherit
  :font-weight bold

  &:hover
    :color= !color2
    :background-color inherit

.small
  :font-size 0.9em
```

■**Note** The references to & in the Sass file are just a useful shorthand way of referring to the parent selector.

In this Sass file, we define two colors: color1 and color2. The first represents the blue color used as the background of the header region, which is also the color of most links. The second represents the white background of the content area, and the color of text and links in the areas whose background color is color1.

There are a number of places where we want a color that is just a shade darker than color2 or a bit lighter than color1. An example is the background color of the currently selected menu item, which is naturally just a bit darker than the normal color.

Try out this style sheet by accessing http://localhost:3000/content in a web browser. The result should look the same as before.

"Wait!" you say, "We just did all this work, and the template looks exactly the same as it did before?"

Well, yes. But from this point forward, making any changes to the CSS becomes much easier. We've also made it simple to change the color scheme. Test this by substituting a dark red color, #800000, for the value of color1, and a light yellow, #FFFFF0, for the value of color2. Now, when the Sass file is saved and the page is reloaded, the color scheme should be updated accordingly.

■**Note** If nothing changes when you modify the color values, the .sass file is not being processed. Try checking that the file is in the correct location and/or restarting your Rails application server instance.

Wasn't that easy? That's the power of Sass. Consider using it the next time you start a CSS-heavy project. It can be even more useful when you're dealing with pixel calculations for column placement, floating sidebars, and other visual elements whose width or height depends on neighboring elements.

Summary

In Rails, the plugin system provides us with a number of different options when it comes to rendering view templates. In this chapter, we took a look at Haml, a markup language for constructing clean, DRY view templates in Rails. Haml's syntax is denser and more concise than standard ERb and avoids the need to mix HTML with in-line Ruby code snippets in the same template. Instead, it provides a more abstract templating language interface that you can use with Ruby to describe and generate HTML output.

We also examined Sass, an accompanying library for generating CSS, which adheres to the same principles: eliminating repetition and beautifying markup. Sass also allows you to use variables in the style sheet templates, which can be very helpful, particularly in complex style sheets.

Haml and Sass can be used separately or together on the same project. We find that using one or both of them can make complicated HTML views and style sheets much easier to read, write, and maintain. However, ultimately, the templating language you choose to use in your projects is a personal choice and boils down to whatever feels most natural to you, which may be Haml, Markaby, stock RHTML/ERb, or something entirely different. Regardless of which you prefer at the moment, it's certainly good to have options, and the Rails plugin system delivers a number of appealing choices that you can investigate.

For more information about both Haml and Sass, visit `http://haml.hamptoncatlin.com`, where you can find tutorials, full documentation, and community resources.

CHAPTER 21

■■■

Graphing and Charting with CSS Graphy and ZiYa

We've said it before, and we'll repeat it here: *it's all about the data*. Having the right data is important. It can enable us to analyze even the most complicated situations and make informed decisions. But it's often difficult to stare at a spreadsheet full of numbers or a series of XML files and see the big picture. For that, you need proper visualization, which can be provided by charts, graphs, and other tools to interpret definitive but otherwise unpalatable information. Charting and graphing tools plot points, create legends, and connect the dots. They make data presentable, and therefore, they make it useful. They allow us to see beyond the numbers to spot trends and draw conclusions.

Graphing and charting can be useful in many types of web applications. Perhaps you need charts to frame data in your user interface, such as to show cash income/expenses in a financial application or technical analysis for stock tracking. Even more common is the use of graphing tools for internal administrative purposes, such as to view and analyze activity logs in a web statistics package, as shown in the example in Figure 21-1. Another common use is to track and analyze performance of specific web advertisements. There are countless possibilities. Anywhere that there is data to be analyzed, there are visualization tools that can help us determine exactly what it means to us.

In Rails, we have access to a variety of plugins that help us visualize data quickly and easily. In this chapter, we'll use two different plugins for this task, with sample data supplied from a real-world application. First, we'll take a look at Brian Kaney's CSS Graphy package (http://oss.vermonster.com/css_graphy). It creates lightweight vertical and horizontal bar graphs using only HTML markup and CSS. Then we'll demonstrate the use of a popular Flash graphic/charting package called ZiYa (http://ziya.liquidrail.com), developed by Fernand Galiana and Delynn Berry, which is also available as a Rails plugin. ZiYa allows for more feature-rich charts to be rendered as SWF files and displayed using the Flash web browser plugin.

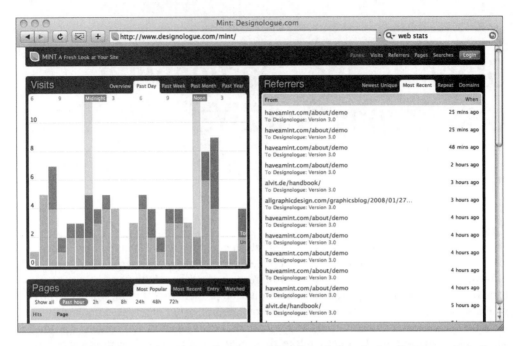

Figure 21-1. *Charts used in the Mint web stats package (http://www.designologue.com/mint/)*

Our Task: Analyze Publishing Trends with Graphs

Ink19.com is an online webzine about music, art, and culture. When it first started as a print publication (in 1991), articles were submitted by mail, carefully retyped, cut and pasted into a layout, and photocopied for distribution. Ink19 has been publishing a web version since 1996, and since 2000, all writing, editorial, and publishing tasks have been handled in a browser, with daily updates.

One particularly fortuitous side effect of running the magazine as a database-backed web application is that it's easy to gather statistics about which articles are popular, which articles have the highest ratio of referrals from other sites, and which ads have the most impact. Fortunately, analysis of this data is already handled quite nicely by existing web statistics packages such as Mint (http://www.haveamint.com) and AWStats (http://awstats.sourceforge.net), and hosted solutions like Google Analytics (http://google.com/analytics). However, these packages are limited to fairly general-purpose analysis.

Since Ink19 has developed its own proprietary publishing system, certain types of reporting tools need to be designed from scratch in order to be effective. The magazine's publisher has asked us to do just that. Ink19 wants to add some extra reporting tools to an administrative interface that will allow the editors to see, in a quick snapshot, the average monthly output of each of their writers over time, and the number of articles published in each section of the online magazine every month.

Preparing the Graphs Application

Let's create a new Rails application for the Ink19 data analysis project:

```
rails inkgraphs
cd inkgraphs
```

Next, install the CSS Graphy and ZiYa plugins by executing the following commands inside the new application root directory:

```
ruby script/plugin install http://oss.vermonster.com/css_graphy/svn/css_graphy
ruby script/plugin install svn://rubyforge.org/var/svn/liquidrail/plugins/ziya/trunk
```

We'll also use the Ruby FasterCSV library to help with parsing and importing the comma-separated values (CSV) file that has been provided by Ink19's staff. Install it via RubyGems with the following command:

```
gem install fastercsv
```

Note FasterCSV is a faster and more powerful replacement for Ruby's built-in CSV parsing library. Depending on your system configuration, you may also need to install the `sqlite3-ruby` gem in order to use FasterCSV (in case you don't already have it). For more information about FasterCSV, see `http://fastercsv.rubyforge.org`.

The CSV data itself can be obtained from `http://railsplugins.com/files/ink19.csv` (or the Source Code/Download section of the Apress web site, `http://www.apress.com`). Save it as `db/ink19.csv`. This data was exported from a legacy database table, and includes a legacy identifier, the path of the article, the article title, the author, the section, the issue, and the publication date. In order to work with it, create the database migration shown in Listing 21-1. Also create models for articles, authors, and sections, as shown in Listings 21-2, 21-3, and 21-4, respectively. In addition to these models, we'll need to create a quick routine to import the CSV data for easy analysis. Since we're going to perform this import only once at migration time, we'll add this routine directly to the migration.

Listing 21-1. *Ink19 Article Data Migration (db/migrate/001_create_articles.rb)*

```
require 'fastercsv'

class CreateArticles < ActiveRecord::Migration
  def self.up
    create_table :authors do |t|
      t.string :name
    end
```

```ruby
    create_table :sections do |t|
      t.string :name
    end

    create_table :articles do |t|
      t.integer  :legacy_id
      t.string   :title
      t.string   :path
      t.string   :section_id
      t.string   :author_id
      t.datetime :published_on
    end

    FasterCSV.foreach("db/ink19.csv", :headers => true) do |row|
      author = Author.find_or_create_by_name(row['author'])
      section = Section.find_or_create_by_name(row['section'])
      article = Article.create(:legacy_id => row['id'],
                               :title => row['title'],
                               :path => row['path'],
                               :published_on => Date.parse(row['date']),
                               :author => author,
                               :section => section)

    end
  end

  def self.down
    drop_table :authors
    drop_table :sections
    drop_table :articles
  end
end
```

Listing 21-2. *Ink19 Article Model (app/models/article.rb)*

```ruby
class Article < ActiveRecord::Base
  belongs_to :author
  belongs_to :section

  validates_presence_of :legacy_id, :title, :path, :author_id,
    :section_id, :published_on
  validates_uniqueness_of :legacy_id
end
```

Listing 21-3. *Ink19 Author Model (app/models/author.rb)*

```
class Author < ActiveRecord::Base
  has_many :articles
  validates_presence_of :name
end
```

Listing 21-4. *Ink19 Section Model (app/models/section.rb)*

```
class Section < ActiveRecord::Base
  has_many :articles
  validates_presence_of :name
end
```

When you run the migration, it will use FasterCSV's foreach method to iterate over each line of the CSV file. For each row that it processes, the author and the section will be retrieved, or created if the retrieval fails. Then a new article will be created with the appropriate data and saved to our database.

Run the rake db:migrate task to execute the migration and populate your database with new Article models. (Note that it may take several moments to complete.)

```
rake db:migrate
```

```
== 1 CreateArticles: migrating ====================================
-- create_table(:authors)
   -> 0.0026s
-- create_table(:sections)
   -> 0.0030s
-- create_table(:articles)
   -> 0.0038s
== 1 CreateArticles: migrated (53.9038s) ===========================
```

Once the task is finished, you will have all the Ink19 article, author, and section data that you need available in your models, and can move on to visualizing and analyzing it.

Creating CSS Graphs with CSS Graphy

Our next step will be to create a simple controller, called ReportsController. This controller will house the actions that we'll need for displaying the required graph data. Ink19's publisher wants to see the following graphical reports produced:

- The number of articles published in each section, rendered as a bar chart. The data displayed should be selectable by year.

- The article contribution trends of significant authors, plotted on a line chart over time and compared against the average of all other author contributions during that period. This should also be displayed a year at a time (with months of the year plotted on the x axis).

We'll use CSS Graphy to produce the bar chart. Later, we'll use the Flash charting package to produce the more complicated line chart. These two graphs will correspond to two different actions on the ReportsController. For now, we'll define just the first action, sections. Save the code in Listing 21-5 as app/controllers/reports_controller.rb.

Listing 21-5. *Reports Controller (app/controllers/reports_controller.rb)*

```ruby
class ReportsController < ApplicationController
  before_filter :get_year

  def sections
    @data = Section.find(:all).map do |section|
      { 'label' => section.name,
        'value' => section.articles.count(
          :conditions => ["published_on >= ? and published_on < ?",
            @start_date, @start_date+1.year]) }
    end

    @data = @data.select { |section| section['value'] > 0 }
  end

  protected

  def get_year
    @year = params[:id] || Article.find(:first).published_on.strftime("%Y")
    @start_date = Date.strptime(@year, "%Y")
    @years = Article.find(:all, :select => "strftime('%Y', published_on) as year",
      :group => "year").map { |a| a.year }
  end
end
```

We want to be able to pass a string representing a year to the sections action to specify the year for which we want to see statistics. We use params[:id], since we aren't dealing with a typical RESTful resource here. If it's not explicitly specified, we set the year to the publication year of the first article we find (which should be the first year for which Ink19 has data available). This is handled by our before filter, get_year, which also sets up a @years instance variable to contain all available years found in the database's articles table. We'll use this @years variable later, in our view, to construct a selection widget that visitors can use to choose a data set. Since our authors action will also need to perform these same tasks later on, it makes sense to handle these tasks in a separate protected method and run it as a before filter, thus keeping our controller as duplication-free as possible.

The sections action itself is quite simple. CSS Graphy expects the data it's being asked to graph to be formatted as label/value pairs. Therefore, we prepare a @data instance variable that will contain an array of hashes, each of which has a label and a value key:

```ruby
[ {:label => "Section 1", :value => 100}, {:label => "Section 2", :value => 85} ]
```

We construct this array by iterating through each `Section` model in our database, and using the `map` method to create the two-element hashes. The first element, the `label`, represents the name of the section. The second element, the `value`, is the number of articles published in that section during the given date range. We determine this value by calling the `count` method on the section's `articles` association and passing it conditions that specify the date range (articles in that section that were published during the specified year).

When this is finished, the `sections` method will render the template found in app/views/reports/sections.html.erb, where we'll call the view helper installed by CSS Graphy to create the first graphical report. The code listing for this view is shown in Listing 21-6.

Listing 21-6. *Sections Graph View Template (app/views/reports/sections.html.erb)*

```
<%= graphy_stylesheet %>
<%= vertical_graph(@data, :caption => "Articles in Sections, #{@year}") %>
<p>Select Year: <%= select_tag('year', options_for_select(@years, @year),
      :onchange => "document.location = '/reports/sections/' +
          this.options[this.selectedIndex].value") %></p>
```

The call to `graphy_stylesheet`, a helper method provided by the plugin, would usually be found in a layout template, but for demonstrative purposes, we render it directly in the view. By doing this we import the styles listed in the stock CSS style sheet (provided by CSS Graphy and installed to `public/stylesheets` when the plugin script is run), thus ensuring that the graph output is styled correctly in the visitor's browser.

■Tip You can also supply your own style sheet-driven themes for CSS Graphy and include them by passing a parameter to the `graphy_stylesheet` method, in this form: `<%= graphy_stylesheet theme_name %>`.

The `vertical_graph` helper method is one of two main helper methods available through CSS Graphy. The other is `horizontal_graph`. They both work the same way, rendering a graph that is either vertically or horizontally oriented. Both take a number of optional parameters. In our case, we just supply a caption. We could also include a scale, values for width and height, and labels for the x and y axis. For more details, see the documentation at `http://oss.vermonster.com/css_graphy`.

We render the `select_tag` with an option list of available years, and set the `:onchange` JavaScript callback so that when the selection is changed, the action will once again be called, this time with the updated parameter. The view will then refresh (this could also be done via Ajax) to show a new bar chart for the newly selected year. You'll see this technique used again in the ZiYa example later in this chapter.

You can now start our Rails application using `ruby script/server` and view the results. Navigate to `http://localhost:3000/reports/sections`, and you will see a display similar to the one shown in Figure 21-2.

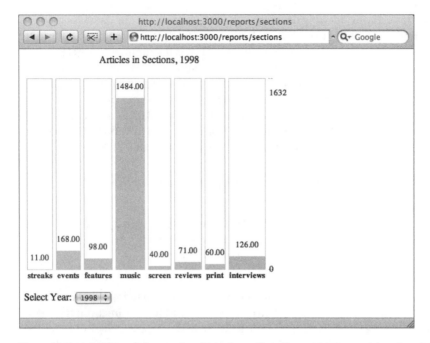

Figure 21-2. *A CSS graph for section data (http://localhost:3000/reports/sections/1998)*

Creating Flash Charts with ZiYa

Using the CSS graphs helper is great. CSS is extremely lightweight and well suited for simple data representation. No images need to be generated! However, the kind of data we can visualize using only CSS and HTML markup is limited. If you want to represent anything more complicated, you can either create image data using a library, and then display it, or use a Flash-based charting solution to generate graphs on the fly. Adobe Flash content, available in the form of SWF movies, is cross-platform and available on almost all modern web browsers and operating systems. It's estimated that Flash content is viewable by 98% of all Internet users, which is why Flash is the dominant format for displaying animated vector graphics and other rich media on the Web.

■**Tip** There are a number of ways to generate images (PNG, JPG, GIF, and so on) for graph data. Popular Ruby solutions include Gruff (`http://nubyonrails.com/pages/gruff`) and Scruffy (`http://scruffy.rubyforge.org`). Both packages require installing ImageMagick or a similar image-manipulation library on your server. You can also use other Flash charting packages, such as Open Flash Chart, which has a Rails plugin (`http://pullmonkey.com/projects/open_flash_chart`). You can learn more about these options at their respective web sites or by reading *Practical Reporting with Ruby and Rails* by David Berube (Apress, 2008).

We'll be using the ZiYa plugin to produce Flash charts. ZiYa is wrapped around the popular XML/SWF Charts library (http://www.maani.us/xml_charts), which includes a number of fancy features, such as clickable graph elements and graph animations. Also, since XML/SWF Charts takes XML as input to describe what it should render, it's a natural fit for Rails, which allows us to easily render XML representations of our data within a respond_to block.

Adding the Authors Action and View

Let's get to work. Modify the ReportsController so that it resembles the code shown in Listing 21-7.

Listing 21-7. *Updated Reports Controller with Authors Action (app/controllers/reports_controller.rb)*

```
class ReportsController < ApplicationController
  include Ziya
  ARTICLE_MIN = 120 # number of articles per year for "core" contributors

  before_filter :get_year

  def authors
    respond_to do |format|
      format.html # render authors.html.erb
      format.xml do
        graph = Ziya::Charts::Line.new(nil, "author_chart", "ink")
        graph.add(:axis_category_text, ["Jan", "Feb", "Mar", "Apr", "May",
          "Jun", "Jul", "Aug", "Sep", "Oct", "Nov", "Dec"])

        authors_to_graph = Author.find(
          :all).select { |author| author.articles.length > ARTICLE_MIN }
        authors_to_graph.each do |author|
          graph.add(:series, author.name,
            monthly_articles(@start_date, author.articles))
        end

        graph.add(:series, 'AVERAGE',
          monthly_articles(@start_date, Article, :average => true))
        render(:text => graph.to_xml)
      end
    end
  end
end
```

```ruby
def sections
  @data = Section.find(:all).map do |section|
    { 'label' => section.name,
      'value' => section.articles.count(
        :conditions => ["published_on >= ? and published_on < ?",
          @start_date, @start_date+1.year]) }
  end

  @data = @data.select { |section| section['value'] > 0 }
end

protected

def get_year
  @year = params[:id] || Article.find(:first).published_on.strftime("%Y")
  @start_date = Date.strptime(@year, "%Y")
  @years = Article.find(:all, :select => "strftime('%Y', published_on) as year",
    :group => "year").map { |a| a.year }
end

def monthly_articles(year, articles, options = {})
  res = []
  0.upto(11) do |i|
    articles_this_month = articles.find(:all,
      :conditions => ["published_on >= ? and published_on < ?",
        year + i.months, year + (i+1).months])
    if articles_this_month.length > 0
      if options[:average]
        res << articles_this_month.length /
          articles_this_month.map { |article| article.author_id }.uniq.length
      else
        res << articles_this_month.length
      end
    else
      res << 0
    end
  end

  res
end
end
```

We've added two new methods to this controller: the public authors action and a protected method called monthly_articles. We've also added a constant, ARTICLE_MIN, and mixed the Ziya module into our controller class by using the include directive. This mixin is required in order to access the methods provided in the plugin's module and create charts with ZiYa.

The `authors` action uses a `respond_to` block to discriminate between requests for XML content and HTML content. If the user requests HTML, our application will simply render the `authors` view template, shown in Listing 21- 8 (save it as `app/views/reports/authors.html.erb`).

Listing 21-8. *Authors Graph View Template (app/views/reports/authors.html.erb)*

```
<%= ziya_chart(
    url_for(:controller => 'reports', :action => 'authors', :format => :xml),
    :id => 'authors_chart', :bgcolor => "white",
    :width => 800, :height => 600 ) %>
<p>Select Year: <%= select_tag('year', options_for_select(@years, @year),
        :onchange => "document.location = '/reports/authors/' +
        this.options[this.selectedIndex].value") %></p>
```

This view calls the `ziya_chart` helper provided by the plugin. The helper method takes a URL and a number of formatting options (the DOM ID for the element to be created, and other instructions passed to the SWF file, including a preferred width and height). The URL references the very same action for which we're rendering the current template, but specifies that the format should be XML. Therefore, when the SWF file loads, it makes another request to the `authors` action, this time specifying the XML format.

The `respond_to` block, this time handling the request for XML content, creates a new ZiYa line chart object named `graph` and sets the x-axis labels to the months of the year. Next, it fetches any authors who have a number of articles exceeding the minimum we've set in our constant (our publisher really cares only about the contribution trends among the core contributors, and therefore we discard contributors with low article numbers).

For each of the authors that matter, we install a new data series using the `add` method on our `graph` object and pass it the `:series` symbol, followed by the author's name as a label and the data points for this series, in the form of an array. The data points are generated by the `monthly_articles` method, and correspond to the author's publishing statistics for each month of the specified year.

After we've finished adding each author to the chart, we make one more call to `monthly_articles`, this time specifying an option to compute the average output of *all* authors for the set of months. The resulting array is used to specify yet another series, this time labeled "AVERAGE." This additional metric will allow Ink19's publisher to see where his core contributors stand in comparison to the average writer output for each month.

Finally, an explicit call is made to the `render` method, instructing it that the content type should be text and that the response body should contain the XML representation of the ZiYa graph object. This XML data will be used as input to the SWF file, allowing it to generate the custom graph dynamically (at runtime) in the browser. Users may experience a slight delay, accompanied by a loading cursor display, while the XML data is requested and the graph is generated.

Try it by accessing `http://localhost:3000/reports/authors/1998` in a web browser. The result should look similar to Figure 21- 3. Note that during the years for which data was available, Ink19 did not publish a January issue. Therefore, writer output during the month of January will show as 0 in the chart.

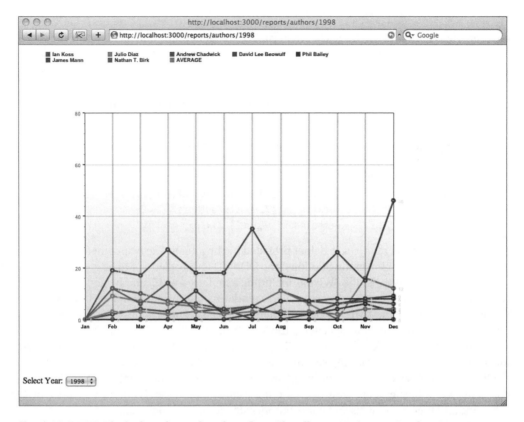

Figure 21-3. *ZiYa Flash chart for author data (http://localhost:3000/reports/authors/1998)*

■**Caution** Although the XML/SWF Charts library is available free of charge, users are encouraged by the library's creators to purchase a registered copy. Copies of the unregistered version will redirect the user to the XML/SWF Charts home page if they click the chart. For more information, see `http://www.maani.us/ xml_charts/index.php?menu=License`.

Adding Some Style

With ZiYa, themes are used to specify the look and feel of a chart. Themes can be used to change chart elements such as the colors for the axes and legends, the spacing of elements, and the font sizes, and even introduce animations and effects. ZiYa comes with two stock themes, named `default` and `commando`, and you can also create your own themes. All theme data is stored in the `public/charts/themes` directory in YAML format, making them easy to edit, update, and create.

If a theme is not explicitly specified, the default theme is used. To specify an alternate theme, add the following line in the authors action of ReportsController (you need to place it immediately after the line that initializes the graph object):

```
graph.add(:theme, "theme_name")
```

Set commando as the theme name, save the file, and reload the browser. The graph will be rerendered using the new theme.

Now let's add our own theme to customize the look and feel of the Ink19 author output graph. Save the code in Listing 21-9 as public/charts/themes/ink/base_chart.yml.

Listing 21-9. *Custom ZiYa Chart Theme (public/charts/themes/ink/base_chart.yml)*

```
<%= chart :base %>
  <%= component :axis_category %>
    size: 12
    color: 000000
    orientation: diagonal_up

  <%= component :axis_value %>
    color: 000000
    size: 12

  <%= component :chart_rect %>
    positive_color: ccffcc
    positive_alpha: 60
    negative_color: ccffcc
    negative_alpha: 40

  <%= component :legend_rect %>
    line_color: 999999
    line_thickness: 3
    line_alpha: 100

  <%= component :axis_ticks %>
    major_color: 999999
    minor_color: 999999
    value_ticks: true

  <%= component :chart_border %>
    color: 333333
    left_thickness: 3
    bottom_thickness: 3
    top_thickness: 0
    right_thickness: 0
```

```
<%= component :chart_grid_h %>
  thickness: 3
  color: 000000
  alpha: 20

<%= component :chart_grid_v %>
  thickness: 3
  color: 000000
  alpha: 10

<%= component :chart_transition %>
  type: slide_left

<%= component :chart_pref %>
  point_shape: none

<%= component :legend_label %>
  color: 000000
  size: 10

<%= component :legend_transition %>
  type: dissolve

<%= component :series_color %>
  colors: 008000, 808000, 008080
```

■**Tip** You can create a theme for your chart interactively using the theme designer provided by the plugin's creators at `http://ziya.liquidrail.com/train`. At this site, you can also find a handy reference that demonstrates the different parameters that can be set in the YAML files.

Now update the name of the theme listed in `ReportsController`. Set it to `"ink"`, as follows:

```
graph.add(:theme, "ink")
```

This will instruct ZiYa to retrieve theme information from the file you just saved, and to use those configuration options to style the graph you're rendering.

Reload the browser once more. The new graph will look similar to Figure 21-4. Notice that, in addition to an updated look and feel, the transitions animate as well. The graph itself should slide in from the left, while the legend dissolves into place.

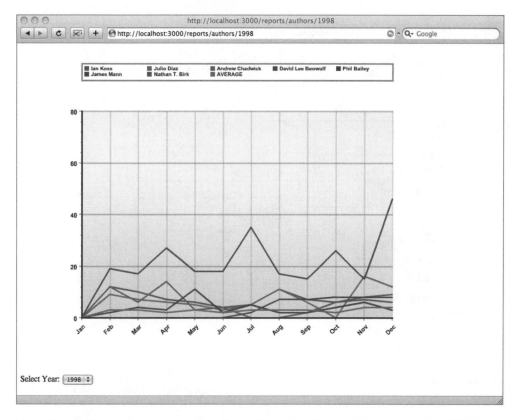

Figure 21-4. *ZiYa author chart with new theme (http://localhost:3000/reports/authors/1998)*

As you can see, ZiYa charts are very flexible and easy to style with themes. It's also easy to switch between the different graph representations that are supplied. Do you want a bar chart instead of a line chart? Change `Ziya::Charts::Line.new` to `Ziya::Charts::Bar.new` in the `ReportsController`, save the file, and reload the web browser to reveal a bar chart representation of that same dataset, as shown in Figure 21-5.

For more information about the different chart and graph types supported by ZiYa (which include pie charts, scatter charts, and even mixed-type charts) and all the theme configuration options, see the gallery at `http://ziya.liquidrail.com/tutor` and the API documentation at `http://ziya.liquidrail.com/rdoc`.

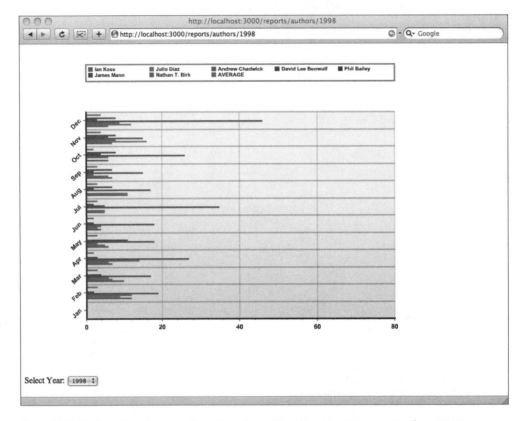

Figure 21-5. *ZiYa author data as a bar chart (http://localhost:3000/reports/authors/1998)*

Summary

Graphs and charts are useful tools for visualizing data that might otherwise be difficult to grasp. Whether the charting is for end-user consumption or administrative statistic gathering and trend analysis, it's important to have access to these facilities. The specific plugin or library that you choose depends on your requirements, of course.

In this chapter, we looked at two different plugins that can be easily dropped into an existing Rails project. ZiYa provides easy access to a flexible charting library for creating truly complex visualizations. On the opposite end of the spectrum, CSS Graphy allows you to create simple, lightweight bar charts, which don't require generation of even a single image. These plugins cover a number of common cases and are certainly useful plugins to have in your Rails development toolbox.

For more information about ZiYa Charts and the XML/SWF Charts library, see http://ziya.liquidrail.com. Documentation and examples for the CSS Graphy plugin are available at http://new.vermonster.com/2008/02/13/ css-graphy-bar-graph-plugin-for-rails.

■■■

## CHAPTER 22

Safe User Templating with Liquid

Social networking is an increasingly important aspect of the Internet. After the mammoth success of sites like Facebook and MySpace, traditional social networking startups are on the rise. Consequently, many Rails developers are spending more and more time developing social networking applications. Additionally, social networking and related technologies are expanding into unfamiliar development territory. In fact, many large companies are advertising on social networking sites and even building social networking components into their own sites.

The upshot of these trends is that if you're developing a social networking site or component, you must work very hard to meet the demands of its users. After all, if you don't, you'll likely find that your users will migrate to a site that does. One of the ways to do this is by offering a higher level of customizability than your competitors. Originally, such customizability was offered by allowing users to directly create HTML templates. Although this technique is fine for static home pages, it doesn't work well for today's complicated sites, which have a huge degree of customizability, often allowing for blog posts, RSS aggregations, lists of links, comments, and more. The client should be able to customize each of these items, and it's difficult to allow this with traditional CSS and HTML combinations.

Rails has a powerful templating system, ERB, but the problem is that it's too powerful. Because it uses the eval statement, which gives access to anything you can do in Ruby, your users could use it to run shell commands on your server, leading to massive security problems. (Even if you manage to isolate users, by giving each a different Unix user—in and of itself a nontrivial task—you would still be escalating local privilege security bugs into remote exploits, which could be a huge problem.)

Fortunately, the Liquid plugin, created by Tobias Luetke, is a great solution to the templating problem. It allows users a limited degree of control so they can do simple tasks like loop over their blog posts and print them, but can't perform more advanced functions that might jeopardize the security of your system. In this chapter, we'll take a look at an example of using Liquid to create safe user templates.

■Note Liquid does not protect against cross-site scripting (XSS). There is basic XSS protection built into Rails via the `sanitize` helper, but it's not particularly secure. If you need this protection, a better alternative is the White List plugin (`http://weblog.techno-weenie.net/2006/9/3/white-listing-plugin-for-rails`).

Our Task: Create a User Templating System

Suppose we're running a social networking site, Exabandsite, designed to empower small, independent touring bands, and we want to give each of them control over their layout. A typical social networking site gives you a URL and the chance to skin a static layout. Instead of giving them a page on our site, we intend to give them an entire subdomain. Instead of letting them theme data, we're going to use Liquid to give them access to their own data, such as blog posts containing announcements.

Eventually, multiple types of data and multiple pages will be added, so that users can, for example, export their data as a custom XML format. For now, they'll be able to present their data using Liquid on a single home page. Our goal is to create a single, customizable page, where the users can choose exactly where their data goes, without letting them execute arbitrary code on our server.

Building the Liquid Example

Begin by adding the following to your `/etc/hosts` or your `C:\windows\system32\drivers\etc\host` file on OSX/Linux and Windows, respectively:

```
127.0.0.1 localhost.localdomain
127.0.0.1 test1.localhost.localdomain
127.0.0.1 test2.localhost.localdomain
```

This allows you to access two sample accounts at either `test1.localhost.localdomain` or `test2.localhost.localdomain`, which lets you simulate having multiple subdomains.

■Tip In production, you'll probably use a DNS wildcard, which means you will just have a single DNS entry, instead of a separate entry for each user, as we have here. To do that, you'll need to set up both your web server and your DNS with a CNAME (for Canonical Name) wildcard. See the documentation for your DNS software for more information. You can also find out more about how to set up Apache for DNS wildcards, and about domain wildcarding with Rails in general, at `http://wiki.rubyonrails.org/rails/pages/HowToUseSubdomainsAsAccountKeys`.

Setting Up the Liquid Example Project

Now we're ready to create a new Rails project:

```
rails liquid_example
cd liquid_example
```

Next, install the Liquid plugin:

```
ruby /script/plugin install \
http://liquid-markup.googlecode.com/svn/trunk
```

For this example, we'll create two tables: the first will hold our users, and the second will hold each user's blog posts. For now, we'll have only one type of dynamic data that Liquid templates can access: blog posts. Of course, you could easily add more. Listings 22-1 and 22-2 show the code for the users and posts tables.

Listing 22-1. *Users Migration (db/migrate/001_create_users.rb)*

```
class CreateUsers < ActiveRecord::Migration
  def self.up
    create_table :users do |t|
      t.string :username
      t.string :password
      t.text :profile
      t.timestamps
    end
  end

  def self.down
    drop_table :users
  end
end
```

Listing 22-2. *Posts Migration (db/migrate/002_create_posts.rb)*

```
class CreatePosts < ActiveRecord::Migration
  def self.up
    create_table :posts do |t|
      t.integer :user_id
      t.text :content
      t.timestamps
    end
  end

  def self.down
    drop_table :posts
  end
end
```

We'll store Liquid code in both the profile and content fields. Note that these two fields are of type text. Under MySQL, this translates into a TEXT column type, which gives you 64KB or so of storage. You can override this, if you would like, by adding a :limit=>*some_large_ number_of_bytes* argument to the lines creating the fields. (During testing, we'll use SQLite, which has a maximum column length of about 2GB—far more than we'll use.)

▪Note The dynamic data types in SQLite are one of the reasons it's slower than a full relational database management system like MySQL, PostgreSQL, or Oracle.

Run the migration using rake db:migrate.

Creating the User and Post Models

Now that we've set up our project, let's create our models. Listings 22-3 and 22-4 show the code for the User and Post models.

Listing 22-3. *User Model (app/models/user.rb)*

```
class User < ActiveRecord::Base
  has_many :posts
  def to_liquid
    { 'username'=>self.username,
      'url'=>self.url }
  end

  def url
    "http://#{self.username}.localhost.localdomain:3000/"
  end
end
```

Listing 22-4. *Post Model (app/models/post.rb)*

```
class Post < ActiveRecord::Base
  belongs_to :user
  def to_liquid
    { 'author'=>self.user.username,
      'body'=>self.content,
      'posted_at'=>self.created_at.strftime('%D') }
  end
end
```

These models are fairly simple, except for the to_liquid method. Liquid expects hashes or arrays full of items that respond to the method to_liquid. Out of the box, Active Record objects do not respond to to_liquid, which is why we've explicitly defined to_liquid methods on our models. You could do this more generically by adding a to_liquid method to

ActiveRecord::Base, but you probably want to exclude some data from being passed to the user, so it's wise to define them manually.

Let's add some data by running ruby script/console, and then entering the following commands:

```
>> User.create(:username=>'test1',:password=>'test' )
>> User.create(:username=>'test2',:password=>'test')
>> test_user = User.find(1)
>> test_user.posts.create(:content=>"New Show at the RXZ " <<
   "Super Stadium on Jan 35 2015!")
>> test_user.posts.create(:content=>"Band broke up; I'll never talk to scum " <<
   "like that again.")
>> test_user.posts.create(:content=>"Band back together; sorry guys!")
```

Creating the Profile Controller

Our profile controller fulfills three functions: the first shows a list of all user profiles on the system, the second shows a particular profile, and the third lets a user edit a profile. Listing 22-5 shows the code for our controller.

Listing 22-5. *Profiles Controller (app/controllers/profiles_controller.rb)*

```
class ProfilesController < ApplicationController
  before_filter :get_user
  def index
    if @user
     render :action=>'show'
    else
      @users = User.find(:all)
      render :action=>'index'
    end
  end
  def edit
   if @user
     if authorize(@user)
        if request.post?
          if @user.update_attributes(params[:user])
            flash[:notice] = "Profile saved; " <<
                            "you can view your profile at " <<
                            "<a href='#{@user.profile_url}'>" <<
                            "<%=@user.profile_url%></a>"
          else
            flash[:notice] = "Profile not saved."
          end
        end
     else
       render :text=>"Not authorized."
     end
```

```
      else
        render :text=>"Profile not found!"
    end
  end
  protected

  def get_user
    @user = User.find_by_username(request.subdomains.first)
  end

  def authorize(user)
    authenticate_or_request_with_http_basic("Profile") do |username, password|
      username == user.username && password == user.password
    end
  end
end

end
```

Two protected methods, get_user and authorize, are used by the show and index actions. Protected methods cannot be called by the user as part of a URL, so they are for internal use only. The get_user protected method retrieves a user based on the subdomain of the site. For example, if you go to example1.localhost.localdomain, it will retrieve the profile for the user with the username example1.

■**Note** The authentication for this example is very simple. It uses HTTP Basic authentication to check that the username and password are correct. In a production environment, you would probably use a more full-featured system, like that provided by the RESTful authentication plugin (covered in Chapter 11).

Constructing the Views

Let's take a look at the view for the first action, index. It uses Liquid, instead of ERB, and it looks like this Listing 22-6.

Listing 22-6. *Band Index (app/views/profiles/index.html.liquid)*

```
<h1>Bands on Exabandsite</h1>

<style>
  li { padding :1em; }
  li.odd { background-color:white }
  li.odd { background-color: #eee6ff; }
</style>
<ol>
```

```
{%for user in users%}
  <li class="{% cycle 'even', 'odd' %}" >{{user.username}} -
    <a href="{{user.url}}">{{user.url}}</a></li>
{%endfor%}
</ol>
```

As you can see, Liquid syntax is reasonably clear. It provides a `{%for.. endfor%}`
construct that loops over members of collections. The `cycle` command is a built-in convenience tag provided by Liquid. It loops through its arguments one at a time, so the first
time `{% cycle 'even', 'odd' %}` is called, it returns even, the second time odd, and so forth.
Note that the `{{variablename}}` syntax is used to include the variable. The full details on the
Liquid markup can be found at `http://www.liquidmarkup.org/`.

Of course, typically you would use Liquid views to render user data only, but some developers strongly feel that having any complex logic in your views violates MVC separation. If you
feel that way, using Liquid templates may be a good choice. (Personally, we feel it's wiser to
separate concerns rather than statically assigning "levels of complexity" or other concepts to
given layers.)

Remember that for Rails 2.0 views, the last part of the file name specifies the interpreter,
so `.html.liquid` means that this view is an HTML format view to be interpreted by Liquid.

Next, let's take a look at our `edit` action view, shown in Listing 22-7.

Listing 22-7. *Edit Profile Page (app/views/profiles/edit.html.erb)*

```
<h1>Edit my Profile</h1>
<%if flash[:notice]%>
   <p><%=flash[:notice]%></p>
<%end%>
<% form_for 'user' do |f|%>
<p>Profile:<br> <%=f.text_area 'profile'%></p>

<p>TIP: You can use Liquid code in your profile. You can find out
 about Liquid's syntax at
<a href="http://info.getcashboard.com/topics/liquid_basics">
Cashboard's site</a>.</p>

<%=f.submit%>
<%end%>
```

As you can see, the page for editing profiles is relatively simple. It has a form with a text
area, and bands can enter their Liquid code in the text area.

The show action view is shown in Listing 22-8. This actually shows a band's profile.

Listing 22-8. *Show Profile View (app/views/profiles/show.html.erb)*

```
<%=Liquid::Template.parse(@user.profile).render 'posts'=>@user.posts%>
```

This code is an ERB template that renders a Liquid template. Although in this case it takes
up the entire template, you could also have the Liquid template be just part of the overall
page—a sidebar, for example.

The call to `Liquid::Template.parse` in Listing 22-8 creates a `Liquid::Template` object. We can then call `render` on it. `render` takes a hash of variables that are passed to the Liquid template.

Next, let's take a look at our routing, as shown in Listing 22-9.

Listing 22-9. *Route Configuration (config/routes.rb)*

```
ActionController::Routing::Routes.draw do |map|
  map.root :controller=> 'profiles'
  map.connect ':action', :controller=>'profiles'
  map.connect ':controller/:action/:id'
  map.connect ':controller/:action/:id.:format'
end
```

The routes are fairly standard. Note that the profile controller is the default, and we add a custom route, which lets us access methods of the profile controller without explicitly specifying the controller. This means we can say /edit instead of /profile/edit.

■**Note** If you're used to setting up Apache, note that nothing special is done to get Rails to accept the new subdomains. Unlike Apache, Rails responds to requests from all hostnames. If you wanted only a Rails application to respond to some requests, you would usually take care of that in your web server or reverse proxy configuration.

Testing the Liquid Example

Let's take the app for a spin. You can launch it using `ruby script/server`. Point your browser to `http://test1.localhost.localdomain:3000/edit`. You'll be prompted to enter a username and password. Enter `test1` and `test`.

Enter the Liquid code shown in Listing 22-10 in the text area, as shown in Figure 22-1, and then click the Save changes button.

Listing 22-10. *Sample Liquid Template*

```
<style>
body {font-family: helvetica, verdana, sans-serif; }
</style>
<h1>Andy "Catskillfish" Thomas And The Tangoleers </h1>

Here's the latest news from Andy and the Tangoleers:
```

```
<li>
{% for post in posts %}
 <li><strong>{{ post.posted_at }}</strong>
<p>{{ post.body | prettyprint}}</li>
{% endfor %}
</ul>
```

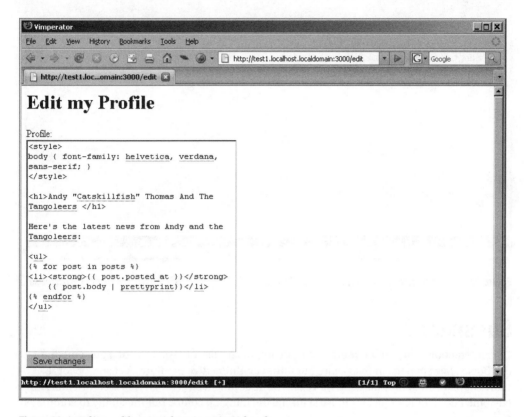

Figure 22-1. *Edit profile page showing Liquid code*

Now visit `test1.localhost.localdomain:3000` with a web browser. You should see a page similar to Figure 22-2.

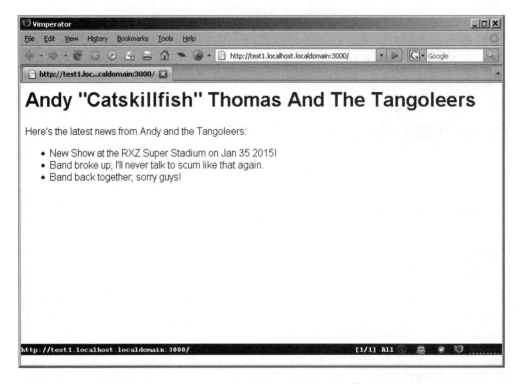

Figure 22-2. *Profile page showing output of Liquid code dynamically pulling from the database*

Summary

User interaction is becoming more and more important on the Web. It's not a push medium, like books, newspapers, or television, but rather an interactive medium. As users become more sophisticated, they demand more and more sophisticated tools. This includes tools for customization, and not just for loose skinning or changing colors, but the ability to completely rearrange a page. For that purpose, Liquid is a great choice. It's easy, it doesn't give the user too much power, and it's flexible.

## CHAPTER 23

Creating Dynamic, Reusable Web Application Sidebars

Sidebars are everywhere: on your desktop, on the Web, in print brochures and coffee shop menus. Sidebars are a design element used to add context, or to supplement the main flow of information, without interrupting it or detracting from it.

In the realm of web sites and applications, sidebars often contain menus, submenus, advertising, quotes, polls, pictures, or other related contextual information that doesn't fit into the flow of the main content area. However, this doesn't mean that the information is any less important. It's common to see sidebars used for search entry and login boxes, for example, which are clearly very necessary functional elements. In blogs, sidebars frequently play host to information related to the main content area such as a tag cloud of terms used in the site (see Chapter 3), an archived list of recent articles by month, information about the blogger, and so on. Sidebar data found in portals and blogs is also commonly culled from other sources, such as recent updates made by fellow bloggers, things they've recently bookmarked through a social bookmarking service, or photos they've recently posted to a photo sharing site.

In the world of Rails application development, sidebars need to be flexible. Sometimes you'll need a sidebar to display a flat collection of links. When we're dealing with this sort of sidebar, it functions much like a partial template. On the other hand, sometimes sidebars are used to display a dynamic element such as a poll, in which case they're most likely rendered as a component. In either case, they need to be easy to declare, easy to bind to a specific view (or many views), and easily reused. Fortunately, there's a Rails plugin that makes this easy for us: Simple Sidebar (`http://mabs29.googlecode.com/svn/trunk/plugins/simple_sidebar`) by Matthew Abonyi.

Our Task: Define a Sidebar Solution

Our friend Steve is just getting started with Rails, and as a learning experience, he's decided to rebuild his personal web site. The site is going to have a little bit of everything, including a simple blogging platform, a mechanism to browse his web portfolio sites, and another to allow him to update pictures of the cars that he restores in his spare time. Steve has multiple controllers in this application, each of which has multiple actions, and he's trying to think up a way to create a modular set of sidebars that he can add to each of them in any fashion he desires.

Having had this same scenario pop up with our own web applications in the past, we suggest that he might want to look into the Simple Sidebar plugin, which provides an easy way to add reusable sidebars to any Rails-based application. The sidebars are flexible and can take many forms; they can be a list of links, an ad, a poll, a login box, and so on. It's up to you to define what your sidebars *do*; the plugin just provides you with a framework for creating and displaying them.

Usage is simple: just create reusable sidebars in code fragments and then attach them to any number of actions within a given controller class, extending the controller DSL in a logical manner. Sidebars can also be called conditionally. Much like Rails handles rendering controller actions, it seems logical that sidebars might be declared at the controller level for each action whose view needs them, for instance, only if a certain precondition is met ("Is the user logged in?"). Using this filtering capability and the fact that any number of sidebars can be attached to an action, we can build a pool of sidebars to render for each action. Then, to display the currently relevant sidebars to a visitor, we can just call the render_sidebars method in the application layout, and the appropriate sidebars will be automagically rendered for us.

In this chapter, we're going to write a bit of code to help Steve get started with Simple Sidebar. First, we'll install the plugin, and then we'll get to work on building three demonstration sidebars for Steve's personal web portal. The first will display a static list of links to some of our favorite blogs, the second will be a login sidebar to interoperate with an existing authentication system, and the final one will demonstrate how to create a sidebar that polls a remote web service in order to create a list of music that we've been listening to recently.

Preparing a Sample Application for Sidebars

Let's create a new Rails application for the sidebar project:

```
rails sidebarsite
cd sidebarsite
```

We can then install the Simple Sidebar plugin by executing the following command inside the new application root directory:

```
ruby script/plugin install ➥
http://mabs29.googlecode.com/svn/trunk/plugins/simple_sidebar
```

In order to retrieve Steve's recent listening history for our third example, we'll leverage an existing Ruby library that interfaces with Last.fm's web service API, Audioscrobbler. The gem that allows us to access the Audioscrobbler data is called Scrobbler, and you can install it using the following command:

```
gem install scrobbler
```

■**Note** Last.fm is a web service that builds a social network around the music that you and your peers listen to, and gives you personal top artist and album charts and recommendations. For more information, visit http://last.fm. For more information on the Scrobbler gem and using Last.fm web services in Ruby, visit http://scrobbler.rubyforge.org/.

Since Steve has already written a fair bit of code for his project, and we want to demonstrate how he can add sidebars, we'll just mock up some of his controllers and views with a stock `ArticlesController`, shown in Listing 23-1, and two stock views for the `index` and `show` actions, in Listings 23-2 and 23-3, respectively.

Listing 23-1. *Dummy Controller for Sidebar Examples (app/controllers/articles_controller.rb)*

```
class ArticlesController < ApplicationController
  def index; end
  def show; end
end
```

Listing 23-2. *Dummy Index View for Sidebar Examples (app/views/articles/index.html.erb)*

```
<p>This is the index view.</p>
<p><%= link_to('link to show', :action => 'show', :id => 1) %></p>
```

Listing 23-3. *Dummy Show View for Sidebar Examples (app/views/articles/show.html.erb)*

```
<p>This is the view for article <%= params[:id] %>.</p>
<p><%= link_to('link to index', :action => 'index') %></p>
```

Obviously, you'll want to insert your own application logic in place of this dummy controller and views; their purpose here is simply to provide context for the sidebars we'll build in this chapter. We'll also use the default (preexisting) Rails routes, which means that the URLs for our `index` action will look like `http://localhost:3000/articles`, and a sample `show` action might look like `http://localhost:3000/articles/show/1`.

Start your Rails server now using `ruby script/server` and visit these URLs. What you should find there will be profoundly uninteresting. Our next task is to change that by adding sidebars.

Building a Truly Simple Sidebar

If you just want to create a simple, static list of your favorite blogs and include it in a number of different templates, two techniques will immediately spring to mind: using your application's built-in layouts and using partial view templates. In order to see why we might use Simple Sidebar to augment these built-in facilities, let's examine how we might proceed without the sidebar plugin.

First, we would simply create a layout for our application that includes a sidebar column, and the layout will yield to our per-action views, displaying them wherever we position the `yield` statement in the template. This works great if our sidebars are static and don't vary from controller to controller (or action to action). Even if they do vary, we could consider creating multiple layouts with different static sidebars, which might work well if the layouts are different anyway. But this starts to feel un-DRY very quickly, especially if we want different actions in the same controller to have different sidebars.

The next step we'd take would be to create separate partial templates for each sidebar. For our reading list, the first iteration of that partial might look something like the code in Listing 23-4. Save it as `app/views/sidebars/_blogs.rhtml`.

Listing 23-4. *Blog Reading List Sidebar Partial Template (app/views/sidebars/_blogs.rhtml)*

```
<div class="sidebar">
  <div class="title">Reading List</div>
  <ul>
    <li><a href="http://www.readwriteweb.com">ReadWriteWeb</a></li>
    <li><a href="http://www.mashable.com">Mashable</a></li>
    <li><a href="http://www.smashingmagazine.com/">Smashing Magazine</a></li>
    <li><a href="http://boingboing.net/">Boing Boing</a></li>
    <li><a href="http://icanhascheezburger.com">I Can Has Cheezburger?</a></li>
  </ul>
</div>
```

■**Caution** Make sure to note the leading underscore in the partial template name. Also, at the time of this writing, Simple Sidebar uses only old-style `.rhtml` templates rather than new-style Rails 2.0 `.html.erb` templates. Therefore, templates must begin with an underscore and end with `.rhtml` to work with Simple Sidebar.

This template could then be rendered into the layout(s) using a bit of conditional logic:

```
<%= render(:partial => "sidebars/blogs") if controller.controller_name ==
"articles" %>
```

Although this will work, it's clearly not very elegant, nor is it maintainable for any significant number of cases. And adding an enormous case statement won't help much, either.

The core advantage to using Simple Sidebar becomes very clear here; it allows you to create sidebars independent of application-level views and render them on a per-controller/action basis, with any relevant conditional logic provided at the controller level, outside of the view, where it belongs.

Using Simple Sidebar, we can reuse that same partial we just defined in Listing 23-4, but declare it within the context of our controller. See the updated ArticlesController in Listing 23-5 for how we might declare this.

Listing 23-5. *Updated Controller with Blog Sidebar (app/controllers/articles_controller.rb)*

```
class ArticlesController < ApplicationController
  sidebar :blogs

  def index; end
  def show; end
end
```

As you can see, this is a clear way of declaring the presence of a sidebar. It feels very much like part of a domain-specific language and fits quite naturally with the Rails

`ActionController` syntax, which it extends. This particular sidebar declaration means that any action rendered from this controller will also render a sidebar named `_blogs.rhtml` in the `app/views/sidebars` directory, as long as there is a corresponding call to the special `render_sidebars` method somewhere in the layout.

Embedding the Sidebar in a Layout

Let's add a standard layout now so we can see our sidebar in action. Save the code in Listing 23-6 as `app/views/layouts/application.html.erb`.

Listing 23-6. *Sidebarsite Application Layout (app/views/layouts/application.html.erb)*

```
<html>
<head>
  <title>Sidebarsite</title>
  <style type="text/css">
    .sidebar {
      border: 2px solid black;
      background-color: yellow;
      margin: 10px;
      width: 200px;
      min-width: 200px;
    }
    .sidebar .title {
      color: yellow;
      background-color: black;
      font-weight: bold;
      padding: 8px;
    }
    .sidebar ul {
      list-style-type: none;
      margin: 0;
      padding: 5px;
    }
    .sidebar ul li {
      margin: 3px;
    }
    .sidebar a {
      color: black;
      text-decoration: none;
    }
    .sidebar a:hover {
      text-decoration: underline;
    }
```

```
    .sidebar input[type=text] {
      width: 160px;
      margin-bottom: 10px;
    }
  </style>
</head>
<body>
  <div style="float: right;"><%= render_sidebars %></div>
  <%= yield %>
</body>
</html>
```

As you can see, the body of our HTML layout calls the render_sidebars method and wraps it in a div element, which is floated to the right of the main content area. We've also added some CSS that will provide basic formatting for our sidebars. Feel free to move this to a proper style sheet if you like.

Now, if we visit http://localhost:3000/articles, we'll see the appropriate sidebar floating to the right of the content area as shown in Figure 23-1.

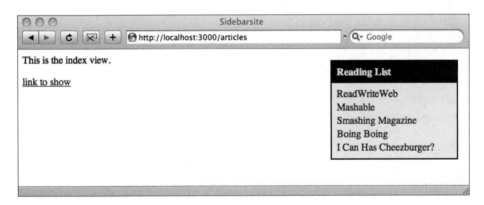

Figure 23-1. *A very simple sidebar (http://localhost:3000/articles)*

Note that render_sidebars will render as many sidebars as there are listed for a given controller/action, and it will render them in the order that they are declared in. That is, if you include two sidebar statements in your controller, it will render the first one above the second. You'll see this in practice momentarily.

■**Tip** You can change the order that sidebars are displayed in using the sidebar_sort method. For instance, to invert the display order of the sidebars listed in your controller, you could sort on the implicit priority property of the sidebars by calling sidebar_sort { |sb1, sb2| sb2[:priority] <=> sb1[:priority] }.

Filtering Options

We can also use filtering options to limit the display of a sidebar to specific actions within the controller using :only and :except. If you've used before, after, and around filters in ActionController, this practice should be familiar. Change the sidebar declaration in the controller to look like the following:

```
sidebar :blogs, :only => :index # or :except => [:new, :show]
```

If we reload our web browser now and visit the index view, the sidebar will still be present. However, if we reload the show view, the sidebar will no longer be displayed.

Our next sidebar example, although not much more complicated than the first, presents an even more common use case.

Enabling User Authentication with Login Sidebars

Many applications that support user logins provide users with numerous opportunities to log in. In addition to providing a link to a separate login page or an Ajax pop-up, it's common to find login boxes displayed directly in the page layout or in well-positioned sidebars. For instance, Slashdot, a popular technology news portal, has an omnipresent user authentication sidebar box in a persistent right-hand column.

To add this capability to our sample portal site with Simple Sidebar, we can create another partial template; this time that partial will contain a login form, as shown in Listing 23-7. Save it as app/views/sidebars/_login.rhtml.

Listing 23-7. *Login Sidebar (app/views/sidebars/_login.rhtml)*

```
<div class="sidebar">
  <div class="title">Your Account</div>
  <% form_tag('/session') do -%>
    <ul>
      <li>Login:<br/>
        <%= text_field_tag(:login) %></li>
      <li>Password:<br/>
        <%= text_field_tag(:password) %></li>
      <li><%= link_to("&raquo; New Account", "/signup") %></li>
      <li><%= submit_tag('Do It!') %></li>
    </ul>
  <% end -%>
</div>
```

The form in this partial posts the login and password fields to the create action of a pre-existing SessionController, mimicking the same form that might exist in the controller's native new action view (for more information on building a functional SessionController and handling user authentication, see Chapter 11 and the sidebar "Integrating RESTful Authentication with the Login Sidebar" a little later in this chapter).

Note that we're reusing the CSS classes we defined previously, since we generally want all of our sidebars to have the same basic look and feel. We're also reusing the app/views/ sidebars directory for template storage; this is the default location where Simple Sidebar looks for partial templates to render, and it's a good idea to store any sidebar views here.

Using Conditional Logic to Display Sidebars

In order to display this new sidebar, we'll need to add it to our controller. However, it doesn't make sense to show a login box if a user is already logged in, so we'll also use this opportunity to demonstrate the use of conditional logic for sidebar display.

Simple Sidebar provides :if and :unless options that we can use to control the display of sidebars. If we have an authentication system like RESTful Authentication installed, a method like logged_in? may already be available that we can use to determine the user's authentication status. But for our example here, let's define it in the local controller as a protected method, so we can give Steve a demo without worrying about integrating a proper authentication system. The code for our updated ArticlesController is shown in Listing 23-8.

Listing 23-8. *Controller with Login Sidebar (app/controllers/articles_controller.rb)*

```
class ArticlesController < ApplicationController
  sidebar :login, :unless => :logged_in?
  sidebar :blogs, :only => :index

  def index; end
  def show; end

  protected

  def logged_in?
    !params[:logged_in].nil?
  end
end
```

The logged_in? method we've mocked up here simply checks the parameter string for the presence of a parameter, logged_in, and, if found, it assumes the user has already logged in. This means that the logged_in? method will return true if the string is found and false otherwise.

Now, if we reload http://localhost:3000/articles, we'll see the updates shown in Figure 23-2, which includes both the login sidebar and the blogs sidebar, in the specified order. If we modify the URL in our browser so that it reads http://localhost:3000/articles? logged_in=1 and reload, the logged_in? method will return true, and the conditional logic on our login sidebar will prevent it from being shown.

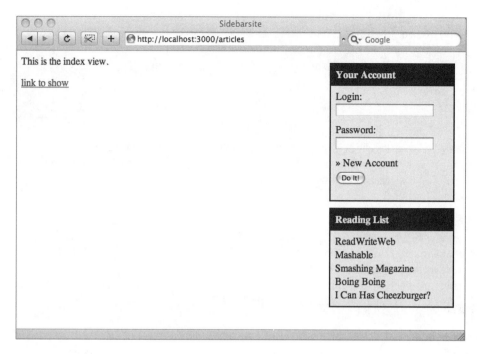

Figure 23-2. *Sidebars with login box (http://localhost:3000/articles)*

INTEGRATING RESTFUL AUTHENTICATION WITH THE LOGIN SIDEBAR

One of the nice things about Rick Olson's RESTful Authentication plugin is the `store_location` facility. If you set a `:login_required` before filter in your controller, the `access_denied` method will be called if the user isn't logged in. This will store the requested URL in the session, and the user will be redirected to a login page. Then, when the user is successfully authenticated, the `redirect_back_or_default` method is called by `SessionController#create`, which pulls the stored location out of the session and redirects the user back to where he or she intended to go in the first place.

However, if you're using a login sidebar, Restful Authentication really has no idea where the user is coming from before the post to the `create` action (because `access_denied` was never called!). This means the user will be redirected to the default path (usually /) instead, when the user probably expects to be returned to the page he or she was looking at before logging in. We can fix this with just a few simple changes to `lib/authenticated_system.rb`.

First, the `store_location` method should be modified so it can optionally take a location to store as a parameter. Using the current `request_uri` as a parameter default maintains backward compatibility with existing code:

```
def store_location(location = request.request_uri)
  session[:return_to] = location
end
```

Next, the create method in `SessionController` should be changed so it checks the HTTP referrer. All that needs to be done here is to add a single line to the top of the method:

```
def create
  check_referer
  ...
end
```

Finally, implement the `check_referer` method, which should be a protected method in `lib/authenticated_system.rb`. The purpose of this method is to check the HTTP referrer and store it for redirect purposes after authentication, as long as it is from the current domain and is NOT a well-known login URL such as `/login`:

```
def check_referer
  referer = request.env['HTTP_REFERER'] || ""
  if referer.match(request.domain) &&
     !referer.match(session_url) &&
     !referer.match(login_url)
       store_location(request.env['HTTP_REFERER'])
  end
end
```

The stored URL will later be plucked out of the session by `redirect_back_or_default` and used to redirect the user to the location he or she expects to return to after authentication.

Using Component Rendering in a Sidebar

Our final sidebar uses the Scrobbler gem to retrieve our listening profile information from Last.fm (via Audioscrobbler) and display our top artists for the current week. This is a cool feature you might find on more progressive music-lover blogs. Because of the power afforded by the Simple Sidebar plugin we're using and the Scrobbler gem, this is truly trivial to implement, and we think Steve will be excited about it.

However, this time around our sidebar has a bit more logic to it than the examples we've dealt with previously. First, we have to use the Scrobbler library to retrieve an object identifying a Last.fm user. Once we have that, we can use it to retrieve the user's weekly artist chart, and then truncate it to reflect only the top ten artists.

Could we do all this in a partial? Yes, but MVC principles tell us that we're crossing a line by putting what is clearly controller logic in a view. Instead, we'll use a style of rendering that is often referred to as "component rendering." That is, we'll associate the sidebar to a specific controller action and let the output of that action dictate what's shown in the resulting sidebar view template.

Since we're already using an `app/views/sidebars` directory to store our sidebar views, it makes sense to create a `SidebarsController` with actions whose names map to the more complicated sidebar view templates that might need to be rendered. In this case, we'll call our sidebar "music," and we'll create the `SidebarsController` with a `music` action to set up the instance variables we'll need in the view, as shown in Listing 23-9.

Listing 23-9. *SidebarsController (app/controllers/sidebars_controller.rb)*

```
require 'scrobbler'
class SidebarsController < ApplicationController
  def music
    user = Scrobbler::User.new('zapnap')
    @artists = user.weekly_artist_chart[0..10]
  end
end
```

The `music` action creates a `Scrobbler::User` object given a Last.fm username, and then makes an API call to retrieve the weekly artist chart for that user. It places the artist chart, an array of `Scrobbler::Artist` objects, in the instance variable `@artists`, and we limit the number of results to the indicated range (the top 10 artists of the week). Note that we also `require` the Scrobbler gem at the top of the controller, which is what gives us access to the library in the first place.

Now all our view has to do is iterate through each of the artists in `@artists`, and for each, create a list element with the artist name and link to their Last.fm profile. This view is shown in Listing 23-10. Make sure to save it as `app/views/sidebars/music.rhtml`. Note that the file name should *not* be preceded with an underscore this time, as this is the view rendered from the component, rather than a partial template like our other sidebar views.

Listing 23-10. *View for Favorite Artist Template (app/views/sidebars/music.rhtml)*

```
<div class="sidebar">
  <div class="title">Now Playing...</div>
  <ul>
    <% @artists.each do |artist| -%>
      <li><%= link_to(artist.name, artist.url) %></li>
    <% end -%>
  </ul>
</div>
```

With this in place, the only remaining task is to add the sidebar declaration to our example articles controller, as shown in Listing 23-11. The syntax is slightly different this time around; we're specifying a controller and an action that will render the sidebar component, which will then be displayed like any other sidebar. The controller specified here doesn't have to be the `SidebarsController`; it could be anything. We've just used `SidebarsController` because it's a convenient, logical convention, and we like conventions that make our lives easier.

Listing 23-11. *Updated Controller with Music Sidebar (app/controllers/articles_controller.rb)*

```
class ArticlesController < ApplicationController
  sidebar :login, :unless => :logged_in?
  sidebar :music, :component => { :controller => 'sidebars', :action => 'music' }
  sidebar :blogs, :only => :index
```

```
def index; end
def show; end

protected

def logged_in?
  !params[:logged_in].nil?
end
end
```

Refresh your browser after saving the code changes. The new index view should look similar to what you see in Figure 23-3, with the artists displayed matching the interests of the user specified in the controller action. Feel free to substitute your own Last.fm username if you don't like our musical tastes!

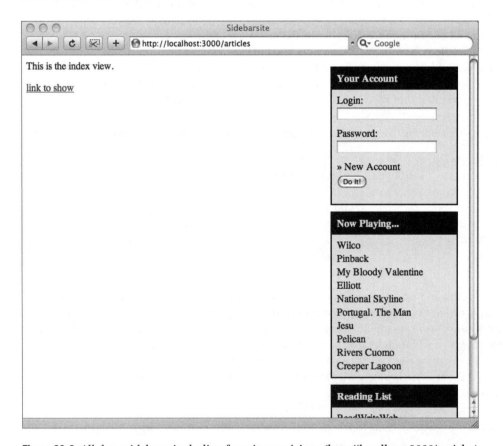

Figure 23-3. *All three sidebars, including favorite musicians (http://localhost:3000/articles)*

Summary

Sidebars are found in all sorts of web applications, ranging from portals to personal blogs to niche business applications. If they're relatively static, they can be baked right into a layout. But if you want to render sidebars dynamically based on the controller/action that's being called, the Simple Sidebar plugin can save you a good deal of work. It's simple, flexible, and easily reusable, which are all hallmarks of a well-designed Rails plugin.

You can find more information about the Simple Sidebar by visiting `http://mabs29.googlecode.com/svn/trunk/plugins/simple_sidebar`.

■■■

## CHAPTER 24

Quick PDF Generation with RTex

PDF files are a ubiquitous, somewhat open standard from Adobe for creating, printing, and exchanging documents. They are much more cross-platform than, say, Microsoft Office documents. PDFs will typically look (and print) the same almost everywhere, and a free PDF viewer is available from Adobe for most platforms. The reason that we call PDF a "somewhat open," rather than "open," standard is that not all of the features commonly associated with PDFs, such as limits on user activities and e-book encryption, are part of Adobe's PDF specification. On the other hand, a number of open source PDF generation applications, libraries, and toolkits are widely available. You can also download an open source PDF viewer, such as Ghostview or Xpdf.

Part of the reason for the popularity of PDFs is that they provide features that are missing from HTML documents. HTML has no header/footer control, no reliable way to print background colors or images, no control over the paper size or margins, and no way to easily e-mail a document. You can e-mail a link, but e-mailing a document is harder. If you want to, say, take a report from your account on a site and send it to someone else in your organization without giving that person your authorization credentials, you're more or less stuck with PDFs.

■Note Although it's still not enough, HTML and CSS now offer better control over the printed page. You can specify separate size sheets for printing, which lets you, for example, hide user interface elements when a user prints a page. You can also manually create page breaks using the `page-break-after` and `page-break-before` CSS attributes. CSS3 also has a module called Paged Media, which may eventually solve even more of these problems. This module lets you specify page sizes and margins. It also allows you to keep page breaks from happening inside a given element, which lets you keep together, say, figures and their captions. At this time, however, support for CSS3 in general, and Paged Media in particular, is virtually nonexistent.

Generating PDFs is quite a task, partly because the PDF standard is print-oriented. PDF viewers do not wrap words or lay out elements for you, which is quite different from HTML. The upside of this is that a PDF document is likely to print the same on your printer as it would if you ordered 10,000 copies from the local Kinko's. The downside is that you often need a preprocessing engine to do the layout for you.

Of these engines, there are a few you are likely to use in Ruby. The first, and most common, is PDF::Writer (http://ruby-pdf.rubyforge.org/pdf-writer/), which is written in pure Ruby and has no outside dependencies. Unfortunately, PDF::Writer is quite limited. As of this writing, it has only basic support for tables, and it is completely lacking in many other areas. If you're interested, see Chapter 10 of *Practical Reporting with Ruby on Rails* (Apress, 2008) for more on using PDF::Writer to create reports.

Another common approach is to keep your views in HTML and use an HTML-to-PDF converter to convert them into PDFs on request. The disadvantage of this approach is that you're typically not able to take full advantage of the features of PDFs. HTML is designed so that any device can reformat HTML content to have it display correctly according to the device's limitations. PDFs are designed to appear the exact same under any circumstances. As a result, viewing a PDF on a cell phone or widescreen monitor may be awkward. Furthermore, HTML gives rendering engines, typically web browsers, wide latitude in exactly how HTML elements should appear; PDF does not. However, if you want a PDF page that roughly resembles a web page, using an HTML-to-PDF converter can be a workable solution.

▪Tip A popular and freely available converter, called HTML2PS, is available at http://user.it.uu.se/ ~jan/html2ps.html. Chapter 8 of *Practical Reporting with Ruby and Rails* covers using HTML2PS, although it's within the context of a script, rather than a Rails application.

This chapter covers generating PDFs with the RTex plugin, by Bruce Williams. The RTex plugin uses LaTeX, an older technology that can be relatively hard to learn, particularly compared with Ruby. However, LaTeX has two large advantages over the alternatives: it's fast, and it's flexible. LaTeX can perform a huge array of PDF-formatting tasks—ranging from automatic page numbering, to footnotes, to mathematical formulas, to printing address labels and envelopes—and it can create even very large PDF reports quickly. These advantages are why LaTeX remains one of the most popular typesetting tools for many scientific and technical documents.

On the other hand, LaTeX is not the most user-friendly tool. If you're looking for another solution, you can try the PDF:Writer or HTML-to-PDF converter approach.

Our Task: Automate Creation of Overdue Billing Notices

For this chapter's example, let's suppose we have been contracted by a company to create a system that automatically writes collection letters to clients who have overdue invoices. We can use RTex to create both the envelopes and the letters themselves. As a bonus, because the PDFs are cross-platform, the company could easily outsource its printing to another firm by simply e-mailing the PDFs.

Preparing for the Overdue Billing Application

Before we get started, you need to install LaTeX. The LaTeX distribution you use depends on your operating system:

Windows: You can obtain 2.340MiKTeX, a TeX/LaTeX distribution for Windows, from http://miktex.org.

Mac OS X: You can obtain a TeX/LaTeX distribution for OS X at http://tug.org/mactex/. If you have a preferred ports manager for OS X, such as Fink or MacPorts, you can install LaTeX using that as well.

Linux: If you're running Linux, LaTeX may already be installed. If not, you should be able to install it easily using your system's package manager.

- The command for Debian Linux and related distributions (Ubuntu, for example) is apt-get install texlive.

- For Red Hat–based distributions, you should be able to use the command sudo yum install tetex-latex.

After you install LaTeX, create a blank Rails application:

```
rails overdue_billing
cd overdue_billing
```

You also need to install the RTex gem:

```
gem install rtex
```

You next need to install the RTex gem as a plugin into your Rails application:

```
rtex --install .
```

Now you're ready to build the application.

Building the Overdue Billing Application

The overdue billing application will have two tables: one for customers and one for invoices. Listings 24-1 and 24-2 show the two migrations.

Listing 24-1. *Create Customer Migration (db/migrate/001_create_customers.rb)*

```
class CreateCustomers < ActiveRecord::Migration
  def self.up
    create_table :customers do |t|
      t.string :name, :limit=>40
      t.string :street_address
      t.string :city
      t.string :state
      t.string :zip
```

```
        t.string :phone_number
        t.timestamps
      end
    end

    def self.down
      drop_table :customers
    end
  end
```

Listing 24-2. *Create Invoices Migration (db/migrate/002_create_invoices.rb)*

```
class CreateInvoices < ActiveRecord::Migration
  def self.up
    create_table :invoices do |t|
      t.date :due_on
      t.decimal :amount, :precision => 8, :scale => 2
      t.integer :customer_id
      t.timestamps
    end
  end

  def self.down
    drop_table :invoices
  end
end
```

Run the migrations as follows:

```
rake db:migrate
```

Creating the Customer and Invoice Models

The application also has a model for customers and a model for invoices. Listing 24-3 shows the code to create the Customer model.

Listing 24-3. *Customer Model (app/models/customer.rb)*

```
class Customer < ActiveRecord::Base
  has_many :invoices
  def past_due_invoices
    self.invoices.find(:all, :conditions=>['invoices.due_on < date("NOW")'])


  end
end
```

As you can see, the `Customer` model is fairly simple. It has a `has_many` relationship with invoices, and has a single method, `past_due_invoices`, which finds all of the invoices that are past due.

Next, let's take a look at our `Invoice` model, shown in Listing 24-4.

Listing 24-4. *Invoice Model (app/models/invoice.rb)*

```
class Invoice < ActiveRecord::Base
  belongs_to :customer
end
```

This model, with just a single `belongs_to` relationship, is self-explanatory.

Adding Some Data

Next, we'll need to create some sample data. We can use the Faker gem, which creates fake names and addresses, to create some fake names for our customers. You can install the Faker gem as follows:

```
gem install faker
```

You can find out more about faker at `http://faker.rubyforge.org/`.

Listing 24-5 shows our test data script. Save it as `script/create_test_data.rb`.

Listing 24-5. *Create Test Data Script (script/create_test_data.rb)*

```
require 'faker'
Customer.delete_all; Invoice.delete_all

100.times do
  c = Customer.create!(:name=>Faker::Name.name,
                       :street_address=>Faker::Address.street_address,
                       :city=>Faker::Address.city, :zip=>Faker::Address.zip_code,
                       :state=>Faker::Address.us_state,
                       :phone_number=>Faker::PhoneNumber.phone_number)
  rand(10).times do
    c.invoices.create!(:due_on=>(Date.today + (rand(200) - 170)),
                       :amount=>(rand(1000)+25))
  end
end
```

The test data script creates 100 sample customers, each with an invoice due between 170 days ago and 30 days from now. You can run it using the following command:

```
 ruby script/runner script/create_test_data.rb
```

Creating the Billing Controller

The application has only a billing controller. It's shown in Listing 24-6.

Listing 24-6. *Billing Controller (app/controllers/billing_controller.rb)*

```
class BillingController < ApplicationController
  def index
  end
  def envelopes
    @customers = get_delinquent_customers
  end
  def letters
    @customers = get_delinquent_customers
  end
protected
  def get_delinquent_customers
    Customer.find(:all,
                      :include=>[:invoices],
                      :conditions=>['invoices.due_on < date("NOW")'],
                      :group=>['invoices.customer_id ' <<
                                  ' HAVING count(invoices.id)>0']
                )
  end
end
```

The first action, index, just shows a few navigational links. The next two actions are identical except for which view gets displayed. The final method, get_delinquent_customers, is protected, which means it's for internal use by methods only and can't be viewed in a web browser. This method returns a list of customers who have outstanding invoices.

■**Note** If you so desired, you could easily put the get_delinquent_customers as a class method of the Customer model. Arguably, that could be considered to be more MVC, although you could also view get_delinquent_customers as simply DRYing up actions that, taken alone, would not normally be considered to violate MVC.

Using RTex Views

We have three views, two of which use RTex. First, let's take a look at our index view, which is simple, as you can see in Listing 24-7.

Listing 24-7. *Billing Index View (app/views/billing/index.html.erb)*

```
<h1>Billing</h1>

<p><%=link_to 'Envelopes', :action=>'envelopes', :format=>'pdf'%></p>
<p><%=link_to 'Letters', :action=>'letters', :format=>'pdf'%></p>
```

Note that we need to include the :format parameter. Even though pdf is the only available format, Rails won't look for it by default.

Listing 24-8 shows the first of our two RTex views, for envelopes.

Listing 24-8. *Envelopes RTex View (app/views/billing/envelopes.pdf.rtex)*

```
\documentclass{article}

\usepackage[margin=0.3in,papersize={3.25in,9.5in},landscape]{geometry}
        % Sets the margins and paper size to
        % fit an envelope:

\usepackage{times} % Use the font Times.

\pagestyle{empty}  % No headers or footers.

\begin{document}   % Start our document.
\large             % Set our font.

<%@customers.each do |c|%>
\parbox{4.0in}{ %  A parbox is a box of text, or, as the name implies,
%                  of paragraphs. This parbox will contain the return
%                  address.
\textbf{%          Put our address in boldface...
\raggedright{%     and align it to the left. The name might be a bit confusing;
%                  "ragged right" is typically called "left alignment" by word
%                  processors.
J.X. Heating and Cooling Company \\
89 Bog Rd \\
Arctainville, New Glockenshire
} } }
```

```
\vspace{0.5in}%        Put some extra vertical space between this box and the last,
\hspace{3.8in}%        and move this box over a few inches.
\parbox{4.0in}{
\raggedright{<%=l c.name%> \\
<%=l c.street_address%> \\
<%=l c.city%>, <%=l c.state%> <%=c.zip%>
} }

\newpage%              Start a new page for our next envelope.
<%end%>
\end{document}
```

Note that % is a comment symbol in LaTeX, and, for that matter, the TeX environment on which it's built, which is why all of the comments start with a %. The first few lines set up our environment, using the \usepackage command to set the geometry and the font. Note that the \usepackage command pulls in code, just like Ruby's require statement. However, unlike with Ruby's require statement, you can pass arguments to the packages, and our file uses that to set the exact dimensions of our envelopes.

Additionally, note that the l method is analogous to the h command in erb: it escapes a string so that it doesn't contain any LaTeX special characters.

Our code then loops through each delinquent customer and creates an envelope for that customer's notice. Note that we create a parbox for the return address and another one for the recipient's addresses. A parbox is used to group text into boxes, and we use it to conveniently place groups of text. The \vspace and \hspace commands create vertical and horizontal space, respectively, and we use both to position the recipient's address parbox.

Finally, let's take a look at the LaTeX template for our letters view, shown in Listing 24-9.

Listing 24-9. *Letters RTex View (app/views/letters.pdf.rtex)*

```
\documentclass[12pt]{letter}
\usepackage[margin=1.0in]{geometry}
\usepackage{times}
\pagestyle{empty}

\address{% This is a special command provided by the letter document class,
%          and will be used in all of the different letter environments in our
%          document. Since we have only one letter environment,
%          this will specify the return address for our single letter.
%          If we had more than one letter, the address would be shared among
%          them.
```

```
J.X. Heating and Cooling Company \\
89 Bog Rd\\
Bogville\\
Arctainville, New Glockenshire}
\signature{ R.F. Sutton, \\
J.X. Heating and Cooling Company } % Another special command; this is the name
%                                    of the sender of the document, and is
%                                    displayed right below the space where the
%                                    sender can sign.

\begin{document}
<%@customers.each do |c| #Loop through all of our customers... %>
\begin{letter}{%  Start a letter environment for each; note that the argument
<%=l c.name%>,\\% we pass to the \begin{letter} command is the address of
%                 the recipient.
<%=l c.street_address%>\\
<%=l c.city%>, <%=l c.state%> <%=l c.zip%>
}

\opening{ Dear <%=l c.name%>: }

I am writing to you on behalf of the J.X. Heating and Cooling Company,
the world's oldest and most powerful Heating and Cooling company
specializing in the heating and cooling of antique electronic mechanisms.

% Note that a blank line creates a new paragraph automatically.
%
Most of our clients have electronic mechanisms in need of heating and cooling
that are at least tens of years old, and many are several tens of years old.
Such devices in need of said cooling/heating/etcetera functionality include such
wonders of the ancient world as 8-track players, Betamax players, computers powered
by Microsoft operating systems, and HD-DVD players. As you can imagine, such items,
while antiquated and almost useless by the standards of today's more fast-paced
world, are difficult to come by and often irreplaceable, so even the slightest
mistake could diminish the world forever by destroying a priceless piece of history.
Please support our efforts by promptly paying your bills.
```

```
The following invoices are past due:

\begin{itemize}  % The itemize environment is similar to the <li>,
%                    or unordered list, tag in HTML.
<%c.past_due_invoices.each do |i|%>
\item Invoice <%=i.id%>, in the amount of <%=i.amount%>,
      which should have been dutifully paid on the day of <%=i.due_on%>
% The \item command corresponds to the <li> element in HTML.
<%end%>
\end{itemize}

Please pay immediately.

\closing { I hope you pay soon,} % This is automatically followed by a space,
%                                   typically used to sign the letter,
%                                   then the name from the \signature command above.
\end{letter}

<%end%>
\end{document}
```

The document in Listing 24-9 has a few notable features. First, the \documentclass statement tells LaTeX that we wish to use the letter document class. This class gives us a number of special commands, such as \opening, \signature, and so forth, which are designed for writing letters. Next, we use several \usepackage statements to import LaTeX packages; \usepackage is analogous to Ruby's require statement.

The \begin{document} command starts our document. You can think of it as an HTML <body> tag. Our document is later ended by a \end{document} tag, which is similar to a </body> tag.

The code in Listing 24-9 uses a few other features of the LaTeX letter class, such as the \opening command, used to specify an opening for a letter, and the \address command, which specifies a return address for the letter. Each command is briefly commented in the code listing. You can find the full gory details about the LaTeX letters class at http://en.wikibooks.org/wiki/LaTeX/Letters.

Finally, let's take a look at our routing file, shown in Listing 24-10.

Listing 24-10. *Routes File (config/routes.rb)*

```
ActionController::Routing::Routes.draw do |map|
  map.root :controller => 'billing'

  map.connect ':controller/:action.:format'
  map.connect ':controller/:action/:id'
  map.connect ':controller/:action/:id.:format'
end
```

Note that we added a default route that allows for actions without an ID to be given a format. Delete public/index.html.

Testing the Billing Application

At this point, your application should be ready to go. Launch the application using `ruby script/server`, then point your web browser to `localhost:3000`. You should see a page similar to Figure 24-1. Click the Envelopes link to see the Envelopes page, shown in Figure 24-2. Click the Letters link to see our letter, as shown in Figure 24-3.

Figure 24-1. *Index page*

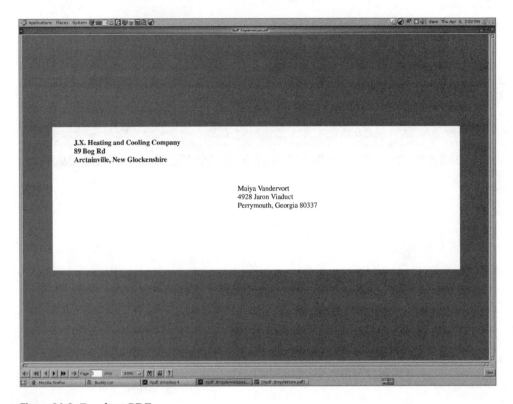

Figure 24-2. *Envelope PDF*

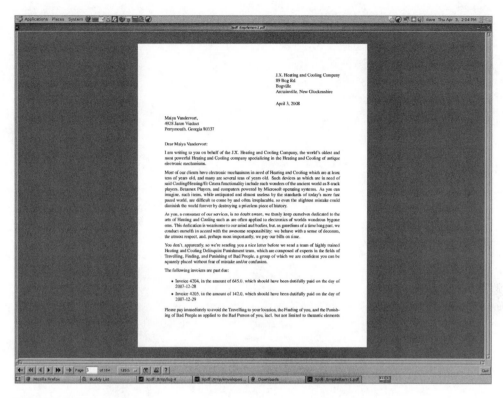

Figure 24-3. *Letter PDF*

Summary

Although the initial learning curve can be steep, the rewards of LaTeX are great. LaTeX is a relatively high-performance, powerful way to create even complicated PDF documents. RTex makes using LaTeX from Rails applications easy and powerful, using ERb style embedding of Ruby code.

PART 8

■■■

Testing with Plugins

Automated testing is one of the cornerstones of agile software development, and Rails' support for testing is often given as one of its greatest strengths. Testing has a number of benefits: it can prevent old bugs from reentering your codebase, detect new bugs, and give you more confidence in your code. In fact, testing can even speed up your initial development of a project by allowing you to solve problems quicker, since debugging code is a large part of even initial software development.

A number of plugins can make your tests easier to write, easier to read, and more efficient. In this part, we will cover a few of these plugins: Rcov for checking the code coverage of your tests, RSpec for behavior-driven development, and Assert Valid Asset for validation testing.

CHAPTER 25

■■■

Testing Code Coverage with Rcov

Agile testing is an important part of Rails development. It can help you keep your code free of bugs, speed up your development, serve as a form of documentation, and provide other benefits. However, all its advantages come with one overriding prerequisite: your tests must cover your code adequately. Untested code gains none of the advantages of testing. In fact, code that is not fully covered by your test may be even worse than equivalent code in a completely untested project. If you labor under the false assumption that your code is tested, you might neglect to test it even manually before deployment.

Rcov, created by Mauricio Julio Fernandez Pradier, is a tool for Ruby that can help check the code coverage of your tests. Specifically, it can detect *line code coverage*, which means that it can produce a list of which lines in your program have been run and how many times. Of course, this is not a guarantee of coverage. If a given line contains an execution branch, for example, only one of those branches may be tested, but Rcov will report the entire line as having been tested. Additionally, Rcov does not ensure that your program has been run across its entire range of input data, and even though a line of code may be tested, it may behave very differently with different input data.

Like all testing, using Rcov is no substitute for an effective knowledge of your codebase and problem domain. Nonetheless, Rcov is very valuable as a general gauge of testing completeness, and you can easily and effectively use it to judge which areas of your codebase need more testing.

In this chapter, we'll examine how to use the Rcov plugin to test the coverage of code in a simple Rails application.

Our Task: Check Code Coverage in a Rails Application

For this chapter's example, suppose we have a site where users can enter a long, tedious URL and receive a permanent short link to that URL, like TinyURL.com or RubyURL.com. We want to use Rcov to ensure that we're testing our single model thoroughly.

However, before we examine the Rcov plugin in the context of testing a Rails application, let's see how Rcov works in a simpler example.

Using Rcov to Test Coverage of a Ruby Script

To demonstrate the results you can expect from Rcov, we'll walk through using it on a Ruby script. First, install the Rcov gem, as follows:

```
gem install rcov
```

Next, save the short test script shown in Listing 25-1 as rcov_test_1.rb.

Listing 25-1. *Rcov Test Script 1 (rcov_test_1.rb)*

```
 puts 'starting'
def do_something(something)
  if something == 'branch'
    puts 'true'
  else
    puts 'false'
  end
end
do_something 'branch'

puts 'all done'
```

Now let's run Rcov on this script:

```
 rcov -T rcov_test_1.rb
```

```
starting
true
all done
+----------------------------------------------------+-------+-------+--------+
|                        File                        | Lines |  LOC  |  COV   |
+----------------------------------------------------+-------+-------+--------+
|rcov_test_1.rb                                      |   11  |    10 |  70.0% |
+----------------------------------------------------+-------+-------+--------+
|Total                                               |   11  |    10 |  70.0% |
+----------------------------------------------------+-------+-------+--------+
70.0%   1 file(s)   11 Lines   10 LOC
```

The -T flag runs a text summary, as you see here. It shows statistics on each of the files analyzed.

Rcov offers a number of other modes. For example, the following shows which lines are executed:

```
rcov --text-coverage rcov_test_1.rb
```

```
starting
true
all done
================================================================================
rcov_test_1.rb
================================================================================
puts 'starting'
def do_something(something)
  if something == 'branch'
    puts 'true'
  else
    puts 'false'
  end
end
do_something 'branch'

puts 'all done'
```

In your display, the bolded lines will show up in red. This indicates that the given lines were not executed.

Rcov also has an HTML output mode, which is the default. Let's take a look at that next:

```
rcov rcov_test_1.rb
```

```
starting
true
all done
```

If you open the file coverage/index.html in a web browser, you should see a screen similar to Figure 25-1. This shows a brief summary of each file tested (only one in this example). Click the link rcov_test_1.rb, and you will see a screen similar to Figure 25-2. Like the --text-coverage option output, it highlights several lines in red, indicating that they were not successfully run.

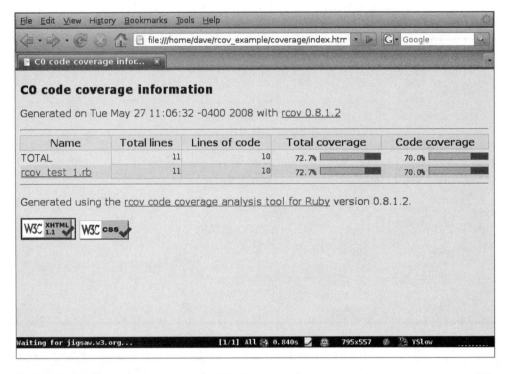

Figure 25-1. *Code coverage summary in HTML*

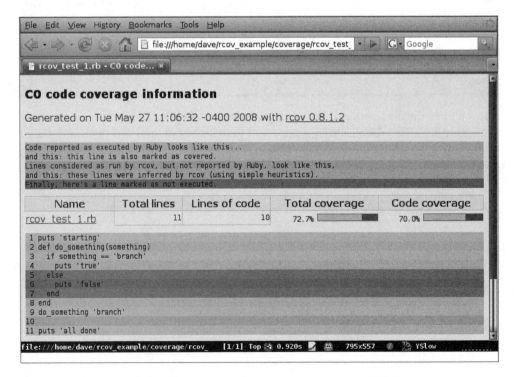

Figure 25-2. *Color-coded, line-by-line breakdown of code coverage in HTML*

Let's adjust the file to run all of our code. Save the code shown in Listing 25-2 as
rcov_test_2.rb.

Listing 25-2. *Rcov Test Script 2 (rcov_test_2.rb)*

```
puts 'starting'
def do_something(something)
  if something == 'branch'
    puts 'true'
  else
    puts 'false'
  end
end
do_something 'branch'
do_something 'do_not_branch'

puts 'all done'
```

Now, let's rerun the Rcov testing, as follows:

```
rcov rcov_test_2.rb
```

```
starting
true
all done
```

If you open the file coverage/index.html in a web browser again, you will see a screen
similar to Figure 25-3. The code coverage page for rcov_test_2.rb looks like Figure 25-4. Just
as before, it lists our source file, but this time, we have 100% coverage, since all of the lines of
code in our program are executed.

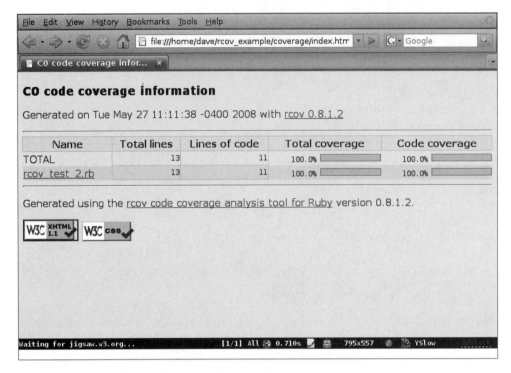

Figure 25-3. *Summary of code coverage for second test in HTML*

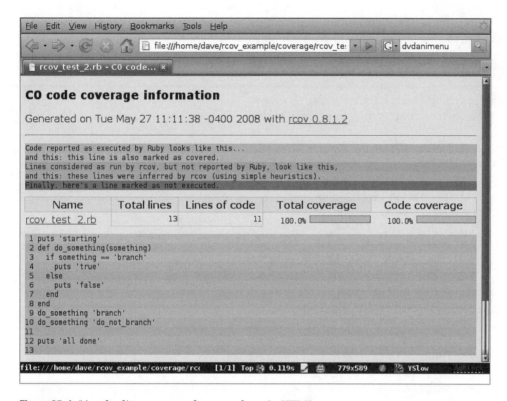

Figure 25-4. *Line-by-line coverage for second test in HTML*

Now that you've seen Rcov in action, let's try it out on a simple Rails application.

Using Rcov in a Rails Application

As described earlier in the chapter, we're going to use Rcov on an application that generates short links for URLs.

First, let's generate the Rails application:

```
rails rcov_url_shorten_example
```

Next, install the Rcov plugin:

```
cd rcov_url_shorten_example
ruby script/plugin install http://svn.codahale.com/rails_rcov
```

```
+ ./MIT-LICENSE
+ ./README
+ ./tasks/rails_rcov.rake
```

As you can see from the output, the only thing the Rcov plugin provides for us is Rake tasks. You can find out exactly which tasks it provides as follows:

```
rake -D rcov
```

```
rake test:functionals:clobber_rcov
    Remove Rcov reports for functional tests

rake test:functionals:rcov
    Run all functional tests with Rcov to measure coverage

rake test:integration:clobber_rcov
    Remove Rcov reports for integration tests

rake test:integration:rcov
    Run all integration tests with Rcov to measure coverage

rake test:plugins:clobber_rcov
    Remove Rcov reports for plugin tests

rake test:plugins:rcov
    Run all plugin tests with Rcov to measure coverage

rake test:recent:clobber_rcov
    Remove Rcov reports for recent tests

rake test:recent:rcov
    Run all recent tests with Rcov to measure coverage

rake test:test:clobber_rcov
    Remove Rcov reports for test tests

rake test:test:rcov
    Run all test tests with Rcov to measure coverage

rake test:uncommitted:clobber_rcov
    Remove Rcov reports for uncommitted tests

rake test:uncommitted:rcov
    Run all uncommitted tests with Rcov to measure coverage

rake test:units:clobber_rcov
    Remove Rcov reports for unit tests

rake test:units:rcov
    Run all unit tests with Rcov to measure coverage
```

This output reveals that the Rcov plugin includes quite a few Rake tasks. Notably, it has tasks to create functional, integration, unit, and plugin test reports, along with a few others. We're going to be focusing on unit tests, but the other types of tests are very similar.

■**Note** If you're not familiar with Rails testing terminology, note that according to standard industry usage, what Rails calls *unit tests* and *functional tests* are both, strictly speaking, unit tests. The former are unit tests of a model, and the latter are unit tests of a controller. To fit in with the official documentation, we use the Rails terminology throughout this book, but you should note the difference between normal software testing terminology and Rails terminology.

Next, let's generate our model:

```
ruby script/generate model url url:string shortcode:string
```

Rails automatically creates the migration for us based on the string url:string shortcode:string. This table has just two fields other than those for the timestamps and IDs. One holds the URL, and the second holds the short code, which is the identifier that will be used to uniquely identify the URL.

Run the migration as follows:

```
rake db:migrate
```

Enter the code shown in Listing 25-3 to create our model (app/models/url.rb).

Listing 25-3. *URL Model (app/models/url.rb)*

```
class Url < ActiveRecord::Base
  validates_presence_of :url
  validates_uniqueness_of :shortcode

  after_validation :ensure_shortcode_exists

  def ensure_shortcode_exists
    if self.shortcode.nil?
      until !self.shortcode.nil?  && Url.find_by_shortcode(self.shortcode).nil?
        self.shortcode = Digest::MD5.hexdigest("#{self.url}_" <<
                                     "#{Time.now.to_f.to_s#{rand(1024)}}"
                                   ).to_i(16).to_s(32)
      end
    end
  end
end
```

This model is fairly straightforward. It has two tests and an after_validation callback. This callback is called after the model is validated but before it has been saved. The callback checks if the short code is nil; if it is, it generates a new short code. The short codes are generated by taking the hexadecimal MD5 digest of the URL, followed by the time in milliseconds, followed by a random number. Presumably, that's going to be reasonably random. We then convert the hexadecimal digest into an integer by calling to_i(16)—16 for base 16, or hexadecimal—and then calling to_s(32), which is a fairly uncommon base, but used here because it's shorter.

Now, let's write a simple test. Save the code shown in Listing 25-4 as test/unit/url_test.rb.

Listing 25-4. *URL Test (test/unit/url_test.rb)*

```
require File.dirname(__FILE__) + '/../test_helper'

class UrlTest < ActiveSupport::TestCase
  def test_url_is_required
    test_url = Url.new(:url=>nil, :shortcode=>'very_short_code')
    assert !test_url.valid?
    assert test_url.errors.invalid?(:url)
  end
end
```

As you can see, this does not test the ability of our model to automatically create short codes. Let's run Rcov and see if it detects our omission:

```
rake test:units:rcov
```

```
Loaded suite /usr/bin/rcov
Started

.
Finished in 0.060374 seconds.

1 tests, 2 assertions, 0 failures, 0 errors
```

File	Lines	LOC	COV
app/controllers/application.rb	10	4	100.0%
app/helpers/application_helper.rb	3	2	100.0%
app/models/url.rb	15	12	66.7%
Total	28	18	77.8%

```
77.8%   3 file(s)   28 Lines   18 LOC
View the full results at <file:///path/to/rcov_example/coverage/units/index.html>
```

It looks like Rcov noticed the missing test. Let's amend our unit test to test the missing short codes. Save the code shown in Listing 25-5 as test/unit/url_test.rb.

■**Note** The Rails task includes both a textual summary and a full HTML report. You can see the HTML report at the address included in the output.

Listing 25-5. *URL Test, Second Draft (test/unit/url_test.rb)*

```
require File.dirname(__FILE__) + '/../test_helper'

class UrlTest < ActiveSupport::TestCase
  def test_url_is_required
    test_url = Url.new(:url=>nil, :shortcode=>'very_short_code')
    assert !test_url.valid?
    assert test_url.errors.invalid?(:url)
  end

  def test_shortcode_is_automatically_generated
    test_url = Url.new(:url=>'http://apress.com')
    test_url.save
    assert test_url.valid?
    assert_not_nil test_url.shortcode
  end
end
```

Let's see if Rcov detects the change:

```
rake test:units:rcov
```

```
(in /path/to/rcov_example)
/usr/bin/ruby1.8 "/path/to/rcov_example/vendor/plugins/rails_rcov/tasks/ ➥
rails_rcov.rake" --run-rake-task=test:units
(in /path/to/rcov_example)
rcov -o "/path/to/rcov_example/coverage/units" -T -x "rubygems/*,rcov*" --rails ➥
-Ilib:test "/usr/lib/ruby/gems/1.8/gems/rake-0.8.1/lib/rake/rake_test_loader.rb" ➥
 "test/unit/url_test.rb"
Loaded suite /usr/bin/rcov
Started
..
Finished in 0.053616 seconds.
```

```
2 tests, 4 assertions, 0 failures, 0 errors
+--------------------------------------------------+-------+-------+--------+
|                      File                        | Lines |  LOC  |  COV   |
+--------------------------------------------------+-------+-------+--------+
|app/controllers/application.rb                    |   10  |    4  | 100.0% |
|app/helpers/application_helper.rb                 |    3  |    2  | 100.0% |
|app/models/url.rb                                 |   15  |   12  | 100.0% |
+--------------------------------------------------+-------+-------+--------+
|Total                                             |   28  |   18  | 100.0% |
+--------------------------------------------------+-------+-------+--------+
100.0%   3 file(s)    28 Lines    18 LOC
View the full results at <file:///path/to/rcov_example/coverage/units/index.html>
```

As you can see, Rcov now displays a 100% coverage figure—it works. Of course, in a full application, you would have more tests, but you can use the same techniques to work with any number of files.

GENERATING SHORT URLS

Since this chapter is about testing, not URL-shortening, we've covered only part of the code required. If you want to extend this application to be a full short URL-generating application, you could use a controller like this:

```
class UrlController < ApplicationController
  def go
    url = Url.find_by_shortcode(params[:id])
    redirect_to url.url
  end
end
```

However, if you're only interested in generating short URLs, and don't care if you control the domain they come from, you may want to consider using the Acts As Tiny URL plugin, which lets you add TinyURL.com links to your models. For more information, see http://code.google.com/p/acts=as-tiny-url/.

Summary

Testing is a very important part of Rails, and Rcov lets you quickly get an indication of the quality of your testing. Like testing as a whole, Rcov is not a perfect indicator, but it's an extremely important tool, and, fortunately, it's easy to use.

CHAPTER 26

■■■

Behavior-Driven Development with RSpec

Rails comes with baked-in support for the popular Test::Unit testing framework, and that's A Good Thing. Having testing present as a core part of the framework makes test-driven development (TDD) easier than ever before.

Rails has clearly embraced TDD as a best practice, and for good reasons. Developing your application test first has a number of advantages. Above and beyond just helping you catch bugs, effective use of TDD practices lets you improve your designs and write cleaner, more concise code.

Behavior-driven development (BDD) represents a further evolution of the TDD model. Rather than thinking about how you can test your application before building it, with BDD, you focus on how you can specify behavior that an application should possess. This process of writing "specs" tends to be much more natural than writing tests for code that doesn't yet exist. It also serves as a form of documentation, since your specs describe exactly how your model should work.

On the surface, differences between TDD and BDD seem largely syntactical, related to how the problem is approached and framed. BDD relies heavily on a common English language approach to constructing specifications. For instance, a controller spec might specify that the index action *should* render the index.html.erb template, or that the result of submitting some data to a create action *should* result in a redirect back to the index action. Since its focus is on defining behavior rather than testing, the use of mocks and stubs to isolate the testing of component parts is also a central tenet of BDD. These differences may seem minor at first, but anything that makes tests easier to write as precursors to actual code also helps make that code more understandable.

For these reasons and many more, BDD has become a popular topic in the world of Ruby, and a number of BDD-related libraries also integrate nicely into Rails. Of all these, RSpec (a large project with a substantial core team and many contributors; see http://rspec.info/ community) is probably the most popular, and it is the one that we'll be examining in this chapter. We'll demonstrate how to use RSpec, as well as how to apply the BDD philosophy to creating a simple application, spending time on both model and controller specs along the way.

Our Task: Write Some Useful Specs

We've been ignoring tests throughout the majority of this book, in order to maximize the time we spend talking about plugins. However, in our own real-world projects, we never, ever ignore testing.

In this chapter, we'll walk you through the typical process that you might take with RSpec as we develop a simple application. The usual approach goes something like this:

- Stub out the list of behaviors that describes some part of the system we're building.

- Write the tests (specifications) for those behaviors.

- Run the specs we've written. They will fail because we haven't implemented code to satisfy them yet (red light!).

- Implement the model, view, or controller code to make the specs pass.

- Rerun the specs and verify that they work as expected (green light!).

- Repeat until finished.

Tip To automate this process, we use Autotest, part of the ZenTest package. Install the package as a gem (gem install ZenTest) and then, in your project directory, type autotest to start it. Autotest runs continuously, monitoring your files for changes. Whenever you modify a file, it will run the corresponding tests (or, in this case, specs) within moments. If the test fails, you can see results immediately, without needing to manually rerun the Rake tasks.

To keep our discussion centered around BDD itself, our example will be a brief one. We'll create an online petition to save our favorite canceled television show, *The Adventures of Young Banzai Cooper* (affectionately referred to as TAYBC by the superfans). Visitors will be able to come to the site and add their names to the petition.

This project will involve the creation of two models: a petition model and a signature model. It will have a single controller that interfaces with the models and exposes just two actions: the ability to view the list of all signatures for the petition and the ability to sign the petition.

Often, when we're working on a larger project, we start with a series of wireframes and work backward from the views to create controller and model specifications. However, this example is very simple, so we'll start by specifying the behavior of our models, which will lead us to implementing the code for those models, and then we'll do the same with the required controller.

Bootstrapping an RSpec Project

Let's create a new Rails application for the television show petition project:

```
rails tvpetition
cd tvpetition
```

Next, install the RSpec and RSpec on Rails plugins by executing the following commands inside the new application root directory:

```
ruby script/plugin install ➥
svn://rubyforge.org/var/svn/rspec/tags/CURRENT/rspec
ruby script/plugin install ➥
svn://rubyforge.org/var/svn/rspec/tags/CURRENT/rspec_on_rails
```

Note that RSpec is also available as a gem for use in non-Rails projects. However, when using RSpec in a Rails project, it is suggested that you install the plugin version. You can learn more about RSpec and alternative installation methods at http://rspec.info.

When you install the RSpec plugin, a number of new Rake tasks are made available, such as rake spec, which you can use as a replacement for rake test to run the specs you've created. A number of new generators are installed as well. We'll use the new generators to create models and controllers for this project. But first, we need to use the generator to RSpec-enable our application:

```
ruby script/generate rspec
```

```
create  spec
create  spec/spec_helper.rb
create  spec/spec.opts
create  spec/rcov.opts
create  script/spec_server
create  script/spec
create  stories
create  stories/all.rb
create  stories/helper.rb
```

This bootstrapping task prepares our application to work with RSpec by creating a number of files and directories in our project directory. Two new top-level directories are created:

- spec, which will contain model specs, controller specs, fixtures, and so on

- stories, which houses RSpec stories for the optional Story Runner facility

---

■**Tip** Since version 1.1, RSpec has also provided the RSpec Story Runner for developing integration tests in a very natural way. For more information, check out the resources at http://rspec.info/documentation/stories.html.

Petition Model Specs

If you're a fan of Rails' generators, you'll be happy to learn that RSpec provides replacement generators that produce specs in place of tests. We'll use the rspec_model generator provided by the plugin to create two models, including the appropriate specs and migrations. The first of these models will represent our petition, and the second will represent a signature contributed to the petition.

```
ruby script/generate rspec_model Petition name:string description:text
```

```
exists   app/models/
create   spec/models/
create   spec/fixtures/
create   app/models/petition.rb
create   spec/fixtures/petitions.yml
create   spec/models/petition_spec.rb
create   db/migrate
create   db/migrate/001_create_petitions.rb
```

```
ruby script/generate rspec_model Signature name:string email:string ➥
comment:string petition_id:integer
```

```
exists   app/models/
exists   spec/models/
exists   spec/fixtures/
create   app/models/signature.rb
create   spec/fixtures/signatures.yml
create   spec/models/signature_spec.rb
exists   db/migrate
create   db/migrate/002_create_signatures.rb
```

If you examine the database migrations created by this process, you'll find that they include all the fields you specified on the command line, as well as created_at and updated_at timestamps, as you would expect. Migrate the database using the rake db:migrate task:

```
rake db:migrate
```

```
== 1 CreatePetitions: migrating ================================================
-- create_table(:petitions)
   -> 0.0034s
== 1 CreatePetitions: migrated (0.0036s) =======================================

== 2 CreateSignatures: migrating ===============================================
-- create_table(:signatures)
   -> 0.0036s
== 2 CreateSignatures: migrated (0.0040s) ======================================
```

Now, let's take a look at the specs that the generator created for us. Specs live in the spec directory, in which you'll find models and fixtures subdirectories. Later, when we get to specifying and implementing a controller, subdirectories for our controllers and views will be added to the spec directory as well. Note that spec files for our models are named after the model, with _spec appended to the end of the file name by convention.

Understanding Basic Model Specs

Open the file spec/models/petition_spec.rb. It contains a very simple boilerplate spec for the petition model, as shown in Listing 26-1.

Listing 26-1. *Boilerplate Petition Model Spec (spec/models/petition_spec.rb)*

```
require File.dirname(__FILE__) + '/../spec_helper'

describe Petition do
  before(:each) do
    @petition = Petition.new
  end

  it "should be valid" do
    @petition.should be_valid
  end
end
```

The syntax in use here is clearly quite different from that of Test::Unit. This *spec* is used to *describe* the behavior of a class using a number of *examples*. The boilerplate spec specifies only a single example, which states that a newly created model should be valid. As you can see, individual examples such as this make use of the it "*string*" { *block* } syntax within a describe *Class* block, which results in very natural-sounding statements, such as "A petition should be valid" (which will be true, at least for now, since we used the generator to produce the model code and its migration).

The before(:each) block in this listing runs before each example in the spec. In this case, it is used to set up a @petition instance variable that we can use in subsequent examples. RSpec also defines other hooks like this, such as before(:all), after(:all), and after(:each). For more information about these and to view the full RSpec documentation, refer to http://rspec.info/documentation.

Inside the "should be valid" example, you see our first use of an RSpec *expectation*: @petition.should be_valid. This is nice, natural-looking syntax for making an assertion that reads like an English sentence. In fact, it's so natural that we immediately know, just by reading it, what its purpose is: it asserts that the @petition variable we've set up is valid. What this really means is that @petition.valid? should return true, but nowhere here have we called valid? directly.

So how exactly does this work then? Some people say it's magic, but really, it makes a lot of sense once you see what it's doing. RSpec takes advantage of the metaprogramming capabilities of Ruby to define the methods should and should_not on every object for testing purposes (that is, only in the test environment, of course). should and should_not each accepts either an expression using a subset of Ruby operators (for example, `@petition.name.should == 'foo'`) or an RSpec expectation matcher.

RSpec defines a number of expectation matchers out of the box, such as `be`, `be_close`, `change`, `have`, `have_at_most`, `include`, `match`, and many others. These matchers can be used to create powerful but easy-to-read assertions in a behavioral style, like this:

```
@proposal.should have(1).error_on(:name)
lambda { @proposal.create }.should change(Proposal, :count)
```

RSpec also creates custom matchers on the fly using any arbitrary Ruby predicate. This means that any method on an object that ends with a question mark (?) and returns true or false can be used in this manner. This is exactly how the `should_be valid` syntax works. The combination of the `should` method with the `be_valid` matcher translates to a call to the `valid?` method on the `@petition` object, and that response is tested to determine whether the result is true:

```
@petition.should be_valid # => @petition.valid?
@petition.should_not be_important # => @petition.important?
```

■**Tip** For a full list of matchers, see `http://rspec.info/rdoc/classes/Spec/Matchers.html`. You can also add your own custom matchers as needed if none of the stock matchers feel natural enough for your particular situation.

Although the differences from the unit testing syntax you're used to seeing can make using RSpec awkward at first, this is quickly overcome with practice. We believe that it results in more natural-sounding assertions and easier to fathom requirements when writing code. And we all aspire to writing the cleanest code possible, right?

The boilerplate spec for the `Signature` class will look similar. If we go ahead and run these specs as is, they should pass, as we haven't added any custom validation logic or other code that would cause a newly instantiated `Petition` or `Signature` object to fail validation. Try this now by using the `rake spec` task:

```
rake spec
```

```
..


Finished in 0.118926 seconds

2 examples, 0 failures
```

■**Tip** You can also specify that you want to run only model specs by using `rake spec:models`, or run only controller specs by running `rake spec:controllers`.

Our specs are passing. Congratulations! Of course, we haven't specified any actual functionality yet, other than noting that a newly created Active Record model should be valid when it's instantiated. Let's remedy that now.

Specifying Our Model Behaviors

Now we'll start adding specs that describe the behavior of our `Petition` class. First, let's consider what we know about the nature of a petition:

- It should require a name.

- It should require a description.

- It should require a name that is unique among the set of all petition names.

- It should be associated with any number of signatures.

Eventually, our model will need to be able to do more than this. But let's start here. The key to proper BDD is breaking down development into small, workable (testable) pieces and implementing it a step at a time.

We can implement our petition requirements as examples in our specification by transcribing them quite literally. To do so, modify your spec/models/petition_spec.rb file so it resembles the code shown in Listing 26-2.

Listing 26-2. *Petition Spec with Pending Examples (spec/models/petition_spec.rb)*

```
require File.dirname(__FILE__) + '/../spec_helper'

describe Petition do
  before(:each) do
    @petition = Petition.new
  end

  it "should be valid" do
    @petition.should be_valid
  end

  it "should require a name"
  it "should require a description"
  it "should require a unique name"
  it "should have many signatures"
end
```

Even though we haven't implemented our examples yet, just stubbing them out can be useful. If we run this spec as is, the Rake task will inform us that all specs are still passing but that we have four *pending* specs that have yet to be implemented:

```
rake spec
```

```
PPPP..

Pending:
Petition should have many signatures (Not Yet Implemented)
Petition should require a unique name (Not Yet Implemented)
Petition should require a description (Not Yet Implemented)
Petition should require a name (Not Yet Implemented)

Finished in 0.2387 seconds

6 examples, 0 failures, 4 pending
```

Marking specs as pending can be a useful way to keep track of your running TODO list of features, even when you haven't yet figured out the specifics of how those behaviors will work.

So, our next step is to fill in the spec examples we've defined. In order to DRY up the spec, we'll also implement a short spec helper module that can be used to selectively choose valid attributes to test. Listing 26-3 shows the updated spec/models/petition_spec.rb file.

Listing 26-3. *Updated Petition Spec (spec/models/petition_spec.rb)*

```ruby
require File.dirname(__FILE__) + '/../spec_helper'

module PetitionSpecHelper
  def valid_petition_attributes
    { :name => "Petition to Save TAYBC",
      :description => "Please don't cancel our favorite show!" }
  end
end

describe Petition do
  include PetitionSpecHelper

  before(:each) do
    @petition = Petition.new
  end

  it "should be valid" do
    @petition.attributes = valid_petition_attributes
    @petition.should be_valid
  end
```

```ruby
  it "should require a name" do
    @petition.attributes = valid_petition_attributes.except(:name)
    @petition.should_not be_valid
    @petition.should have(1).error_on(:name)
    @petition.errors.on(:name).should == "can't be blank"
  end

  it "should require a description" do
    @petition.attributes = valid_petition_attributes.except(:description)
    @petition.should_not be_valid
    @petition.should have(1).error_on(:description)
    @petition.errors.on(:description).should == "can't be blank"
  end

  it "should require a unique name" do
    @petition.attributes = valid_petition_attributes
    @petition.save!

    @petition = Petition.new(valid_petition_attributes)
    @petition.should_not be_valid
    @petition.should have(1).error_on(:name)
    @petition.errors.on(:name).should == "has already been taken"
  end

  it "should have many signatures" do
    Petition.reflect_on_association(:signatures).should_not be_nil
  end
end
```

Here, we're using the valid_petition_attributes method provided by the helper to return a hash of valid attributes. The except method (added to the Hash class by the Rails Active Support library) is used to selectivity exclude an attribute in certain examples in order to test that the attribute is required.

Let's examine a couple of these spec examples. First, we've modified the "should be valid" example, using our helper to assign a batch of attributes before checking to see if the model is valid. Our assumption is that it is valid if all these attributes are supplied.

In the "should require a name" example, we need to illustrate the behavior of the Petition model when it is lacking a name, and demonstrate that such a petition should be invalid. So we set the attributes of the @petition instance variable to the hash of valid attributes, excluding only the name. Then we assert that it should_not be_valid, which means that the valid? instance method is called on @petition (and that we expect it to return false). Since we know that running validation should populate the Active Record errors object too, we can assert that it should have exactly one error on the description attribute, and that the error should be "can't be blank".

Many of the other examples in our spec mirror this approach, as we're just testing simple model validation logic at this juncture. But the "should have many signatures" example is a bit different, and we've added it in here just to show the different types of specs that can be used.

The purpose of the "should have many signatures" example is to illustrate that a petition should always have some number of signatures (0 through *n*) associated with it. To specify this behavior, we can call the reflect_on_association method on the Petition class itself (rather than the instance variable) and assert that the signatures association should not be nil. This will mandate that an association with the Signature model must be present, and perhaps prevent us from accidentally removing that association at some later point.

Tip We haven't used any fixtures In our example, but should you need them, they're available in spec/fixtures in the familiar YAML format. They can be loaded in your specs by adding a fixtures :*your_model_names* declaration at the top of the spec, just as you would do in a unit test in Test::Unit.

Passing Model Specs

If you're the motivated type, you've no doubt already leapt ahead and ran the rake spec task again. Your output probably looks something like this now:

```
rake spec
```

```
FFFF..

1)
'Petition should have many signatures' FAILED
expected not nil, got nil
./spec/models/petition_spec.rb:46:

2)
'Petition should require a unique name' FAILED
expected valid? to return false, got true
./spec/models/petition_spec.rb:40:

3)
'Petition should require a description' FAILED
expected valid? to return false, got true
./spec/models/petition_spec.rb:31:

4)
'Petition should require a name' FAILED
expected valid? to return false, got true
./spec/models/petition_spec.rb:24:

Finished in 0.134804 seconds

6 examples, 4 failures
```

This is (in most cases) where the real work starts. We must implement the features in our codebase to get the specification code we wrote to pass. In our case, it's actually quite simple to do, as we're just specifying that the `Petition` model is associated with some number of signatures and that certain Active Record validations should be present. We'll modify the model in app/models/petition.rb to resemble the code in Listing 26-4.

Listing 26-4. *Updated Petition Model (app/models/petition.rb)*

```
class Petition < ActiveRecord::Base
  has_many :signatures

  validates_presence_of :name, :description
  validates_uniqueness_of :name
end
```

Now rerun the `rake spec` task:

```
rake spec
```

```
......

Finished in 0.183428 seconds

6 examples, 0 failures
```

Our specs should now pass with flying (green!) colors. Wash, rinse, and repeat for any other features that you want to add to the model, or any other models. In fact, we'll leave creating a spec for the `Signature` model as an exercise to the reader. (The full source code is available from the Source Code/Downloads section of http://www.apress.com.)

RSPEC OUTPUT FORMATS

RSpec defaults to showing a textual progress report as specs are run, but it supports a variety of output formats. You can use the `--format` option to the `spec` command to specify an alternative or additional (formats can be combined) output format.

Within your Rails application, you can specify the format, as well as other spec processing options, in the `spec/spec.opts` file:

```
--colour
--format
specdoc
--loadby
mtime
--reverse
```

This version of `spec.opts` changes the default output format from the standard progress report (`progress`) to the spec doc (`specdoc`) format. A spec doc outputs the behavior specifications in a human-readable text format. Here is an example of the spec doc output for a version of the project that has specs written for both the `Petition` and the `Signature` model:

```
Petition
- should have many signatures
- should require a unique name
- should require a description
- should require a name
- should be valid

Signature
- should belong to a petition
- should require a unique email to this petition
- should require a petition id
- should require an email
- should require a name
- should be valid
```

Alternatively, you can specify the `html` format to generate a color-coded HTML summary. Replace the line that reads `specdoc` in the `spec.opts` file with `html:doc/spec.html` to generate an HTML report in the doc directory when the `rake spec` task is run. The following is an example of an HTML report for a full suite of specs (with 22 examples total; 2 failing, 1 pending).

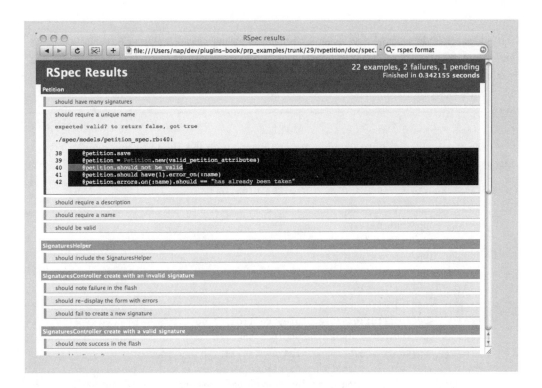

Signatures Controller Spec

Now that we've reviewed the basics of RSpec syntax and have implemented specs and working models, let's turn our attention to controller specs. Much like functional tests with `Test::Unit`, controller specs exist to specify the behavior and test the functionality of the code that interfaces user actions with your system's models, meaning your controllers.

By default, and unlike their functional test corollaries in `Test::Unit`, controller specs do not actually render views. RSpec emphasizes testing each component of the MVC triad (models, views, and controllers) in isolation from one another, and this means separating functional tests into controller specs and view specs, rather than grouping the two together as `Test::Unit` does. The behavior that we want to specify in our controller specs is just what's happening in the controller: what methods are called, what variables are assigned, and what templates will be rendered. (It's important to test that a controller method renders the correct template, but at this point, we shouldn't worry about the contents of that template.)

Whatever behavior belongs in the view is specified elsewhere, in view specs. This approach keeps each component nicely isolated, and prevents our controller specs from failing when the errors are actually in the view templates. We'll talk more about view specs in the next section.

Tip If you prefer to integrate view testing with controller testing, as with traditional Rails functional tests, the integrate_views directive can be used in a controller spec to override the default behavior. For more information, see http://rspec.info/rdoc-rails/classes/Spec/Rails/Example/ControllerExampleGroup.html.

Let's use the RSpec controller generator packaged with the plugin to create our SignaturesController. Run the following command:

```
ruby script/generate rspec_controller Signatures index
```

```
exists  app/controllers/
exists  app/helpers/
create  app/views/signatures
create  spec/controllers/
create  spec/helpers/
create  spec/views/signatures
create  spec/controllers/signatures_controller_spec.rb
create  spec/helpers/signatures_helper_spec.rb
create  app/controllers/signatures_controller.rb
create  app/helpers/signatures_helper.rb
create  spec/views/signatures/index.html.erb_spec.rb
create  app/views/signatures/index.html.erb
```

This time, the generator creates a controller and its corresponding spec, as well as a helper and its spec. (We won't discuss creating specs for helpers here, but RSpec most certainly provides facilities for this.) It also creates a view spec for the index action view, which we'll examine later. Open spec/controllers/signatures_controller_spec.rb. It should resemble the code in Listing 26-5.

Listing 26-5. *Boilerplate Controller Spec (spec/controllers/signatures_controller_spec.rb)*

```ruby
require File.dirname(__FILE__) + '/../spec_helper'

describe SignaturesController do
  it "should use PetitionsController" do
    controller.should be_an_instance_of(PetitionsController)
  end

  describe "GET 'index'" do
    it "should be successful" do
      get 'index'
      response.should be_success
    end
  end
end
```

Note the nested describe declaration present here. The outer one describes the controller itself, and any inner ones can be used to break up specs into manageable chunks, or contexts, by actions or behaviors that they are intended to represent. In our case, we'll have two actions, index and create, and we'll expect certain behaviors from each of these, so we'll ultimately want a nested describe block for each of them. Furthermore, we may have different expectations of our create action, depending on what kind of data is handed to it: valid data or invalid data.

Another thing worth noting in Listing 26-5 is that we're using some special matchers specific to the Rails request/response cycle. In the boilerplate "should be successful" example, we see that the response is specified as successful by using the be_success matcher on response.should. Later in this section, you'll see a couple more custom Rails matchers (provided by the RSpec on Rails plugin) that deal with response, rendering, and routing expectations. For a full list and other helpful examples, consult http://rspec.info/documentation/rails/writing/controllers.html.

Mocking and Stubbing

Remember how we mentioned that RSpec emphasizes testing each component in isolation? Well, in addition to separating controller and view specs, a few other techniques can be used to promote that agenda. Ideally, we would like to not only separate our controller and view specs from one another, but also to isolate the controller spec from model implementations and any underlying database activity. We can achieve this by taking advantage of RSpec's built-in mocking and stubbing capabilities.

Mocks are "fake objects" used to set and verify expectations. *Stubs* are a way of specifying canned responses to messages. Mocking and stubbing are central tenets of BDD. We use stubs to intercept calls to methods on our models like new, create, and find. By intercepting these calls, we can replace real instances of Active Record objects with mock instances, thus isolating our controller specs from the model code and freeing us from reliance on fixtures. This is considered a best practice in RSpec, and it is intended to make us focus on specifying actual controller behavior, rather than navigating the eccentricities of particular model logic. Model logic is best specified in the model specs themselves, after all!

To illustrate how we might use mocks and stubs in our specs, let's consider for a moment how we might specify the fact that our SignaturesController should create a new signature for a petition. Following our RESTful conventions, this should occur when the create action is called and passed some valid data. We've already tested our model creation/validation elsewhere, so we don't need to repeat that here. In fact, we would prefer not to hit the database at all.

We know that a signature must be associated with some petition, so our controller will need to look up the appropriate Petition somehow (probably by using an ID supplied in the parameters). The usual way to do this is by using Petition.find, but if we want to write a controller spec without relying on the behavior of the model at all, we'll want to stub find to return a mock object that we can use to test our controller in isolation. We can do this by using the stub! method that RSpec makes available on all objects. We tell stub! to return a mock created with the mock_model method:

```
Petition.stub!(:find).and_return(@petition = mock_model(Petition,
  :name => "name", :description => "description", :signatures => []))
```

This code stubs the find method and returns a mock object of the class Petition with name, description, and signatures methods that return the canned responses that we've specified.

▪**Tip** RSpec includes its own mocking and stubbing facilities, but many other popular Ruby implementations are available, including Mocha (http://mocha.rubyforge.org) and FlexMock (http://onestepback.org/software/flexmock). If you would prefer to use Mocha or FlexMock instead, you can set the config.mock_with :mocha or :flexmock directive in the Spec::Runner.configure block in your spec/spec_helper.rb file.

We also know that we'll need to add a new signature in the create action. Since we'll want to add a new element to the existing signatures association, we'll logically use @petition. signatures.build. The build method returns a new object of the collection type (Signature) that has been linked to the object with the correct foreign key but has yet to be saved. Since we're striving for complete model isolation in this controller spec, we'll stub that as well, returning another mock object:

```
@petition.signatures.stub!(:build).and_return(
  @signature = mock_model(Signature, :save => true))
```

This time, the mock object should be of the Signature class, and we've supplied a canned response for a single method, save. We're testing the context where the data supplied is valid, so we know that save is always going to return true in this context. Remember that we're testing the controller logic, *not* the model! Therefore, we don't want anything to do with validation in this spec. In the other context, where we're dealing with responses to invalid Signature data, we'll create a mock object whose save method always returns false instead.

We usually specify our mocks/stubs in a before(:each) block within a given describe context. With those in place, we can now tackle our "should create a new signature" example simply by checking to see if our @signature mock receives a call to the save method. We can do this by using RSpec's special should_receive expectation, which allows us to verify that the controller action being executed calls the named method on a particular mock object and also to check that method's return value:

```
it "should create a new signature" do
  @signature.should_receive(:save).and_return(true)
  post(:create, :petition_id => @petition.id)
end
```

This particular type of expectation is very powerful. If we want to specify that certain arguments to the method call are also expected, for instance, we can use a syntax like this:

```
should receive(:method).with(arg1, arg2)
```

We can also specify additional constraints, including the number of times the method is received:

```
should receive(:method).at_least(:twice)
```

or that the method should cause an exception to be raised:

```
should receive(:method).once.and_raise(<exception>)
```

For more information about these and other options, see `http://rspec.info/rdoc/classes/Spec/Mocks.html`.

Specifying Our Controller Behaviors

Now that you understand the roles of mocks and stubs in specs, let's write that controller spec. As before, we'll follow the BDD paradigm in defining the behavior of our controller before actually implementing it in code. Here are the initial behaviors we might want our controller to possess:

- The `index` action should render the index template.

- The `index` action should locate the appropriate `Petition` model and assign it to an instance variable. (Actual display of the signatures associated with that petition will be something the view is responsible for, so we don't worry about that here.)

- The `create` action, given a valid signature, should create a new signature associated with the current petition.

- The `create` action, given a valid signature, should redirect the visitor back to the index page.

- The `create` action, given a valid signature, should place a success message in the flash (which will be displayed on the index page).

- The `create` action, given an invalid signature, should fail to create a new signature.

- The `create` action, given an invalid signature, should redisplay the index page so the information can be corrected and another attempt can be made to submit the signature.

- The `create` action, given an invalid signature, should place a warning message in the flash.

As you can see, these items can be cleanly broken down into three contexts: the context in which we've asked to see the index of signatures, the context in which we've been asked to create a new signature with valid signature data, and the context in which we've been asked to create a new signature but have been given incomplete (or invalid) data. For the sake of brevity, we'll examine only one of these contexts here. However, you can find the full specs with the sample code for this book at `http://www.apress.com` (in the Sources/Download section of the Apress web site). Listing 26-6 contains a spec for the context in which the `create` action is called with valid `Signature` data.

Listing 26-6. *Partial Signatures Controller Spec (spec/controllers/signatures_controller_spec.rb)*

```
require File.dirname(__FILE__) + '/../spec_helper'

describe SignaturesController do
  describe "create with a valid signature" do
    before(:each) do
      Petition.stub!(:find).and_return(
        @petition = mock_model(Petition, :name => "name",
          :description => "description", :signatures => []))
      @petition.signatures.stub!(:build).and_return(
        @signature = mock_model(Signature, :save => true))
    end

    def do_create
      post(:create, :petition_id => @petition.id)
    end

    it "should create a new signature" do
      @signature.should_receive(:save).and_return(true)
      do_create
    end

    it "should redirect after create" do
      do_create
      response.should be_redirect
      response.should redirect_to(petition_signatures_path(@petition.id))
    end

    it "should note success in the flash" do
      do_create
      flash[:notice].should_not be_empty
    end
  end
end
```

We've illustrated three examples within the chosen context. Each of them demonstrates one aspect of the create action's behavior when it is supplied with valid signature data. At this point, the basic RSpec syntax shouldn't seem quite so foreign.

The first example, "should create a new signature", was already covered in our discussion of mocks and stubs. It asserts that our create action should create a new signature. We express this simply by checking to see if our @signature mock receives the save method and returns true. This example, as well as the others shown in Listing 26-6, makes use of a do_create method that we've within the describe block. This method is what actually posts the data to our controller action, and we've made it its own method in order to keep things DRY.

```
it "should create a new signature" do
  @signature.should_receive(:save).and_return(true)
  do_create
end
```

The second example, "should redirect after create", is pretty straightforward as well. To express it, we use the Rails-specific expectation matcher be_redirect and then use redirect_to, specifying the location where users should be taken once they have entered valid data (back to the list of signatures seems like a good place to us!):

```
it "should redirect after create" do
  do_create
  response.should be_redirect
  response.should redirect_to(petition_signatures_path(@petition.id))
end
```

The final example, "should note success in the flash", is the simplest of the three and warrants no further explanation.

Passing Controller Specs

If you run these specs before implementing the controller, they'll fail, of course. So our next step is to write the first iteration of our controller to satisfy these specifications and also to install some routes. Our very basic SignaturesController is shown in Listing 26-7, and the routes for the application are shown in Listing 26-8. Save both before continuing.

Listing 26-7. *Signatures Controller (app/controllers/signatures_controller.rb)*

```
class SignaturesController < ApplicationController
  before_filter :find_petition

  def index
    @signatures = @petition.signatures
  end

  def create
    @signature = @petition.signatures.build(params[:signature])
    if @signature.save
      flash[:notice] = "Thank you for your support"
      redirect_to(:action => 'index')
    else
      flash[:error] = "Please check the form for errors"
      redirect_to(:action => 'index')
    end
  end


  protected
```

```
  def find_petition
    @petition = Petition.find(params[:petition_id])
  end
end
```

Listing 26-8. *Routes for Signatures Controller (config/routes.rb)*

```
ActionController::Routing::Routes.draw do |map|
  map.resources :petitions, :has_many => :signatures
end
```

■Note SignaturesController is defined as a RESTful resource nested on another resource,
Petitions. We do this in order to scope the list of signatures to the correct petition through the
petitions_id that will be available in the params. We have not, however, at this point, implemented
a PetitionsController, but this will work fine as is. If you want to allow your users to create arbitrary
petitions, you can implement your own PetitionsController. Make sure to write a spec for it first, of
course!

With the routes in place and the controller implemented, rake spec should once again
show us passing specs.

Signatures View Specs

So far, we've covered two of the three parts of the MVC triad. As mentioned, RSpec provides
isolated view specs for us as well. When writing view specs, you should generally be careful
to test only for the presence of certain business logic and key data in the views, and resist the
temptation to specify theme or other design-oriented traits. From our experience, specifying/
testing too many nonessential traits can be almost as bad as not specifying any at all, and the
last thing we want is for our specs to be brittle and difficult to maintain.

As you my recall, a boilerplate spec for the index action view was generated for us when
we created our controller with the generator script earlier. It should resemble the code in
Listing 26-9.

Listing 26-9. *Boilerplate Index Action View Spec (spec/views/signatures/index.html.erb_spec.rb)*

```
require File.dirname(__FILE__) + '/../../spec_helper'

describe "/signatures/index" do
  before(:each) do
    render 'signatures/index'
  end
```

```
  it "should tell you where to find the file" do
    response.should have_tag('p', /Find me in app\/views\/signatures\/index/)
  end
end
```

Note that a new expectation matcher is shown in the lone example here: have_tag. It simply tests for the presence of a particular tag and markup content in the template (as rendered in the before(:each) block). For a full list of expectations and helpers for view specs, refer to http://rspec.info/documentation/rails/writing/views.html.

Specifying Our View Behaviors

Before diving into the view spec, let's once again take a moment to think about the responsibilities of this particular piece. The following might be a few necessary behaviors of the index action view:

- It should have a form for submitting a new signature.

- It should show the list of all current signatures for the given petition.

- It should show an error message if invalid data was submitted previously.

With these behaviors in mind, we can create our view spec, as shown in Listing 26-10.

Listing 26-10. *Updated Index Action Spec (spec/views/signatures/index.html.erb_spec.rb)*

```
require File.dirname(__FILE__) + '/../../spec_helper'

describe "/signatures/index" do
  before(:each) do
    @signatures = []
    @petition = mock_model(Petition, :name => "name",
      :description => "description", :signatures => @signatures)
    assigns[:petition] = @petition
  end

  it "should have a form for submitting a new signature" do
    render 'signatures/index'
    response.should have_tag('form[action=?]', petition_signatures_path(@petition))
  end

  it "should show the full list of all signatures" do
    @petition.should_receive(:signatures).at_least(1).times.and_return(@signatures)
    render 'signatures/index'
  end
```

```
  it "should show an error message if invalid data was submitted previously" do
    flash[:error] = "Please check the form for errors"
    render 'signatures/index'
    response.should have_tag('div#messages')
  end
end
```

Once again, we use the before(:each) block to set up shared environment data used by each of our examples—this time for mocking the @petition instance variable used throughout the views. Since this view spec is completely isolated from our controller, the presence of that variable is necessary in order to test view concerns. We use assigns[:petition] to assign it to the template variable so our view can access it. A similar convention exists for setting flash variables that would normally be set in the controller.

At this point, everything else should seem relatively straightforward:

- In the first example, we specify the form action URL to make sure that we're submitting it to the correct place.

- In the second example, we specify that the signatures association should be called *at least once.* We know that we'll need to iterate through it to display each signature, but we may also want to display the number of signatures above the list, and that would entail another call to the association.

- In the third example, we specify that a div with an ID of messages should be displayed in the view if there is an error or some other informational message within the flash. Therefore, we populate the flash[:error] object before rendering the template, and then check to make sure that the appropriate div exists in the output.

Passing View Specs

The view that satisfies the view spec that we've created is shown in Listing 26-11. If you rerun the rake spec task after saving the updated template, all specs should once again pass.

Listing 26-11. *Signature Index View (app/views/signatures/index.html.erb)*

```
<% if flash[:notice] || flash[:error] %>
  <div id="messages" style="margin: 10px; padding: 10px; border: 2px dashed;">
    <%= flash[:notice] || flash[:error] %>
  </div>
<% end %>

<h2><%= h(@petition.name) %></h2>
<strong><%= h(@petition.description) %></strong>
<hr/>
```

```
<h3>Sign the Petition!</h3>
  <%= error_messages_for(:signature) %>
  <% form_for(:signature, :url => petition_signatures_path(@petition)) do |f| -%>
    <label for="signature_name">Name: </label><br/>
    <%= f.text_field(:name) %><br/>
    <label for="signature_email">Email: </label><br/>
    <%= f.text_field(:email) %><br/>
    <label for="signature_comment">Comment: </label><br/>
    <%= f.text_area(:comment, :rows => 2) %><br/>
    <%= submit_tag('Do it!') %>
  <% end -%>
<hr/>
<h3>Signatures (<%= @petition.signatures.length %>)</h3>
<% @petition.signatures.each do |signature| -%>
  <div class="signature" style="margin-left: 10px;">
    <div class="scomment"><em><%= h(signature.comment) %></em></div>
    <div class="sname"><%= h(signature.name) %></div>
    <br/>
  </div>
<% end -%>
```

To see all this actually working in your browser, you first need to manually create the petition for our television show (since we haven't implemented an actual `PetitionsController`). You can do this using the Rails console script. In your main project directory, execute the following commands:

```
ruby script/console
>> Petition.create!(:name => "Save The Adventures of Young Banzai Cooper!",
      :description => "Help us save the show by signing this petition. Thanks!")
>> exit
```

Now you can fire up a web browser and point it to `http://localhost:3000/petitions/1/signatures`. You should be able to add any number of signatures to the petition. Figure 26-1 shows an example with several signatures added. If everything went according to plan, this simple application should work exactly as we've specified, which is, after all, the whole point!

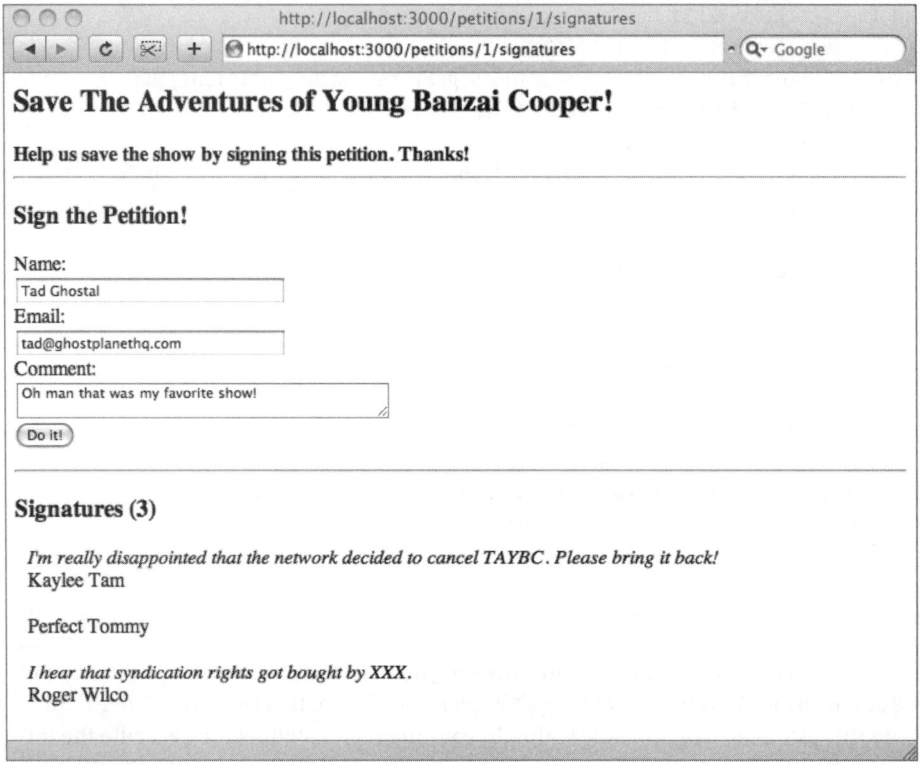

Figure 26-1. *Petition with signatures (http://localhost:3000/petitions/1/signatures)*

Summary

Test-driven development is a central tenet of the Rails framework and the Ruby way of thinking. Behavior-driven development stays true to the core TDD philosophies but improves on TDD in many ways. With a more natural syntax, it's easier than ever to specify behavior before writing actual code (and easier to maintain, too!).

RSpec, a popular BDD package for Ruby, allows you to express your goals very succinctly. Using RSpec's friendly syntax and logical conventions puts you on the right path to thinking about what kind of behavior your system should exhibit, in a natural way, rather than just diving into coding. Throughout this chapter, you've seen how to use RSpec to write specs for models, controllers, and views, and noted the many ways that it differs from Test::Unit. You've also had a chance to examine RSpec's powerful built-in stubbing and mocking capabilities.

RSpec is not the only BDD library available for Rails. Other plugins, such as Test/Spec (http://test-spec.rubyforge.org/test-spec) and Shoulda (http://www.thoughtbot.com/projects/shoulda), build on the foundation provided by Test::Unit and allow you to slowly mix in elements of BDD. If you're in a situation where you must maintain and work with existing test suites while transitioning (rather than just starting from scratch), you may want to evaluate one or more of these alternatives.

RSpec and BDD are rich, important topics, and there is a lot to learn that we couldn't possibly hope to cover in a single chapter. Indeed, just documenting the set of powerful Rails expectation matchers alone could fill several chapters. However, we hope that we've presented a solid introduction.

For more information about RSpec, make sure to check the official RSpec home on the Web at `http://rspec.info`. This site contains a wealth of knowledge, including full library documentation, community resources, examples, and even a table of RSpec equivalents for standard `Test::Unit` assertions (`http://rspec.info/documentation/test_unit.html`), which can be particularly helpful for new users. For more information about BDD in general, we encourage you to visit `http://behaviour-driven.org`.

■ ■ ■

Preventing Validation Errors with Assert Valid Asset

Validation is the process of checking the documents you develop against a standard. When we talk about validation in the context of web development, we're usually referring to the process of validating your HTML views and CSS against standards maintained by the World Wide Web Consortium (W3C).

Are you validating your views? If not, we strongly encourage you to consider it. Validation can help us identify when we've forgotten to close an HTML tag, misspelled a tag attribute, or made other garden-variety hand-coding mistakes. Not only is this useful during the development process, but it can also help us ensure cross-browser and cross-platform compatibility, as well as future compatibility. If your HTML is not validated against a document standard, then when it comes to rendering results, all bets are off.

Think of validation as a form of quality assurance. You want to ensure that the web property that you've developed not only looks and works correctly in your local environment, but also behaves properly for everyone else. If your document isn't valid, there's no telling what issues might crop up or how any given browser might choose to render a mistake you've made. Remember that an HTML document in your Rails application isn't something a user sees; rather, it's just a set of rules that governs how information is structured. And, when combined with CSS display properties, these rules dictate how a browser should format and display a document.

In order for browsers to render the information you want to communicate in a reliable, predictable manner, both the HTML and CSS for an application view need a well-defined syntax and structure. The various HTML and CSS standards, combined with validation, help us make sure we meet those requirements.

There are other reasons to validate your document as well. Search engines that crawl your web site expect documents to be valid, for example, and your rankings may suffer if your documents do not validate. Support for mobile devices, and even screen readers, can be tripped up by badly structured documents, so validation is also of use in those areas. Another reason is pure and simple professionalism. After all, our web properties reflect the quality of our work and demonstrate our knowledge of best practices.

The W3C provides a validation tool online at `http://validator.w3.org` and also maintains a number of other web-based tools for checking the validity of CSS, RSS/Atom, and alternative formats. You can use the tool by uploading a file, by entering the HTML text to validate directly, or by specifying a public URI. Figure 27-1 shows the result of validating the US government's official web portal at http://www.usa.gov. It informs us that the document is not valid XHTML 1.0 Transitional, and gives a detailed report on each element that does not comply with the standard. There were 14 errors at the time of writing.

■Note Many different document type declarations (DOCTYPEs) are in common use today. DOCTYPEs inform the browser which version of (X)HTML is in use, so it can render document contents correctly. Common document types include HTML 4.01 and XHTML 1.0 (both Strict and Transitional). For more information, see http://www.alistapart.com/articles/doctype.

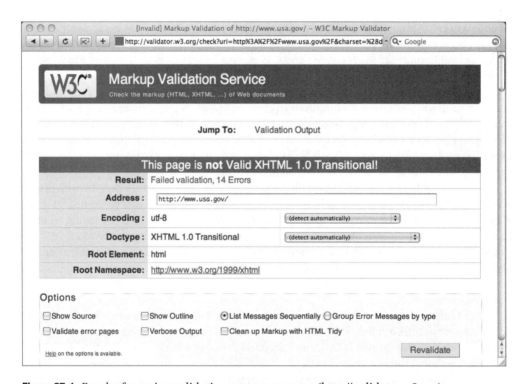

Figure 27-1. *Result of running validation on www.usa.gov (http://validator.w3.org)*

As you can see, the validator service is extremely useful. It can not only be used to determine whether your document is valid, but will also inform you of exactly which errors are preventing it from validating so you can locate and fix them.

When we're developing new web properties, we're often doing it from the comfort of our own private network, and therefore we can't simply give the validator service a URL and let it go to town. To use this service as we've described it, we would need to cut and paste or upload a file to revalidate each time, and this would be painful. What we would really like to do is to integrate validation into our testing process, so when we edit our HTML views, we can be notified immediately if we've done something invalid that might not render as expected in a browser.

Fortunately, we're not the first people to have felt this pain. First, Scott Raymond released a plugin called Assert Valid Markup (`http://redgreenblu.com/svn/projects/assert_valid_markup`), which integrated view document validation testing into the Rails suite of tests. Peter Donald later released an improved version called Assert Valid Asset (`http://www.realityforge.org/svn/code/assert-valid-asset`), adding CSS validation support and numerous other niceties. In this chapter, we'll demonstrate how this latter plugin can be integrated into your application's testing strategy with the Rails standard `Test::Unit` facilities.

Our Task: Integrate Validation Tests

Since our focus here is on showing a testing strategy, we'll use a basic example that consists of a barebones `ArticlesController` and two sample views. Those views will contain a number of intentional markup errors. We'll demonstrate how we can catch those errors easily using the Assert Valid Asset plugin, and we'll also validate the associated application style sheet while we're at it.

Creating the Validation Example

Let's create a new Rails application for the validation testing project:

```
rails validex
cd validex
```

We can then install the Assert Valid Asset plugin by executing the following command inside the new application root directory:

```
ruby script/plugin install ➥
http://www.realityforge.org/svn/code/assert-valid-asset/trunk
```

To generate our simple boilerplate sample controller and its views, we'll use the standard Rails generator script. The generator also creates a stock functional test that we can modify later.

```
ruby script/generate controller articles index show
```

We'll need to create a layout for this project as well. As we've done in previous chapters, we'll create a generic application layout in `app/views/layouts/application.html.erb` and use it to wrap the output of both the `index` and `show` action templates. The markup for this layout is shown in Listing 27-1.

Listing 27-1. *Application Layout with Markup Errors (app/views/layouts/application.html.erb)*

```
<!DOCTYPE html PUBLIC "-//W3C//DTD XHTML 1.0 Transitional//EN"
  "http://www.w3.org/TR/xhtml1/DTD/xhtml1-transitional.dtd">
<html>
<head>
  <title>Validation Example</title>
  <%= stylesheet_link_tag('application') %>
</head>
<body>
  <div class="container">
    <div class="header"><h1>Validation Example</h1></div>
    <div class="leftcol">
      <ul>
        <li><a href="http://www.w3.org">World Wide Web Consortium</a></li>
        <li><a href="http://validator.w3.org">Markup Validator</a></li>
        <li><a href="http://jigsaw.w3.org/css-validator">CSS Validator</a></li>
        <li><a href="http://www.realityforge.org/svn/code/assert-valid-asset"> ➥
Assert Valid Asset</a>
      </ul>
    </div>
    <div class="rightcol">
      <%= yield %>
    </div>
    <div class="footer">&copy; <%= Time.now.strftime("%Y") %> Your Name</span>
  </div>
</body>
</html>
```

Since our purpose is to demonstrate that we can detect and prevent validation errors, we've intentionally added some bad markup to Listing 27-1. We'll also add a couple of errors to our index template (we'll leave the other view template, show.html.erb, as is). Open app/views/articles/index.html.erb and replace the contents with the code shown in Listing 27-2.

Listing 27-2. *Index View Template with Markup Errors (/app/views/articles/index.html.erb)*

```
<p>Main content area text of the #index page. This is the first paragraph.
  Change this text to something you like.</p>
<p>Second paragraph</p>
<hr>
<p position="bottom">Third (and final) paragraph</p>
```

Before we can move on, we'll also want to create a style sheet in order to satisfy the stylesheet_link_tag used in the layout. Save the code in Listing 27-3 as public/stylesheets/application.css. The keen observer will note that we've created a few small errors in our CSS as well. If you spot them early (good for you!), don't fix them. We'll be using them later to demonstrate how the plugin can also detect invalid CSS.

Listing 27-3. *Style Sheet with CSS Errors (public/stylesheets/application.css)*

```
.container {
  width: 90%;
  border: 2px solid #666;
  margin: 10px auto;
}
.header {
  padding: 5px;
  border-bottom: 2px solid #666;
}
.footer {
  border-top: 2px solid #666;
  font-size: small;
  padding: 5px;
  margin: 0;
  clear: both;
  text-align: middle;
}
.leftcol {
  float: left;
  width: 240px;
  margin: 0
  padding: 10px;
}
.leftcol ul {
  list-style-type: none;
  margin: 0;
  padding: 5px;
}
.leftcol ul li {
  margin-top: 3px;
}
.rightcol {
  margin-left: 250px;
  padding: 0 20px;
  border-left: 2px solid #666;
}
a {
  text-decration: underline;
  color: blue;
}
a:hover {
  color: purple;
}
```

```
h1 {
  padding: 0;
  margin: 0;
}
```

Now that we have a working web site with some (subtly) bad markup, let's see how these problems can be detected using Assert Valid Asset in our functional tests.

Detecting Invalid Markup

Adding tests to check for valid markup is straightforward. The most basic version can be integrated by adding a single line to a functional test. Open the stock functional test created by the generator in `tests/functional/articles_controller_test.rb` and replace it with the contents of Listing 27-4.

Listing 27-4. *Functional Test for Markup Validity (tests/functional/articles_controller_test.rb)*

```
require File.dirname(__FILE__) + '/../test_helper'

class ArticlesControllerTest < ActionController::TestCase
  def test_index_markup
    get :index
    assert_response :success
    assert_template 'index'
    assert_valid_markup
  end
end
```

Our sole functional test contains a typical check for document validity. The `assert_valid_markup` method call runs a validity check on whatever markup exists in the response body (as populated by the preceding call to `get` or `post`) and asserts that it is error-free. If errors in the markup cause validation to fail, the test case will fail and alert us. It's really just that simple.

■Tip If a string is passed to the `assert_valid_markup` instance method, the document markup in that string will be tested for validity in place of the response body.

Even more conveniently, a class-level method can be called to validate any number of actions at once. In fact, let's modify that code fragment to use the class-level variant and assert the validity of both the `index` and `show` templates at once. The result is shown in Listing 27-5.

Listing 27-5. *Simplified Functional Test (tests/functional/articles_controller_test.rb)*

```
require File.dirname(__FILE__) + '/../test_helper'

class ArticlesControllerTest < ActionController::TestCase
  assert_valid_markup :index, :show
end
```

To run the test, we'll use the `rake test:functionals` task, which should alert us that we have two failing tests at this time. In the following output, we're listing the details of only the first of the two test failures.

```
rake test:functionals
```

```
Loaded suite /opt/local/lib/ruby/gems/1.8/gems/rake-0.8.1/lib/rake/rake_test_loader
Started
FF
Finished in 0.157463 seconds.

1) Failure:
test_index_valid_markup(ArticlesControllerTest)
Invalid markup: line 3: Missing xmlns attribute for element html.
    The value should be: http://www.w3.org/1999/xhtml
Invalid markup: line 17: end tag for "li" omitted, but OMITTAG NO was specified
Invalid markup: line 16: start tag was here
Invalid markup: line 23: end tag for "hr" omitted, but OMITTAG NO was specified
Invalid markup: line 23: start tag was here
Invalid markup: line 24: there is no attribute "position"
Invalid markup: line 28: end tag for element "span" which is not open
Invalid markup: line 30: end tag for "div" omitted, but OMITTAG NO was specified
Invalid markup: line 9: start tag was here
Invalid markup: line 17: XML Parsing Error:  Opening and ending tag mismatch: ➥
li line 16 and ul
Invalid markup: line 18: XML Parsing Error:  Opening and ending tag mismatch: ➥
ul line 12 and div
Invalid markup: line 27: XML Parsing Error:  Opening and ending tag mismatch: ➥
hr line 23 and div
Invalid markup: line 28: XML Parsing Error:  Opening and ending tag mismatch: ➥
div line 28 and span
Invalid markup: line 30: XML Parsing Error:  Opening and ending tag mismatch: ➥
div line 11 and body
Invalid markup: line 31: XML Parsing Error:  Opening and ending tag mismatch: ➥
div line 9 and html
Invalid markup: line 31: XML Parsing Error:  Premature end of data in tag body line 8
Invalid markup: line 31: XML Parsing Error:  Premature end of data in tag html line 3.
<false> is not true.
...snip!...

2 tests, 2 assertions, 2 failures, 0 errors
```

Tip If you want to see even more detailed information from the test, you can add the line `self.display_invalid_content = true` to the body of the `ArticlesControllerTest` class. With that in place, test output will be even more verbose, showing the entirety of the response body in the output, along with line numbers that are easily matched with the validation results. This can be invaluable when troubleshooting.

So, our markup validation failed, and we receive a nice, concise report of exactly which elements in the document caused the failure to occur and why. This is exactly the same output we would receive if we copied the response body from a browser and pasted it into the W3C validator service (see Figure 27-1). Having this done automatically for us when our test suite is run is clearly much more convenient. It also provides us with another advantage: whenever our view templates change and our tests are run, we'll be automatically alerted if something is amiss.

Since we're using a third-party web service to obtain these results, it's natural to wonder what kind of effect this has on test performance. Indeed, it does slow down testing somewhat, since the validator service needs to be contacted. However, because results from the validation service are cached by the plugin, there is no need to contact the service each time the functional test is run, unless the view template in question has changed. If nothing has changed, the plugin will use the results cached in the `tmp/markup` directory. This cache is updated transparently whenever the template is modified and results are rerun.

WORKING OFFLINE

Assert Valid Asset assumes that you have a working network connection so that it can contact the remote validation service. If you want to override this so that the remote service is not contacted, you can set the NONET environment variable to `true`. This is handy, for instance, when working offline.

If you find yourself working offline frequently, you may want to consider installing a local standalone validation service. We recommend Validator S.A.C. (`http://habilis.net/validator-sac`), a popular option for OS X users.

You can configure Validator S.A.C. to be available as a local web service (follow instructions on the web site) and then instruct Assert Valid Asset to query it by making a few small changes to `test/test_helper.rb`. Add the following inside the class definition in that file:

```
MARKUP_VALIDATOR_HOST = "localhost"
MARKUP_VALIDATOR_PATH = "/w3c-validator/check"
```

With these changes in place, Assert Valid Asset should validate your view templates against the local validation service. Since Validator S.A.C. contains a complete working version of the W3C Validator, this approach will let you validate documents just as if you were online!

In any case, the errors themselves are quite descriptive. Among them, the validator notes that we seem to have omitted the html tag's namespace (xmlns) attribute, missed a couple of closing tags, and tried to close a tag that was never opened in the first place. These can be common mistakes when hand-coding HTML without the proper tools or reference materials. The validator also notes that there is no attribute named position available on the p (paragraph) tag—oops!

Since the validation is run on the entirety of the response body as it would be viewed by an end user (or browser), markup issues can reside in the view action template, its layout, or any partials that are rendered by either. In our case, we have a mix of mistakes in our template and the index action view.

Let's edit our layout to remove the errors noticed by the validation tool, and then run the test again. Three of our errors are in the layout: the missing xmlns attribute on the html tag, the fact we haven't closed the final li tag, and the mistake we made trying to close a div tag in the footer with a span tag. The corrected version is shown in Listing 27-6 (the changes are in bold).

Listing 27-6. *Application Layout with Valid Markup (app/views/layouts/application.html.erb)*

```erb
<!DOCTYPE html PUBLIC "-//W3C//DTD XHTML 1.0 Transitional//EN"
  "http://www.w3.org/TR/xhtml1/DTD/xhtml1-transitional.dtd">
<html xmlns="http://www.w3.org/1999/xhtml">
<head>
  <title>Validation Example</title>
  <%= stylesheet_link_tag('application') %>
</head>
<body>
  <div class="container">
    <div class="header"><h1>Validation Example</h1></div>
    <div class="leftcol">
      <ul>
        <li><a href="http://www.w3.org">World Wide Web Consortium</a></li>
        <li><a href="http://validator.w3.org">Markup Validator</a></li>
        <li><a href="http://jigsaw.w3.org/css-validator">CSS Validator</a></li>
        <li><a href="http://www.realityforge.org/svn/code/assert-valid-asset"> ➡
Assert Valid Asset</a></li>
      </ul>
    </div>
    <div class="rightcol">
      <%= yield %>
    </div>
    <div class="footer">&copy; <%= Time.now.strftime("%Y") %> Your Name</div>
  </div>
</body>
</html>
```

Rerunning the `rake test:functionals` task should now reveal that we have only one failing test instead of two. The remaining failures are in the `index` template itself: an improperly formed `hr` tag and a paragraph tag with an unrecognized attribute named `position`. Maybe the coder meant to specify a CSS class or property? Or maybe he was just plain sloppy? In real life, we would probably ask him, but for the purpose of this example, we'll just remove the erroneous attribute. The corrected template is shown in Listing 27-7.

Listing 27-7. *Index Action Template with Valid Markup (app/views/articles/index.html.erb)*

```
<p>Main content area text of the #index page. This is the first paragraph.
  Change this text to something you like.</p>
<p>Second paragraph</p>
<hr/>
<p>Third (and final) paragraph</p>
```

With these changes in place, our markup should now be valid XHTML 1.0 Transitional. We can test this by rerunning the functional tests. The results should speak for themselves:

```
rake test:functionals
```

```
Started
..
Finished in 0.744128 seconds.

2 tests, 2 assertions, 0 failures, 0 errors
```

■**Tip** You can also enable automatic validation on the content output of each functional test by adding the line `self.auto_validate = true` in into `test_helper.rb` in the `Test::Unit::TestCase` class. For more information, see the plugin's `README` file in your project, in `vendor/plugins/assert-valid-asset/README`.

Detecting Invalid CSS

Now that we've covered how to detect invalid markup in view templates, it's time to show how you can use similar facilities to test style sheet validity. The Assert Valid Asset plugin provides the `assert_valid_css` method to do just this.

As with `assert_valid_markup`, there is both an instance method and a class-level variant. We'll use the latter here, `assert_valid_css_files`. We've added it to our existing functional test and specified the name of the style sheet to test, as shown in Listing 27-8.

Listing 27-8. *Functional Test with CSS Validation (test/functional/articles_controller_test.rb)*

```
require File.dirname(__FILE__) + '/../test_helper'

class ArticlesControllerTest < ActionController::TestCase
  assert_valid_css_files 'application'
  assert_valid_markup :index, :show
end
```

Let's run our functional tests again and see if we find any problems with our CSS. We're willing to bet there are at least a few mistakes!

```
rake test:functionals
```

```
Loaded suite /opt/local/lib/ruby/gems/1.8/gems/rake-0.8.1/lib/rake/rake_test_loader
Started
F..
Finished in 0.164453 seconds.

  1) Failure:
test_application_valid_css(ArticlesControllerTest)
...snip!...
CSS Validation failed:
Invalid CSS: line 16 .footer Value Error : text-align middle is not a text-align ➥
value : middle
Invalid CSS: line 22 .leftcol Value Error : margin attempt to find a semi-colon ➥
before the property name. add it
Invalid CSS: line 38 a Property text-decration doesn&apos;t exist : underline .

3 tests, 3 assertions, 1 failures, 0 errors
```

This output tells us that we have three errors in our CSS. The first issue is that we've incorrectly specified the value of the text-align property for the footer class. It should be center. The second is a very common CSS mistake: forgetting to end a line with a semicolon. Finally, we've misspelled a property of the a (anchor) element—it should read text-decoration. The corrected style sheet is shown in Listing 27-9.

Listing 27-9. *Application Style Sheet with Valid CSS (public/stylesheets/application.css)*

```
.container {
  width: 90%;
  border: 2px solid #666;
  margin: 10px auto;
}
.header {
  padding: 5px;
  border-bottom: 2px solid #666;
}
```

```
.footer {
  border-top: 2px solid #666;
  font-size: small;
  padding: 5px;
  margin: 0;
  clear: both;
  text-align: center;
}
.leftcol {
  float: left;
  width: 240px;
  margin: 0;
  padding: 10px;
}
.leftcol ul {
  list-style-type: none;
  margin: 0;
  padding: 5px;
}
.leftcol ul li {
  margin-top: 3px;
}
.rightcol {
  margin-left: 250px;
  padding: 0 20px;
  border-left: 2px solid #666;
}
a {
  text-decoration: underline;
  color: blue;
}
a:hover {
  color: purple;
}
h1 {
  padding: 0;
  margin: 0;
}
```

We'll save the changes and rerun our tests one final time to make sure that all the HTML and CSS in our project validates and is error free. Everything should pass with flying (green!) colors.

```
rake test:functionals
```

```
Loaded suite /opt/local/lib/ruby/gems/1.8/gems/rake-0.8.1/lib/rake/rake_test_loader
Started
...
Finished in 0.950108 seconds.

3 tests, 2 assertions, 0 failures, 0 errors
```

Now that both our markup and our CSS have been validated, we can be confident that the document that visitors' browsers are receiving is error-free and standards-compliant, and it also should render correctly across browsers present and future. To see the index view, start the server using `script/server` and point a web browser at `http://localhost:3000/articles`. It should resemble the screen shown in Figure 27-2.

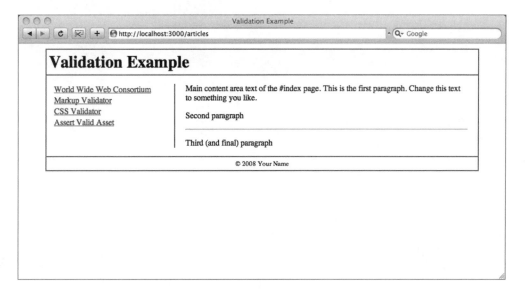

Figure 27-2. *Articles index view (http://localhost:3000/articles)*

■**Caution** Just because your document validates doesn't mean that certain browser quirks won't prevent it from rendering correctly! Especially for complicated views, it's of the utmost importance that the developer checks the site that's being developed by hand in each browser that needs to be supported. Many browsers have certain display quirks that need to be coded around. Also, particular browsers may not support the entirety of some of the newer W3 specifications (such as CSS3).

Summary

The W3C has established a set of standards for web pages, including rules for markup syntax and code structure. Any web property you develop should conform to these standards. Of course, standard conformance isn't just a way to assert your professionalism; it's also important for ensuring cross-platform and cross-browser compliance (both present and future), support for alternative display devices, and search-engine friendliness.

There are a number of existing tools for validating HTML and CSS, but the advantage of using a plugin like Assert Valid Asset in your Rails project is that it makes the process of validating user-visible content as easy as running your existing functional tests. Whenever your views change and a mistake in markup is accidentally introduced, you'll know immediately. The verbose output also simplifies the task of finding and fixing any validation errors.

For more information about the Assert Valid Asset plugin, see `http://www.realityforge.org/svn/code/assert-valid-asset/trunk/README`. For more information about web standards in general, visit the W3C site at `http://www.w3.org`.

PART 9

■ ■ ■

Plugin Development Strategies

Throughout this book, you've seen a number of powerful plugins that cover a broad spectrum of use cases, including model enhancement, request/response cycle modification, performance optimization, and testing. We sincerely hope that some of these plugins prove useful to you and help accelerate the development of your own Rails-based web sites and applications.

But no matter how useful the plugins we've discussed here are, perhaps the most important plugin of all may be the one you have yet to write. Perhaps you've devised a new action-caching strategy, or come up with a recommendations system framework, or developed an attractive new media player package that you want to share with others.

Whatever it is that you've come up with, if it can be sufficiently generalized and turned into a plugin, there is a good chance that someone else may be able benefit from it. In this final part of the book, we'll examine the process of taking a simple idea and packaging it as a plugin for sharing and easy installation. Along the way, we'll also discuss plugin testing strategies and distribution resources.

## CHAPTER 28

Creating and Distributing Your Own Plugins

The true power of the Rails plugin system lies in the fact that not only can you consume any number of terrific third-party plugins, but you can also create and share your own code with ease. This is one of the key aspects that makes the Rails ecosystem so powerful: plugins allow us to both give and take, offer suggestions, and demonstrate ways of improving on the status quo. The plugin system is a great way to introduce new concepts and ideas without modifying the core itself.

There are various strategies for developing all sorts of plugins that do vastly different things. However, the core technique for creating these extensions tends to be the same: you load a piece of code that, using Ruby's powerful metaprogramming capabilities, overrides the default functionality of some core piece of Rails, replacing or extending it with your own functionality.

In this chapter, we'll examine the structure of a typical plugin (including the installation and initialization hooks provided by the framework) and walk you through the process of creating, testing, and distributing a simple example.

Our Task: Whitelist IP Addresses

Because our purpose here is to focus on the process rather than the particulars of the plugin itself, we'll keep our example relatively basic. We're presently working on a super top-secret project and have decided that when we deploy our applications to a staging server, we would like to be able to limit the range of remote IP addresses that can access them to our own address and maybe one or two other IPs (clients, bosses, and other stakeholders). Therefore, we'll design a plugin that we can use in our controllers to restrict access to visitors who have an IP that is in a predefined whitelist.

Note There are various other more intelligent ways to restrict access to an application. A number of them have been showcased in previous chapters, including Chapters 11 and 13. The Rails Basic HTTP authentication facility can also be used for this (see `http://api.rubyonrails.org/classes/ActionController/HttpAuthentication/Basic.html`). On the other hand, if you just want to limit access by IP addresses as we'll be doing here, you might want to consider installing a basic firewall in front of your deployed application.

Often, plugins start innocuously enough as regular application features or code snippets. We begin by implementing a routine in one place, maybe in one of our application's controller actions. Then, later on, we determine that the same functionality is needed in another controller, and we move the behavior to a self-contained module to keep things DRY. We may also consider reimplementing this as a plugin in order to use it across other applications that we may be building, and also to release it so that other developers can enjoy the same benefit.

With this mind, we'll start by implementing our IP whitelisting functionality in the form of a `before_filter` on an arbitrary controller.

Creating the IP Whitelisting Functionality

Let's get started by creating a sample Rails project for this task:

```
rails topsecret
cd topsecret
```

Listing 28-1 shows what an initial version of an articles controller for this project might look like. Save this code as app/controllers/articles_controller.rb.

Listing 28-1. *ArticlesController with before_filter (app/controllers/articles_controller.rb)*

```
class ArticlesController < ApplicationController
  WHITELIST = ["127.0.0.1", "192.168.1.1", "69.55.226.90"]
  before_filter :check_whitelist

  def index
    render(:text => "It works!  Your IP must be in the whitelist.")
  end

  private

  def check_whitelist
    if WHITELIST.include?(request.remote_ip)
      true
    else
      render(:nothing => true, :status => 401)
      false
    end
  end
end
```

The check_whitelist method shown here is the heart of our simple example; it will check incoming requests to make sure their IP address is included in our WHITELIST constant before passing control on to the appropriate controller action. If the IP address is not in the list, the method halts the filter chain by returning false and renders an empty template, with a status code of 401, indicating that the request was unauthorized.

After you create the articles controller, start the server by using script/server. Accessing http://localhost:3000/articles in a browser should display the line of text shown in the index action, since your current IP (the loopback address, 127.0.0.1) is included in the whitelist.

Now remove the 127.0.0.1 address from the WHITELIST array and reload the page in your browser. This time, a blank page should be shown. Since the address was not found in the whitelist, the server has returned a 401 unauthorized response code and rendered a blank page. You can verify this by looking at the server console output (or the development log in logs/development.log), which should show the filter chain halting when your IP is not found in the allowed list:

```
Processing ArticlesController#index (for 127.0.0.1 at 2008-06-18 11:11:38) [GET]
  Session ID: ( ... )
  Parameters: {"action"=>"index", "controller"=>"articles"}
Filter chain halted as [:check_whitelist] rendered_or_redirected.
Completed in 0.00061 (1650 reqs/sec) | Rendering: 0.00039 (64%) | DB: 0.00000 (0%) |
401 Unauthorized [http://localhost/articles]
```

This simple routine does just what we need. In fact, it might be quite suitable as-is if our use of it were limited to this single controller. To use it with different controllers in the same application, we could just move the logic into our ApplicationController, from which all controllers in a Rails application inherit. However, if we want to reuse the same code across multiple applications, it may be time to create a plugin that wraps up this functionality into a neat, easily reusable package—a Rails plugin.

Creating the IP Whitelist Plugin

For the first version of our IP Whitelist plugin, we'll keep things simple. At a conceptual level, we'll just want to add a new type of before_filter to ActionController::Base: a class-level method that can be called in our controllers (which inherit from ApplicationController, making them direct descendants of ActionController::Base) to indicate that requests should be processed only if the remote IP is in the whitelist.

We'll implement this with a bit of syntactical sugar by adding a single class-level method to ActionController::Base that can be called in any controller to initialize a whitelist and install the appropriate filter method. Our goal is to make adding this capability to a controller as simple as possible for an end user. To this end, we've decided that it should allow us to declare a whitelist using the DSL-style syntax shown in Listing 28-2.

Listing 28-2. *ArticlesController with ip_whitelist Plugin (app/controllers/articles_controller.rb)*

```
class ArticlesController < ApplicationController
  allow_from_ip ["127.0.0.1", "192.168.1.1", "69.55.226.90"]

  def index
    render(:text => "It works!  Your IP must be in the whitelist.")
  end
end
```

In order to make this possible, we'll need to create an `allow_from_ip` class-level method on `ActionController::Base`. That method should do two things when it's called:

- Store the list of IP addresses we want to add in a `whitelist` array, much like the constant in our original version.

- Install the method `check_whitelist` as a `before_filter`.

The `check_whitelist` method will work pretty much as it did before, but instead of checking a class-level constant to find addresses in the whitelist, it will need to check an accessor method that we'll create.

So let's get to work. First we'll create a standard plugin skeleton, and then we can fill it in with our whitelisting magic.

Generating the Plugin Structure

If you've been using Rails for any amount of time, it should come as no surprise that generating a stock plugin skeleton is a feature built right into the framework. That's right—in addition to the standard generators that you're already familiar with, Rails provides a plugin generator.

Inside the `topsecret` project directory, issue the following command to create the plugin skeleton for our new plugin, `ip_whitelist`:

```
ruby script/generate plugin ip_whitelist
```

```
create  vendor/plugins/ip_whitelist/lib
create  vendor/plugins/ip_whitelist/tasks
create  vendor/plugins/ip_whitelist/test
create  vendor/plugins/ip_whitelist/README
create  vendor/plugins/ip_whitelist/MIT-LICENSE
create  vendor/plugins/ip_whitelist/Rakefile
create  vendor/plugins/ip_whitelist/init.rb
create  vendor/plugins/ip_whitelist/install.rb
create  vendor/plugins/ip_whitelist/uninstall.rb
create  vendor/plugins/ip_whitelist/lib/ip_whitelist.rb
create  vendor/plugins/ip_whitelist/tasks/ip_whitelist_tasks.rake
create  vendor/plugins/ip_whitelist/test/ip_whitelist_test.rb
```

The generator creates the plugin directory for us, in `vendor/plugins/ip_whitelist`, and also populates the plugin with a standard structure and a number of boilerplate files to get us started.

Plugin Directories

By convention, each plugin directory contains three top-level directories:

- The `lib` directory will contain the core of our IP Whitelist plugin logic. The code that we'll be inserting into `ActionController` will reside here.

- The `test` directory will contain tests for that code.

- The `tasks` directory provides a useful extra feature: it contains Rake tasks that will automatically be made available in any Rails project that installs the plugin (much like those tasks you might place in `lib/tasks`).

You can expand on this skeletal structure as needed, of course, adding subdirectories to the `lib` directory, a `public` directory to contain images or other assets at the top level, and so on. The plugin generator merely gives you a skeleton to get started with, much like the `rails` command itself gives you a skeleton that you can use to start building a web application.

Plugin Files and Hooks

The plugin structure also contains a number of files at the top level. These include a `README` file that should describe installation and usage of the plugin, a standard software license (the stock MIT license, also used by Rails itself), and a `Rakefile`. The `Rakefile` can contain any number of tasks, but has two useful ones defined by default: the first will allow users to run the tests you've built for the plugin, and the second will generate RDoc documentation.

The three remaining files have special significance. They serve as hooks that run at particular times, as follows:

- The `install.rb` script contains code that is automatically run when the plugin is installed. This might involve copying certain assets required by the plugin to the `lib` or `public` directory in your application, for example. Or it might simply dump the contents of the `README` file to the terminal to display installation and usage information.

- The `uninstall.rb` script (predictably) tells the application what to do when the plugin is uninstalled. Remember that these files are standard Ruby scripts, so you can do anything with them that you can do in Ruby, including manipulating files, creating directories, templates, processing data, and so on.

- The `init.rb` script provides the most important hook. It runs whenever your application is started. Therefore, it's the hook that is used to inject your plugin code into the framework in whatever manner is desired.

> **■Caution** Since init.rb is run only when the server is started, this means you must restart your server when a new plugin is installed, even if it's running in development mode. This also explains why changes to your installed plugins require a server restart.

In our case, init.rb simply needs to insert a few new methods into Rails and make them available to all our controllers; that is, any descendant of ActionController::Base. Assuming that those methods are all self-contained within a single module called IpWhitelist (which we'll build shortly), we can do this using a single line of code, as shown in Listing 28-3. Save it as vendor/plugins/ip_whitelist/init.rb.

Listing 28-3. *Plugin Initialization Hook (vendor/plugins/ip_whitelist/init.rb)*

```
ActionController::Base.send(:include, IpWhitelist)
```

All the line in Listing 28-3 does is to instruct ActionController::Base to include the IpWhitelist module. It does this by sending a message to the class, instructing it to call the private include method. The job of include is to "mix in" the contents of the named module, thus making any methods in that module available on ActionController::Base and all of its descendants.

> **■Note** The send method is used here because include is a private method. In Ruby, a private method cannot be called with an explicit receiver; therefore, we cannot access it directly from outside the class definition. This technique is standard fare in Ruby metaprogramming. We need to send a message to a private method from outside the class, so we just use send to navigate around normal method visibility rules.

Creating the IpWhitelist Module

Before we take a look at the IpWhitelist module itself, we should first note the difference between classes and modules in Ruby. It's a subtle but important one. A *module* is something like a degenerate abstract class; it cannot be instantiated and cannot be inherited from, but can contain any number of methods. When a module is "mixed into" a class using the include method, the module methods become instance methods on the class. Since Ruby does not implement multiple inheritance, this approach allows you to add behavior to any number of classes, while still allowing them to inherit from some other logical parent class.

It should be clear from this description why we've made IpWhitelist a module. Its purpose, after all, is to extend an existing class or module (in this case, ActionController::Base), grafting this new whitelisting capability onto it. Implementing these add-on features as a class would require a much different approach.

Now let's look at the code for our module. It's an adaptation from our previous check_whitelist controller filter, as shown in Listing 28-4. Save it as vendor/plugins/ip_whitelist/lib/ip_whitelist.rb.

Listing 28-4. *IpWhitelist Module (vendor/plugins/ip_whitelist/lib/ip_whitelist.rb)*

```ruby
module IpWhitelist
  def self.included(base) #:nodoc:
    base.extend(ClassMethods)
  end

  module ClassMethods
    def whitelist #:nodoc:
      @whitelist ||= []
    end

    # Limit controller action access to remote IPs specified in the whitelist.
    # Accepts all the standard before_filter options (:except, :only, etc)
    #
    # Example:
    #
    #   allow_from_ip ["192.168.0.1", "192.168.0.2"], :except => [:index, :show]
    def allow_from_ip(access_list, options = {})
      whitelist.concat(access_list)
      before_filter(:check_whitelist, options)
    end
  end

  def whitelist #:nodoc:
    self.class.whitelist
  end

  def check_whitelist #:nodoc:
    if whitelist.include?(request.remote_ip)
      true
    else
      logger.error("WHITELIST: ACCESS DENIED FOR [#{request.remote_ip}]")
      render(:nothing => true, :status => 401)
      false
    end
  end
end
```

The first method in the module is the special `included` class method. A Ruby method callback, `self.included` is executed whenever the module is mixed in with the `include` method. It's used to set up or initialize certain facilities that should come into existence at that time. Here, we are using a common Ruby idiom by employing the `included` method to extend the base class with a new set of *class methods* (represented by the `IpWhitelist::ClassMethods` module) in addition to the *instance methods* we already added.

■**Note** The extend and include methods are closely related. The difference is that include adds all the module methods as instance methods, whereas extend adds module methods at the class level.

The new class methods include a whitelist accessor and the allow_from_ip method. Both of these methods will be available on any controller that inherits from ActionController::Base, and can be used in a declarative manner. However, allow_from_ip is the only one these methods that our clients—end users who are developing controllers— will really care about. When this method is called, it adds whatever addresses are passed in as the first array parameter to the whitelist's class-level accessor. It then installs a before_ filter, instructing the controller to run the check_whitelist instance method and to pass it any additional options that were specified in the invocation. Thus, standard filter options such as :only and :except are preserved and can be used to easily scope the filter to specific actions.

The remaining methods in IpWhitelist—those outside the inner ClassMethods module— are "normal" instance-level methods. Note that the previously mentioned check_whitelist method looks pretty much the same as it did in its original incarnation, except for the fact that it checks the whitelist accessor instead of an array constant in the controller. That instance-level accessor is simply a convenience method for retrieving the whitelist from the class level where it was originally set.

The result of all this work is that controllers receive an important new class method, allow_from_ip, and the rest of the underlying implementation logic is hidden away from framework end users. To the developers using our plugin, the IP Whitelist plugin just works— like magic!

After stopping and restarting script/server, you should be able to see that our updated articles controller (shown back in Listing 28-2 with the modified DSL-style syntax) works in the same manner as the original before_filter version did. If the 127.0.0.1 address is listed in your allow_from_ip array parameter, the text should be displayed. If not, an unauthorized status code should be returned, and your browser will display a blank screen.

Testing Plugins

As you may have observed when poking around the plugins we've used in this book, many plugins don't ship with tests. This is unfortunate but surprisingly common. It's often attributed to the fact that writing tests for plugins is somewhat less straightforward than writing normal unit and functional tests, due to the nature of plugins and their use of metaprogramming practices. But this is clearly no excuse! Testing a plugin is just as important as testing any other piece of code. With that in mind, let's see how we can create a sample unit test to verify the behavior of our new plugin, using the Rails standard Test::Unit test suite.

When testing how your plugin overrides some piece of Rails itself, you need to include your module or changes explicitly in order to test them. We've demonstrated how to do this in some tests for our ip_whitelist plugin, as shown in Listing 28-5. Save the code in this listing as vendor/plugins/ip_whitelist/test/ip_whitelist.rb. Notice that not only does the ip_whitelist module itself need to be explicitly loaded (via require), but that we also load the environment.rb file of the host Rails project in order to provide the routes and other necessities for reaching a sample controller.

Listing 28-5. *Tests for the ip_whitelist Plugin (vendor/plugins/ip_whitelist/test/ ip_whitelist_test.rb)*

```
require File.expand_path(File.join(
  File.dirname(__FILE__), '../../../../config/environment.rb'))
require File.dirname(__FILE__) + '/../lib/ip_whitelist.rb'

require 'test/unit'
require 'action_controller'
require 'action_controller/test_process'

class IpWhitelistTest < Test::Unit::TestCase
  class ::SampleController < ::ActionController::Base
    include IpWhitelist
    allow_from_ip ["127.0.0.1"], :only => :acta

    def acta; render(:nothing => true) end
    def actb; render(:nothing => true) end
  end

  def setup
    @controller = SampleController.new
    @request = ActionController::TestRequest.new
    @response = ActionController::TestResponse.new
  end

  def test_action_protected
    get :acta # addr not in whitelist (0.0.0.0)
    assert_response 401
  end

  def test_remote_addr_in_whitelist
    @request.remote_addr = "127.0.0.1"
    get :acta # addr in whitelist
    assert_response :success
  end

  def test_not_included
    get :actb # unprotected
    assert_response :success
  end
end
```

Rather than testing the eccentricities of the module itself, the three sample tests presented here are intended to test the *behavior* of a controller when IP whitelisting functionality has been loaded into it. Therefore, we want to assert the fact that it should protect actions from firing if the requester isn't in the whitelist. We also want to assert that it should not interfere with the display of templates if the requester is in the whitelist or if the action is unprotected.

To accomplish this, we create a sample controller for the test (SampleController) and use include to mix in the IpWhitelist module. This provides the sample controller with the same methods and functionality it would receive if the plugin's init.rb were loaded, but is easier to test and less "magical." The implementation of the tests themselves is then straightforward and should be familiar to anyone who has ever written a Rails functional test.

You can run the tests from the vendor/plugins/ip_whitelist directory using the rake test task in the provided Rakefile. It's also possible to run plugin tests directly from the Rails project root directory with the rake test:plugins task. You can run rake test:plugins PLUGIN=ip_whitelist to specify that only the tests for the named plugin should be run, or run tests for all plugins installed in the host Rails project at once by omitting the optional parameter:

rake test:plugins

```
/opt/local/bin/ruby -Ilib:test "/opt/local/lib/ruby/gems/1.8/gems/rake-0.8.1 ➥
/lib/rake/rake_test_loader.rb"
"vendor/plugins/ip_whitelist/test/ip_whitelist_test.rb"
Loaded suite /opt/local/lib/ruby/gems/1.8/gems/rake-0.8.1/lib/rake/rake_test_loader
Started
...
Finished in 0.005698 seconds.

3 tests, 3 assertions, 0 failures, 0 errors
```

When testing a more complex plugin, you'll most likely find a good mocking/stubbing library, such as Mocha (http://mocha.rubyforge.org) or the built-in mocks/stubs that come packaged with RSpec (covered in Chapter 26), to be an invaluable resource. The purpose here is, after all, to isolate just the behavior provided by the plugin code, rather than attempting to test an entire system end to end.

Distributing Plugins

Distributing plugins couldn't really be much easier. To distribute a plugin, you just place the entire contents of that plugin in a publicly accessible Subversion or Git server, and then distribute the URL.

You may already be managing your own repositories, in which case you can host your plugin there. For those who don't have their own facilities, plugins are commonly hosted at RubyForge (http://rubyforge.org) and Google Code (http://code.google.com), which both provide free Subversion repository access and administrative tools for open source projects.

A growing number of plugins are also being hosted at GitHub (http://github.com), which provides similar facilities for managing Git-based projects and is also free for open source projects.

SUBVERSION OR GIT?

Subversion and Git are both powerful revision-control systems. However, they are also very different. The solution that you choose to manage your own source code repositories is a matter of project requirements and personal taste.

More information about Subversion is available at http://subversion.tigris.org. Also, check out *Version Control with Subversion* (http://svnbook.red-bean.com), a free book available in HTML and PDF formats.

For more information about Git, visit http://git.or.cz. We also recommend Scott Chacon's excellent Git Internals mini-book, available through PeepCode Press (http://peepcode.com/products/git-internals-pdf).

Whichever you decide to use—Subversion or Git—you can often install it through your operating system's package management facilities. Alternatively, you can download and install a binary version from one of the web site addresses mentioned earlier, or download the sources and build the binaries yourself.

Using Subversion (Google Code)

To distribute your plugin through Google Code, first make sure that you have Subversion itself installed. Next, log in to your Google account or sign up for one at http://code.google.com/hosting. If you're a new user, you will need to confirm your e-mail address. Once you've clicked the link in the e-mail, you should be taken back to the Google Code Project Hosting page. From there, you can choose to create a new project. Do this now.

On the Create Project page, enter the name of the project, a summary, and description, and then select the appropriate license. Note that the name we've chosen for our plugin, ip_whitelist, is not a valid Google Code project name because it uses an underscore. You could use a name like ip-whitelist instead (Google Code project names must be unique, so this exact name may be unavailable).

After creating your project, click the Source tab in the Google Code web interface. It should show you a command you can use to check out a working copy of the repository. This will usually be of the following form:

```
svn checkout https://your-project-name.googlecode.com/svn/trunk/ your-project-name ➥
--username your.email@address.com
```

■Note You'll need to click the link provided in the Google Code Source page to obtain your password for the checkout operation.

Change to a directory outside your Rails project and issue this command now. A new directory will created—this is a working copy of your new Subversion repository. The next step is to recursively copy the vendor/plugins/ip_whitelist directory from your Rails application into this new directory. Once you've done that, you can add the files to the repository and commit them. The following commands do just this on a standard Unix system:

```
cd your-project-name
cp -R /path/to/your/rails/application/vendor/plugins/ip_whitelist .
svn add ip_whitelist
svn commit -m 'first commit'
```

At this point, you've successfully committed your plugin code to the Google Code repository. Back in your browser, if you click the Browse submenu, you can browse the plugin source from the Web, as shown in Figure 28-1.

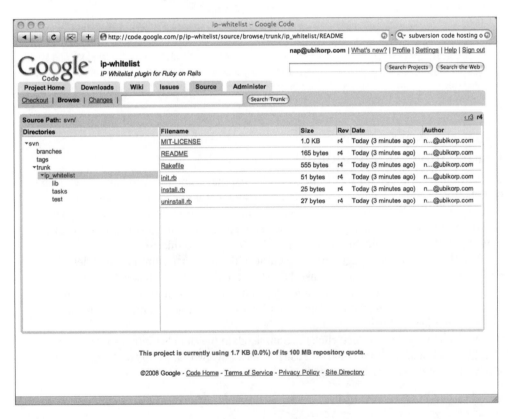

Figure 28-1. *Browsing your plugin source repository at Google Code (http://code.google.com/p/your-project-name/source/browse)*

Other developers can now install our plugin by using the following command:

```
ruby script/plugin install ➥
http://your-project-name.googlecode.com/svn/trunk/ip_whitelist
```

To test this, let's uninstall the `ip_whitelist` plugin from the `topsecret` project (run `ruby script/plugin remove ip_whitelist` from the Rails project directory), and then reinstall it from the new Subversion repository:

```
ruby script/plugin install  ➡
http://your-project-name.googlecode.com/svn/trunk/ip_whitelist
```

```
+ ./MIT-LICENSE
+ ./README
+ ./Rakefile
+ ./init.rb
+ ./install.rb
+ ./lib/ip_whitelist.rb
+ ./tasks/ip_whitelist_tasks.rake
+ ./test/ip_whitelist_test.rb
+ ./uninstall.rb
```

The reinstalled plugin should work as expected.

Using Git (GitHub)

If you're using Git to manage your development projects, you'll probably prefer to use it for hosting any plugins you're developing as well. If you're not interested in hosting your own servers, you may want to investigate GitHub, a particularly useful service that makes finding, forking, and managing Git-based development projects more palatable than ever before.

To distribute your plugin through GitHub, first make sure that you have Git itself installed. Next, sign up for a GitHub account at `http://github.com/signup`. Make sure to enter your SSH key at this time, as this is what GitHub uses to identify you when using Git's `push` and `pull` commands. If you're unfamiliar with this process, GitHub provides a quick-and-dirty primer at `http://github.com/guides/providing-your-ssh-key`.

Once you've signed up, you'll be instantly logged in to your account. You will then be invited to create a new repository. During this process, you'll be prompted to enter the name of the repository (`ip_whitelist` for this example), a description, a home page URL, and repository status: public or private. Make sure to specify that the repository is a public one; you want to allow anyone to access your repository if you're distributing a Rails plugin.

After you click the Create button, GitHub will give you a list of instructions you need to follow to get your existing project into Git. First, copy your `ip_whitelist` directory from `vendor/plugins` to somewhere else on your system. Change your current working directory to that directory, and then follow these steps:

```
git init
git add .
git commit -m 'first commit'
git remote add origin git@github.com:your_user_name/ip_whitelist.git
git push origin master
```

Once you've completed these steps, return to the repository URL in your browser and click the Continue button. You should now be taken to the repository main page, where you'll see the files that constitute your plugin listed in the source browser, as shown in Figure 28-2.

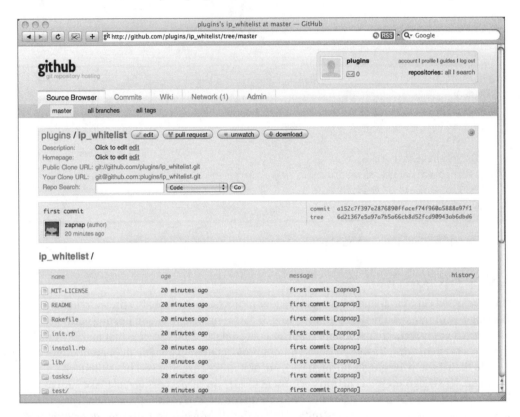

Figure 28-2. *Browsing your plugin source repository at GitHub* *(http://github.com/your_user_name/ip_whitelist)*

You can now distribute the public clone URL listed at the top of the screen to anyone who wants to use your plugin. It should be something like `git://github.com/your_user_name/` `ip_whitelist.git`. So, to install your new plugin, a developer would use the following command:

```
ruby script/plugin install git://github.com/your_user_name/ip_whitelist.git
```

■**Note** Git repository support for plugins was added in Rails 2.1. Older versions of Rails do not support plugin installation from Git, and you may want to note additional installation options in your plugin's README file if you choose to go this route. (GitHub offers an automatic tarball download option that can be useful for this!)

Other Plugin Distribution Resources

You'll want to notify a number of web-based plugin directories when you've created a new plugin that can be useful to other developers. The following is an incomplete list of some of the more frequently searched destinations:

- The Official Rails Wiki Plugins page (`http://wiki.rubyonrails.org/rails/pages/Plugins`)

- The Agile Web Development Plugins database (`http://agilewebdevelopment.com/plugins`)

- The RailsLodge Plugin directory (`http://www.railslodge.com`)

When you list your plugin with these resource and directory sites, those who need the functionality you're providing will be able to find it easily. Win!

Extending the IP Whitelist Plugin

Our goal throughout this chapter has been to keep things simple in order to illustrate the basics of plugin development. Clearly, a number of different features could be added to the IP Whitelist plugin. A couple quick extensions to the core idea will be useful in illustrating the user of installation hooks, Rake tasks, and generators.

First, we could use the plugin install hook to automatically display the contents of the `README` file (containing installation and usage instructions) when the plugin is installed. This is easily accomplished using the following line of code in `install.rb`:

```
puts IO.read(File.join(File.dirname(__FILE__), 'README'))
```

We can also provide very useful statistics-gathering and troubleshooting tools for developers who are using this plugin in their staging environments. For instance, we might find that legitimate users (like our boss or clients!) are having trouble accessing the system when the whitelist protection is present.

Since we're already logging requests that fail the whitelist check to the standard Rails logging facilities, it might be nice for the developer to be able to ask for a summary of all remote IPs that are making these failing requests. This could be useful for locating legitimate users who are having trouble (perhaps they reported an incorrect IP address to us), as well as just for seeing general statistical information. Since the plugin's architecture autoloads any Rake tasks found in the `tasks` directory of any given plugin, we can easily add a Rake task to do just this by copying the code in Listing 28-6 into `vendor/plugins/ip_whitelist/tasks/ip_whitelist_tasks.rake`.

Listing 28-6. *Whitelist Rake Tasks (vendor/plugins/ip_whitelist/tasks/ip_whitelist_tasks.rake)*

```
namespace :whitelist do
  desc "View whitelist access denied statistics"
  task :stats do
    hosts = {}
    pattern = /WHITELIST: ACCESS DENIED FOR \[(.*)\]/
    File.open("#{RAILS_ROOT}/log/#{RAILS_ENV}.log").each do |f|
      match = f.match(pattern)
      if match && hosts[match[1]]
        hosts[match[1]] += 1
      elsif match
        hosts[match[1]] = 1
      end
    end
    puts "The whitelist has denied the following requests:"
    hosts.each do |ip, hits|
      puts "#{ip}: #{hits} requests denied"
    end
  end
end
```

With this code in place, our Rails project gets a shiny new Rake task: `rake`
`whitelist:stats`. This command will return statistics about the number of illegal access
attempts that were blocked by the plugin, listed by offending IP.

```
rake whitelist:stats
```

```
The whitelist has denied the following requests:
10.0.0.2: 1 requests denied
127.0.0.1: 3 requests denied
```

Of course, to obtain meaningful snapshots of denied requests over time is a slightly more
challenging problem. To use this system as is, the log would have to be cleared (using `rake`
`log:clear`) from time to time.

If this proves worthwhile, it might be worth considering a more robust solution in which
denied requests are recorded to a database. In this scenario, a `DeniedRequest` model, as well
as a generator, could be added to the plugin. The generator could be run to produce a database migration, similar to the Comatose migration shown in Chapter 9.

Once the database is migrated, requests could be recorded with a small modification to
the existing `IpWhitelist` module. The `rake whitelist:stats` task could then be modified
to pull statistics from the database in any number of ways, and an optional `rake`
`whitelist:clear` command could be added to clear current statistics.

Of course, these are just a few ideas. You could extend the IP Whitelist plugin in many
other ways. Equipped with the assortment of examples found throughout earlier chapters in
this book, you should be well on your way to plugin development mastery.

Summary

As you've seen throughout this book, Rails plugins come in a variety of shapes and sizes. In this chapter, we've designed and developed a simple plugin that extends Action Controller with an IP whitelisting capability. Although this particular plugin was used to extend the DSL used in Rails controllers, other plugins are just as likely to add features to Active Record models, provide a set of helpful Rake tasks, replace a caching mechanism with something more specialized or optimized, or add a new type of generator.

In the preceding chapters, we've discussed plugins that fit into all of these niches and many others. We strongly encourage you to use the other plugins showcased in this book as examples for your own plugin development experiences. Step back from what they do for a moment, and consider how they do it. Open those vendor directories and study their contents. Analyze how the plugins work—how they inject themselves into the framework and override existing functionality.

Don't be trapped by limitations of current conventions (within Rails or otherwise). With a firm grasp of Ruby metaprogramming techniques and the know-how to manipulate the underlying components through the plugins system, you'll find that you have the tools necessary to make Rails do just about anything you want. And, better yet, to easily share your innovations with others.

Index

■M

You Need the Companion eBook

Your purchase of this book entitles you to buy the companion PDF-version eBook for only $10. Take the weightless companion with you anywhere.

We believe this Apress title will prove so indispensable that you'll want to carry it with you everywhere, which is why we are offering the companion eBook (in PDF format) for $10 to customers who purchase this book now. Convenient and fully searchable, the PDF version of any content-rich, page-heavy Apress book makes a valuable addition to your programming library. You can easily find and copy code—or perform examples by quickly toggling between instructions and the application. Even simultaneously tackling a donut, diet soda, and complex code becomes simplified with hands-free eBooks!

Once you purchase your book, getting the $10 companion eBook is simple:

❶ Visit **www.apress.com/promo/tendollars/**.

❷ Complete a basic registration form to receive a randomly generated question about this title.

❸ Answer the question correctly in 60 seconds, and you will receive a promotional code to redeem for the $10.00 eBook.

THE EXPERT'S VOICE™

2855 TELEGRAPH AVENUE | SUITE 600 | BERKELEY, CA 94705

All Apress eBooks subject to copyright protection. No part may be reproduced or transmitted in any form or by any means, electronic or mechanical, including photocopying, recording, or by any information storage or retrieval system, without the prior written permission of the copyright owner and the publisher. The purchaser may print the work in full or in part for their own noncommercial use. The purchaser may place the eBook title on any of their personal computers for their own personal reading and reference.

Offer valid through 1/09.